Hardship and Hope

Hardship and Hope

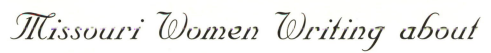

Missouri Women Writing about Their Lives, 1820-1920

Edited with an Introduction by

Carla Waal and Barbara Oliver Korner

University of Missouri Press

Columbia and London

 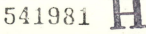

Library of Congress Cataloging-in-Publication Data

Hardship and hope : Missouri women writing about their lives,
    1820–1920 / edited with an introduction by Carla Waal and Barbara
    Oliver Korner.
        p.   cm.
    Includes bibliographical references and index.
    ISBN 0-8262-1120-8 (pbk. : alk. paper)
    1. Women—Missouri—Biography.   2. Missouri—Biography.
3. Missouri—History.   I. Waal, Carla, 1933–   .   II. Korner,
Barbara Oliver, 1950–   .
CT3260H33   1997
920.72—dc21   97-6859
                                                                  CIP

∞™ This paper meets the requirements of the
American National Standard for Permanence of Paper
for Printed Library Materials, Z39.48, 1984.

Text Design: Elizabeth K. Young
Jacket Design: Susan Ferber
Typesetter: BOOKCOMP
Printer and binder: Thomson-Shore, Inc.
Typefaces: Meridien Family, Nuptual Script

FOR CREDITS, SEE PAGE IX

THIS BOOK IS DEDICATED TO OUR MOTHERS

Esther Christiansen Waal

Vonda Jenkins Oliver Mallon

AND TO OUR GRANDMOTHERS

Anna Ludvikke Loberg Waal (1871-1955)

Hattie Klingenberg Christiansen Felt (1888-1978)

Della Kelton Oliver (1897-1965)

Allie Lawrence Jenkins (b. 1903)

CONTENTS

ACKNOWLEDGMENTS

$\mathcal{I}$t has been a pleasure to discover the stories of women's lives that we present in *Hardship and Hope*. We appreciate the help given to us by many people during the years of research. Some individuals we especially wish to thank are Elizabeth Bailey, Martha Clevenger, Lawrence Cott, Mary K. Dains, Robert Dyer, Ree Green, Michele Hansford, Gary R. Kremer, Linda Lambert, Nancy Lankford, Linda Lunyou, Julie March, Ann Morris, Frank Spina, and Vicky Riback Wilson. Above all we thank James R. Korner and Esther C. Waal for their patience and help.

Librarians and archivists at many institutions have assisted us with our research. We thank especially those at Ellis Library, University of Missouri–Columbia; State Historical Society of Missouri, Columbia; Western Historical Manuscript Collection–Columbia (WHMC-C); Missouri Historical Society Archives, St. Louis; Marshall Public Library; Daniel Boone Regional Library, Columbia; and Seattle Pacific University Library.

For permission to quote from unpublished documents, we wish to thank the following: Barry S. Wilderman and Leroy Wilderman (Vanarsdale diary); Elizabeth Willis Buchanan (Frances Gates Willis and A. J. Willis letters); Georgia Bates Creel (Virginia Fackler Creel diary); Scott Jones (Elvira Scott diary); John L. Oliver, Jr. (Marie Watkins Oliver letters); Paul T. Jones, Fern Nance Shumate, and Robert K. Gilmore (Margaret Gilmore Kelso memoirs); Charles E. Leonard (Margaret Nelson Stephens diary); Powers Museum (Marian Wright Powers journal); G. Delany Dean (Anna Dierssen diary); and Mary Margaret Ellis (her own memoirs).

We also express appreciation to the archives in which copies of the unpublished documents are located. At the Western Historical Manuscript Collection–Columbia: Genevieve Bennett Clark Diary and Essay, Champ and Bennett Champ Clark Papers, 1853–1973; Virginia Fackler Creel Diary, 1864; "The Wednesday Club in Person: A Diary," Anna Dierssen Papers, 1907–1965; Marie Watkins Oliver letters, Oliver Family Papers, 1805–1977; Elvira Ascenith Weir Scott Diary, 1860–1887; Margaret Nelson Stephens Diary, 1897–1903; Susan D. [B.] Vanarsdale Diary, 1847–1855; Laura Ingalls Wilder Diary, microfilm, Laura Ingalls Wilder Papers, 1894–1943; Willis Letters, Willis Family Papers, 1843–1908; Martha J. Wood [Woods] Diary, Arrow Rock Tavern Board Papers, 1826–1923. "Grandmother, Mother and Me: 1856–1946" by Mary Ezit Bulkley is located with the Bulkley Family Papers, Missouri Historical Society, St. Louis. Mary Margaret Ellis's "That's the Way It Was" may be found at the Western Historical Manuscript Collection, University of Missouri–St. Louis. "Family History" by Margaret Gilmore Kelso is at the History Museum for Springfield–Greene County. The Powers Museum, Carthage, has "Talks on Self" by Marian Wright Powers.

Permission has been granted to use certain published materials; as follows:

The letters of Philippine Duchesne from *Philippine Duchesne: Frontier Missionary of the Sacred Heart, 1769–1852* by Louise Callan, published by Newman Press in 1957, are reprinted by permission of the Paulist Press.

Phoebe Couzins's speech, an unidentified newspaper clipping, is in the J. E. D. Couzins Papers, Missouri Historical Society, St. Louis.

Letters by Jette Bruns are reprinted from *Hold Dear As Always: Jette, A German Immigrant Life in Letters* edited by Adolf E. Schroeder and Carla Schulz-Geisberg, by permission of the University of Missouri Press and Carla Schulz-Geisberg. Copyright 1988 by the Curators of the University of Missouri.

Excerpts from *On the Way Home: The Diary of a Trip from South Dakota to Mansfield, Missouri, in 1894* copyright 1962 by Roger Lea MacBride. Copyright renewed 1990 by Roger Lea MacBride. Used by permission of HarperCollins Publishers.

Excerpts from *Anatomy of Me: A Wonderer in Search of Herself* by Fannie Hurst are reprinted by permission of Brandeis University and Washington University as co-holders of the copyrights.

HARDSHIP AND HOPE

INTRODUCTION

*O*ne afternoon we were having tea in Columbia, Missouri, discussing plans for developing a script we could perform together. The two of us are actors and directors who had previously created one-person shows featuring the lives and writings of famous women. Looking for challenging and interesting material, one of us had recently read Joanna Stratton's *Pioneer Women: Voices from the Kansas Frontier.* What about presenting pioneer women from our own state, Missouri?

Eighteen months of research followed before we presented the first performance.[1] *Hardship and Hope: Heroines in Life and Art* opened in Mountain View, Missouri, on March 12, 1988. By the fall of 1989, *Hardship and Hope* was performed more than thirty times in all corners of the state and at a theatre in Bergen, Norway. Performance spaces in Missouri ranged from historic theatres in Boonville and Memphis to the public library in Columbia, college auditoriums in Moberly and Springfield, historic churches in Arrow Rock and Kennett, a high school gymnasium in Hannibal, banquet rooms in St. Louis and Kansas City hotels, and the rotunda of the state capitol.

In the creative and performing arts, scholarship is always interdisciplinary. *Hardship and Hope* allowed us to give full rein to interdisciplinary instincts, bringing history alive on stage. We chose a readers theatre format for maximum flexibility in addressing the social and historical context of our selections. Because the cultural background was woven from literary and musical threads in women's lives, the script incorporated songs and literature along with unpublished letters, diaries, and journals. The flexibility had an added benefit: as the show grew in popularity and we traveled to different parts of the state, we added examples of local women and historical events.

During the years of writing and performing *Hardship and Hope,* we came to appreciate the fascinating individuals whose lives were too varied and complex to present in a one-hour show. We continued to discover letters, diaries, and memoirs that draw us into the private thoughts of the writers and teach us about their society. Encouraged by people who saw *Hardship and Hope* and aware that many share their enthusiasm for Missouri history and their empathy for the experiences of women, we decided to edit this anthology. The readers theatre program with its historical framework,

1. The original script was a project of the Missouri Cultural Heritage Center and the Department of Theatre at the University of Missouri–Columbia, and was funded in part by a grant from the Missouri Humanities Council, the state affiliate of the National Endowment for the Humanities. Additional assistance for performances of *Hardship and Hope* was provided with the cooperation of the State Historical Society and the Missouri chapter of the American Association of University Women.

humor, music, movement, and pathos has grown into a book. It may be enjoyed as a collection of interesting life stories, yet it may also be used by students of history, women's studies, or oral interpretation.

This anthology covers roughly a century, starting just prior to Missouri's admission into the Union as the twenty-fourth state in 1821. As the century progressed, the position of women in society gradually changed. Although the women introduced in *Hardship and Hope* vary in personality and the circumstances of their lives, a number of them became convinced that winning the right to vote was symbolic of the opportunity and responsibility women deserved. The 1920 ratification of Amendment 19, giving women the right to vote, is the milestone that provides a suitable stopping place for this biographical sampler. From the years since 1920 there are many interesting Missouri women whose stories deserve telling in another anthology. In the present volume, however, the reader will find diversity and drama in the episodes from women's history leading to passage of the amendment. The significance of that event is analyzed by Mary Ezit Bulkley in the book's final selection.

The private writings of women shed light on and place history in a different perspective than selective histories that focus on masculine-oriented public activities such as war, diplomacy, and affairs of state. Increasingly, women's private writings are being published. Lillian Schlissel is among those who have edited significant collections of frontier women's diaries, calling attention to the ways in which they can alter our perceptions of the past and deepen our historical understanding. In Schlissel's words, "We are beginning to recognize that more should be known about the interaction between family roles and social roles, between social dynamics and human dynamics."[2] The writings selected here reflect the larger patterns of American society, but capture personal perspectives on events and evolving culture. For instance, many of our selections show how ideals were dashed as middle-class women who had enjoyed relatively unencumbered lives in Europe or the Eastern United States found themselves catapulted into the exhausting manual labor required to eke out an existence on the frontier. The selections of Mother Duchesne, Jette Bruns, Margaret Gilmore Kelso, and Mary Margaret Ellis illustrate the lifestyles of immigrants and settlers.

In the nineteenth century, woman's role was circumscribed to the "private sphere." In Barbara Welter's classic and oft-cited essay, "The Cult of True Womanhood: 1820–1860," she illustrates, from a thorough survey of women's magazines and books of the period, the four cardinal virtues that worthy women were to exhibit: piety, purity, submissiveness, and domesticity. Frances Cogan, however, poses an alternative ideal

---

2. Schlissel, "Diaries of Frontier Women: On Learning to Read the Obscured Patterns," in Mary Kelley, *Woman's Being, Woman's Place*, 53.

also drawn from popular literature in *All-American Girl: The Ideal of Real Womanhood in Mid-Nineteenth-Century America*. In contrast to the delicate image of the "True Woman," the ideal of the "Real Woman" stressed physical fitness and health, higher education, a cautious approach to marriage for the "right reasons," and an openness to employment for a variety of reasons and not just economic need as a single woman. Marriage remained the norm for most women, but "Real Womanhood" allowed for a middle-of-the-road position between the demureness of the "True Woman" and the inflammatory tactics of activists for women's rights. Susan Vanarsdale, although talented and strong-willed, is one who would not let go of the ideal of the "True Woman." On the other hand, Marie Watkins Oliver's letters during her courtship show the impact of the "Real Woman's" perspective on courtship and marriage.

Early feminists argued that while woman's role in the private sphere was significant, she should not be kept from public roles. Sarah and Angelina Grimké, Amelia Bloomer, and others challenged the theological arguments that placed woman under man's domination. Rather, they insisted that woman as well as man was created in God's image and was capable of reflecting God's creative and intellectual work. Woman was accountable directly to God, not to God indirectly through man. Several ministers denounced the Grimké sisters' work in a *Pastoral Letter*. Sarah Grimké responded:

> No one can desire more earnestly than I do, that woman may move exactly in the sphere which her Creator has assigned her. . . .
> The Lord Jesus defines the duties of his followers in his Sermon on the Mount. . . . I follow him through all his precepts, and find him giving the same directions to women as to men, never even referring to the distinction now so strenuously insisted upon between masculine and feminine virtues: this is one of the anti-christian "traditions of men" which are taught instead of the "commandments of God." Men and women were CREATED EQUAL; they are both moral and accountable beings, and whatever is *right* for a man to do, is *right* for woman.[3]

As the abolition movement gathered steam, so did the movement for woman suffrage. While many women working for temperance and the abolition movement were welcomed by church congregations, the issue of women's rights was another matter. The Seneca Falls convention of 1848 sent out shock waves with its declaration of women's rights: "We hold these truths to be self-evident, that all men and women are created equal, that they are endowed by their creator with certain inalienable rights. . . ." In the 1850s, women's rights conventions began to be held

---

3. Grimké, letter to Mary S. Parker, July 1837, in *Letters on the Equality of the Sexes, and Other Essays*, 38.

in an effort to assure that the cause for woman suffrage did not get lost in the battle for abolition.

During the Civil War, many women became heads of their families as the men went off to fight, some never to return and some to return severely injured. The role women played during the war gave them individually and collectively new confidence and courage to play more public roles, although for many this did not mean "giving up" their important private roles as wives and mothers. Elvira Scott and Virginia Fackler Creel represent Southern sympathizers whose lives were deeply affected by the Civil War. A young single woman, Creel approached her adventure on the wagon train with great optimism; the determined and spirited Scott did not kowtow to the Union soldiers who tried to intimidate her and her family.

After the war, women increasingly moved into the public arena. No longer were they limited to influencing men through family life; women became crusaders for temperance, for the regulation of child labor, for public health and education, and other worthy causes. Their work in church Sunday school programs and in literary societies, such as Anna Dierssen's Wednesday Club, helped them develop organizational and networking skills that they put to good use in the Woman's Christian Temperance Union, the National Association of Colored Women, the National Woman Suffrage Association, and other organizations.

New public roles did not preclude important private ones in marriage. Quite the contrary, as Blanche Glassman Hersh points out, the nineteenth-century feminists often enjoyed marriages in which "they achieved a notable degree of equality and sharing. The models of egalitarian marriage they created represented a pivotal reform in the nineteenth-century women's movement which has gone unnoticed by historians."[4] As the twentieth century approached and there was a renewed emphasis on temperance and woman suffrage, marriage remained for many women the desired goal in life. But with the opening of more public doors, there were new opportunities for single women also. Genevieve Bennett Clark, Phoebe Couzins, Kate Chopin, Margaret Nelson Stephens, Marian Wright Powers, Emma J. Ray, and Fannie Hurst represent women who claimed more public roles during the decades when one century was drawing to a close and a new one was beginning.

Carolyn Heilbrun has called attention to the difference between women's public and private scripts. In published autobiographical material, women in public leadership roles often downplay their efforts in setting

4. Hersh, "The 'True Woman' and the 'New Woman' in Nineteenth-Century America: Feminist-Abolitionists and a New Concept of True Womanhood," in Kelley, *Woman's Being*, 279.

and reaching goals. "Well into the twentieth century, it continued to be impossible for women to admit into their autobiographical narratives the claim of achievement, the admission of ambition, the recognition that accomplishment was neither luck nor the result of the efforts or generosity of others. . . . Letters and diaries are usually different, reflecting ambitions and struggles in the public sphere . . . ," while in their published autobiographies women portray "themselves as intuitive, nurturing, passive, but never—in spite of the contrary evidence of their accomplishments—managerial."[5]

Hardship and Hope: Missouri Women Writing About Their Lives, 1820–1920 takes its place among those works that may illuminate the lives of earlier generations. Through the words of Missouri women we become acquainted with distinctive individuals—their families, their experiences, and their thoughts. Most of these women were not trying to change American society, yet they experienced growth in self-esteem and confidence. Some recognized how they might play a role beyond the private sphere, challenging society's male orientation and serving causes in which they believed.

In this anthology we present primarily private writings and keep editorial intrusion to a minimum. We have changed original spelling and grammar only as needed to make the meaning clear. Many of the selections have not been previously published or have been out of print for years. We have included an introductory essay to each entry that places it within its historical context, gives a personal history of the writer, and draws links among the various selections. Some of the women, such as St. Philippine Duchesne, Carry Nation, and Laura Ingalls Wilder, are known for their achievements; they have received public recognition and scholarly treatment. Some of our women, like Elizabeth Keckley, spent only a brief time in Missouri, but comments written during their sojourn in the state warrant inclusion in this anthology.

While we consider *Hardship and Hope* to be a contribution to a fuller understanding of American history, particularly in Missouri, we have maintained our approach as interdisciplinary theatre artists. That is, we have chosen material that can be performed effectively through oral interpretation techniques. Many of the selections contain theatrical elements and reveal that the women saw themselves as playing a role in the drama of their own lives. Our criteria for selection, therefore, have included the documents' significance in the light they shed on history, their dramatic content, and their relevance to women's concerns of the late twentieth century.

A popular song of the nineteenth century, "Whispering Hope," begins:

5. Carolyn Heilbrun, *Writing a Woman's Life,* 24.

Soft as the voice of an angel
Breathing a lesson unheard
Hope with her gentle persuasion
Whispers her comforting words.[6]

A universal pattern of human experience emerged in our program and continues in the majority of selections in this anthology: even at difficult times, the women express hope. Hope whispered to themselves in a diary or journal. Hope shared with a friend or loved one in a letter. Hope proclaimed for all women.

6. By Alice Hawthorne, published in 1868.

SAINT ROSE PHILIPPINE DUCHESNE (1769–1852)

*O*n April 9, 1682, René Robert Cavelier, Sieur de la Salle, took possession of the Mississippi River and all its tributaries in the name of the French king, Louis XIV, establishing the Louisiana Territory.[1] Jesuit missionaries and other early visitors reported on the rich resources of the new territory. They described the "delightful [Mississippi] valley, where winds one of the most majestic rivers of the globe," and where "small lakes and villages [are] intersperced with woods and natural meadows . . . level as the surface of a calm ocean. . . ." Soil was so fertile that it "yields two Crops every Year without Ploughing or Sowing," bringing "forth in great Abun[d]ance, Sugar-Canes, Tobacco, Cotton-Trees, Silk-Worms, Corn, Hemp, and Vines." There was plentiful fish and game, and there were rich deposits of copper, iron, and silver.[2] St. Louis became a center of travel and commerce as settlers were enticed to the Louisiana Territory.

In the late 1700s, a Jesuit working in Louisiana, Father Jean-Baptiste Aubert, returned to France with stories that kindled the imagination of a young girl in Grenoble. Rose Philippine Duchesne, who was born in 1769, determined to become a missionary.[3] Asserting herself against the advice of many, at the age of forty-eight in 1818, she immigrated to St. Louis, Missouri, to establish in this country the Society of the Sacred Heart, the only European order founded prior to 1830 that would achieve permanent stability in the United States.[4] St. Philippine Duchesne died on November 20, 1852, at the age of eighty-two. On July 3, 1988, she was canonized by the Roman Catholic Church.

In *The Female Experience in Eighteenth- and Nineteenth-Century America*, Jill Conway concludes that "religious culture provided the most striking opportunities for new roles and new authority for women of talent."[5] Although this was generally truer for women working within the Protestant denominations than for Roman Catholic nuns, Duchesne's strong character and pioneering spirit led her to accomplish much on the frontier.

Her faith, determination, and hope never faltered, although plans were sometimes thwarted by hardships, circumstances, and male authority figures. After the Louisiana Purchase in 1803, there was an influx of American Protestants into the predominantly Catholic Louisiana Territory. In 1815, the new Catholic Bishop, William Louis Valentine Du Bourg, began

1. William E. Foley, *A History of Missouri*, 1:3.
2. Victor Collot, *A Journey in North America*; and [Anon.], *Some Consideration on the Consequences of the French Settling Colonies on the Mississippi . . .*, both cited in "The Missouri Reader: The French in the Valley," part 1, ed. Dorothy Penn, in *Missouri Historical Review* 40 (October 1945): 92–93.
3. Louise Callan, *Philippine Duchesne: Frontier Missionary of the Sacred Heart, 1769–1852*, 23.
4. Mary Ewens, *The Role of the Nun in Nineteenth-Century America*, 32.
5. Conway, *The Female Experience in Eighteenth- and Nineteenth-Century America*, 49.

a campaign to revitalize local parishes from New Orleans to St. Louis.[6] Duchesne played a key role in this campaign, starting three convents in the St. Louis area and three in the vicinity of New Orleans. Although the latter enjoyed more financial stability in her lifetime, one of the academies she started in St. Charles still trains young children. The educational seed she planted grew into nineteen schools and four colleges throughout the United States.[7]

Duchesne never would have claimed success, for she struggled constantly to bring financial stability to her convents and schools. Work in the more populated centers around St. Louis was far from her dream of ministering to Native Americans. Although she maintained a Euro-centered cultural perspective, Duchesne's letters also reveal sympathetic insights into changes forced upon them by the United States government. Only for a brief time, in 1841, at an advanced age and in ill health, was she able to realize her dream and travel with a Jesuit missionary, Father Pierre De Smet, to work among the Potawatomi Indians in Sugar Creek, Kansas. The Indians named her *Quah-kah-ka-num-ad*, the "Woman-Who-Prays-Always."

Her prayer life strengthened Duchesne to stand up for her ideas and overcome objections. Born into a wealthy family of merchants and lawyers, she resisted her parents' wish that she give up the life of a religious and marry well. In the 1790s she defied the French Revolutionary government and cared for priests who had been forced into prison or hiding after the banning of religious orders. Against the wishes of some of her religious superiors, she used the influence and money of her family to obtain the old monastery of Ste. Marie du Haut near Grenoble in 1801. She tried to reestablish the Visitation order that was in residence at Ste. Marie's before the French Revolution, but her attempts ended in disputes with her former sisters. In 1804, the nuns remaining at Ste. Marie with Philippine joined the Society of the Sacred Heart under the direction of Mother Madeleine Sophie Barat. After serving in several capacities for the society and making numerous pleas to Mother Barat, Duchesne was allowed to fulfill her lifelong dream of mission work in the New World.

Influenced by the Jesuit tradition of contemplation mixed with activism, Duchesne dedicated herself to both a consistent devotional life and hard work. She had dedicated Ste. Marie's reestablishment at the turn of the century to St. Francis Regis, a French Jesuit missionary to the poor. Claiming him as her patron saint, she took a portrait of St. Regis to enshrine at the new convent in Missouri.[8]

6. Catherine M. Mooney, *Philippine Duchesne: A Woman with the Poor,* 111.

7. There are still nineteen Sacred Heart schools. The four colleges are now considered to be "affiliated" with the order.

8. Mooney, *Philippine Duchesne,* 76–77, 215–16, 224, 241–43. Mooney discusses Duchesne's 1801 promise in prayers to St. Francis Regis that she would offer a novena of masses at his tomb; fast and receive communion on his feast each year; establish an oratory in

In spite of her middle-class upbringing, Duchesne exhibited an unusual devotion to the poor. Charity was her way of life.[9] She disregarded all physical risks to tend to the needs of the poor, whether in nursing the sick or setting up new schools. In spite of Father Du Bourg's insistence that she concentrate on boarding schools for the wealthier classes, she started the first free school for girls west of the Mississippi. She became an ardent campaigner for U.S. government funds for schools for Native American girls, because federal policy favored schools for boys.

Nor did her middle-class upbringing hinder Duchesne when it came to the physical hardships of convent life in the New World. Her involvement in the everyday life of the convent was a sermon in itself. One of Duchesne's pupils, Ellen Mullanphy Chambers, paints a picture of Duchesne's influence on the lives she touched:

> . . . She had a great love for little children, gathering them around her whenever possible. . . . She was an excellent needlewoman and taught the children sewing. . . . Her days were spent in unending labor. The rising sun found her in the garden, digging, planting, or gathering the ripened fruit and vegetables. On washdays she hung out the clothes, took them in, and sprinkled them so they would be ready for those who were to do the ironing. Besides her manual labor, she taught the higher classes several hours each day and found time to read aloud for half an hour or so each day from some spiritual book to her little community. Holidays found her in the convent parlor making vestments for the altar, and canopies and banners for the many processions that used to take place in the little church and village. No work was too hard for her, and no matter how much there was to do, nothing however small was neglected. No matter how crowded the day with busy tasks, she found time for many little visits to the chapel. . . .
>
> Nothing made me happier than to plod along beside her in the garden, picking up the potatoes as she dug them and listening to her quaintly told stories of France and the convents there, of the children in that land which seemed so far away. . . . She was a noble and brilliant woman, but withal as simple as the child who followed her along the potato row.[10]

Since Duchesne wrote in French, the editors have relied primarily on translations found in Louise Callan's book *Philippine Duchesne: Frontier Missionary of the Sacred Heart 1769–1852*.[11] The editors have selected letters

---

his honor in the convent; and provide religious instruction for poor people—if she could be back in Ste. Marie's within the year. In later years she attributed convent closings and other catastrophes to her inability to keep those promises and to Mother Galitzin's removal of St. Regis's shrine in Florissant in 1840. Mooney notes that "the doubts and fears which appear in her later years with regard to the promise to Regis are simply one more indication that Philippine's holiness can never be understood apart from her very human experiences" (77).

9. Mooney, *Philippine Duchesne*, 63, 68–76.

10. Archives of the Society of the Sacred Heart, St. Charles, Missouri, cited in Callan, *Philippine Duchesne*, 433.

11. Permission to reproduce the letters in this volume has been granted by the Paulist Press. Page references for the letters found in Callan will be identified in the text. Passages

(1) that describe the cultural changes Duchesne faced as an immigrant pioneer to the St. Louis area, including the role her faith played in meeting the challenges of a new frontier; (2) that reveal her administrative and managerial practices; and (3) that illustrate her devotion to education for women and the poorer classes. The selections also reveal her determination not to play the role prescribed for her in a script that someone else had written. She followed the dictates of her own heart, which was devoted to the Sacred Heart of Jesus.

—————————— LETTERS OF PHILIPPINE DUCHESNE ——————————

Paris, France
FEBRUARY 1, 1818

[TO HER SISTER AMÉLIE, MADAME JOSEPH-CONSTANS DE MAUDUIT][12]
    . . . For a long time a very strong and definite attraction has drawn me to the teaching of the infidels. I even thought of going to China, but that is not practicable, as women cannot appear in public there. God has listened to my prayers and has let me find nearer home and at less financial cost the happiness for which I prayed. In Paris I met the Bishop of Louisiana, and it is in his diocese that I shall work to instruct the savages and found a house of the Society. . . . I wish you would send me a supply of seed of all the kinds you have, labeled and marked with the time for sowing. The land is so fertile in the area where we shall live that the cattle are entirely hidden in the prairie grass. (206–7)

New Orleans
JUNE 3, 1818

[TO THE CHILDREN OF THE BOARDING SCHOOLS IN PARIS AND GRENOBLE]
    . . . I have already seen the savages for love of whom we have undertaken this difficult journey. A great number of them come here to sell small baskets . . . or the blackberries they gather in the woods. The skill with which they make these baskets and the shrewdness with which they do their trading prove that they are quite intelligent and so they are able some day to attain to a knowledge of God, if only they are brought to civilization and are thus enabled to become Christians.

    But in this city, which is more corrupted by luxury and magnificence than any city in France, people are accustomed to treat the Indians like

—————————

quoted from *Philippine Duchesne: A Woman with the Poor* by Catherine M. Mooney are identified in a note.
    12. Callan spells the name *Amelie;* Mooney gives it with the accent.

animals. They have only huts to live in, and they are much more wicked than those we shall deal with in Upper Louisiana. . . .

. . . All along the Mississippi [on the way up to New Orleans (Callan's brackets)] I saw plantations where there are as many as one hundred slaves. For that alone the master would have to be worth a million francs, since each Negro is worth more than ten thousand francs In this country some planters make two hundred and fifty thousand francs' worth of sugar a year. Does that bring them happiness? I would much rather teach a little savage and eat the same kind of food she does than see myself in such great abundance and with the responsibility of so many persons, for whose salvation many masters are so indifferent, they leave them without instruction and without any practice of religion. (733–34)

New Orleans
JUNE 7, 1818

[ADDRESSEE UNKNOWN]
Here is a quite astonishing incident, one which has indeed moved me. These ladies [the Ursulines of New Orleans] wanted to have all our laundry done at their own expense and by their Negresses in order to help us in every way possible. I had Catherine [Lamarre] do just the soaping. She was doing the wash in the same shed [as the Negresses]. After several quarrels, she came to tell me that she did not like being with these Negresses, and that here the whites did not mix with them. I answered her that they have the same soul as she; that they have been redeemed by the same blood and received into the same Church; and in view of the fact that she and we had come for the Blacks, that if she did not want to keep company with them, it would be well to avail herself of the ships about to return.[13]

Bishop Du Bourg ignored Duchesne's expressed desire to do mission work among the Indians. He dispatched the sisters to the small and remote village of St. Charles to start a boarding school for Creoles and Americans.

OCTOBER 8, 1818

[TO MOTHER BARAT]
. . . Divine Providence has brought us to the remotest village in the United States. It is situated on the Missouri, which is frequented only by those trading with the Indians who live not very far away from here, but I have not seen any little Indian girls since we came here. . . . Against this race there is not the same prejudice as there is against *Negroes* and

---

13. Brackets are Mooney's. Mooney, *Philippine Duchesne,* 128.

mulattoes. Monseigneur Du Bourg has said positively that we may not admit them to either of our schools [boarding or free], and he has appointed one day a week for the instruction of the colored people; otherwise, he says, we should not hold the white children in school. He told us of an experience he had in the college in Baltimore, which shows how difficult it is to overcome race-prejudice in this country. He consulted the Archbishop of Baltimore on the matter and was told that this attitude would have to be maintained as the last safeguard of morality and manners in this country.[14]

This letter also reveals the tension between the bishop's desire to provide schooling for the American settlers and Duchesne's desire to reach the Indians.

. . . A few years ago . . . one might have witnessed conduct comparable to pagan bacchanalia: girls scantily clad, holding a bottle of whisky in one hand and a man with the other, dancing every day of the year and never doing any work. Now there is more exterior decency, but these people are as ignorant of morality as the Indians are. In our free school we now have twenty-two children, and in proportion to the population this equals a school of one hundred in France. These children have never heard of our Lord, of His birth or His death, nor of hell, and they listen open-mouthed to our instructions. I have to say to them continually, "Yes, this is really true." All except two are learning the alphabet. Among the children who pay a little fee there is the same ignorance. When we complain to the Bishop that we have no savages, he replies: "Indeed you have, and your work among these children will be wider and more lasting because of the influence of the rich over the poor." (277–78)

NOVEMBER 20, 1818

[TO MOTHER BARAT]
. . . Living in this remote corner of the world, cut off by the Mississippi and the Missouri rivers, I do not know whether you have received a single one of the letters we have written, but I have had the inexpressible consolation of receiving several from you. . . .

Among all the things we shall need and those I have already asked for, the essentials are such as may keep us alive. . . . We look on potatoes and cabbage as you in France regard rare delicacies. . . . The gift of a pound of butter and a dozen eggs is like a fortune received. . . . During the hunting season, which we are in now, we can procure venison and ducks, but in

14. Duchesne, *Philippine Duchesne*, 277; Mooney, *Philippine Duchesne*, 129. Mooney interprets this letter as revealing Duchesne's ambiguous attitude toward racial prejudice and acceptance of the conventions of the time.

the spring and summer one can get only salted fish and meat. Many of the cows are almost dry. . . . If we have to buy milk, it costs twelve cents a bottle, and fifteen cents in winter. And with all the salt diet we lack water. The well in our garden is dry and it costs twelve cents every time we send someone to the Missouri to get us two little buckets of water. (279 80)

DECEMBER 1818

[TO MOTHER THÉRÈSE MAILLUCHEAU IN FRANCE]

. . . I do not know how to describe the place in which we live. Its population is made up of a mixture of American emigrants from the East, French and Canadian Creoles, German, Irish, and Flemish settlers, along with half-breeds. . . . As for real Indians, we never see them because the Americans from the East are pushing them out and making war with them. They are withdrawing further away. . . . We would attract them more quickly with liquor than with sermons. . . . But in conscience no one should give it to them, seeing what a state it puts them in and how dangerous it makes them. God allows some faint light of religion to shine amongst them and bring about conversions, but these are very rare. . . .

We have had the privilege of doing without bread and water. I had expected the former privation, but I never dreamed that on the banks of the Missouri we should lack water with such an abundant flow of it in sight. . . . The Missouri is almost frozen over, and it is so cold that the water freezes beside the fire. . . . We have logs, but they are too large, and there is no one to chop them for us and no saw with which we might cut them ourselves. Laziness is the vice of this region; it belongs to the way of life. People work only when obliged to do so, and pride keeps many from working for wages. *[She asks for some seeds and other items.]* . . . We should also value a case of altar wine and one of olive oil—the only edible oil to be had here is bear grease, which is disgusting. . . . I do not see how we shall survive Lent with only fish cooked without either butter or oil, and not an egg to be had till spring. But we are willing and glad to be in want. (283–85)

FEBRUARY 15, 1819

[TO MOTHER BARAT]

. . . If our sisters in France imagine us surrounded by savages, they are quite mistaken. I have seen only a few old ones who made their first Communion at fifty or sixty years of age, when temptations to passions had passed. But to compensate for our disappointment we have new employments: we dig in the garden, carry out the manure, water the cow, clean out her little stable. . . . And we do all this with as much joy as we would have if we were teaching Indians, for God wills it this way, and our poverty, along with the false pride of the settlers, prevents us from getting servants. (289)

Duchesne was quite content in St. Charles, where the nuns were on friendly terms with the townspeople, many of whom appreciated being able to send their children to the free school. Since the amount paid by boarding students could not support the entire operation, there were such financial difficulties that Bishop Du Bourg ordered the Sacred Heart sisters to move their school to St. Ferdinand's in Florissant. Duchesne had some authority to administer the business of the school; her options were limited, however. Du Bourg had control of several thousand francs of the nuns' money; also, Duchesne had no access to her family fortunes, nor did she receive much funding from the mother house in France. She asserted her business acumen when responding to the contractor's proposal for the new convent.[15]

MARCH 15, 1819

[TO FATHER BARAT][16]

. . . When I saw the contractor's plans and estimate for a convent there, I realized it was simply extortion—excessive expenditures that would bring ruin on us. I wrote to the Bishop, refusing the services of the contractor and telling him that we had no other funds than those we had placed in his keeping. He replied that he had weighed the matter well and, being unable to assist us, he thought it best to drop the undertaking at Florissant. (296)

Later, when the Bishop changed his mind and insisted on a move to Florissant, Duchesne describes in her journal the situation that caused her to submit.

Monseigneur came to make his retreat at Father Richard's house. He spent one whole day upsetting all our plans, as well as the desires of Fathers Richard and Acquaroni, who have simply exhausted themselves in their efforts to get us firmly established here at St. Charles. The Bishop has in his keeping the sum of $2,000, which was sent to him from France by Mother Barat for us at the time of our departure for America. He declares he will use it only at St. Ferdinand's [in Florissant] and that he will borrow the rest of the money needed for the erection of the new building. (298)

They finally moved to Florissant in the fall of 1819. Beset by money troubles with his several building projects, Bishop Du Bourg required Duchesne to write a letter

---

15. Barbara O. Korner, "Philippine Duchesne: A Model of Action," 353.
16. Father Louis Barat was the brother of Duchesne's Mother Superior, Sophie Barat. He had been instrumental in convincing his sister to let Duchesne go to America.

to Mr. Mullanphy, a wealthy Irish merchant, for a loan of $2,000 to finish their building. Difficulties with insufficient funds would plague Duchesne throughout her life.

OCTOBER 8, 1821

[TO MOTHER BARAT]

. . . Our boarding school must inevitably diminish, as the Bank of Missouri has failed, and so have the banks of many other states. Money is so scarce, even the largest landowners have none. All trade is carried on by barter and we are getting absolutely nothing. There is some question of a new issue of bank notes. . . . Until these notes appear, we shall receive little money from anyone. As creditors may even refuse to accept them, only by a stroke of Providence shall we be able to pay our debt that falls due in November, 1821. . . .

The money shortage has made the price of produce drop very low. Corn is down to 25¢ a bushel, meat to 2 1/2 or 3¢ a pound; soap is only 8¢. (350–51)

Mission work among Native Americans remained of vital interest to her.

Florissant
JULY 1822

[TO MOTHER D'OLIVIER]

. . . The Osage Indians have promised to receive the priests who are going amongst them. This is a savage tribe that sets the example for many others. A priest is going there to establish a mission soon. . . .

. . . [T]he savages in this region like the French and what they bring them better than the Americans, as they call the people of the United States. They tell a story of an Indian who said to one of them: "They told us the great father of Spain had given the land to the great father of France; then the forest trees fell in a great heap and there was a great fire and dancing around it. But then they told us the great father of France had given the land to you, the Americans; then no trees fell and there was no fire and no dancing, but only the ashes of great grief." (744–45)

JANUARY 4, 1823

[TO MOTHER BARAT]

. . . There is no denying the fact that temptations are great in St. Louis, and it adds to our distress to realize what we have to fear for the girls who are still in our school. I consider St. Louis as bad as Malacca in the days of St. Xavier. After a short period of fervor, or rather effervescence, there has followed a time of great indifference as regards religion and of excess in the pursuit of pleasure. Our children are taken to balls, shows, speeches, have bad books in their hands, live in idleness. Already several vocations have been undermined in these surroundings, and I foresee that here, as in the time of Jesus Christ, the poor will be chosen to work for Him in preference to the rich. (374)

Florissant
DECEMBER 28, 1823

[To her sister, Amélie de Mauduit]

. . . The village in which we live is five leagues from St. Louis, the principal town in the new state of Missouri, and about the same distance from St. Charles, our first place of residence, which has been for some time the capital of the State.[17] . . . Our convent is built of brick and joins the newly erected parish church. . . . Monseigneur gave the land for the church and made us a gift of the property we own, consisting of a big meadow, a small woodland along a creek, and a garden with a courtyard and a pasture for our animals. We have about 100 chickens, 7 cows, 1 horse. We do not have to buy feed for the animals—we just open the gate and let them out; in the evening they all return to exactly the same gate without shepherd or shepherdess. I forgot to mention our five lambs and sheep and some very handsome geese. In good weather all the livestock graze in the common fields and woods, and in winter these animals have no shelter except a shed covered with thatch. (394)

JANUARY 2, 1824

[To Mother Eugenie de Gramont]

. . . We make our soap, candles for both the house and the church, altar-breads, our butter, woolen yarn, and cotton and linen thread. We sowed some cotton this year, but had no success with it, as the seeds were not suited to this climate. We hope to succeed better another year and to purchase a loom for weaving cotton and woolen cloth. We know how to dye in several colors—black, grey, and yellow. There is no expense in this as we obtain the dye from native wood or plants. We are going to plant some indigo to obtain a blue coloring matter which is easy to use. Salted pork, milk, vegetables from our garden make up our food supply. But I have written enough about the animal side of life. I beg you, pray to the Sacred Heart of Jesus for us, that He may assure us of one day possessing eternal life. There we hope to see you again someday. (395)

17. Missouri had become a state on August 10, 1821.

As nearby Jesuits started a seminary for Native American boys, Duchesne's hopes revived that she might realize her dream of a similar seminary for girls.

Florissant
JUNE 10, 1824

[To MOTHER BARAT]

. . . Government aid for the civilization of the savages will be given only after the work has been undertaken. Then the missionaries must follow the plan outlined by the Secretary of War in what regards both the boys and the girls. As the Father Rector cannot take the latter group, we hope to do so, trusting in the help of Divine Providence. Food will cost very little; we have a place to house them; and we shall beg clothing for them. The chief agent of Congress for treating with the tribes in this part of the country [Gen. William Clark] approves of this plan. He is going to Washington and will see whether the Secretary of War [John C. Calhoun] is willing to appropriate money for the traveling expenses of some more of our religious to help with this work. That would be an unprecedented favor for Indian girls, and the agent has little hope of obtaining it. But we must do everything in our power to further this important work which has been the object of so many prayers, which really brought us here, and which is in itself so interesting and offers us more hope of success than anything else does. . . .

If my skin were worth any money, I should willingly sacrifice it to support our missions. (399–400)[18]

JULY 25, 1824

[To MOTHER BARAT] .

. . . The five Indian boys the Fathers have give them a great deal of trouble now . . .

I do not know when we shall be able to take the Indian girls. We are all eager to do so, but this has been a year of disasters. The Missouri has flooded to a great width and carried off the farmhouses and cattle of many settlers and ruined the crops. There will be almost no grain or vegetables, and we shall soon have only three or four pupils. . . .

Here at Florissant we are no longer afraid of starving to death, and that is something. (404)

In March of 1825, she reports that the Fathers have received $500 from the Government for the Indian boys. In April one of the Fathers brought her two girls,

---

18. Callan's brackets.

and Duchesne started a Female Indian Seminary. By June there were six girls at the school.

JUNE 8, 1825

[To MOTHER BARAT]

. . . The government has appropriated a sum of money for the civilization of the Indians. As the Secretary of War is in charge of this, I am writing to him to ask support for four teachers and money to help erect a school building which will cost at least three thousand francs. The policy of the government is to give aid and encouragement only to associations which have means to found institutions. So even if he gives us something, it will be but a fraction of our expense. But we must rely on Divine Providence and not do less for God than the Protestants, who have schools for the Indians in many sections of the states. (420)

JULY 3, 1825

[To MOTHER BARAT]

. . . I intended writing to the Secretary of War to obtain help for the Indian girls. But the Father Superior [Van Quickenborne], who is acquainted with the government's intention of putting the boys and girls together here as in other *seminaries* of this kind, told me that I should be cutting his throat if I did so. That was enough to stop me. He wrote instead and stressed the advantage of separate education for the two sexes. I have small hope of success. The Presbyterians watch keenly for any advantage, and they will make an outcry against the novelty of the plan. (423)

DECEMBER 27, 1825

[To MOTHER BARAT]

. . . The policy of the United States government is to drive all the Indians out of the settled states. Agents buy their lands and push them into uninhabited regions. The chiefs say: You are stronger; we must give way to you—and they withdraw, but not without great suffering, for they have not enough room for hunting. The Sac tribe has made a treaty with the government and reserved a large area of land . . . outside the present territory of the United States. The head man there would be glad to have a priest in residence, but the people are so poor, they could not assure him a living. . . . The Osage are farther away and much more savage, for they have not been brought into contact with ideas of the true religion as have the tribes near Canada. Take this matter to heart, Reverend Mother, and may all turn out well. (429)

During the summer of 1826, it became clear that the school for Indian girls would have to be closed, but there was good news, too. Enrollment in the boarding school was increasing.

JANUARY 1, 1827

[TO HER COUSIN JOSEPHINE PÉRIER, MADAME JACQUES-FORTUNAT DE SAVOYE-ROLLIN][19]

. . . The American government has followed the policy of buying up the Indian lands within the boundaries of the states in order to secure public peace. . . . This is the last year the savages will be allowed to hunt in, or even to travel across, the state of Missouri. Having been herded together in restricted areas, they no longer have sufficient land for the hunt, and this makes them more and more miserable. Some efforts have been made to get the Indian children into schools, but the parents only allow them to remain for a short time, then come and reclaim them. The children are worse off then than before, because when they take up the old licentious life, they act with more knowledge of right and wrong. Some Presbyterian missionaries, supported by a society in New York, took up residence near the Osage Indians, but they complained loudly about the conditions in which they had to live. They could not hold the Indian children in the school and had only half-breeds. It is rumored that they will give up the mission. Some Lazarist Fathers who journeyed along the Arkansas River . . . were begged by the pioneers in that region, which is being opened to settlement, to reside among them, . . . but there was no means of subsistence for the Catholic missionaries, while those of the Methodist sect . . . are supported either by the government or by different organizations. All this is a reason for greater zeal on our part. (444)

Duchesne felt that there was a need to establish a City House in St. Louis. This would provide a stronger financial base in a more populated area. A boarding school could accommodate both poor and wealthy students. She received little encouragement from the Jesuit Father Superior, Van Quickenborne, so she wrote to Mr. Mullanphy, the wealthy St. Louisan who had helped to establish the Florissant boarding school. He made an offer, and she exercised the authority bestowed on her by Mother Barat to sell or acquire property in the name of the Society of the Sacred Heart.

MARCH 1, 1827

[TO MOTHER BARAT]

. . . After making many inquiries, I realized that we should need at least 30,000 francs on hand in order to procure a house in St. Louis as

---

19. Callan spells the name *Perier;* Mooney uses the accent.

good as this one, that we could not count [on others for help]. . . . So I wrote to Mr. Mullanphy, asking him if he would not give us a house, as he owns a great many, and that on favorable conditions in view of our intention of opening a free school for the children of the poor. He answered by asking in turn how many orphans we would house on the following conditions: 1. that he would give us a brick house built about seven years ago, situated at a distance of a fifteen-minute walk from the Catholic church with 24 arpents of land around it . . . the house having 12 fairly large rooms, but not being as large as our convent here; 2. that he or his heirs would give each orphan at her entrance the sum of 50 francs for her bed, etc., and 25 francs yearly for clothing; and 3. that he would give 5000 francs cash for the initial expenses of the foundation. I replied that we would accept 15 or 20 orphans; he wanted 20, and they were to be presented by himself or his oldest daughters.

I went to inspect the house and found the site somewhat similar to that of Ste. Marie, though less attractive. It is high, solitary, and in a healthful location overlooking the Mississippi and the city, from which it is well removed. It seemed to me we should be going against our own best interests to refuse this offer. True, we are taking on a burden for which we shall be responsible, but think of a debt of 20 or 30 thousand francs, or the necessity of being confined to a village where we are shut in by six feet of water up to our door five or six times a year, and that quite suddenly and with such force as to wash away the bridge leading to our house, to flatten all our fences, to destroy our entire garden, which has produced nothing these last two years, as the vegetables have rotted in the water. Besides that, there is the probability that if we do not take the lead [in opening a school],[20] someone else may do so, and we shall be without any means of supporting ourselves. Are not these facts worth taking into consideration?

You counseled me to ask advice, and I did so. At first the Father Rector [Van Quickenborne] was opposed to the plan, then he thought better of it, though he was not enthusiastic. . . . I told him that you considered an establishment in St. Louis necessary, that you had told me to make plans for it, and that this should come before any other undertaking. The other Jesuit Father [De Theux][21] is wholly in favor of the St. Louis foundation. So I accepted, and things are getting under way. . . . It was impossible for me to wait for an answer from you in this matter, as several parties were interested in the property—and how could I say when your answer would reach us, with the dangers and delays of sea travel? I am sorry you are not sending a good superior. . . . The people of St. Louis would certainly appreciate a religious who is American in both language and character.

20. Callan's brackets.
21. Callan's brackets.

No other nation in the world admires itself as this one does. . . . I cling to the thought that the religious who are coming are younger than I and may be able to learn the language and customs of the country.

I think it best for me to go to St. Louis for the foundation. The position might offer some dangers for others, as it is unwise to be too friendly at first with people, lest one make undesirable intimacies. Then, too, there are many well-educated people in St. Louis, and some of our religious might not make a good impression. (446–47)

Duchesne's spunk and diplomacy stand out in one of the few letters she wrote in English.

[SPRING] 1828

[To WILLIAM CARR LANE, THE MAYOR OF ST. LOUIS]

I have recourse to your authority for the redress of an abuse which I look upon as very much against the welfare of our establishment. You know, Sir, that our young ladies, day schollars [*sic*], . . . have to pass the creek that runs all around our house. The warm weather invites a number of men and boys to swimming in the creek, and every day our young ladies meet with that disagreeable sight, both coming [to] and leaving the house; and as I understand that some regulation of court forbids swimming in public places, I suppose that it is merely by some negligence of the sheriffs in discharge of their duty that it takes place.

As you are Sir, the father of an amiable family I need not say how much that rudeness is against the delicacy of sentiments we strive to endow our young ladies with, and I am convinced that you will be so good as to use your power to remove that obstacle. (475)

St. Louis
MAY 18, 1830

[To MOTHER BARAT]

We have had the cross of poverty this year to such an extent as to prohibit us from writing to you, as we had not the money to spare for the postage and were not able to get some mail out of the post office for the same reason. The convents at St. Ferdinand and St. Louis have often been several days without a penny, and we have had to pretend that things were otherwise, so as not to lose credit at the stores. At last, however, Mother Eugenie [overseer of the Louisiana convents] wrote me to draw on her for the money which you were so good as to instruct her to give us . . . [W]e have such scanty resources—eight boarding pupils, twenty-seven people to feed, nineteen of them to support entirely, and 1250 francs to be paid to the hired man. The eighteen day pupils who pay tuition have kept us alive this winter. Day pupils also support St. Charles, where there is only 1 boarding pupil, along with several orphans who are cared for gratis . . .

We have sixty children in the free school, and within a year that school will have given us four postulants. (487)

When more nuns arrived from France in 1831, Mother Duchesne, now over sixty years old, hoped to be relieved of her duties as mother superior of the Missouri missions.

AUGUST 28, 1831

[TO MOTHER BARAT]

Do name Mother de Kersaint superior. I shall keep so quiet in my corner as never to be in her way. I should add that I am ready to go anywhere you may send me, though I realize that wherever I go I may be in the way because of my age and my years as a professed religious. And, too, I can never deal easily with the parents of our children. The Americans do not understand me. The Creoles want good looks and attractive manners. The best thing for me to do is to disappear, either teaching a class or caring for the sick. I tell you this in all sincerity, and I shall act accordingly. (523)

Because some of the nuns sent recently from France wrote back with complaints about the condition of the St. Louis house and the low enrollment, Mother Barat reluctantly agreed to replace Mother Duchesne as American superior. But Bishop Rosati, Bishop Du Bourg's successor, argued persuasively to leave Mother Duchesne in place. His letter of protest provides a picture of the differences one could expect in American and European standards for convents.

[FEBRUARY] 1832

[BISHOP ROSATI TO MOTHER BARAT]

Madame, Mother Duchesne has informed me, according to your instructions, of your latest letter to her and of the changes you believe it proper and even necessary to make in regard to the government of your institutions in Missouri. . . . I have begged Mother Duchesne to suspend its execution until she heard from you again. I want you to think over what I am going to tell you.

In the first place, I believe there is no one among your religious who can gain as much confidence as Mother Duchesne justly receives here. All who know her respect and venerate her because of her virtues, which, joined to age and the experience she has acquired during her long sojourn in this country, make her esteemed by all. . . . In the next place, I see by the complaints that have moved you to decide on the proposed changes that things have been misrepresented to you. I am well aware that no one wished to deceive you, but rather spoke from a lack of insight into the matter. . . . You have been told the property has not been properly cultivated; one of your religious newly arrived from France told me the same thing. I replied that after she had been here a while and had made attempts like mine, she would realize that in America, where land is cheap and labor expensive, a religious community cannot obtain profits from its farm produce, for this must be sold at a very low price. . . .

With regard to the religious sent from France, whom Mother Duchesne has not kept here—this action was not prompted by the fact that she did not need them, but rather by her desire to work for the general good of all your convents. This generosity . . . led her to make sacrifices in order to satisfy the demands of the superiors of the Louisiana houses. These demands were such that had they always been heeded, the houses here would be empty. I speak from firsthand knowledge on this point. More than once she has had to make a change of house or climate to satisfy some of the religious or to prevent complaints. You yourself know that this is not rare in communities, where we feel the effects of human weakness unless we are well advanced on the way of perfections. Religious are also children of Adam, so this is not to be wondered at. On this point in particular Mother Duchesne has suffered very much. . . .

I am speaking very frankly, Madame, because I have at heart the happiness and prosperity of your houses in my diocese. I believe that the contemplated change will in no way contribute to this end. No religious whom you may designate to fill the position now held by Mother Duchesne could really replace her. I greatly fear this excessive desire to enlarge the house, to make it appear more like the French houses, and to put the houses here on the same footing with them. . . . In this country we have not the resources nor many wealthy Catholics. At present the Protestants have their own schools and they fear to send their daughters to a convent lest they be converted to Catholicism. That is the real reason for the small boarding school. Is it prudent to go into debt and pay a high rate of interest to build new additions? As things are now, much good is being done with the orphans and in the crowded free school, and there are others who could pay if you received them as day pupils.

In all the convents good is being done and more is hoped for in the future. With the growth of population and wealth will come increased opportunities for good. . . . Let us follow, then, the guidance of Divine Providence; it will not fail to uphold us. That is what those newly come from Europe do not know and do not want to know. But we know it after years of experience. Their views must not be placed before those of experienced persons. I pray you to pardon me if I speak so frankly. I sincerely desire the prosperity of your convents. (526–27)

Barat was persuaded and left Duchesne in place as superior. She proceeded to fight the good fight with unfailing dedication, hanging on to her dream to reach the Indians.

JUNE 23, 1833

[To JOSEPHINE PÉRIER]

You simply overwhelm me, dearest Cousin, with your friendship and your gifts. . . .

I hope you do not mind if I decline your invitation to return to Sainte Marie and rest. I prefer to die at work and, as they say, "in the fight." . . . It has always been my ambition to die among the Indians, and in my youthful enthusiasm I thought this an easy thing to attain. But at close range one sees that one cannot hope for that, and where there seemed to be reality, one finds only a beautiful dream. . . . I am not holy enough to gather about me a school for Indian girls. We find closer at hand a kind of white savage, who lives without faith or in deadly indifference to religion. Of course, one can always win a few children, but how difficult it is to raise them to the level of generous virtue. (543)

By September, 1840, Duchesne's health reached the point where she had to be relieved of her duties as superior. After a trip to Florissant to gather her scant belongings, she "took her place [in the City House in St. Louis] without distinction except that of seniority in profession, in the ranks of the community among the Mothers and Sisters who had for so many years looked to her as the representative of the foundress herself in the American convents of the Society" (622).

She spent much of her time in the infirmary, but Duchesne never fully gave up her dream of traveling to an Indian mission. The Jesuit missionary, Father De Smet, saw an important role for her to play. De Smet and Duchesne, encouraged by favorable responses from both Bishop Rosati and Mother Barat, decided to press the matter.

St. Charles
JANUARY 7, 1841

[To MOTHER ELIZABETH GALITZIN, THEN IN NEW ORLEANS]

. . . So far we have been disappointed in our hopes—at least I have, for all my inclinations and desires urge me to work among these tribes. . . . Yesterday, the feast of the Kings, a visit from Father De Smet, who has come back from the Rocky Mountains, roused my ardor once more, and that to such an extent that I experienced a sort of physical resurrection as a result of the hope I feel that I may be among those chosen for a mission that is now offered to us under very favorable auspices.

Beyond the western boundary of Missouri, this Father tells me, there is a very good tribe that comes from Canada, already partly converted to Christianity. They are called the Potawatomi. A holy Breton priest . . . now lives the same hard life as his new charges and finds great consolation in working among them. . . . The Government has contributed to the expense of building a log church and may also help build us a house. The missionary whom I saw yesterday considers it a duty for us to seize this opportunity before others of non-Catholic faith do so. I showed him the letter you brought me from Bishop Rosati, in which he wrote to me so positively: *Follow your attraction.* At the time I received it, I did not pay much attention to it; for my soul was crushed and all my offers were rejected. Now I think it really is the voice of God. Our Mother General [Barat] has often expressed this desire, and our Lord will so arrange matters that you will lend a hand in this enterprise. (629)

Duchesne was among the four nuns who traveled with the Jesuit missionaries to Sugar Creek, Kansas, in June 1841.

From the Tribe and Village of the Potawatomi
[JULY 21, 1841]

[TO MOTHER BARAT]
    . . . This tribe, which like many others was driven out of Michigan by the Americans, is now about half Catholic. These people have built their village at a distance from the pagans, who are being converted gradually. Once baptized, they never revert to drunkenness or stealing. Whatever is found is placed at the door of the church to be claimed by the owner. Not a single house has locks on the doors, yet nothing is ever missing. The Indians gather in groups . . . for morning prayers, Mass, and catechism. In the evening they assemble again for prayers. They eat seven times a day. (638)

While Duchesne was unable to do much physical labor, her constant prayers were appreciated by the religious who accompanied her and by the Indians. Mother Galitzin visited Sugar Creek on Palm Sunday in 1842. Alarmed at Duchesne's deteriorating health, she recalled her to St. Charles, where Duchesne would spend her final days.

In 1843 Duchesne learned that her long campaign for federal support for a school for Indian girls had resulted in the Potawatomi mission school for girls receiving federal funds. An Indian agent visited the school and, pleased with what he saw, ordered necessary school supplies and "promised to recommend the school to Congress."[22]

22. Letter to Euphrosine Duchesne, May 5, 1843, in Duchesne, *Philippine Duchesne,* 666.

St. Charles
APRIL 22, 1852

[TO MOTHER BARAT]

I was astonished and greatly consoled on receiving your letter. Since Easter of last year I have not been expecting to live through another twelve months; especially during last summer there were times when I could not even write my own name. When the weather got cool, that gave me back some strength, but my memory has been failing more and more, and also my eyesight. . . .

The charity of our Mother Superior is a wonderful example for all. She sleeps in the same room with me, and this gives her an opportunity to exercise her charity. She has also had still more opportunities because of the illness and death of one of our Sisters and a pupil. . . .

We have enrolled a good number of new pupils, but we cannot take more than thirty-five without being greatly overcrowded and risking fresh cases of illness. There is real need for an addition to the building; and since I am so useless, I have begged God to take me to Himself, as that would give place for two more people. . . .

Duchesne describes the achievements of various schools and Jesuit missions serving Native Americans.

My letter is very badly written, but I cannot see to rewrite it. I have strength, however, to kneel in spirit at your feet to receive your blessing with all possible love and respect in the Heart of Jesus. (713–15)

St. Philippine Duchesne died on November 20, 1852. On October 9, 1872, Father De Smet remembered her as he wrote from St. Louis:

. . . Her praise has been and is on the lips, not only of her own Sisters in religion, but of all those who had the honor and the happiness of her acquaintance. On every return from my Indian missionary visits, I deemed it a most agreeable duty to pay my respects to good Mother Duchesne, and I never returned from one of these visits but with an increase of edification, with a higher opinion of her virtues and sanctified life, and always under the full conviction that I had conversed with a truly living saint. I always considered Mother Duchesne as the greatest protectress of our Indian missions. For years she offered two Communions a week and daily prayers for the conversion of the Indians. . . . I can entertain no doubt, many were brought over to the Holy Faith of Christ by the many acts of mortification she performed, and by the constant prayers she offered up for the salvation of these, her dearly beloved Indian children. (686)

On July 3, 1988, Rose Philippine Duchesne was canonized by the Roman Catholic Church. Her remains are buried in the Shrine of St. Philippine Duchesne at the Convent of the Sacred Heart in St. Charles.

SUSAN B. VANARSDALE (1824–1856)

*I*n 1820 the Missouri Constitution provided for the establishment of free public schools, which were controlled at the local level for decades. There were also private academies and denominational institutions, separate schools for boys and girls, and those that were coeducational. There were notable women educators, such as Mary Easton Sibley, whose private school for girls in St. Charles developed into Lindenwood College; Eliza Ann Carleton, the founder and president of Carleton College in Farmington; and Susan Blow, who established the first public kindergarten in the nation at Carondelet, a suburb of St. Louis. The achievements of these women of vision tend to overshadow the work of numerous others in towns and rural areas, who won permission to work in a field that was dominated by men and often had to raise subscriptions from parents to earn a modest salary. For young single women, teaching was one of the few opportunities for employment. Some were truly dedicated to their task; others dreamed of the day when they would leave the classroom and marry. Often a young woman would spend school terms far from home, boarding with families of the children she was teaching.[1] The experiences of Susan B. Vanarsdale were typical of those of many teachers, but the account of those experiences found in her diary is exceptional because of Susan's literary talent and emotional complexity.[2]

Susan was born on a farm near Harrodsburg, Kentucky, on March 2, 1824. Wanting to live in a non-slave state, her father Peter took his wife Charity, their son, and seven daughters to Carrollton, Illinois, in 1836. Another daughter, Ida, with her husband George W. Cardwell, had moved to Missouri in 1832. Susan's father recalled, "The beginning of the year 1845 we received letters from Missouri from Cardwell and family insisting our daughter Susan come over to that region and teach school and as she wished to go and try it I went with her in a carriage starting the last day of January 1845."[3] For four years Susan taught school, earning her living from what parents of the pupils paid her. She boarded with several families, and was popular with a large circle of friends. They would attend church services, eat meals together, and enjoy wholesome party games. Having strict ideas of proper behavior, Susan frowned on dancing and

1. On the experiences of Justina Woods and her teaching in the mining area of Caledonia and Big River Mills from 1849 to about 1853, see the Woods-Holman family papers at WHMC-C.

2. The family name is spelled variously as "Van Arsdalen," "Van Arsdale," "Van Arsdall," "Vanausdale," and "Vanausdoll." For information about Susan Vanarsdale's family we thank June Wilderman of the Brighton Heritage Group, Brighton, Illinois. Susan's middle initial sometimes appears as *D*.

3. "Autobiography of Peter Van Arsdall," typed transcript.

gambling. Her attitudes were influenced in part by Christianity and in part by popular sentimental literature.

Susan must have been attractive, for she had many suitors during the four years in Mexico and after she returned to her family in Illinois. Only one touched her heart, Dr. Louis Nathaniel Hunter. Susan referred to him in the diary as L., L. N., and Dr. H. One evening Dr. Hunter made improper advances and shattered Susan's illusion that he was the "beau ideal" of whom she had dreamed. She never gave him a second chance after that evening when he asked her, as she confided in the diary, "to be his mistress." Yet no one else ever took his place in her affections. After returning to Illinois, Susan led a busy life, performing domestic tasks for her parents, studying at a normal institute, teaching school, seeing friends, and helping to care for nephews and nieces. In January 1856 she nursed a nephew, who died of typhoid fever; a month later Susan also died of typhoid fever.

Writing in her diary allowed Susan to indulge her talent for writing and to analyze her moods of melancholy and self-denial. Often she chose to stay at home alone to write lengthy entries pondering her fate, in which she saw herself as the noble heroine of a sentimental drama. Through reading the diary in its entirety one learns about Susan's thoughts, the communities in which she lived, historical events, and vivid details of social life.[4] The excerpts which follow are highly selective, presenting primarily passages that illustrate Susan's social activities and the unhappy turn of events that caused her to leave Missouri and the man who loved her.

_____ **DIARY OF SUSAN B. VANARSDALE** _____

Mexico, Audrain County, Missouri
MONDAY, JUNE 21, 1847

. . . Mr. Redman came. Spent the night. Preached in Mexico. He is a widower of fifty, his wife has been dead about six months. He is after a wife again. He gallanted me to church. It was a lovely evening, soft and delicious moonlight, how could one help talking of love. I was surprised. . . .

4. The copy of Susan Vanarsdale's diary used by the present editors found its way to Mexico, Missouri, where for a while it was probably in the possession of a descendant of Ida Cardwell. It was acquired by L. M. White, who presented it to WHMC-C in 1951. Another copy is held by the Audrain County Historical Museum. Susan had no direct descendants; excerpts from the diary appear here with the permission of descendants of her father's brother Symon. The niece who transcribed the diary provided genealogical information in the introduction and in an afterword told about Susan's death and the family's appreciation of her talents and personality.

Saturday, June 26, 1847

. . . I received a ticket to a cotillion party next Thursday at Shelton Pearson's tavern. Old Mr. Levaugh gives a Birthday dinner, and Pearson has a ball in the evening. I shall not think of attending. . . .

July 4, 1847

At the Prairie House. A warm clear Sunday. A hundred and twelve took dinner at Pearson's last Thursday at Lavaugh's expense, then they danced till Friday evening. [F]olly!

Sunday, July 11, 1847

. . . [T]he Cumberland Presbyterians are holding a meeting in Mexico. . . . I do not attend. [T]hey have all gone today and I am all alone. . . .

I have received much for which I should be thankful, kind friends have ever been around my way, Christian parents who brought me up in the fear of the Lord; education and manners which have secured for me the good will and respect of all, there is no one in the world whom I wish ill, nor do I know that I have an enemy; yet what avails all this to me now. [T]ime seems to pass quickly away and I am glad of it; three months of my school are gone, my home here at Mr. White's is as pleasant as can be—my life has not been a monotonous one, I have more than realized the fondest dreams of my youthful days. [T]hat is, I have been more highly esteemed and praised by others, as they are pleased to say for my intelligence and moral worth. Several of my most intimate acquaintances have called me talented, that surely was but flattery. As for Romance, I am fully satisfied with it. [M]any have sought to win my heart and hand, Lawyer, Doctors, Preachers, etc., and more than one has gone partially deranged because they could avail nothing. I have never received a proposal that I felt the least inclined to accept; if I were a Roman Catholic, I would *now* certainly enter a nunnery, for the world has no charms for me; but no, this is wrong. I have a great work to do, to stand in my lot and wait my Father's time. . . .

Wednesday, [July] 21, 1847

J. K. Hawkins spent the night at Mr. White's on his way to the camp meeting. [H]e took occasion to hand me a note which I read the next morning, very politely asking if I have any objection to being addressed on the subject of matrimony by the writer. Well, I have no objection to being addressed on the subject, but I certainly have objections to marrying him. He deserves some attention from me for his politeness last winter. . . .

Saturday, [July] 24, 1847

. . . George Evans and Elizabeth Sims was married last March, they have parted, he has gone off. She is at her father's, so goes the world. . . .

Tuesday, [July] 27, 1847

. . . Hawkins spent the night here. I handed an answer, telling him that I know of no reason that would justify me in refusing to receive his addresses,—Oh folly. [H]e is not smart—nor am I. . . .

Saturday, [August] 14, 1847

. . . I saw Hawkins the evening before, and gave him my final answer. I am *not* the person, etc. . . .

Friday, September 3, 1847

[V]ery warm. Stopped school early and went to town with Mrs. White to attend meeting of the Bible society. Hawkins was to give an address. No one attended. . . .

Sunday, [September] 5, 1847

Clear and cool. We attended love feast[5] in the morning, then Redman preached to a crowded house, he is an excellent preacher. —[H]ome to dinner. . . . Mr. Redman and some others came out to spend the night. Mr. Redman, Mr. White and myself had a discussion about marriage. Mr. R. contended that *piety* should be the first essential qualification in the companion of a Christian, in preference to much common sense or attainments or any or everything else. We took the contrary; that intelligence, good common sense, energy, etc. were to be first. We talked two or three hours and then could not agree. . . .

[Friday,] September [17], 1847

. . . My school closed on Wednesday . . . by my having a chill, and there were only two more days. [I]t averaged 18 1/2 scholars, amounting to 64 dollars. [H]ad a slight chill Friday. [W]as very sick all day. [C]ould hardly be sick now, as I had engaged a company to go to Mr. Blue's Saturday to eat peaches and watermelon. . . .

---

5. A "love feast" was a gathering imitating the occasions when early Christians would eat together to celebrate their sense of community and friendship.

Sunday, [October] 3, 1847

They killed a pig and churned before breakfast. We all went to meeting at Liberty school house. . . . Mrs. Muldrow spent half the week out here helping me quilt. . . .

Monday, [November] 22, 1847

Rainy. . . . I am to teach school in the neighborhood of Blue's this winter, commence next week.

[Undated]

Commenced school Nov. 29, boarding at Mr. Blue's. But few scholars. Have a good home. . . .

Saturday, December 25, 1847

Christmas Day. Cloudy snowy day. . . . They were dancing in two rooms at Morris's. We looked on a few minutes. It was the largest party ever has been in Mex. More than a hundred attended. . . .

Monday, [December] 27, 1847

Had a candy pulling at Prairie House at night. What a jam and what sport. Upward of fifty persons. I had my full share of fun. . . .

Friday, December [31], 1847

Mrs. Morris had a sewing. Thirteen there. An excellent dinner. Came home in the evening worn and muddy. . . .

March 6, [1848]

At the Prairie House once more. My school closed last Thursday, March 2. The winter has passed away very pleasantly. I had a good home. There has been a good deal of sickness of late. One of my scholars, Victoria Blue, [became ill] the 15th of Feb. of Head Disease and died on the 20th. A smart child. . . . I quit school and watched at her bedside day and night. . . . Mr. Blue would charge me nothing for my board. They were all so kind. . . . Dr. Hunter returns to Mexico. The winter has been warm and wet. Some snow fell last week. Not enough for sleighing . . .

MONDAY, [MARCH] 27, 1848

. . . Tomorrow we start to Illinois. Anxious as I am to see [all] at home, I cannot start without some misgivings. The last few days have passed so pleasantly. The company of L., [h]is attentions have convinced me that I am weak as the weakest. Yes, my heart is won completely, and were it not for one thing I would be as happy as mortal need be. But I must not complain. . . .

Mexico, Audrain County, Missouri
SATURDAY, [APRIL] 8, 1848

. . . I am as homesick as ever I was. Do wish I had stayed in Illinois. . . .

APRIL 27, 1848

Circuit Court adjourned today. It has been a busy time. A great many people in town. . . . I bought of a book peddler the other day two books, *The Honeysuckle* and *The Physiology of Love*. I was sick all last week. Had an attack of chills, the worst I have ever had. I expect to commence school next Monday. Dear Life!

[UNDATED]

Commenced school in Mexico, May 1st, 1848. 26 scholars the first week. No other school in town. . . .

SUNDAY, MAY 7, 1848

. . . In the afternoon we young folks went out in the prairie gathering flowers. Then Dr. H and I rode home with Jane. We came back home. A pleasant ride. Mr. Harrison and Dr. H. spent the evening here. What does it mean? . . .

SATURDAY, [MAY 13], 1848

. . . [M]y school now numbers 38 scholars. . . . A most lovely moonlight night. I wrote half a page by moonshine. . . .

SUNDAY, MAY [14], 1848

[After a church service and dinner in Concord, Susan, Will Day, Mary Ward, and Dr. L. N. Hunter rode home by moonlight.]
. . . It was a beautiful night, and it might have been a lovely ride but [for] the turn the conversation took. Oh, I felt so dreary. As though the light of hope was extinguished forever. . . .

THURSDAY, [MAY] 18, 1848

. . . Dr. H. called at dusk, we talked by moonlight till half past ten. I cannot account for my weakness the other evening. I just felt as though the Angel of Despair had fanned his wings so near to me that I felt their cold breeze enter my soul; I tried to exert myself to appear cheerful, but it was a vain effort. It just then struck me that I had been mistaken. That L. cared nothing for me, and well might it sadden me. I was truly glad when we reached home, for the first time when in his company, and when alone, I she[d] bitter tears, I knew not why. The days have passed slowly since then and I believe I was glad to hear him say they had been the longest four days he had ever experienced. . . .

SUNDAY NIGHT, JUNE 4, 1848

. . . Took a ride this evening with Dr. Hunter. We took walks almost every evening last week. . . .

JULY 4, 1848

[A] clear pleasant day. It was celebrated by a barbeque at Mexico. Upwards of six hundred attended. The Declaration of Independence was read by Mr. Mansfield. Jim Jackson then spoke fifteen minutes, then Dr. L. N. Hunter made an oration, which of course was good. . . .

SUNDAY, JULY 16, 1848

. . . L. came over and we sat in the moonlight till almost two o'clock. Time passes, oh, how swiftly. I believe I am doing wrong in some things, but how to do better I hardly know. . . .

THURSDAY, [AUGUST] 10, 1848

I am surely the veriest fool that ever did exist. Raised as I have been, knowing what is right and proper, yet acting as though I were infatuated. L. was here last night. How weak I am. I am afraid I have been deceived in regard to him. *[A sentence is marked out.]* And I have always thought him so superior to all other mortal men, but he is a man. My friends are forsaking me and my prospects never were so dark.

SATURDAY, AUGUST 19, 1848

. . . Many have sought to win my heart and hand but have never made any impression on my hard heart till I met with *L.* He more than realized the Beau Ideal of my peculiar fancy, and how could I help loving with all my soul? His manner and attention convinced me that I had won a place in his regard. I thought I should be perfectly satisfied if he would tell me he loved me. He has told me so and sealed it with the seal of love—the first kiss. Now what a dunce I am. The summer of forty-eight will never be forgotten, but will it in coming time, be looked back to with regret or with pleasure? . . .

Monday, [September] 18, 1848

Closed my school of five months. It averaged twenty-five scholars and amounted to almost 90 dollars. . . .

Sunday, [September] 24, 1848

. . . Had the toothache. Last week my face swelled very much. Had the tooth drawn this morning by Dr. Hunter. . . . If I could once more look into my own heart and examine its motives, what would I find. —Alas, my weakness. How far I have wandered into folly and sin. . . . Well, what is to be will be. . . . In the morning rode out with Dr. Hunter to Richmond Pearson's. [G]ot apples and watermelons. . . .

Tuesday night, October 17, 1848

Alas! for me there is no hope. Oh, why was I ever born? Vain dreams, false hopes. I received a letter last week from Brother telling me if I will spend the winter in Illinois, he will come for me. What must I do? I believe it would be best for me to go and never return. . . . I must leave Missouri and forget that I ever knew ——— then farewell to hope and happiness. . . .

Sunday, [November] 12, 1848

. . . L. N. spent the evening with me. I can no longer be mistaken. He has changed or else he has always been trifling. Such is my destiny. . . . That he should prove to be like other men—win but to deceive. . . . Dear life; adieu to hope. . . .

Sunday, [December] 3, 1848

. . . L. N. spent the evening and half the night here. I guess I will not see Illinois this winter. . . .

SUNDAY, [DECEMBER] 31, 1848

The close of the year! How has it passed. I have enjoyed much for which I desire to be thankful. Uninterrupted health and all the common blessings of Providence. . . . Spent a few days at home, then taught school in Mexico five months. . . . What of the future? None can tell. This much I know. God reigns, all will be well. Time has passed very pleasantly the past year. The society of L. made life seem as a pleasing dream, and if I have been mistaken—but I will still hope. The cholera has been raging in Europe and has lately appeared in New York. In all probability, it will visit us in the coming year. I tremble to think of the desolation it will make. Oh, that I may be prepared for whatever my fate may be! . . .

MONDAY, JANUARY 15, [1849]

Very cold. In the evening attended an exhibition of wax figures and a cosmorama, Queen Victoria, King Solomon and several others. Music on an organ and some songs by Mr. Blake.

TUESDAY, [JANUARY] 16, 1849

. . . L. N. spent the evening with me. I don't know what to think of him. I have always thought him almost perfection, and can I have been mistaken? Time will show. Almost every person is sick with colds. Billy Cardwell's youngest son, Thomas, was taken sick on Wednesday, the head disease. Dr. Hunter was with him almost all the time till he died. Friday his sister Malinda was taken and died at ten o'clock that night, a few hours before Tom breathed his last. I rode out on Saturday morning on horseback before breakfast. . . . The road just caked with ice. Oh it was a sad melancholy sight. Two children laid on the same board. . . . They were buried in the village graveyard late in the evening, both laid in one wide grave. A good many persons attended the funeral. I rode in with Dr. Hunter in his sleigh. It upset twice. . . .

FEBRUARY 18, 1849

. . . The California gold fever has been raging here for some time. A meeting was held yesterday to organize a company to start out the last of March. Men are going from all parts of the Union. . . .

MONDAY MORNING, [FEBRUARY 19], 1849

. . . L. N. was with me till almost morning. It is all over now. There is not a lingering ray of hope left to light my way. Yes, I have been mistaken. We talked on all sorts of subjects till a late hour, and he was about starting home when he said something to me which I thought almost insulting. I burst from him (his arms were round me and mine had been round his neck, not for the first time) and started into the other room. He stopped me at the door, "Susan, forgive me for hurting your feelings. After what has passed it would perhaps be best if we should never meet again. We cannot meet again as we have met." "Oh, Dr. Hunter," I answered, "I just want to die," and burst into tears. I could not help it. All that made life bright and happy swept away. Oh, it was agony. He led me back to the fire, and for some time nothing was said. "I have never thought I was capable of inspiring love in the breast of anyone. I have thought you were indifferent to all. I may have been mistaken." "How could you think so? I, too, have been mistaken. I thought you loved me." "I may; I do not know. I certainly think more highly of you than of any other, but I have not dared think of love. My circumstances would not allow that." Much more was said but it does not matter. He begged me to forgive and forget and let our future conduct be as it had been. I said I would try, but it will be in vain. And this is the end of my life romance. I have not deserved it of him. Why did he act as he did, why talk as he did? And now what is there on earth worth living for? Can I forget? No, I do not wish to. His image shall ever reign supreme in my heart, and may *he* ever be happy is my first wish. For myself I ask nothing. A castaway, nothing can affect me more.

TUESDAY, [FEBRUARY] 20, 1849

. . . Jim Sulleger and Dr. Hunter called and sat till bedtime. L. tried to appear as usual and succeeded better than I did. I was sad and half sick. I hardly know how I ought to act. . . . Why did I ever leave my own dear home, where I was loved and respected by all who knew me. . . . Is it wrong, then, ever to *love?* The only one whom I ever could love has proved false. . . . I am not well, but none shall hear a vain regret, and none shall hear a sigh. In silence I will endure the bitterness of my dark fate. . . .

SUNDAY, MARCH 11, 1849

. . . I have been sick all the week. In bed half the time for some days past. Why wish to live when hope is dead? . . . L. told me that if he loved any one on earth it was me; he never had loved any other, but that I was worthy of a better destiny. . . .

FRIDAY, MARCH 23, 1849

. . . Every day but confirms more fully that I have been mistaken in his character. Spending half his nights at the card table, "only for amusement." I did hope he would see and turn from his follies and yet be all I had thought him. . . . I used to tell him if he would only quit playing cards, he would be without a fault. At last I told him if he would quit it entirely I would do anything he would ask, and what did he ask? What no gentleman would stoop to think of, and what I thought no one on earth would dare have thought of asking of me. When I fully comprehended his meaning, I exclaimed, "I would die first," and burst from his arms. . . .

SATURDAY, APRIL 4, 1849

. . . Old Duncan Blue even had the assurance to address me on the subject of love. It is almost insulting. He handed me a note today telling me that he loved me, etc. etc. I wrote a few words on it and sent it back to him in short order; an ugly old gray-headed widower, with four children and nothing else, himself the very personification of laziness. Oh, dear, what next! . . .

SUNDAY, MAY 13, 1849

. . . Oh, I have been so infatuated. I could see no fault in him; though I knew I was acting improperly, that it would be wrong for others to do so, but I had as much confidence in him as in myself. I knew he had no wish to marry now, and I was willing to lengthen the days of courtship, believing what others tell me—that they are happier than married life. . . . I granted him so much that at last he thought I would refuse him nothing. . . . I was doubtless some to blame for tempting him as I did. That does not excuse him, for I did it through ignorance. I had lived in so pure a sphere that I did not know the meaning of some things as I have since heard them explained. . . . I will try, by word and example, to incline him to walk in the paths of virtue and happiness. I believe I have friends here, who, did they but know, would not let him go unpunished, and that would be worse than death to me. . . . Our conduct when in company is the same as it ever was, but when we are alone it is so different. . . . Everybody thinks we are engaged. For almost three years it has been the constant talk and they have had reason to think so, if actions meant anything. . . .

TUESDAY, [MAY] 22, 1849

. . . What is this world coming to? Old Mr. Powell called here this morning and spent an hour, and *he* did actually ask to be permitted to pay his addresses to me. I never was more astonished. I looked up at him and told him he was certainly joking. No, he said, he was not. We talked for half an hour on the subject. . . . I told him *no* very decidedly before he left. I was very sober; but when he was gone I indulged in a fit of laughter. How very ridiculous. To think of my being the third wife of an old weakminded ignorant man of sixty, with twelve living children and I don't know how many grandchildren; whose last wife has been buried but six weeks. . . . I told him I had thought he surely would not think of such things any more. He said perhaps he ought not, and if he could be content without, he would not, but so it was. Surely I ought not to wonder at anything any more. I told Ida and George the circumstances at night. It amused me to see how warm it made them. They said I ought to have considered it as nothing short of *insult* and ordered him from my presence; but I think forbearance is best. He did not intend it as an offense, and I can excuse the silly old man. . . .

SUNDAY, MAY 27, 1849

. . . I told L. N. in the morning I had some good news to tell him. He came over at night. Was anxious to know what it was. I told him I had received an offer of marriage not long since which I had accepted. "Accepted! Susan!" he exclaimed. I bowed. He appeared thunder-struck. For a minute we gazed at each other in silence. "[A]nd this is the news you had for me, *good* news, you said?" "Well, is it not good news?" "It may be to *you;* I hope it is. And you are to be married," he continued in a tone of such bitter sadness that I could hardly proceed. "Yes," I said, "but not for love; no, not for *love*, I assure you." There must, then, be some other strong inducement which he hoped would secure my happiness. "I would have a home, and a protector; but happiness, no, I never expected to be happy, never." . . . We sat for some time in silence, then I asked if he did believe what I had told him. Yes, he said, how could he doubt my word. I told him I just wished to see if he could not believe a falsehood more readily than the truth, and did he think I would accept such an offer from anyone. . . . Though I told him it was part *truth*, I had received an offer, etc. . . .

SUNDAY, [JUNE] 10, 1849

. . . L. N. spent the evening with me. He answered my verses by writing me a long piece of poetry; speaks of friendship as the dearest tie which can bind hearts. I do not exactly understand him. He says, "No, we cannot, must not part," and what must I do? . . .

SUNDAY, JULY 5 [8?], 1849

. . . L. came over in the evening and stayed till a late hour. [H]e had written me another acrostic, and I gave him a piece of twenty verses. [J]ust before he started home I wrote a *wish* for him to read the next morning. . . . It was this, "That *your* name may be written in the Book of Life."

TUESDAY, [JULY] 10, 1849

. . . [A]t dusk took a ride in a buggy with L. [H]e spoke of that *wish* and thanked me for taking so much interest in his welfare. . . . I told him that it did seem to me that Heaven could hardly be a place of joy if not shared with *him*. . . . Saturday night, midnight. . . . [Mr. Bill Cardwell, the old widower] stopped here for dinner. As soon as he left, I sat down and wrote a piece of poetry, "Old Widowers." They provoke me too much. . . .

SATURDAY, JULY 21, 1849

. . . My piece, "Old Widowers," was published in the *Fulton Telegraph*.[6] L. sent it without my consent. I guess the Widowers will pester me no more (29–30). . . .

FRIDAY, AUGUST 3, 1849

This day was set apart by proclamation of President Taylor as a day of fasting and humiliation and prayer, that the great scourge [cholera] that has been desolating our land may be moved. I suppose it has been generally observed all over the land; but *here* the people were too busy, could not spare the time, breakfast bells rang all over town as usual, and work did not cease. Oh, I was *so* grieved. We have been blessed with a healthy season, and the people now feel secure. L. told me the other night that if I would abstain from food entirely all day, he would also. I agreed to it for I had intended doing so anyhow. . . .

SUNDAY, AUGUST 12, 1849

Went to the Baptist Association ten miles from town at the Prairie church. A very large congregation there. Heard five sermons. . . . Wrote a long piece of poetry last week. "A Fancy Sketch, Irena." It is little else than my own experience. . . .

Susan's lengthy poem begins,

> Why sits Irena thus apart,
> With wearied look and saddened heart?
> Why wanders from the crowd away,
> To spend in solitude the day?

6. July 20, 1849. In ten verses Susan writes about old widowers who court young women: "Old Widowers—how they swarm around, / Like birds on summer's day. . . ." Although she credits the widowers with being "gallant," Susan describes how ridiculous they are, "their wrinkles clothed in smiles." She ends with a plea for them to "stand back" and "let young men have a chance. . . ."

The infatuation and disappointment Irena experiences with her unnamed suitor mirror the course of Susan's relationship with Dr. Hunter. She describes the brave mask presented to the world:

> She held her grief in her own heart,
> And tried to hide the inward smart;
> That none might know the keen despair
> That brooded deep in silence there.
> In smiles her face was clothed again,
> That none might see a trace of pain.

The last 106 lines of verse describe Irena's farewell to her family from her deathbed, and a prayer "that he might be forgiven."

THURSDAY NIGHT, AUGUST 23, 1849

And it is done at last. I returned to L. his borrowed books and his New Year's gift and wrote him a farewell. I sent him a copy of "Irena." He can understand it. I had to come to the conclusion that his whole course of conduct towards me has been deliberate, determined villainy. . . . To think of all the past almost crazes me; the many rides and walks we have taken together, the many hours we have spent reading and writing poetry by moonlight when all other eyes were slumbering and none but the lights of Heaven were looking on us, when I did not doubt that he loved me, with my cheek resting to his and his arms around me, those were blissful hours. . . .

THURSDAY, [AUGUST] 30, 1849

Today L. returned the New Year's gift. In it was a scrap of poetry and a communication, which only mystified the mystery. . . . Can it be possible that I misunderstood him?. . . .

THURSDAY, [SEPTEMBER] 13, 1849

. . . Camp meeting closed this morning. Fifty persons united with the church, many of whom we had thought hopeless cases. Malinda was immersed this morning by Mr. Redman. . . . There was no levity even in the outskirts of the crowd. All were serious. . . .

SUNDAY, SEPTEMBER 16, 1849

. . . Dr. McConnell gave offense by preaching about church discipline. He also spoke of the sin of murmuring against Providence, to which my conscience pleads guilty. I cannot but ask why I have to endure so much. . . . Emaline and I talked almost all night. I told her of what has passed between L. and myself. She could hardly believe, and it does seem to me yet as if I must have been dreaming. . . .

Sunday night, [September] 23, 1849

. . . Took a walk this evening with Louis (Brooke). Told some things of what had passed between L. N. and myself. . . . He said L. had told him that he had the highest opinion of me; he respected and esteemed me more highly than he did any other for my superior mind, intelligence and talent, combined with every virtue which should adorn the female character. What mockery! . . .

Tuesday, October 2, 1849

. . . L. N. sent me a note [F]riday morning. . . . He is offended because I told Louis Brooke what I did. I have written him a long answer. . . .

Saturday, October 13, 1849

. . . I received a letter from Brother, says he will be here next week, and I must be ready to start back on Monday. "And must I leave thee, Paradise"? Can I go? Yes, I must. . . . I have spent four years in Missouri. Most of the time passed like a pleasing dream; but clouds dark as despair have hung round my way for the last few months. . . .

Monday, [October] 15, 1849

. . . After dinner went to Morris'. Helped quilt a comfort and put in another and had a quilting at night. All the young folks there. Had a candy-pulling after the quilt was out. It was as pleasant a party as I have ever attended in Mexico. L. came home with me. We were as friendly as in times of old. As it is but a few days that we can be together, I concluded to act as though all was well. He lingered near me all the evening. . . .

Saturday, [October 20], 1849

. . . At night attended a party at Mr. Morris'; about twenty present. It was given by the young gentlemen to the young ladies of Mexico, more especially to me before my departure. It was a pleasant party. We took a walk out in the prairie. L. was with me. We talked over the past. He did not give me as much satisfaction as I wanted, but we explained some things; promised to forgive and forget. I have judged him too severely in some things. Our candy was scorched. Closed the evening by playing

"Old Jake." Very amusing. Then Louis made me a speech, to which I could only bow. We came home at half past twelve. . . .

MONDAY, OCTOBER 22, 1849

. . . Preparing to start home tomorrow, and can I? Must I bid farewell, perhaps a last farewell, to my friends here? I had to promise them and myself that I will return in a year if I live, but what changes may take place in that time! Took supper at Morris'; attended Temperance Meeting at night. . . . L. N. with me. We took a long walk by moonlight alone. Had he made the explanations a month ago which he makes now, I could not have left Mexico. . . .

TUESDAY, OCTOBER 23, 1849

. . . L. N. gave me some verses at parting, "A Gentle Good-by." If he had only told me sooner! . . .

Susan "bade adieu" to everyone in Mexico, and returned to her family's home in Carrollton, Illinois.

SUNDAY EVENING, [OCTOBER 28], 1849

Everything here looks just as it did when I went away. Carrollton has improved a good deal. . . . If I was only at home now, in Mexico! It seems to me as though I cannot live here. . . . I feel so lonely, so far from *home.* . . . I though[t] *he* had changed so much that my absence would be a relief to him. He told me better, but it was too late. How blest, how happy we might have been. . . .

THURSDAY, [NOVEMBER 22], 1849

. . . I weighed yesterday. I used to weigh 145, now 124. The people here tell me I have changed so much they hardly know me. I thought they had only forgotten how I looked, but suppose I am changed, and I have had cause. . . .

TUESDAY, DECEMBER 25, 1849

Christmas, a cold cloudy day. Spending the day at home. . . . Now, while others are spending the day in pleasure and gaiety, I am here alone, fasting; for I have more cause to mourn than to rejoice, for the future to me is so dark, so drear, I do not see what is to become of me. . . .

MONDAY NIGHT, DECEMBER 31, 1849

The close of another year. A time for serious thought. . . . Through this year I have enjoyed a tolerable share of health and many blessings, for which I desire to be thankful. . . . I have found some pleasure in the exercise of a power which I had not dreamed I possessed, writing Poetry. No one could have been more surprised at it than I was myself, for I had never even thought of trying to do it. Since May I have written two hundred and fifty verses, thirteen acrostics, "A Fancy Sketch, Irena," of three hundred and sixty lines, and a Carrier's Address of two hundred and twelve lines. Several pieces have been published and highly spoken of; but what does it profit me? I never wished for fame, nor do I desire it now. Give to me, a woman, waters from the well of affection—nothing else can satisfy the heart's thirstings. . . . When L. found I was certainly going away, he did all he could to effect a reconciliation. We explained to our mutual satisfaction; it was too late for me to alter my decision. I returned to Illinois. He told me that Mexico would be a solitude till I returned for no one could fill my place. I thought him sincere; but he seems to have forgotten me entirely. I promised him that if I lived I would certainly return in a year; but I hardly think I ought to go, and yet I do not see how I can live here. . . .

It is late. I am sitting here alone, all the others asleep. I must close my journal for the year. How different the close from the commencement. I could not record the half that I have endured. . . .

I will put my trust in God, for He reigns over all. May I be accepted of Him and find a home in Heaven, when done with the cares of earth, through Jesus Christ, our Saviour. . . .

SUNDAY, JANUARY 22 [27?] [1850]

. . . [R]eceived a letter from Ida last week. Old man Powell is married at last. . . .

MONDAY NIGHT, JANUARY 28, 1850

. . . I have just been reading a tale in *The Era*, "The Temptation." One sentence fixed my attention: "To everyone who has passed unsullied through the lesser temptations of this world . . . there comes once in life one trial of preeminent strength, . . . a temptation through the most powerful passion of the soul, of the weakest point in the character." How does this apply to me? . . . My affections were too entirely placed on an earthly object. That idol proved to be but clay. . . . The folks on String Prairie wish me to teach school for them next summer. I had thought I would rather stay at home, but I do not think I could stand it to do the housework in warm weather, and I know it would be best for me to engage in some employment which would occupy my whole attention. . . .

FEBRUARY 19, 1850

. . . Received a letter from Ann Jane Cardwell. Her pa still talking of going to California. I dreaded to hear from Mexico for fear of hearing that L. N. would be going too; but she does not say so. Yet, why should I care? . . . Did ever love meet with such return? By every attention in his power, by every means, to win my heart till he knew it beat for him alone, then —ah, Heavens, I shudder yet when I think of it. That he should be so base and think that I would submit to such degradation, such vileness, to have the assurance to wish me to be his mistress! . . .

SATURDAY, MARCH 2, 1850

My birthday. [D]ark gloomy cloudy day. I am not superstitious, but the day and my destiny are similar. . . .

[MARCH] 1850

A Normal Institute commenced its sessions at Carrollton on the 18th. . . . Upwards of eighty scholars in attendance. I attend. Public discussions of evenings, very interesting. . . . Disappointed again; my school at Walnut Grove is a failure. . . .

SATURDAY, [MARCH] 30, 1850

Well, our Institute has had a glorious termination. I was one of the committee of eight to write reports on the best methods of teaching. I wrote of English Grammar, Composition and Rhetoric. The reports were read Thursday night and are published. . . . At the close of the exercises, a poetical valedictory written by me was read by Mr. Townsend; a unanimous vote of thanks was given to the authoress. At six we met and formed a procession which moved round town, preceded by the brass band. . . .

MONDAY, [APRIL 8?], 1850

I commenced school in the stone school house. Seventeen scholars. I feel alone. Nevermore will my heart meet with a friend. If I may only be enabled to be of service to others, to do some good, 'tis all I ask.

Friday, [April] 26, 1850

. . . In the afternoon a good-looking gentleman walked past the school house and looked in. A few minutes afterward he came back and handed me a note and passed on. I opened it. He offered me a seat in his buggy to Carrollton that evening; signed Temple. I was delighted for I was so anxious to get home. I dismissed school early. . . . Found my new acquaintance, an intelligent pleasing young gentleman. . . .

Sunday, [May] 17, 1850

. . . Temple stopped here only a minute. Oh, why is it so? That I must cause so much unhappiness to others and be so wretched myself? Temple told me as we came along that he loves me alone. I had feared this, little as we have been together. I saw something in his manner deeper than friendship, and I tried to put him on his guard, to let him know that I had no heart to give. I thought I had lost all power to charm. . . . He is a pious young man, well educated, etc. He took it so hard. . . . I have received offers from many men, but none appeared to feel so deeply the disappointment, and I never was so grieved. . . .

Sunday, June 2, 1850

. . . Ward Eldred called again and spent some hours. He is rich; has had four wives and is in search of another. I cannot accommodate him. . . .

Sunday night, [March] 23, [1851]

. . . This evening Walter Hunter called to see me. We parted in Mexico little more than two years ago, and Oh, what changes since then. . . . He says he expects L. N. here in a few days. He begged me to tell him what had passed between us, why we had not married. . . . He said he knew there was no woman on earth whom L. regards as highly as he does me. I could not help saying, "You don't know him as I do." Yet I believe he is right. . . . I slept but little last night, and sleep will be a stranger to my eyelids tonight. . . .

Brighton, Illinois
March 2, [1852]

My Birthday. . . . I believe the horizon of my future appears clear blue. No light of hope illumes it; no cloud of fear shades it. . . . Will try . . . to give to Heaven the whole homage of my soul—the affections that were once lavished on an unworthy mortal. He is nothing to me now. Our paths are far apart. . . . He still inquires about me and says he cares for no one else, but I have almost ceased to care for him. And now, once more, disentangled from the allurements of love, I will try and keep my bark off those dangerous reefs and let it float down the stream of life, unbuoyed by hope, unbecalmed by despair. . . .

Between the last page of the journal and its back cover lies a copy of the Missouri Telegraph, *dated October 11, 1855. The headline on the front page reads "Death of Mexico's Best Loved Citizen, Dr. L. N. Hunter." The obituary reports the doctor's death from consumption at the age of thirty-seven, and pays tribute to "his unselfish devotion to the sick and the needy, his strong courage and good cheer." The writer comments, "For some reason, never divulged even to his closest friends, Dr. Hunter remained unmarried, and thus he belongs equally to us all." On the inside of the back cover of her journal Susan wrote: "Wednesday, October 17, 1855. I thought the Past was dead. How little did I know my own heart."*

The last years of Susan Vanarsdale's life were devoted to her family. Her father wrote, "Susan was so good and neat a housekeeper and of such good judgement pertaining to everything that made for the comfort of her parents that the time from December 1852 till February 1856 was the most pleasant part of my life till the death of that beloved daughter which took place February 27th, 1856."[7] Her family later recalled her as "a very handsome woman and beloved by all who knew her."[8]

7. "Autobiography of Peter Van Arsdall."
8. Susan was buried in the city cemetery of Brighton, Illinois. Seventy years later her niece Fannie Brown said, "The outstanding calamity of our family was the death of Aunt Sue" (editorial comment in manuscript, 238).

FRANCES GATES WILLIS (1825–1867)

$\mathcal{D}$uring the nineteenth century thousands of people traveled westward in search of opportunity, freedom, and wealth. Prosperity came to towns in Missouri where merchants supplied the wagon trains, but that prosperity could fade when the routes changed or a railroad was built. Some settlers found what they wanted in Missouri, while others followed the trails farther west. After 1821, when a party of men from the Boone's Lick area of Missouri established the Santa Fe Trail, traders traveled back and forth, encountering the colorful Mexican culture, taking goods like hardware, furs, and fabrics and bringing back an abundance of silver dollars. A few women traveled the trail, but wives usually stayed at home, caring for children and coping with household responsibilities. Separation strained marriages, when hope of material gain and a zest for adventure lured husbands away for months and years.

Although the mobility of men and the plight of women left alone may be found in many eras, a vivid analysis of this pattern on the American frontier is presented by Linda Peavy and Ursula Smith in *Women in Waiting in the Westward Movement.* They tell the stories of women who felt like widows, raising a family, coping with financial worries, and wondering whether they would ever see their husbands again. While some felt a sense of freedom at first, they "soon realized that life in limbo was only another form of bondage." Mail delivery was unreliable in both directions, and it was difficult to fill months or years of silence with memories of marital happiness or to keep fresh a child's memory of Papa.[1] The stress and challenges faced by women who waited along with the dreams and failures of the men who left them are epitomized in the life of Frances Gates Willis from Fayette, Missouri.

Finding gold and with it financial independence—surely that justified a separation, thought Andrew Jackson Willis. On October 7, 1845, Willis had married nineteen-year-old Frances D. Gates, who was his second wife.[2] Their first son, Oscar Gates, was born on July 10, 1846, and on April 6 the following year a second son, Arthur Fountain, joined the family. Andrew and Frances loved each other intensely, but they were caught up in the excitement of gold fever in 1849.[3] Frances and the children would stay with her Aunt Betsy in Fayette; Andrew would join

1. Peavy and Smith, *Women in Waiting,* 17, 28.
2. According to research done by Marilyn Neathery McCluen of Rockwood, Tennessee, Andrew Jackson Willis was born March 7, 1817, in Roane County, Tennessee. At the age of fourteen, he married Elizabeth Asher, from whom he obtained a divorce in 1838. Willis visited his brother, William Fountain Willis, in Alabama, and then came to Howard County, Missouri, probably in the early 1840s. McCluen, "Andrew Jackson Willis," personal copy.
3. On the Gold Rush, see Donald Dale Jackson, *Gold Dust;* and Joann Levy, *They Saw the Elephant: Women in the California Gold Rush.*

a group of "gold hunters" who intended to try their luck in mines along the Santa Fe Trail. Others in his party might go on to California, but Andrew promised to turn back when he reached Santa Fe.

Unaccustomed as they were to writing to each other, Frances and her husband filled their letters with passionate expressions of love and colorful descriptions of events.[4] Their worlds were so different. Andrew saw breathtaking scenery, faced physical danger, struggled to earn money, dreamed of finding gold, and repeatedly delayed his return. He wrote from Santa Rosa, California, that he felt like an exile from his family, but dreaded coming home "with so little money so long as there is a chance to make some at least enough to render independance for it chills my blood to think of being dependant" (July 3, 1851). Frances, surrounded by friends and family, watched her sons develop and reminded them daily of their father, attended church services, and struggled with loneliness and disappointment, wondering if she would ever see her husband again. Since the Willises depended on acquaintances to carry letters for them, there were long months of silence and uncertainty. Frances must have become capable and independent during the two years and five months her husband was away. After a brief reunion she was left alone again, a grieving widow, for Andrew died in March 1852. Frances died on January 14, 1867, and was buried next to Andrew on the Gates family farm northeast of Fayette.

LETTERS OF FRANCES GATES WILLIS ---

Fayette, Howard County, Missouri
MAY 5, 1849

DEAR HUSBAND

I with pleasure take my pen in hand to inform you that we are in good health as when you left us, hoping to find you enjoying the same. I have nothing of importance to write. I feel quite melancholy when I think of your long absence. I am all alone in the room steadying [studying?]

---

4. Some of the original handwritten correspondence, which began in the spring of 1849, may be found at WHMC-C. The correspondence was given to the State Historical Society in 1947 by the grandson of Frances and Andrew, Colonel Prior Fristoe Willis. His daughter, Elizabeth Buchanan, has granted permission for inclusion of selected letters in this anthology. For ease in reading, the editors have added capitalization and periods to indicate the beginnings and ends of sentences. However, other punctuation and spelling have been retained from the original letters. The *Willis Family Papaers, 1843–1908* at WHMC-C contain, in addition to the letters, the following items: a family record with birth and death dates for Frances, A. J., and some of their descendants; letters written by other family members; and miscellaneous items including an article on the engineering career of Prior F. Willis, the son of Arthur Fountain Willis.

about you and feel as though it would be the greatest source of pleasure in existence to have you with us tonigt, Oscar and Fountain are both a sleep. Oscar has had qite a merry time in mud and water today, I fear they will both forget you although I remind them of you often, we had qite a shower the evening you left here. [I]t has been qite showery since, I want you to write to me the first opportunity and let me know all about how you are getting along and write often all the particulars of your travels, and try to avoid all difficulties should there be any. [T]ry and take good care of yourself. [C]heer up and think of prospects ahead far more flattering than those of old Howard. You must excuse bad writing and green composition. [I]t is getting late and I must bring my letter to a close while I remain your most affectionate and loveing wife until death.

FRANCES D. WILLIS

PS [A]unt Betsy sends her best respects to you and says you must think of us all often. [W]e often ask Oscar where Pa is. [H]e will make a bow and grunt, Fountain screams as loud and kicks as hard as ever and says Pa qite plain. [W]e should like to hear something about our crackers. [Au]nt Betsy speaks of going to Doct. Dinwiddie on . . . next. I should like to have you here wih myself and children. I know it will be a long and lonesome day with me.

A. J. Willis had started toward Santa Fe in an exhilarated mood, writing on May 9 that he and his companions "set sail on our tour of the golden west." He even reports feeling in better health than when at home. Seeing many families on the trail, he wishes that he could have taken Frances along. On May 24, Andrew writes from Big John Creek near Council Grove, delighted to have heard from his wife: "[I]t being the first letter I ever receved from one of whom my affections were all concentrated that its peculer pleasures are beyond expression." Sending "ten thousan kisses" to his sons and "hoping you will take the same to yourself," Willis closes with a reminder that she should write to him next in Santa Fe by way of Fort Leavenworth.

By the time her husband writes on July 7, the company has grown to 130 "gold hunters," who stop to explore mines along the route. Andrew has sad news to report, for he has accidentally shot one of his traveling companions. In addition to reporting the calamity, he tells about spending the Fourth of July "eating snow diging gold & drinking water" and describes the terrain as "delitefull country."

Fayette, Howard County, Missouri
AUGUST 12, 1849

DEAR HUSBAND

I have heard of another opportunity sending another letter to you. I heard there would several leave Fayette next week and hope you will get this from some of them, we are all well accept Fountain. [H]e has

been very bad at times with the diarrhae and cutting teeth together. [H]e
has fallen off very much and is qite weak. [H]e still can run about and is
very mischievous at times and tries very hard to talk. Oscar is qite well
and a growing very fast. [H]e improves some in talking and called Fount
this [morning] for the first time that we have heard him. I can't get him
to say Pa but do not think that he has forgotten you. I often ask him if
he dont want to see you. [H]e will laugh and look very wishful. I think
when you get home that we will have chat a plenty from both of them.
[W]e went to church this morning at Gilead and carried both of them.
[T]hey have had a protracted meeting of better than a week and a great
many have joined. [I]t will continue until tuesday if not longer. I have
gone several days and have taken Oscar with me. [H]e is very fond of
going and behaves very well. I often think of you while at church and
wonder how you are and what your employments are. [I]t makes my
heart ache within me when I see other women with their husbands with
them. I allmost envy them their happiness and hope that it will not be
long when we shall meet again and meet to part no more in this world
nor the world to come, I have a great many pleasant dreams about being
with you and conversing with you. Oh that I could only realize some of
them. I would be amongst the happiest bings in the world. [Y]ou are the
last and first object that presents itself to view when I lie down to rest
at knight or rise in the morning, I want you to try and get home this
fall and I will hold myself in readiness to go with you next spring any
place you should choose to go to if it should be to California for I am
wearied of living the life I have been living so long without you. I can
scarcely write without dropping a tear or two in remembrance of you.
I immagine that I gone far enough with this but cannot stop without
warning you against the dangers that you may have to encounter with
in any respect whatever. Mr. Robert Brown has received inteligence of
his son James getting drowned which was thought to be by imprudence.
[I] have been to Pa's once since you left. I heard from there yesterday.
They were all well. William was over in July. He had an attack of cholera
about a month before he was here and looked so very bad. [T]he cholera
has been raging to a great extent in St. Louis. [T]he people fled a great
many of them. John Collinss Mother died there with it and left a babe
about two weeks old. Mr. Potts and his family left there for Fayette and
he died with it on board of a boat and was brought to Fayette and burried.
[H]is oldest daughter died in a few days afterward as Mrs. Doct. Saunders
and a coloured woman died in Glasgow also of the cholera. Mr. Stephens
son in law of John Tolson died about the same time. The last account it
was abating very fast in St. Louis. [T]ell Mr. Shepard I saw Mrs. Shepard
last sunday at church. [H]erself and children were all well. I heard from
Mrs. Saunders also that day. [T]hey were all well. [T]hey are both aging
[aching] to write but for fear of your not receiving our letters we write

for each other. [T]ell Mr. Estell his lady was well the last account I had of her. Give my best respects to all in company and say to them I wish them to return home in good health and with aplenty of gold with them, Aunt Betsy sends her respects to you & wishes you to return home to your family in good health & wealth,

I wrote a letter to you in July but thought it very uncertain whether you would get it or not. I have not heard . . . a word from you since Mr. Douthet returned. [H]e wrote me a letter stating that you was in good health & getting along well. I have received two letters from you one written the 9th of May the other 24th. [Y]ou must be certain to write every opportunity and let me know all about how you are what you are adoing. [Y]ou not [do not know?] how anxious I am to hear from you. [I]t appears like a long time to have received but two letters. I hope you will do better in future, you told me I must remember you to Oscar & Fountain by ten thousand kisses. [W]hile I embrace them I give a portion in remembrance of you. I must bring my letter to a close by bidding you an affectionate farewell until we meet again

FRANCES D. ,WILLIS

OSCAR & FOUNTAIN WILLIS

[P.S.] I will enclose a lock of their hair to remind you of their white heads once more.

By the time she writes again on October 15, Frances has received the letter of July 7, telling about the day when Andrew accidentally shot William Tartenshall while hunting deer and antelope by horseback. "I sprang to his side folding him in my arms & . . . laid him easy on the ground with his head in my lap." The dying man assured Willis that he did not blame him. It is easier for Frances to accept that account calmly than to hear that Andrew will not be coming home.

Fayette, Howard County, Missouri
OCTOBER 15, 1849

DEAREST HUSBAND

I received yours of the second of augst. and was very sorry indeed to hear that you was a going on to California. I had been flattering myself with seeing you this fall without a doubt. [I]t seems as though your mind changed very suddenly affter writing your last letter to me, I was sorry truly sorry to hear of the accident that happened in company although it was great satisfaction to learn that he did not reflect on you in the least. [Y]ou stated in your last you had not received any letters from me. I have written two and sent by companies going out. [T]he first I sent by a company that was a ging [going] from Boonville the second by the

Mr. Coopers from Fayette which I hope you will get when you get to California, Oscar and myself are both in fine health at present. Arthur has not been well since the second wek after you left home which I wrote you in both my last letters. [H]e has very bad bowels and teething together. [H]e has fallen off very much and looks badly. I gave him some vermifuge which brought seven large worms. [H]e seemed to improve for several days after taking it. I hope he will improve as the weather is getting cool. [Y]ou would hardly know him. [H]is features have changed so much. [H]e gave me about a half a dzen kisses this evening without ceaseing. I wish you could be here to share a portion of them with me. Oscar after retiring at knight kisses me again and again and says more Pa. [H]e aims them all for you, his aunt Margaret and aunt Elizabeth stayed here last knight and he went home with them this morning. [H]e was qite anxious to go with them. I expect he will stay a week or so as they are very anxious to have him there. [H]e gave me a sweet kiss and hug when he went to start, they are all well at Pa's accept our Ma. [S]he has had a very bad spell of the fever but is on the mend, aunt Betsy is qite well at present. [H]er family has increased very much this fall. . . . [T]here has been a great many revivals of religion here this summer of every denomination. [T]here has a great many of your acqaintences joined. Mr. Hendvise Judge Hilland his two oldest daughters, Mr. Rich—Joseph Hanson and Holmes. Also James Hachly and his wife have all joined the Methodist besides a great many others, Mr. Rich prays in public every opportunity. I have been weaving some for aunt Betsy to get winter clothing for myself and children. I have wove about 36 yds, and have about 20 yet to weave in the town, Pa sent me word that Detherage had colected a little money on those accounts you left for him and sent me word that he would come and bring it to me when he got through collecting, I have not received a cent from any of your creditors since you left. I want you to make all you can this winter and come home next spring let it be great or small.

Mr. Embry and family left here this morning. [T]hey were all well. Aunt Betsy says she wishes you good luck and health and wants you to return home as [soon] as possible. . . . You wrote of Kit carson haveing his pretty little mexican wife. [D]o pray do not take a liking to them yourself. I have chosen me a bedfellow which I think will be a very good substitute. [D]o not be so brief next letter but give me a little more satisfaction. [S]o fare well my dear util we [meet] again

FRANCES D. WILLIS

OSCAR & FOUNTAIN WILLIS

Ps. [I]t is now all most bedtime. . . . [Y]ou know not how I dread to go to bed without you. [T]ake good care of yourself and be in time against I see you. I hope to realize some of my pleasant dreams about bing with you before next fall. [Y]ou must try and get home next spring anytime. I do not think I can stand it any longer. If you can only get home safe and sound I will be very satisfied. [D]o take good care of yourself and write often. I shall be uneasy until I hear from you again. [A] kind kiss and I will stop

A. J. Willis does not return home in the fall of 1849; he goes on to California. In his next extant letter, written December 26, he promises to return the next fall "with money." Meanwhile he sends Frances $25.00 and a sample of gold which he found on the street. No letters have arrived from her. "For god sake write often to Sacramento."

Fayette, Howard County, Missouri
JANUARY 19, 1850

Dear Husband

It is with pleasure I take my pen in hand to try to write, my self and children are well at present. [H]oping when this comes to hand to find you enjoying the same blessing. I received yours of the 10th of Nov which gave me more pleasure than I am able to express to hear from you, although I was truly sorry to hear of your illness. I fear that you suffered for want of attention & nourishment while sick. I had allmost give up all hopes of ever seeing or hearing from you a gain as being a live for I could not hear anything direct from those that came in. [A]ll the information that I could get was that you had gone to the mines. You stated that Benjamin Embree had left for home. [H]e hasnot arrived that I have heard of yet. Solon Shepard & one of the Furnishes landed a few days ago. Joel Furnish died on his return below St. Louis. I hear of a great many of our acquaintances who have died that went out last spring which has caused a great deal of trouble & distress among their Families & friends who are left behind. I am at Pa's at this time and have been for the last four weeks. [T]hey are all well at this time. I [expect] to go back to aunt Betsys as soon as the weather will admit, Oscar says tell Pa I want to see him mighty bad, they both speak of you very often. Fount says he is a going to eat a heap of meat and grow to be a big man. [H]e makes large calculations him self. [Y]ou would not [know] them. [T]hey have grown so much. Fount can talk as plain if not plainer than Oscar. [H]e will try to say anything we tell him. [H]e is not a fraid nor ashamed of nobody. [H]e loves to talk about the ladies. Oscar is rather on the timid order. I often look at them and wish for you here as I know its a pleasure you delighted in before you went a way. I was sadly disappointed at your not returning last fall. I made sure calculations on haveing you here to spend the Christmas with us. I therefore earnestly entreat you not to delay comeing home this spring. I want you to come Gold or no Gold. [I]f [you] can get enough to get home with I will be satisfied. [H]earing of so many deaths & so much suffering I am always miserable. I have pleasnt dreams of being with you all most every night which I hope [I] realize before a great while if kind providence smiles. [A]s I have but little hopes of your getting this before you start home I will not add a great deal at present. I hope that you will write oftener as I am allways anxious to hear from you. I will add nomore but remain yours truly util death

FRANCES D. WILLIS
TO A. J. WILLIS

Fayette, Missouri
AUGUST 12, 1850

DEAR HUSBAND

I with pleasure take my pen in hand to inform you that we are all in good health at present. [H]oping when this comes to hand to find you enjoying the same blessing. I have waited very impatiently up to the present to hear from you. [T]he last letter I received from you was dated the 19th of april. [Y]ou stated in your letter you expected to start to the trinity mines the next day. Mr. Douglas told me that he heard from you all a few days before he started in that you were in the mines and all were well which I was truly pleased to hear although it is nothing in comparison to receiving a few words of consolation from your own hand and heart. [Y]ou stated in your last letter that you expected to start home the 1st Oct. Mr. Hungerson [?] Shepard returned on monday last. [H]e could not tell anything a bout any of you. [H]e had not heard from you all since in appril. [H]e is perfectly calm on the subject of California. [H]e does not give any satisfaction as to what he has made or done. [H]e has not so much as told his Fatherinlaw. [H]e gives vasive answers to all the questions that are put to him. [Y]ou still speak of moving to California in your last letter and requested me to study on the subject until you returned. I have thought about it a great deal and will prove true to my promise should you have the good luck to get home this fall and want to go back in the spring although I flatter myself that you will not want to go back again. I hope you will prove to be one of the lucky ones and bring enough home with you to render us both comfortable and happy. Oscar and Fountain are both quite well. Oscar speakes of you often and wishes Pa would come home and bring him and [B]ud some gold. [H]e says Pa stays too long. [H]e wants him to come home. I told him that Mr. Shepard had come home. [H]e wanted to know if he brought gold with him. Fountain tries to say anything that is told him. [H]e says Pa done to forny [gone to California]. Oscar says tell Pa he must bring him gold & pony & gun. [A]unt Betsy started last thursday down to Osage on a visit. [S]he was quite well when she started. Pas family were all well on sunday last. [T]hey came down to the association at Mt. Gilead on saturday which lasted three days only. I attended during the meeting and heard some excellent sermons preached. [W]hile under the sound of the gospel I think of you often as bing deprived of that pleasure which I feel assured by your last letters that you would consider it as such and hope the time not far distant when you can be one in our midst and hope that we can enjoying ourselves in that way should we think propper. [D]o not delay comeing home this fall for I cannot stand it any longer. [T]he family is very large and cold weather drawing near it makes me want to see you get home. [Y]ou must to write me what time you expect to get home so that I may be prepared to meet [?] those affectionate embraces you speak of in your letters for I do not know that I can keep my lips closed long enough for a kiss when I see you. I shall be so overjoyed. [D]o not for get to bring Oscar and Founty a present when you come home. [M]y dear you must excuse all errors for I have not language to express my feelings as I would wish to do. [T]herefore I will bid you an affectionate farewell while I remain yours affectionately until death

FRANCES D. WILLIS
TO A. J. WILLIS

The next letter from A. J. Willis is dated November 10, 1850. He has been very ill, delirious for five days, and so reduced that his friends do not recognize him, "but now Frances I am my self a gane & bid fair to be more fleshy than you ever seen me." The gold mines have been a disappointment, and much of the $1,000 he has managed to save has had to be spent on doctor's bills. He regrets not being able to return home this fall, but promises to leave California in February. "Would to god I had an opportunity to test you keeping your lips closed while I would kiss you."

Unfortunately Andrew becomes seriously ill again, with terrible discomfort in his hips and back. He writes to Frances in April from the Santa Rosa Valley that he has progressed from walking with crutches to using only a cane. To earn a modest salary he is working in a store, but by June the store goes out of business and Andrew applies for a mail route. If he cannot get work, he will start for home, "but let me tell you my dear I can not come home with so little money. . . ." He has not received a letter from Frances for six months, but begs her to "forgive my faults & negglect which I have been guilty of by fate not chois" (June 9 [17?], 1851).

A. J. Willis must have returned to Fayette by early October. His dream of becoming independently wealthy was abandoned and his health ruined. The collection of letters ends, but we assume that Andrew did not suddenly strike it rich before leaving California. He was anxious to see his wife, for "the longer I stay from you the more I learn to love & appreciate you & domestic felisity" (July 3,

1851). The reunited couple did not enjoy "domestic felisity" very long, for Andrew died on March 14, 1852. In July Frances gave birth to a daughter, Ida Jackson Willis, who lived only nine months.[5]

5. Ida Jackson Willis died May 13, 1853. A. J. Willis, Frances, and Ida are buried on the Gates farm, now called the Delaney farm. Oscar Gates Willis, the older son, died in 1908. The younger son, Arthur Fountain Willis, who married Nannie Maria Fristoe in 1874, died in 1921. Prior Fristoe Willis, Arthur's son, married Elva C. Moss and became the chief engineer and designer for Xcel Products of the Superior Oxy-Acetylene Company in St. Louis. He was married for a second time to Mary Banks of Piedmont. A Democrat, Willis served as Commissioner of Prison Industries and as chief clerk for Secretary of State Wilson Bell until Bell's death in 1947. Information on the family comes from the "Family Record," in the Bible of Andrew Jackson and Frances Willis, WHMC-C; news stories in the *St. Louis Post-Dispatch*, 1944–1947; and Marilyn Neathery McCluen (correspondence with editors).

MARTHA J. WOOD

$\mathcal{M}$artha J. Wood is one of those anonymous women about whom we know only what can be read in her diary.[1] From 1857–1860, she recorded her impressions as she traveled back and forth between her home in Albemarle County,[2] Virginia, and Saline County, Missouri. Martha left Virginia on March 17, 1857, and arrived in the vicinity of Arrow Rock nearly two months later, on May 9.

Wood's situation was typical of many settlers who came to Missouri from the Southern states of Virginia, Tennessee, or Kentucky. The culture to which she was accustomed was quite different from what she encountered along the trail or found among settlers carving out a new life with few conveniences of the old. The diary reveals that her faith in God's guidance sustained her in the trials of life. She traveled to a location near relatives who had arrived in Missouri earlier; proximity to her relatives provided some comfort as she faced the challenge of a new way of life.

Martha was a young single woman. She traveled to Missouri with a "Brother Cobb," who was probably her brother-in-law, Thomas H. Cobb. He and her sister Mary had six children, and Mary may have needed Martha's help with domestic tasks and child care. We assume that members of the extended Wood family felt Missouri offered advantages and opportunities. Martha's uncle, Milton Wood, who had thirteen children, had come from Albemarle County, Virginia, to Saline County "at an early date," and he permitted Martha's family to farm on some of his land. Census records from Virginia and Missouri do not provide clear documentation about other members of the family.[3]

Early in 1859 Thomas H. Cobb prepared to take over management

1. There are contradictory uses of *Wood* and *Woods* in documents related to Martha J. The editors have relied on the typed transcript found in the Arrow Rock Tavern Board collection at WHMC-C. Although the transcript uses "Woods" for Martha, in other sources the family members are referred to as "Wood." Because *History of Saline County* (1881) lists Martha's family members as "Wood," the editors choose that as the preferred spelling. Punctuation and spelling within the diary have been corrected only as necessary for clarity. Original spellings, as transcribed in 1961, have been retained for the most part.

2. Donald H. Welsh states in "Martha J. Woods Visits Missouri in 1857" that Martha was from Augusta County, Virginia. However, careful reading of the diary reveals that she actually had resided in Albemarle County. After leaving there and traveling a full day, she and her party reached the home of relatives in Augusta County.

3. *History of Saline County* (1881), 639, gives Milton Wood's death as "about 1855," but according to Martha's diary, he was still alive in 1857. Martha's family may be the one listed in the 1850 Albemarle County census: Willis Wood (45) farmer, Emily (43), Martha (16), George (15), John (12), Richard (9), Hilvy [sp.?] (5), Artelia (2), Elizabeth (85). In the 1860 census for Saline County there was a William Wood (33), farmer, and his wife Elizabeth (23), both born in Virginia. They had a daughter Margaret (5) and son Walter D. (3), born in Missouri. William may have been Martha's brother. He is listed immediately before David B. Wood, who was probably his cousin and neighbor. Also living in Arrow Rock in 1860 were families from Virginia named Wood, Cobb, and Grayson, who might have been related to Martha.

of the Arrow Rock Hotel. According to "Podajiah Peasly" in the *Marshall Democrat* of February 25, "friend Cobb is hunting up new feathers and bed quilts to re-clothe it." Preparations being complete in early April, a letter in the Marshall newspaper predicted that "nothing on his part or that of his estimable lady will be wanting to render his guests comfortable. . . ."[4] That winter the mother of Martha and Mary had come for a visit; Martha returned with Mrs. Wood to Virginia, via steamboat and train. The diary does not cover the year at home, but picks up again on March 19, 1860, when Martha once again took leave of her "beloved Mother and dear Sister Grayson and her darling little boy Georgie" and her "beloved native state" to visit her sister Mary in Arrow Rock.

Wood describes the selfless duty that often fell to unmarried women of tending the sick and less-fortunate relatives. "God only knows the agony of such a separation. I have now been in [Virginia] one year after an absence of [two] years in the west and have learned the value of dear relatives and friends. For oh, with what love and kind attention I have been overwhelmed ever since my return. I never appreciated my loved ones in Virginia till I stayed from them so long, but now that they seem so essential to my happiness; duty calls me to leave them to go [to] the deeply afflicted family of my beloved Sister Cobb, for she has been called on to pass through the deep waters and fiery trials of affliction since I parted from her. . . . She has been called on to give up her oldest and youngest born sons and her second daughter to the relentless hand of death. And now she is lying prostrate on the bed of affliction which her Physician and friends fear will be her death bed. So, hard as it is to part, go I must."

The role nineteenth-century women played as sustainers of the family permeates the pages of Wood's diary. Motherhood was a high and sacred calling for the antebellum South; it was the finest "calling" for a woman in a patriarchal society that limited women's options for self-fulfillment.[5] Although single, Martha exemplifies the southern devotion to the caring role assigned to women. She missed her mother and church activities greatly, but she was deeply attached to the nieces, nephews, and other family members who needed her in Missouri. Even the recipes she records in the diary indicate her understanding of women's domestic role. Wood's diary reflects her willingness to fulfill the southern woman's domestic duty to serve her family, although it might mean sacrificing her own desires and emotional needs.

In his introduction to excerpts of the Wood diary published in the *Missouri Historical Review* in 1961, Donald H. Welsh comments that "diaries vary tremendously in value to the historian and to the typical reader.

4. Observer, letter to the editor, *Marshall Democrat,* April 8, 1859.
5. See Sally G. McMillen, *Motherhood in the Old South: Pregnancy, Childbirth, and Infant Rearing.*

Some merely note weather conditions from day to day or trivial incidents in the writer's daily activities, while others demonstrate the author's ability to observe and to record his observations in a style which will interest others. Martha J. Woods' diary falls in the latter category."[6] We get a sense of the writer's individuality through the record of her response to what happens around her. A Christian and a refined southern lady, Martha disliked much of the rugged landscape and the "ruffians" who inhabited the regions she passed through on her journey. There are frequent comments about fashion and suppositions about character and social class. Her colorful expressions of opinion create a vivid and often amusing character that comes to life as one reads the diary.

When the diary ends in 1860, so does our knowledge of what happens to Martha J. Wood. The Cobb family left the Arrow Rock Tavern in 1861, and it is possible that they and Martha went back to Virginia. The diary came into the hands of the Daughters of the American Revolution (D.A.R.), which put it on display in the Tap Room at the Arrow Rock Tavern, probably in the 1920s. Instead of naming a donor, the catalog entry says "came with tavern," suggesting that Martha's diary was left behind when the family moved out in 1861. The hotel register that Thomas Cobb used from 1858 to 1861 also found its way into the D.A.R. exhibit.[7] Although the manuscript of the diary cannot be located, a transcript still allows us to hear Martha's intensely personal voice.[8] The vivacious diarist who recorded her devotion to family and her responses to antebellum Missouri comes to life for us in those pages.

DIARY OF MARTHA J. WOOD

Augusta County, Virginia
MARCH 17, 1857

This day will ever be memorable as having been the most painful of my life. The one on which I left my native County in the Old Dominion for a home in the far west.

---

6. Welsh, "Woods Visits Missouri," 109.
7. Charles van Ravenswaay, "Arrow Rock, Missouri."
8. For his article, "Martha J. Woods Visits Missouri in 1857," Welsh had requested permission to borrow the manuscript and make a typed transcript, which may be found at WHMC-C. Page numbers in the text refer to the transcript. Welsh returned the diary in 1962. When the D.A.R. discontinued its exhibit at the tavern in 1983, some artifacts were given to the Department of Natural Resources for display at the Arrow Rock State Historic Site. The editors thank Mary Louise Fricke of the D.A.R. Headquarters in Boonville and Susan Warner and Richard Forrey at the Arrow Rock State Historic Site for their assistance in searching for the diary. The diary is described in the Missouri State Society, Daughters of American Revolution, Old Tavern, Arrow Rock, Mo., catalog item T-109, 453.

... The separation from many relatives and friends, and above all from the dearest and best of Mothers was almost too much for poor frail human nature to bear. . . .

Pulaski County, Virginia
MARCH 23, [1857], NOON

We have now stopped to dine and feed and while the horses are eating I am scribbling. We have passed through some very mountainous regions this a.m. but portions of it rich and productive. But I have noticed a lamentable scarcity of houses of worship ever since we left Salem. We hardly ever see a church except at the Co. seats, where there are some very handsome ones, though between these towns we sometimes go 26 miles or more and not see more than one church. . . .

Wythe County, Virginia
MARCH 25, 1857

Last night was a terrible one as we had rain and so much wind that I was much afraid the tent would blow over though it was well propped and the storm did not last all night, so we put down some fence rails to keep our mattresses off of the damp ground and we were so tired that we all slept tolerably well. What a change a five days travel makes; before I started I could not sleep until everything about my bed was arranged just to suit me; now I can sleep anyway, even on fence rails. . . .

Sullivan County, Tennessee
MARCH 29, 1857

Another Sabbath finds us in this state and with no opportunity of going to church, but may God watch over and protect us is my prayer for Christ sake. We stopped last night near an old Methodist camp ground and I was much pleased to see it as it proved that this community had religious instruction.

Since we came into this state the country and poeple look rough and uncouth. Yesterday soon after we came into the state we came to a Musterground and such grotesque looking figures I never beheld. Nearly all dressed in homespun clothes of a variety of colors, and pantiloons large enough for petticoats. But they had the fife and drum and seemed to be enjoying themselves very much. The children were highly amused. The most of the houses are about like the ragged mountain huts. But I was gratified to see that they all seemed to be sober with all their roughness. . . .

Knox County, Tennessee
APRIL 4, 1857

We had the misfortune to loose our little black dog Jim in Knoxville and had come out 1 mile from Town when we missed him. [W]e stopped to hold a consultation as to what was to be done when we unanimously decided to send back for him, and away went James Cobb and the boy Fielding to search the town, and to our great joy as well as the dog's they soon found him and overtook us. . . .

Cumberland County, Tennessee
APRIL 6, 1857, AT NIGHT

We have had really a trying day of it today. Just after I had finished writing this morning a lowlife man, a renter on the farm of the gentleman who owns the vacant house we camped in last night, came up and threatened to get a warrant to take the gentlem[e]n of our party. But they were not easily frightened, so they gave him a lecture and paid him for the use of the house and left. The young men that were along were in favor of threshing him instead of paying, but the older ones prudently kept them from it. We then set out and a few miles drive brought us to the Cumberland mountains and here we had times of it climbing the steepest roads and winding along just above roaring catara[c]ts, and steepest precipices, above awful looking cavarns that looked wild and gloomy in the extreme; just my idea of fit hiding places for banditts. I felt awed and fearful indeed and it was withal bitter cold so that we only traveled 12 miles. But fortunately for us and contrary to our effections we met with a man in these wild mountains that had a kind heart and a house large enough to take us in, and we had a comfortable jolly time of it, notwithstanding himself and family looked rough and uncouth. . . .

De Kalb County, Tennessee
APRIL 10, 1857

We have made another days travel a distance of 20 miles and passed over quiet rough country. Ferried Can[e]y Fork River and crossed . . . along the river over Snow hill [mountains], making in all a first rate drive though we have many trials in dealing with cheats and rascals in trying to buy food. I think this certainly beats any State in the Union for swindlers. Nearly all of them have a price for travellers and another for their neighbors. It is only now and then we meet with an honorable man that will sell to us as to his countrymen. It is mainly through them we find out the scamps. So far I have a poor opinion of both country and poeple in this state, with the before mentioned exceptions, one of which is the family we are travelling with. We enjoy ourselves very much of evenings visiting each other. Sometimes chatting sociably and sometimes we have music as one of the young ladies has her accordian and her brother his violin with them, and our boy Fielding occasionally gives us a tune on the banjo by way of variety. Then we have singing and altogether we enjoy ourselves very much. I have enjoyed the music more than usual this evening as it is a beautiful moonlight night and we are camping right on the banks of a rippling stream which sparkles in the moonbeams. These and our tents spread out with large log fires burning at their doors make a fine picture, almost like a fairy scene. It is very pleasant to be with persons whose faces look familiar after being so long with strangers and this family have been with us so long that we feel like old acquaintances. . . .

Davidson County, Tennessee
APRIL 12, 1857

It seems that we have come into a new country and another nation in the last 2 days. The farms are rich looking, the buildings handsome and the poeple look fashionable and are much more genteel and polite than in the Eastern part of the state. The churches are far more plentiful and the people seem to be church going, as we have seen many going to and from church. . . . I think much of dear old Virginia and all my dear friends I have left behind me, and more especially of my beloved Mother. Oh how I wish I could see her tonight. . . . How much I would like to be at dear old Mt. Ed and hear our good pastor preach as he only can! . . .

[Cheatham County,] Tennessee
APRIL 13, 1857

How great a contrast in the appearance of things, will 1 days slow travel bring about! Until late this afternoon we were travelling in the most beautiful and by far most wealthy part of the state I have seen. Splendid farms and princely mansions, with much appearance of wealth and splendor. I think the Goddess of fashion reigns here supremely. We also passed through Nashville the Capitol which is a handsome flourishing city, with the finest state house I ever saw, though the square does not compare with our capitol square in Richmond. . . .

After leaving Nashville we travelled several miles through pretty country and where the poeple live in magnificant style, but this P.M. we came off on another, to us, much dreaded ridges and the whole scene is changed. We came sometimes for 2 or 3 miles without seeing a house and then but a cabin, and to our sorrow night came on and we were compelled to camp right on top of the ridge, though near the best looking house I have seen on these [mountains]. We are now 605 miles on our way. . . .

Henry County, Tennessee
APRIL 17, 1857

Owing to some detainments we have only travelled 18 miles today. . . .
Henry [County] is nearly settled up by Virginians and they are still
Virginians in kindness.

We met with a gentleman whose parents came from Va. who gave us
some nice squirrels for supper, which was a treat to us; and then assisted
us in getting corn for our horses and was very kind and obliging indeed.

We are now camping near an old gentleman from Va. who has sold us
the best bargain in provisions we have had for days. We are now . . . in
the last county we will pass through in this state. . . .

Graves County, Kentucky
APRIL 19, 1857, NOON

This is the [third] Sunday in April the day for preaching at dear old
Mt. Ed. . . . I always think more of loved ones in Old Va. on Sunday than
any other day. . . .

Mississippi County, Missouri
APRIL 22, 1857

This morning we ferried the largest river on the North American
Continent,[9] and it is well calculated to fill the mind and soul with awe and
[reverence], when we remember the Hand that formed this stupendous
river formed also the smallest grain of matter in the Universe. It is indeed
a grand sight to see the noble steamboats gliding on its rolling current,
and just to think of the 100[s] and 1000[s] of people that are constantly
being conve[y]ed on its mighty waters and at the solemn thought that
thousands are sleeping their last sleep on its bottom! How these thoughts
conspire to make us remember our own feebleness and entire dependence
on the Mercies of God. This is certainly the most beautiful river scenery
I ever beheld. The river is 1 mile wide and bordered on either side by
lofty forests just beginning to bud forth. . . . Since leaving the river we
have been passing through the Mississippi bottom which is the richest
land I ever saw, though nearly entirely in woods, only a few huts to be
seen occupied by woodcutters. The trees on this bottom are the tallest
and largest I ever saw and suppose not many larger in the world. It
makes me grow dizzy to look up to their tops. We have now stopped to
feed and dine while we rest our horses as we have just had a terrible
time crossing a slough. One of the Jersey-wagon horses mired and I

9. They crossed the Mississippi River by ferry steamboat from Columbus, Kentucky.

though[t] at one time would never be got out,[10] but by great exertion it was extricated and by hitching on 2 more horses drew the wagon out. . . .

Bollinger County, Missouri
APRIL 27, 1857

We travelled on yesterday all day through this poor hilly part of the state with the roughest, most grotesque, looking set of ruffian settlers imaginable. What would Eastern Virginians think of men being dressed in blue coats, red striped linsey wolsey pants or else blue geanes, pants as well as coats pink shirts red cravats and plaid vests? It is no exageration when I say we have seen many such in the last 2 days. The women about as tastily dressed, if we can use such a term in speaking of such garbs. The poeple seem to be nearly heathens as there are no churches to go to, and they spend the sabbath visiting, hunting, or even in more vicious sport, as we passed some men piching money on Sunday and from their red faces coarse behavior and horse laughter; looked as if the intoxicating draughts had passed freely. . . .

[Crawford or Maries County,] Missouri
MAY 2, 1857

Yesterday afternoon we travelled through some hills and 2 prairies, though neither of them so pretty as the one we saw in the forenoon. We still meet with difficulty in getting provisions for our horses. The poeple are lazy and not at all provident as they never save anything more than for present use, and last year they had in the early part of the year drought and in the fall early frost, so that the crops were cut short, and the long cold winter consumed the most of that. Besides I think they have very little feeling for movers, and not much wonder either, for the whole country is thronged with them. I never saw anything like it, going to and fro in all directions. In addition . . . I think we are passing through a low ignorant set, not much more than savages. The land looks pretty good and I believe if the folks would work they would have plenty. . . .

Saline County, Missouri
MAY 9, 1857

Last evening and night were by far the most trying of my life; the roads were the worst I ever saw and we could not get along. Night

---

10. According to Welsh, "Woods Visits Missouri," 111, a *Jersey wagon* was a "light vehicle especially suitable for use on the loose, sandy soil common to New Jersey."

came on and found us in a strange place not knowing even whether we were in the right road or not. We had run out of provisions for the horses and nearly out ourselves and had been trying all day to buy and could not, and to add to our troubles as they never come alone, the bolt of our Jersey wagon broke and compelled us to camp though it was then late at night. We had beautiful moonlight, which was our only comfort.

But the greatest of our troubles was we heard late in the evening that our Cousin had failed to rent us a home and here we were strangers and Pilgrims in a strange land without home or friends, compelled to stop and take our chances. We sent late at night as it was, to a farm nearby and the gentleman was a Virginian and he sent corn and meal, so that we made out last night, but what we will do now God only knows. We have not yet seen any of our relations and I do not know whether they will prove friends or not. But we have one true Friend that is God. . . .

Saline County, Missouri
JUNE 13, 1857

. . . We have made the acquaintance of many of our relations . . . and all are just as kind as can be, and many that are not related at all equally as much so. Our prospects for a home were gloomy for some days. But our Good Cousin David B. Wood was a friend all the time.[11] He persuaded a bachelor friend to move to live with him and let us have his house, which he did free of charge. Our Uncle Milton Wood who is equally kind, offered a part of his house but we would not accept as we knew it would be doing him [an] injustice with his large family. He also offered land to cultivate free of rent which was accepted very thankfully. We have now been to ourselves about a month and our neighbors are so very liberal that we feel almost ashamed of ourselves as we have been here so short a time we have no means of returning it. Until we could buy cows we had milk and butter given us. Our chickens were furnished to raise from, our ice is given just when we send to get it. Nice fresh meat, fresh fish and many little varieties too tedious to mention are sent us.

We were at first dissatisfied with the country and are now not perfectly satisfied though we like [it] better. The want of Church privileges is our greatest cross. Though we must do in this as in everything else, trust in God. . . .

11. The 1860 census lists David B. Wood (41) as a bachelor, living alone.

Saline County, Missouri
JULY 4, 1857, AT NIGHT

I attended today the first anniversary celebrations of our glorious liberty in this state. There were present a large crowd of people of all sorts and conditions in this region of country.

The Declaration of Independence was read by Dr. Durrett,[12] followed by an Oration suitable to the occasion by Mr. J. V. Price. Then there was a plentiful dinner Barbacued, after which the sentiments were read with responses, some of them very good.

If they had have had music everything would have been fine. As it was all went off pleasantly, though of course I did not enjoy it as I would have done a similar occasion in my native state.

There I would have known nearly every one; here I knew but few and they but slightly. . . .

Saline County, Missouri
JULY 10, 1857

Yesterday three young ladies besides myself started off unattended to go to a picnic on Black Water.[13] [We were] expecting to get company by the way, but unfortunately for us, were too late; as every one had gone before we reached their houses; and we were reduced to the necessity of returning or going on without escorts. The ladies decided on the latter. I of course as a stranger acquiesced though I confess reluctantly, as none of the party knew the way. We thought however we could follow the carriage tracks but soon found we did so to our sorrow, as the roads were almost impracticable. We were now willing to turn back but could not turn the carriage around so had to drive over a road that was dangerous to ride horseback on.

But as troubles never come alone we at length found to our dismay that not one of the party knew their whereabouts. Thus we continued to wander on till our appetites warned us it was dinner time. So we stopped and ate dinner. We then traveled on till we came in sight of a house. We then determined to go and get directions homeward, notwithstanding we felt ashamed to go to it in such a flight; for with walking, watering our horses, perspiration &c,&c, we were the dirtiest sights I ever wish to see. But here we found to our surprise that we were not more than 100 yards from the Picnic party. All covered with dirt, we decided to go on as the gentleman of whom we made inquiries kindly sent a guide with us. We

12. Fountain Durrett (35) is listed in the 1860 census as a "Phisician," born in Virginia, and boarding with Thomas H. Cobb in Arrow Rock.
13. The Blackwater River runs near the southern border of Saline County.

reached the party just as they were dispersing to go to their homes, so it was labor lost at last.

This was a bad beginning for me as it was my first picnic in Mo. . . .

Arrow Rock, Saline County, Missouri
MARCH 22, 1859

It has been nearly 2 years now since the above was written and through how many scenes I have been called on to pass. We have moved twice, and have made many acquaintances, had some joys and many sorrows; but in them all we have great right to be thankful to Divine Providence. And in none of my blessings have I more right to be grateful, than that our dear Mother has been spared to come see us and spend the Winter. . . . *[Martha left Missouri the next week to accompany her mother back to Virginia.]*

[Aboard the steamboat Rowena]
[MARCH] 30, 1859, 10 A.M.

Well we are nearing the great city of the west [St. Louis] after having had a safe pleasant trip down the river on board the *Rowen[a]*. The 1st clerk Mr. Mason has been truly attentive, and some of the passengers agreeable some amusing and some disgusting. . . . [T]here were a married man and woman very attentive to each other as each of their companions were left behind. How loathesome to any one with [?] principles. . . . We arrived just at 11 o'clock at St. Louis and hired a hack and drove over as much of the city as we could and walked over some. Made purchases &c &c and have returned on board. Have had our dinner and are now ready to take the Omnibus to leave Mo. as we will be out of here as soon as we cross the Mississippi. . . .

Nearly a year later, Martha returned to Missouri, this time traveling in greater comfort by train through Ohio, Indiana, and Illinois.

[Aboard the steamboat Spread Eagle]
MONDAY, MARCH 22[?], 1860

We got breakfast at a railroad Hotel [in Illinois] where I saw a painful specimen of white slavery as the table was attended almost alone by white girls. Oh how degrading [degraded?] must a white woman be! To be running around waiting on a large concourse of men with unblushing cheeks.

At 2 o'clock P.M. we reached the Mississippi River where we left the cars and ferried over, and as we were anxious to go on made no stop in St. Louis but went on to the wharf as we had learned through the mornings papers that the *Spread Eagle* would leave that evening. We went straight on board. . . .

[En route to Arrow Rock]
MARCH [24?], 1860

. . . Our Capt[ain] was so kind and obliging that it conduced much to our enjoyment. He asked permission to introduce several gentlemen to us, who proved to be very entertaining. 2 were sweet performers on the guittar and fine singers, another, a comic singer. The rest including my escort were entertaining in conversation so we had a delightful evening on [the] 22nd. But all things come to an end and so did Miss Sitton's trip as she reached her destination on the afternoon of 23d, so I was left without a single unmarried lady that I could associate with. How I did miss her agreeable society. Even the Capt. told me he was sorry for me for he said he had some hard customers on board. . . .

Martha was returning to her family in Arrow Rock after learning that two nephews and a niece, aged sixteen, twelve, and seven, had died in the past year. Her ill sister recovered, but another nephew passed away with typhoid pneumonia shortly after Martha's arrival in March, 1860.[14]

Arrow Rock, Missouri
APRIL 14, 1860

Notwithstanding our many afflictions I feel that I have much to be grateful for, just for the practical restoration of my beloved Sister who has been on the very verge of Eternity. And I do feel thankful for my many kind attentive friends that I have found in this land of strangers. Today I had a drive into the country with our kind Dr. P. who is so entertaining and agreeable, he has been a true friend in many of our trials. He says I need recreation and change and has kindly promised a drive whenever I desire it. He drove me in a nice buggy with a fine trotting horse and entertained me with lively chat. This and the exhilaration of the ride, the fresh air so invigorating to the delicate, the beautiful scenery of the landscape, just putting on the adorning of spring made me for a short time feel cheerful. I was surprised and pleased when on passing the Dr's beautiful residence

14. A notice in the *Marshall Democrat*, April 18, 1860, reads: "Thus, in the short space of eleven months, has a family been called to mourn the death of four children; and while we cannot restrain the sympathetic tear for the bereaved parents, they can find consolation in the reflection that the Savior himself said, 'Suffer the little children to come unto me, for such is the Kingdom of Heaven.' " The name as transcribed in the diary is *Jonnie*. The newspaper gives the boy's name as *Tommie*, and the 1860 census lists him as *Thomas*. There were two surviving Cobb daughters.

his servant came running out with a beautiful bouquet of sweet spring flowers. I felt more complimented than had he presented it himself much as I enjoy and appreciate his attention. . . .

[Arrow Rock, Missouri]
[APRIL] 16, 1860, SABBATH MORN

I am deeply depressed in spirits. I am suffering Mentally and bodily so that I can hardly support under it. It has just been 3 weeks since I arrived here and what have I not endured since then! Non[e] but God knows. Just one week today my idolized nephew was dying, expecting every moment to be his last. Oh the agony of that day! I know I ought to try to bear my troubles better for the sake of the sorrowing ones around me, but the heart will ache on and no power of mine can stay it. My darling ceased to suffer tomorrow week. . . . I should try to submit to God's decree.

Our friends seem very distant. None have been for several days, do they think we do not need a word of comfort or do they wish to shun such sorrows as ours? Oh may they never know from experience what such sorrow[s] as ours are is my prayer for Christ sake.

Recipes
Martha J. Wood

Hair Oil

4 Oz Castor Oil	1 Dram Cantharides
3 Do. Alcohol	Oil Bergamot to perfume

Bed Bug Poison

2 Oz Alcohol

Do, Do, Spirits Turpentine

2 Drams Corosive Sublimate

Wash the bedstead in cold water and apply this preparation to the slats and all the crevices of the bed.

To make Light Cake

Thicken your milk with eggs as you would do to eat. [P]ut as much butter as you think will make your cake rich enough into the milk and eggs. Then wet up your flour with the milk and eggs. [P]ut yeast enough to make it rise and Cloves or mace to your taste. [I]f you have not spice, fenne [fennel?] seed is very good. [D]on't put as much sugar at first as will make it sweet enough but work in a sufficiency [until?] it is light.

To make Trifle

Soak your Naples bisket in sweetned wine. Then boil your milk and eggs and mix your wine. [T]hen pour into your bisket. [Y]ou must grate some nutmeg in your trifle, then frost it with Cream or the white of eggs.

To make a Potato Pye

Slice your potatoes very thin. [P]ut a layer of potatoes, [then?] a layer of sugar, butter and spice. [Then?] layer of potatoes, &c &c in rich puff paste [pastry]. Let your potatoes be baked first.

To make another kind potato pye

Bake your potatoes till they are well done. [P]eall them and mash them well with sugar cream and butter with spice to your taste. You must make it soft enough with cream for it to spread smooth on your paste.

To dress Veals or Shoals [Shoats?] Head

Boil your head till it is well done then pick all the bones out. Chop it up and season it with pepper Butter, &c. Then lay it nicely in your dish on rich paste. [Y]ou may put small slices of liver in if you cho[o]se. Then make your . . . meat balls with some of the head chopped very fine. [S]eason them very high with pepper salt sage and Thyme. Then lay them in your dish and bake it. [Y]ou may slice boiled eggs and lay them over it after it is baked if you choose.

To pickle Cabbage

Split your Cabbage in quarters. [C]over them over with salt. [L]et them stand two or three days then put them in a pot and scald your vinegar with pepper ginger and allspice. [L]et it stand till it is cold then pour it to your Cabbage.

To make very good Cake

Take four ounces of sugar, four ounces of Butter two pints of flour, and one egg, which you must wet with milk and beat like bisket.[15]

---

15. The recipes given here represent a selection from Wood's collection. Among her other recipes are "baked suet pudding," "black bake," "stuffed beef," "quince cream," and "cherry mamblet."

Virginia Fackler Creel (1845–1937)

"$\mathcal{I}$f I came to voting age with a passionate belief in equal suffrage, it was because I *knew* my mother had more character, brains, and competence than any man that ever lived."[1] Her son George paid this tribute to Virginia Fackler Creel, who was born in Boonville, Missouri, in 1845. Her parents, Dr. John Fackler and Amanda Parkes Austin, were married in Staunton, Virginia, where they had been childhood sweethearts. While Virginia was still quite young, they moved to Western Saline County to join Dr. Fackler's parents and siblings, who were living in or near Blackburn.[2]

After Amanda died in 1848, Dr. Fackler entrusted his children's upbringing to his sisters. When the American Civil War shattered their peaceful way of life, the family witnessed guerrilla warfare and terrorism by Union troops. A biographical sketch written by her sons describes the experience surrounding the brief diary Virginia wrote as her family traveled by wagon from Missouri to Salt Lake City, Utah, in 1864. A typescript of the diary was presented to the University of Missouri after Virginia's death by her three sons, Richard Henry, George, and Wylie Creel. In their preface to the diary, the sons tell about the journey:

> During the Civil War, the family, . . . [like] other Southerners, experienced the turmoil and tribulations of border warfare. They were harried by Union "Home Guards" and . . . marauding bands from Kansas. In 1864 the Union forces, then in control of Missouri, had enacted a law that barred professional and business men from practicing or engaging in business unless they could disclaim sympathy with the Confederate cause.[3] . . . John Fackler decided to move to Oregon, where his brother, an Episcopal minister, was living, and

1. George Creel, *Rebel at Large: Recollections of Fifty Crowded Years*, 17.
2. Genealogical information in *History of Saline County* (1881), 650, conflicts to some extent with facts presented by George Creel in his autobiography *Rebel at Large* and by Richard Henry, George, and Wylie Creel in their 1937 preface to Virginia Fackler Creel's diary. Dr. Fackler (1816–1903) received his medical training at the St. Louis Medical College, presumably graduating in 1839, after which he returned to Virginia to marry Amanda Austin (whose last name is given as McClanahan in *History of Saline County* [1881]). According to George Creel, Jacob and Caroline Fackler, Dr. Fackler's parents, came to Saline County in 1842. John and Amanda Fackler had four children: Wylie, John, Virginia, and Amanda (Amy).
3. The convention of the Union's Provisional Government of Missouri, established after Governor Jackson fled to the Confederacy, formulated a loyalty oath for people to swear allegiance to both state and Federal constitutions and avow not to aid the Confederacy. The oath, first required in 1861, was used increasingly throughout the Civil War to punish Southern sympathizers: first, state civil officials had to take it; then it was required of city officials, business and educational leaders, attorneys, jurors, clergy, newspaper editors, and others, including any man registering to vote. The penalty for not taking the oath was severe both financially and personally. See William E. Parrish, *A History of Missouri*, 3:43–45, and Parrish, *Turbulent Partnership: Missouri and the Union, 1861–1865*, 39, 128, 202–3.

to engage in medical practice there. Together with his two daughters . . . , he joined a company of fifty other Missourians and crossed the Plains in the summer of 1864.[4]

Departing from St. Joseph on May 19, the Facklers and their party traveled to the northwest corner of the state of Missouri, reaching the Iowa state line in six days. Virginia and the other women in her family "rode royally in a specially constructed spring wagon with a canvas top, drawn by four fine mules."[5] On May 26 they headed north toward a ferry that would take them across the Missouri River. In Nebraska the major points along their route were Nebraska City and Kearney. Continuing to central Colorado, they saw the imposing Rocky Mountains. The party traveled north to Fort Collins, which they reached by July 7. They then crossed into the southwest corner of Wyoming, where Fort Bridger was the noteworthy stop on July 12. Continuing toward Utah, the wagon train reached the Bear River by July 17. On July 26 they went through Echo Canyon, northeast of Salt Lake City, which they reached two days later.

Lillian Schlissel's groundbreaking work in *Women's Diaries of the Westward Journey* puts the important role women played on the overland journey in the context of the hardships they faced. Most of the women were in their childbearing years. Virginia Fackler Creel was nineteen years old and single, but many women were traveling with small children, and one in five women on the trail was in some stage of pregnancy. Creel's diary reflects more optimism than others do, but it illustrates how she assumed a typical woman's role. Since her mother was deceased, Creel was one of those who tried "to weave a fabric of accustomed design, a semblance of their usual domestic circle," while traveling on the open road.[6]

Virginia Fackler Creel's diary soars with hope above all the difficulties of overland travel. Unlike many women who dreaded the westward journey, but had little choice when the sirens of land and gold lured their husbands and fathers, Virginia traveled with her family to escape the animosities and repression of the Civil War. The family could not deny their allegiance, for Virginia's brother, Wylie, served in the Confederate army from 1861 to 1865. Once, when he was caught behind enemy lines after paying a brief visit to his family, Wylie hid for three days in a hemp shock. Each evening Virginia would walk into the field at dusk to bring him the food and water hidden under her skirt. During the war Wylie

4. Creel, Creel, and Creel, preface to Virginia Fackler Creel Diary. The manuscript is at WHMC-C. Selected passages are included in this anthology with the permission of Virginia's great-granddaughter, Georgia Bates Creel. We have not altered spelling or grammar.

5. George Creel, *Rebel at Large*, 6.

6. Lillian Schlissel, *Women's Diaries*, 15.

was taken prisoner twice and was wounded at Hartville, Missouri, during one of the many battles in which he fought.[7]

The war forced the Fackler family to leave Missouri until peace returned to their home state. Although there may have been external reasons for her optimistic outlook, the excerpts of the diary selected by the editors suggest that the main cause was Creel's buoyant personality, which allowed her to look beyond immediate trials. The diary is sprinkled with literary quotations, and her grammar and spelling indicate an excellent educational background. She had attended a private school at the home of a relative, where she learned "Greek, Latin, and the classics," according to her son George, who tells that even at the age of eighty Virginia remembered her languages and ancient and modern history. In the diary we meet the young Virginia Fackler, enjoying fully her opportunity to experience the "Gypsy Life." Her account reveals Virginia's humor, sympathy, appreciation for the arts and literature, enjoyment of relationships, and faith in God.

─────────── **DIARY OF VIRGINIA FACKLER CREEL** ───────────

MAY 19, 1864

At last we have turned our faces toward the setting sun. Left St. Joseph [Missouri] this morning at ten o'clock and reached our first tenting-ground at half past six. . . . The day has been delightful and I am sure I would have enjoyed the ride greatly, had I not been the victim of a violent headache. O Dear! I trust the motion of the wagon will soon cease to such deathly sea-sickness; 'tis almost unbearable. Fortunately for my poor head, we had a bountiful supply of cold bread, ham, etc., so the coffee was speedily made and our simple repast soon ready. . . . I think our camp with its dozen spacious wall tents; its tables resplendent with new plate (tin), and above all the cheerful faces, everywhere sun [?], flitting busily hither and thither, in the bright moonlight would have been an interesting study for an artist. . . .

MAY 21, 1864

Made fourteen miles today; nearly half of which distance we walked as the roads were in a state of total neglect, having received no attention

7. William Barclay Napton, *Past and Present of Saline County Missouri*, 226. In 1867 Wylie was "slain by Indian savages," according to his tombstone (*History of Saline County* [1967], 35). George Creel suggests this might have occurred on a cattle drive in Wyoming (*Rebel at Large*, 6).

since the War; the road overseer is probably by this time a "Brigadier." Commodore (Mr. Ewing's favorite mule) tumbled through a broken bridge, turning a somersault in harness; he did not injure himself, however, thanks to his own prudence and sagacity. A few hours later, while descending a very steep hill, the family wagon of Mr. Burchell upset— almost killing a fine horse and spilling all the apple butter in the old lady's best bonnet. I was near at the time, and was really touched by the old man's admirable patience; everything for the long journey turned out in a heap. "Oh, Mr. B," I said, "this is so unfortunate! Can we do anything for you?" "Oh! Miss," he replied, "it is nothing, nothing. I felt so thankful when I saw that none of my family were hurt, that I have not thought of the plunder." Passed through a beautiful region today; had a refreshing shower just after we encamped; the air is much purer, but the sun seemed to shine with redoubled warmth after having been veiled for half an hour. This is indeed a lovely spot in which to spend our first Sunday in this, our "Gypsy Life."

MAY 22, 1864

This is a charming morning; did not hope for one so clear and pleasant, as last night was so stormy; our tent not being sufficiently stretched, the water penetrated the canvas, thereby causing Lizzie greatly to bemoan the day she left Loline. I quite enjoyed the novelty, but did not venture to hint such a thing just then. . . .

MAY 23, 1864

Left camp at half past six; the morning cool, I awoke on hearing the guard called at midnight, dressed, looked out the tent, saw no one stirring, went to bed again; but could not sleep well. . . . Mrs. Jones and I took a long walk. . . . I enjoyed it highly. I love Mrs. J. more and more each day. She has rare conversational powers; her sentiments are so noble, yet essentially womanly, and her mode of expression so elegant, that it is no wonder how she wins the hearty love and admiration of all who know her. Beautiful scenery; saw an immense "Box Elder" which could well have afforded shelter for half dozen wagons; did so long to rest in its shadow. Saw a steamer down the river three miles distant; the last that we see I suppose for a long, long while. Stopped at 2 o'clock; hoped to get supper before a storm came upon us; too late for that. . . . Pa held an umbrella over the stove and I made biscuit. . . . O! 'twas funny and yet provoking too, to see what an effort it required for us to eat them; tough, does not give one the faintest idea of what those biscuits were. Johnny said, "Virgie, if I didn't know for certain that you made these biscuit[s] just now, I would say they were mixed in the year One." . . .

May 25, 1864

Last in train this morning to leave camp; could not walk; the pony was in service; in consequence of which I felt as cross as hungry bears are said to be, all day. I hope we'll never again stop in so disagreeable a place as Rockville B[ridge]. Pigs so enormous, almost carried us off. Johnnie brought in a fine rabbit last night, and he and I were up till after eleven, dressing it for breakfast; made every preparation for an early start, but to no purpose; awoke this morn, found the pigs had rooted over the provision box, eaten the rabbit, bothered our chicks and strewn them in all directions; such confusion! Oh, dear! I can't speak of it. 'Tis thought we will reach Nebraska City this eve; hope we will, 'tis disheartening to think we have spent a week in accomplishing two day's journey. . . .

May 26, 1864

8 AM Left camp [on the Iowa line] at four this morning, only crackers and ham for breakfast; object in moving at such an hour was that the Ferry might be reached before 10 AM as it would then be pressed into Government service, to prevent emigration on account of the Draft.[8] Wish we could always drive as rapidly as we have this morn; would soon reach our destination; have traveled 9 [?] miles in 2½ hours. . . .

4 PM In camp ¼ mile from Neb[raska City]. . . . Most of the ladies went shopping today; as it will be the last time they can do so for weeks. Am half-famished; had nothing but water-crackers since yesterday. Gentlemen took dinner in town therefore are in no hurry to take down stove. Must see if I can find Pa, and begin supper, for if I do not, I fear I cannot crowd enough food in our small oven to feed so many hungry mouths.

May 27, 1864

. . . Made some light rolls for supper; hope they rise well; we all have such fine appetites that I am in constant thought I will not have enough for all to eat as heartily as they wish.

It is the intention of Capt. Ewing, I believe, to move camp to a place three miles further on the road where wood and water will be more convenient. Mr. Davison, poor man, returned this morning to St. Joseph. All the family were quite ill with measles. It distressed us to see them so low-spirited.

8. The ferry would cross the Missouri River, taking the party from Iowa to Nebraska.

MAY 28, 1864

. . . [We] are now encamped on a bold ridge of prairie, a few rods from a farm house, at which we can get as much milk and butter as we desire! The children are in ecstasies. There is a beautiful stream skirted with timber a yard or two from our tent door, supplying us with wood and delicious water; luxuries we duly appreciate. . . .

MAY 29, 1864

The most windy day I ever saw; cannot keep dishes on table; tent looks and feels as if 'twould be blown over each instant. . . .

MAY 31, 1864

Very windy and stormy; have seen nothing of interest today.

JUNE 1, 1864

A wintry morning; violent northwest wind during whole night. 80 miles from Neb. City. . . .

JUNE 2, 1864

In camp on Beaver Creek;[9] saw a large dam composed of trees a foot in diameter, cut as smoothly as if by a saw. Passed through a prairie dog town a mile in length; but my curiosity to see owls, rattlesnakes, and dogs living harmoniously together was not gratified; from Washington Irving's description [I] expected to see everything arranged with precision of marks on chess board; [but] saw only innumerable little heaps of earth, from which now and then one of the inhabitants—an animal about the size of a rabbit—would cautiously put forth his nose, but instantly draw it in again. They keep up a perpetual yelping with short, quick, yet weak tones like those of young puppies. . . .

JUNE 5, 1864

. . . After supper, took our chairs and stools over to Mrs. Van Ansdale's tent, where Cousin George [Fackler] preached a short sermon, and offered up one of the most impressively beautiful prayers I ever listened to; perfect silence reigned, and an indefinable feeling of awe crept over as

9. Beaver Creek runs through Nebraska and Kansas.

that solemn chant "Praise the Lord" rose on the evening air. I shall never forget the hour and scene; so many hearts bowed in thankfulness to Him who has thus far safely guided us on our perilous journey. We had just dispersed to our respective tents when a party of Sioux Indians—first we have seen—came into camp. They were going to Neb.; they said on a trading expedition and wanted to stay near our tents but Capt. E ordered them off.

JUNE 6, 1864

A bitter cold morning. . . . Gathered a quantity of beautiful flowers so faded before eve. could not press them. Pass through Fort Kearney at noon. . . . quite disappointed in the appearance of K[earney] City; houses built of sod and logs. I saw only one tasteful building. . . .

JUNE 7, 1864

Mr. Britton took coach for St. J[oseph] this morning; will go by steamer to San Francisco. I do think it selfish and unwomanly in his daughter to consult her feeling on all occasions, so much to the discomfort of all with whom she is connected. Today has been mild and clear.

JUNE 10, 1864

A delightful camping ground; water deliciously cool and clear; had a large piece of ice given us, which we sent to poor Mr. Douglass. He seemed to enjoy it so much; it is saddening to look at his thin face, so pale, save when flushed with hectic. Consumption seems to have marked him for her own; this journey is his last hope. I do hope it will restore his health; he is the object of our warmest sympathy and all vie with each other in showing him kindest attention; passed through Cottonwood Springs at noon; a company of Feds stationed there soon possessed themselves of our Navy revolvers. Spent a very pleasant evening at Mr. Cochrane's tent, with Mrs. Price (a bride of a month) and her sister Miss Louise Kyner. They sing sweetly and are very kind in favoring one with all the music in their power. . . .

SUNDAY, JUNE 12, 1864

Had a gloomy morning; severe storm last night. . . . [H]ad roast elk for dinner; it was delicious. Wrote to Nonn [Nan?] and Marion [Fackler] today as it is their joint birthday. I have been with them in imagination all day. Spent the eve. with Mrs. Sublitte, and stayed to prayers. . . .

JUNE 28, 1864

. . . The scenery, though monotonous, has been beautiful; the region through which we have passed has seemed a gorgeous flower-bed. I found yesterday, a species of the Cactus; quite different from any I had before seen; it is very beautiful indeed; the petals being rose-colored, orange, and white. I wish I could press some; but that seems an impossibility. I cannot think there is any one who is wholly impervious to the subtle, spiritualizing influence of flowers; as an eloquent writer has said, "They are evangels of purity and faith, if we but unlock our hearts to their ministry, and they weave rosy links of imagination more binding than steel, and sometimes of incalculable value." Another has styled them "chalices of Divine workmanship; of purple and scarlet and liquid gold, from which man may drink the pure joy of beauty."

JUNE 29, 1864

Pa says we shall have to remain here several days, which . . . doesn't depress me in the least. Our tents are very comfortable; the scenery so fine, that I am quite content to enjoy this pleasant idleness; the more pleasant since being involuntary, it is no weight upon my conscience. Before us, to the westward, rises the Rocky Mountains, the waving line of the summits being cut here and there by steep gorges, "the gateways of rivers that come down to the plain." Very different indeed do the mountains appear from the view I saw a week ago; then they seemed a mass of pearl-like clouds; tangible, yet intangible. Now a chain of blue, with here and there a loftier peak "climbing to the topmost snows."

JUNE 30, 1864

This morn dawned clear and beautiful. The mountains, except the snowy crests of Fremont's and Pike's Peak, were wrapped in the early shadows. Amy [Virginia's sister, Amanda] and I did a large washing; I brightened my tins and made a huge cherry dumpling, with brandy sauce for dinner; and after everything was in order again I made myself tidy and spent the remainder of day with Mrs. Jones, I sewing while she read aloud, [Tennyson's] "Locksley Hall." I do not know when I have enjoyed anything so thoroughly. I forgot all bodily fatigue in the delight the poem gave. Mrs. J. reads beautifully; "her voice is clear, gentle and sweet, a most excellent thing in woman."[10] . . .

10. William Shakespeare, *King Lear,* 5.3.274: "Her voice was ever soft, / Gentle and low, an excellent thing in woman."

July 3, 1864

Clouds gathered last evening after nightfall and occasionally there was a dash of rain on our tent, but I heard it with the same quiet happiness I have often felt while listening to the beating rain on the roof of my Missouri home. . . . When we arose this morning 'twas damp and cloudy and after an early breakfast were again on our way. During this afternoon the sun came out brightly; two antelopes were brought into camp this eve; a generous share of which we received. . . .

[One mile from Fort Collins]

July 7, 1864

. . . O! If I could but sketch this spot; it is so lovely. The flowers are glistening with dew; the birds are singing and a cool breeze coming down from the hills makes my blood "leap as nimbly and joyously as the young hart on the mountain side."[11] Mrs. J, Amy and I climbed to the summit of a rocky cliff, the broken edges of which rose like terraces to a great height and there opened before us the most beautiful landscape I ever beheld. Away in the distance, eastward, through a rich mosaic of green, brown and yellow, wound the Platte [River] like a thread of silver; while toward the south mountains whose bases were completely enveloped in forests of pine, lifted their snowy summits into the sky.

July 12, 1864

In camp at Bridger's Pass. I arose very early this morning, shivering in the cold air of the mountains. Drank a "julep," [so] that I might say I had taken one cooled with snow on the 12th day of July. Just as the sun, bursting through the pines, looked down the little hollow in which our tents were pitched, the whole train was in motion. Mrs. J, Amy, Lizzie and I walked 12 miles today. I think we are becoming very accomplished pedestrians. . . . I am too tired to write more and would give almost anything for a drink of pure, sweet water. This we have tastes horribly of salt, sulphur and lime.

July 17, 1864

The atmosphere today has been bracing and invigorating. Encamped this eve on Bear River, a tributory of the Weber. Had venison for supper, which rendered our repast a sumptious one. Trout are abundant. Aunt C[arrie Rammage] and Amy caught several fine speckled ones. At sunset

11. Song of Solomon 2:17 and 8:14.

this eve. Mrs. J, Amy and I ascended one of the highest elevations near our camp, and gave a farewell look to the scenery toward the Atlantic. Far to the west lay a vast and seemingly immeasurable plain, over which the sun shed his declining rays, while to the east could only be seen the tops of some of the highest peaks over which lay profound silence.

JULY 26, 1864

Crossed Weber River late this afternoon and are now encamped in Echo Canyon, on each side of which the mountains tower to the height of several thousand feet, exhibiting a succession of richest verdure and then cliffs that at a distance present every variety of animate and inanimate objects in nature. In some spots the reverberation is wonderful. Mrs. J and I tried it, and fancied it quite equal to Mont Blanc.

JULY 27, 1864

A wearisome day.

JULY 28, 1864

Entered this afternoon the City of the Saints [Salt Lake City]. This has been the very perfection of a summer's day. The "drowsy, dreamy sunshine" aroused a million sweet memories of home. Encamped for tonight in "Emigration Square." Will find a more pleasant tenting ground tomorrow. Truly these Mormons have made the "wilderness to blossom as a rose."[12]

Continuing to Dayton, Nevada, near old Virginia City and the Comstock Lode, Dr. Fackler met a boyhood friend from Virginia who persuaded him to stop over and practice medicine during the winter months before attempting the Sierra Nevada passes. During that interval, Virginia Fackler taught a class of small children. In the spring of 1865 the family traveled to Sacramento, California, and there learned that it would be safe to return to Missouri. They journeyed by steamer from San Francisco to the Isthmus of Panama, by train across the isthmus, by ship to New York, and by train to the banks of the Mississippi River. After crossing the frozen river by sleigh, they concluded the trip by train and wagon.

When the war was over, the family returned to Saline County. Virginia married a former Confederate captain, Henry Clay Creel (1828[?]–1906).[13] Creel's attempts at farming and ranching in Lafayette and Hickory Counties failed, and it became

12. Isaiah 35:1.
13. Henry Clay Creel, originally from Parkersburg, West Virginia, graduated from St. Xavier's in Cincinnati and was elected to the Virginia legislature. In 1860 his father, Alexander Herbert Creel, sent him to Missouri, where he purchased land in Osage County.

Virginia's responsibility to support the family by running a boarding house, first in Independence and later in Kansas City. The three sons, Wylie, George, and Richard Henry (Hal), knew Captain Creel as a chronic alcoholic and Virginia as a cultured and courageous woman.[14]

Virginia Fackler Creel experienced marriage, motherhood, and the hardships of poverty. George Creel writes, "It was not only that Mother had the gift of making tasks and hardships seem a game, but she colored our lives with her own eager interest in everything."[15] *Despite her father's disapproval of Henry Clay Creel, Virginia refused to consent to a separation. After the failure of her boarding house in Kansas City, she lived for a while in Odessa, taking in sewing and keeping a large garden. She always treated her husband with respect, calling him "a gentleman farmer temporarily retired on account of ill health."*[16] *Later the family lived again in Kansas City, and as a widow Virginia lived in St. Louis and in San Francisco, where she died in 1937.*

Her sons describe Mrs. Creel as " 'everything a mother should be'—utterly selfless, sacrificing and devoted, not only to her family, but to a large circle of friends. She had an 'infinite capacity for affection'—and an unswerving loyalty to her native state and to the 'Lost Cause.' Until the end, at ninety-two, she was unreconstructed." The bishop who presided at her funeral said, "She gave a fragrance to life."[17]

There were other Creels in Saline County, for when the Episcopal church of St. Thomas (now Waverly) was organized in 1856, its original members included R. H. Creel, as well as Jacob and George Fackler. There was also the family of Alexander and Salina Creel, at whose home Virginia probably received her schooling. (Walter Barlow Stevens, *Centennial History of Missouri*, 3:211; *History of Saline County* [1967], 149; George Creel, *Rebel at Large*, 5, 8–9; J. Adolphus Owens, ed., *Anywhere I Wander*, 362).

14. Virginia's sons had successful careers. Wylie Creel was a shoe manufacturer in St. Louis. George Creel, a journalist and political reformer, served as the Director of Public Information for the United States Government during World War I and published many books. Dr. Richard Henry [Hal] Creel, a specialist in cholera and tropical diseases, served as Assistant Surgeon General of the United States Public Health Service.

15. Creel, *Rebel at Large*, 19.

16. *Ibid*, 21.

17. Creel, Creel, and Creel, preface to Virginia Fackler Creel Diary, 2. Additional biographical information on the Creel family may be found in Stevens, *Centennial History of Missouri*, 3:211–12; Mrs. Creel's obituary, *Kansas City Star*, May 7, 1937; and Ivan H. Epperson, "Missourians Abroad: No. 3—George Creel," *Missouri Historical Review* 12 (January 1918): 100–10. Although the sons were grateful for their mother's devotion, they also admired her individuality. George wrote to his brother Hal after their mother's funeral that the press notices "made me so damned mad by assuming that Mother had no identity except through her sons" (George Creel, letter to Richard Henry Creel, May 14, 1937, WHMC-C).

ELVIRA ASCENITH WEIR SCOTT (1821–1910)

*T*he Civil War swept over the Missouri countryside, through its towns, and across the thresholds of its houses. Everywhere in the nation the war brought separation, suffering, and loss to many families. In the typical pattern of events men rode off to war and women remained behind to take over responsibility for families, farms, and businesses. Some Missouri women performed heroic service as couriers, spies, nurses, and flag-makers. Acts of bravery could happen in an instant, as when a quick-witted homemaker in Hannibal was approached by Federal troops while working in her kitchen; quickly she rolled up her Confederate flag and sealed it in a can of tomatoes.[1] The mission of the Ladies' Union Aid Society (L.U.A.S.) of St. Louis began in 1861, when they met a train bringing the wounded from the battle of Wilson's Creek near Springfield. Throughout the war members of the L.U.A.S. provided shelter to refugees, sewed thousands of hospital garments, visited and nursed patients in military hospitals, and performed other kindnesses. They outfitted not only hospitals in the city, but railway cars and ships to transport the wounded. The most praiseworthy L.U.A.S. member was Adaline Couzins, whose daughter is featured in this anthology because of her achievement in the field of law. Adaline not only worked tirelessly as a nurse on shipboard and at battlefields, but she also suffered a wound at the siege of Vicksburg which entitled her to a disability pension. Women with Southern sympathies also distributed food to prisoners and helped them escape, if possible. There were a number of women's organizations in Missouri, including one devoted to aiding wounded African-American soldiers.[2]

The organizational skills and public action that had marked church work and the abolitionist and women's rights movements were channeled toward mobilizing relief for prisoners and wounded and needy families. The Civil War may be considered a "major watershed" in women's history, for it occurred when women were learning to be socially assertive and politically active. Vigor and stamina are seen in their lives and reflected in the fiction they wrote about the war, where the theme that links individual narratives is a "celebration of *activeness.*"[3]

No one better exemplifies the transformation wrought by the war than Elvira Scott, who had been languid and delicate, bored with domestic and social routine, and content only when playing the piano and guitar or

1. J. Hurley Hagood and Roberta (Roland) Hagood, *The Story of Hannibal: A Bicentennial History,* 1976, 54–55.

2. Paula Coalier, "Beyond Sympathy: The St. Louis Ladies' Union Aid Society and the Civil War," 42–43; 51 n. 19; William E. Parrish, *A History of Missouri,* 3:72–73.

3. Hope Norman Coulter, introduction to *Civil War Women: The Civil War Seen Through Women's Eyes . . . ,* 7–8.

walking in the fresh air. Elvira Ascenith Weir was born on September 22, 1821, in Indiana, where she met her future husband. In 1841 her parents moved to Wapello County, Iowa. Elvira married John P. Scott, a former schoolmate, in March 1844. The next month the newlyweds arrived in Miami, Missouri.[4] In 1846 John announced the opening of his "Cash and Barter" store by nailing a notice to the side of a log cabin by the river.[5] In addition to a son who died in infancy, the Scotts had two daughters: Eva ("Pet"), born in 1845, and Hebe, born in 1855.

On January 9, 1860, Elvira Scott wrote the first entry in her diary, which is extant in typescript as edited by Donald W. Riddle. Riddle, who entitled the manuscript "A Diary of the Civil War on the Missouri Border," supplemented Elvira's entries with editorial comments and documentation.[6] We present selections that show Elvira Scott as a remarkable woman—hardworking, colorful, and brave.

The issue of slavery caused a turmoil of feelings in Saline County, where by 1860 the population was 14,699, of whom 4,876 were slaves. On December 15, 1860, during a mass meeting held at Marshall to discuss the threat of war, a resolution was passed urging support of the U. S. Constitution. Few people in the county were secessionists, but citizens were prepared to withdraw from the Union over the issue of states' rights. The Scotts were typical of the many Southern sympathizers who had relatives in Virginia, Tennessee, and Kentucky.[7] In 1861 Saline County organized troops to resist a Federal invasion, and the ladies of Marshall presented them with a flag. For a while men in the northern part of the county crossed the river to join Union troops; in 1862 the first Federal

4. Information on the Scott family is found in Riddle's manuscript, in the Genealogy Room of the Marshall Public Library, and at the Miami Cemetery. Called *Greenville* in 1838, the town was renamed *Miami* five years later. Miami Indians established a village in the area before 1810. By 1840 Miami was a prosperous shipping port (*The WPA Guide to 1930s Missouri*, 480).

5. *History of Saline County* (1881), 828–29, and item from the *Miami Index*, May 1876, reprinted in *The Marshall Democrat-News*, March 24, 1943, in James T. Thorp scrapbook, WHMC-C.

6. The manuscript was donated to WHMC-C by Mrs. Donald W. Riddle and Scott Jones in 1974. We present selected passages with the permission of Scott Jones. Occasional spelling errors or archaic spellings from the typescript have been retained by the present editors. Riddle was the author of a number of other books, primarily about the Bible, such as *Early Christian Life as Reflected in its Literature* (1936), *The Gospels: Their Origin and Growth* (1939), and *Paul, Man of Conflict* (1940). He also published the historical study *Lincoln Runs for Congress* (1948). Elvira Scott's significance as a source of information about events during the war is acknowledged by Thomas Goodrich, who quotes her diary in *Black Flag: Guerrilla Warfare on the Western Border, 1861–1865*.

7. John P. Scott's birthplace is identified in the Saline County census of 1860 as Kentucky. Actually he was born in Salem, Indiana, and went to live in Kentucky as a child when orphaned. He worked in Boonville, Missouri, for three years before settling in Miami (*Portrait and Biographical Record of Lafayette and Saline Counties Missouri*, 209–10). Both the Scott and Weir families were originally from Virginia.

county company was formed. The war had drawn closer in 1861 as battles were fought in Boonville and Lexington, and raids and skirmishes began to occur in Saline County itself. In the spring of 1862 a Federal regiment, including many Germans from Boonville, set up headquarters in Marshall.[8]

Like Virginia Fackler Creel's father, John Scott was forced to decide if he would take an oath of loyalty to the Federal government. Scott submitted to the requirement in order to continue running his business and living with his family. They were not safe for long, as Elvira's diary tells us. Her adversary was Lieutenant Adam Bax, a German who served with Company I of the Seventh Cavalry Volunteers.[9] At the close of the century John Shaver, who had served as a sergeant, wrote a verse about each of the men in Company I. He recalled Bax:

> Our Lieutenant Bax, a German was he,
> A splendid drillmaster and strict to a T.
> When he first took command we laughed on the sly,
> When he said "audenshun gombany I."[10]

In her fierce loyalty to the Confederate cause, Elvira Scott looked on German immigrant soldiers as mercenaries and thought of herself as a true American.[11] Her days of leisure and ennui were over, and Elvira Scott, like Jette Geisburg Bruns, demonstrated resourcefulness and endurance in a time of hardship.

Elvira Scott and her family were forced to spend most of the Civil War years in St. Louis. In 1865 they returned to Miami, to repair their home and reopen the store. John Scott died in 1888; Elvira, in 1910.[12]

During the "leisure hours" of Elvira Scott's last decade of life, a friend reported, "she transcribed many a page of the recollections of her early years."[13] Although the diary has an air of spontaneity and fresh and vivid details, it may have been revised to some extent during the process of transcription. The diary is partly a narrative, recording dramatic episodes

8. Napton, *Past and Present of Saline County Missouri,* 141–61.

9. Microfilm Index, Record Group 133, Missouri State Archives.

10. John Shaver, *The Company Roll, with a brief comment upon each member of Company I, 7th Cavalry Missouri Volunteers* (Kirksville, Mo.: n.p., 1898), 4.

11. For a different experience of the war, see the first memoir to be written by the wife of a President, Julia Dent Grant (1826–1902). Growing up on a Missouri plantation, Julia had a sentimental view of slavery and the Southern way of life, but loyalty to her husband, Ulysses S. Grant, converted her to a Yankee (*The Personal Memoirs of Julia Dent Grant,* ed. John Y. Simon). See also Jessie Benton Frémont, *The Story of the Guard: A Chronicle of the War.*

12. After the death of her husband, Elvira continued to live in the family home, which she shared with her widowed daughter Pet and Pet's children, Eva Scott Miller and Louise Miller Byers. When Louise died in 1907, her infant son, Edward Scott Byers, was brought to the family home to be raised by his aunt Eva.

13. Obituary, *Miami Weekly News,* December 16, 1910.

such as her fearless encounters with Union troops. It is also a meditation on concerns about her family, determination to exercise her talents, and evaluation of her role as a woman. The diary was to serve a function: "I am very fond of talking, & lest I offend I will talk less & write more. It can do no harm to write; it will be an expression of feeling, an outlet." Elvira struggled to discipline her emotions: "Sometimes in looking back I think I can see some progress. One proof of some change I felt last week, when every feeling of my heart was outraged. I kept back every feeling of resentment, closed my lips . . . & only felt compassion." Calling the diary her "only confidante," Elvira remarked that it was "not a portrait of the inner life, only the outside thread of life—the visible." She vowed to write "when the heart is full, longing for sympathy when it aches, when weighed down, when the cross is heavy. . . ." The diary was her refuge, as she struggled to overcome her "besetting sin" of troubling other people through speech: "If only I could be still. There is such power, sometimes, in silence."[14] And there is power in the personality revealed in this diary.

DIARY OF ELVIRA SCOTT

SUNDAY, [JANUARY] 29, [1860]

A clear beautiful day. Did not go to church or Sunday School because I did not feel well. It was a peaceful, pleasant day. I read in the Bible. . . . The more I read & improve myself on the subject, the more I am convinced that the Episcopal Church has greater claim to being the true church that the Apostles set up on earth than any other in existence. . . . I wish throughout the year 1860 to live a better life than ever before. I wish to read my Bible & Prayerbook daily.

JANUARY 30, 1860

A beautiful day; cool. I do not feel well. I practiced on the piano, commenced learning "The Child's Wish." Finished a pair of stockings for Belle.[15] Mrs. A. called & took tea; M. L. Eager staid all night. Passed the day pleasantly. There are times when it does not seem much trouble to do right. I read three chapters in Ecclesiastes.

JANUARY 31, 1860

. . . I am very unwell; my bones all ache terribly. I got a new number of Harpers. Practiced all morning, read all afternoon. In consequence my

14. Diary transcript, 259, 266, 273. Subsequent page references appear in the text.
15. A black slave.

eyes hurt very much. Except for some trouble with Pet the day passed pleasantly. I find it very hard to get her to mind & speak to me as she should. It really grieves me to be harsh with her, & yet it is my duty to see that she addresses me as she should, especially before her sister, who will certainly follow her example. I begin to feel how precious my eyesight is when I have to spend whole evenings unoccupied. . . .

FEBRUARY 1, 1860

I hurt the first finger of my right hand severely & fear I shall not be able to practice or sew for some time. I read, laid down & slept a little; passed the day pleasantly. . . .

FEBRUARY 4[6?], 1860

. . . It is Saturday night, & thank God I have been able to pass through the entire week without being angry or speaking harshly to anyone, although I have been severely tempted. What a pleasant thing is a clear conscience! I have read in my Bible every day this week & have sought earnestly to do right. . . .

MONDAY, [FEBRUARY 8?], 1860

A clear cold morning, frozen but not very cold. I practiced an hour; felt well yesterday & today. A very pleasant day; practiced on the piano at least two hours, read, did not sew. Camilla B. was here tonight; she & Hebe have gone to dancing school. It goes to my heart to see Pet so disappointed about [not] going. I feel sorry that she ever went at all, but know that it is best at her age to keep her from such places. It takes her mind off her studies. But that is not the greatest consideration: dancing parties, conducted as they are here, will not improve her mentally or morally. She can't appreciate why she is disappointed or thwarted in her inclinations now. It is painful to me to cross her, & nothing but a sense of duty compels me to do it. Oh! for wisdom to guide my children aright, for strength & grace to live daily before them as a consistent Christian, keeping in subjection every evil passion. . . . [I]f we strive to make home Eden-like, if we govern our little ones with no less kindness but more firmness, if we live so that every night we can feel that our peace is made with God: what a happy New Year this one will be—shall we not try?

[FEBRUARY] 6[?], 1860

A clear, pleasant day. I practiced on the piano nearly two hours, some time on the guitar. The day passed pleasantly. I felt languid & my head ached, but after taking a walk felt clear & bright. . . . I think that I am progressing with my music. It is rather strange for one of my age to be spending an hour or two daily studying music, but I like it. It is recreation & amusement. I grant that my time might be employed more profitably, but would it be? Women's lives are generally filled up with household cares, & their leisure with some fancy work & visiting. My eyes are too weak for the former, & as the conversation of ladies visiting is not always the most improving intellectually or morally I have concluded that music is the pleasantest. It cannot possibly be sinful to spend my leisure cultivating it, as my musical education was totally neglected in my youth. I have always been & still am very fond of it, although I expect to make little proficiency. The practice & study is a pleasant pastime, & as long as I live I expect to cultivate the faculties God has given me. . . .

I was reading the other day of an interview with Samuel Rogers,[16] the poet. At the age of 90 his mind was vigorous. What a pleasant thing to look upon is old age after a useful, wellspent life, after, as St. Paul said, one has fought a good fight. . . .

FEBRUARY 7[?], 1860

. . . [C]alled to see a sick child. There were several ladies in the room, all looking feeble & complaining. Is it possible that our Maker intended us to be so frail & so afflicted? The more I think about it, the more I am constrained to believe that a violation of nature's laws, more than anything else, is the cause, & that ignorance is the cause of such violations. We are fearfully in the dark mentally, morally, & physically. It has been a day of serenity of mind. Have not suffered lately from nervous excitability.

FEBRUARY 8[?], 1860

Cold & clear. Practiced two hours or more, read some, sewed a little. Got up this morning feeling nervous & irritable; came near being angry several times. It was rather a trying day. (31–35)

Elvira Scott was well aware of political issues and recorded in her diary news of distant battles in the Civil War. Finally the war reached Miami, and she and her family experienced the threats and demands of Federal soldiers.

MARCH 11[10?], [1862]

Monday morning, a delightful day. I was awakened by the rush of an armed body of cavalry into town—the Federals at last. They have

16. Samuel Rogers, whose works include *The Pleasures of Memory* (1795), *Human Life* (1819), *Italy* (1830), and *Poems* (1834), lived from 1763 to 1855.

surrounded several houses & taken prisoners . . . & are after many others who have escaped.

SATURDAY, APRIL 26, 1862

. . . After some altercation John got parolled to Boonville & started on Saturday evening to St. Louis to stop there on his way, which he did. We had the parole extended until his return. He visited the provost marshall at St. Louis & was told he would have to take the Oath & give bond or go to prison. At Boonville on his return he took the Oath, giving bond for three thousand dollars.

I suppose there is little if any hope of Missouri ever maintaining her independence of the Federal government, & of course every citizen will be obliged to give his allegiance. It seems a terrible state of affairs when all substantial, worthy men must be fettered down from a free expression of opinion, deprived of arms, deprived of the privilege of voting & kept under subjection by the lowest most unprincipled Dutch, with a very few American hirelings.[17] Gentlemen of the highest social &—a year ago—political position are hunted down & shot like dogs if they do not come forward & take the Oath to support these usurpations. A little moral courage in these days of terror is certain to bring ruin on a man. What is to be the end? God only knows. (104–5)

[LATE APRIL 1862]

[The] 28th, 29th & 30th were spent in active preparation to visit Iowa.[18] I started Wednesday morning, the last day of April, feeling very unwell. I left Pet almost sick. The weather was hot & threatening rain. I never started on a journey with more pressure. . . . We got to DeWitt at eleven o'clock, where we waited two hours for the ferry boat. The river was very high & full of drift. We took our dinners on the river bank. While crossing we had a full view of home. I had sad feelings & forebodings, because I had left Pet alone at home. . . .

The morning was very chilly & windy. The horses seemed not well, & Charley took the thumps after travelling a few miles.[19] He gave out

17. Elvira referred to the German volunteers as "Dutch." The regiment that came into Saline County in 1862 was mostly German-speaking. After a skirmish at Rock Creek, the "prisoners and their rescuers indulged in a joyful jabber in German" (Napton, *Past and Present,* 158).

18. Sources give both 1840 and 1841 as the date when Elvira's family moved to the Iowa Territory. She went to visit them in Agency, which is near Ottumwa.

19. Charley was probably suffering from a respiratory disease that makes respiration laborious, causing a thumping sound and heaving of the flanks (William H. Fales, D.V.M., telephone conversation with Carla Waal, March 14, 1994).

entirely, strength was utterly gone, & he could not proceed another mile. Not knowing what to do, we stopped at a farm house. We were only fifteen miles from home, & almost decided to return. The people were very pleasant & kind. He was a Mr. Wilhite; the woman, a second wife with two interesting daughters of a former husband, was ill. She seemed unhappily mated; was delicate & refined, with a baby a year old. We were invited to stay until we felt able to go on our way. . . .

The next day by twelve, feeling much refreshed, we concluded to go on. As they would not charge us, I made some presents, a pair of shoes for the baby, something to the girls, and 50 cents to the man for horse feed. We were invited to return to see them, & were treated with the kindness of old friends. . . .

It grew very cold before night, & we were recommended to stop at a widow's. We traveled late to get there, & I shall not soon forget the scene that met my sight; a little log house without a yard, water standing under it nearly to the floor, the bare floors wet, no fire. It was poverty without cleanliness. There were some big, barefoot boys, women & children "ad infinitum." I walked or tottered to a bed & dropped down, every nerve giving way. For an hour or two I felt as if I must die. I had not strength to raise my hand to my head. The confusion of the noisy family opening & shutting doors was far more terrible than anything I can describe, & to add to it they seemed determined to keep it up all night. But with the aid of valerian & some sleep by morning I could get up. . . . Our bill was $1.75—rather high, considering the acomodations. Felt determined to get away from there at all risks.

They recommended that we go to a Dr. Bryan's. . . . The Dr. felt my pulse & asked some questions; learned that I had eaten hardly anything since we had been on the road, & that everything had combined to press upon the spirits—anxiety for those left behind, fears & dread of the journey before us. He told me to lie still & rest, & he would have a cup of coffee & something for me to eat. . . .

The lady charred some browned coffee & prepared a tempting dinner— delicious coffee & rich cream, fresh fish fried very nicely, brown cream toast, nice broiled ham, the nicest of bread, eggs. I ate a hearty dinner & felt entirely renewed. . . . I told the Dr. that I felt that we had imposed upon a private family, & wished to pay them for their trouble. I was told that all the pay he asked was for me to do the same for any others whom I might find in a like condition. My prescription was—to order a baked chicken & something else good to eat the next time I gave out.

The change in my feelings when we entered & left that house was perfectly wonderful. The power of kindness, sympathy, & something good to eat is wonderful. They had acted to us the part of the Good Samaritan. May they be rewarded. . . .

So far we had stopped only at Southern houses. The Dr. told us there was a majority of Southern Rights men on the railroad, but they had to be very careful what they said. (108–11)

. . . [W]e [stayed] at the house of a violent Union family named Robertson. They commenced on us as soon as we got in the house; were from Kentucky & seemed to be people of some intelligence. They were old, with a daughter, a young lady. They were insulting & abusive. We were only 3 miles from Lancaster, where soldiers were stationed, & the old lady had a good deal to say about "our loyal German citizens," a great deal about "the rebels" and "gorillows." I did not know but what she would have us arrested. She & Sarah quarreled, but I was very tired & told her we each had a right to our own opinions & we differed widely & were not likely to convince each other, so we had better let the subject drop. . . .

TUESDAY, [MAY] 5[6?], [1862]

. . . The Missouri towns looked deserted, with not much going on in the country. Everything seemed paralyzed by the war. . . .

We landed at Agency after two o'clock, tired out. Found the town much improved. Our horses had stood the journey wonderfully, & I had astonished myself. For the last four days I had gained strength while going through great hardships. I stopped in Agency, but found [my sister] Virginia gone to California; had been gone a week & one day. It was a sad disappointment. We had tried so hard to get there before she started. (112–14)

After visiting her mother and other relatives, Elvira Scott and her party began their 160-mile trip back to Miami on May 28. Along the way she found "everywhere the fatherless & widows—victims of this terrible war."

WEDNESDAY, MAY 30[28?], [1862]

. . . The country looked wild & desolate. Caterpillars were literally stripping every leaf from the trees. . . . Got to Unionville [Missouri], a desolate looking place, about 10 o'clock. Just outside this place there were two roads to Milan, one a prairie road over a high ridge & one through timber. After much hesitation we took the prairie road that looked very inviting. We had been told that it was not as much traveled as the other, & might prove rough. Three miles from town we came to a hollow, or creek, with the bridge washed away. We looked upstream for a crossing, & not finding one turned back to a house, tired & much discouraged. It was near noon, & warm. I lost my satchel here. The woman at the house told us that there was a crossing below the bridge. We found it & crossed.

The hills were steep & rough for a few miles. Then we came upon a vast prairie, with a few cabins to be seen. We ate our dinner on the prairie, turning the horses loose to graze. It seemed cool, & we enjoyed it. I had one orange that, divided into four pieces, was our dessert & drink. . . .

JULY 4, [1862]

There was a celebration by the Federal troops at the Fair Ground. Everybody was invited, or rather commanded, to attend. We left town. . . . We did not feel like celebrating, under the circumstances, with danger & death & terror brooding over almost every home in the land. . . .

SATURDAY, JULY 5, [1862]

Lieutenant Bax made a speech in town, so far as his broken Dutch could be understood, stating that His men had not been treated with proper respect & attention. He said that they could be mild, but they could & would be severe. . . .

MONDAY, [JULY] 7, [1862]

. . . At nearly 10 o'clock the Federals fired off their pistols, just near the gate. It was a signal, I learned afterwards. In a few minutes from twelve to fifteen more, with their Lieutenant, appeared & sprang over the fence, one speaking out on the pavement that he wanted to hear the piano. Mrs. Parsons & I arose, said good-evening, asked them in, & went into the parlor [ourselves]. John, who had been lighting his pipe, asked them to be seated on the porch. I went for Pet, who had undressed, to come & play. She was excited & opposed to it, but her father insisted, & she played some time. They then left as abruptly as they came. There seemed to be some unusual excitement in town, as they were out all night in unusual numbers, & frequently firing their pistols. I did not sleep for the fright & excitement. . . .

WEDNESDAY, [JULY] 9, 1862

. . . I was busy cleaning up my room, when one of the soldiers came in & handed me a document. I thought it was something for John, & was going to lay it on the table, when I discovered that it was directed to Mrs. Jno P Scott. I sat down to peruse it. To my amazement it was a military arrest, stating that the time had passed when treasonable conversation would be allowed. But I will hand down to posterity the Original Document, first stating that I had been careful to give no offence to the military authorities, although they had annoyed us by calling at all hours. We had never failed to treat them politely, playing when they asked us, for the soldier is merely the instrument in the hands of others. They were all an ignorant, degraded class of men, many of them never having seen a piano before. (115–18)

The notice, signed by Adam Bax, reminded Mrs. Scott that "a Ladies place is to fulfill her household duties, and not to spread treason and excite men to rebellion." She was ordered to report to the commanding officer every Friday morning until he was "fully convinced that you behave yourself as a Lady Ought" (119). If she did not comply, her husband would be sent to the military prison at Marshall.

To say that I was *indignant, outraged* would express nothing of the tempest raging within. My first impulse, of course, was to carry it to the store. It was wrong. I should have waited until I was composed, & not gone to excite John in business hours, with soldiers coming in & out of the house. I repented it after coming home.

I thought that there must be other ladies treated in the same manner. I went to Mrs. Pendleton's; found that she had a like Document; also Mrs. Lewis & Mrs. T. P. Bell.[20] They took it coolly; said they would report without their husbands, & before we separated we arranged how we should go, & I came home more composed, but had a bad headache.

After dinner the mail came & I was reading the paper when three soldiers came in. John had told me at dinner not to speak to another one, or to play for them. I had made up my mind that Pet should play no more for them. I asked them to sit down & they asked me if there was any news. I remarked that if there were perhaps I had better not tell them, as I had been arrested that morning & I did not know the offense, that it might be telling them some contraband news, as Mr. Parsons had been reprimanded for telling news the day before. They looked amazed & one said to the other, "Jim, don't that get you, arresting women? Lieut. Bax must be a damned fool & will get himself in a scrape. But after that I suppose we can't ask you for any music." I told them that I played but little & was not well, but would play them a tune or two if they wished it, & did so. I thought of the *captives* in the *Scripture* who were commanded to sing to amuse their captors. My heart was full. This playing to amuse them had been a daily going on for weeks. I felt no animosity to the poor, ignorant soldiers, but could not but feel it a degradation to be intruded upon. Home was no longer a safe asylum, a sacred place. These were the last I had to play for. They thanked me kindly. The rudest & lowest can be touched by kindness.

20. Donald Riddle gives no information on Mrs. Lewis or Mrs. Bell, but identifies Mrs. Pendleton as Mary Hicklin Pendleton. She was married to Curtis Pendleton, a native of Kentucky and a storekeeper, who had lived in Miami since 1849. Like John Scott, Pendleton took the loyalty oath and then went to St. Louis for the remainder of the war.

THURSDAY, [JULY] 10, 1862

One of the most eventful days of my life, & one never to be forgotten
for its suffering if I should live a hundred years. . . . About 10 I went out
to iron some ruffled pillow cases, as Margaret went to the burying of a
black man. While coming in to change my iron I heard a pistol go off, &
looking out saw a crowd of soldiers around the store, as if guarding it,
some with their weapons pointing in at the window.

My first thought was that they had killed or wounded John. . . . My
first impulse was to rush to the scene, so I passed through the crowd at the
back window & ran to the front porch. It was covered by armed, excited
soldiers. The clanking of sabres & clicking of pistols was the first thing I
heard. I tried to step up on the step, & saw John in the midst looking pale
& excited. I tried to approach, but soldiers thrust themselves between us.
I asked what it all meant & what was the matter. John answered that
Mr. ———[21] had him arrested. My strength was failing, & I turned to
cross the street to sit down. As I turned I asked if it took all those armed
men to take care of one unarmed helpless man.

Just then I saw Lieutenant Bax rushing across from the other side in
an excited manner. He approached me & threw up his hand in my face.
He held three pistols in it. "Madam, you shall not insult the flag of my
country. . . ." I answered, "I have insulted no flag—but I have neither
country nor flag to protect me." I was beyond fear, & would not have
feared a hundred bullets. . . . I suppose it is something of the feeling that
soldiers have on the battle field. . . .

. . . Many came to me & offered their sympathy, but advised me to go
home; my presence seemed to excite John more, for when Bax pointed
his pistols at me he called to me to go home & not face a mob. In an
instant a dozen pistols were pointed at him. The excited crowd of soldiers
took him to the Fair Ground & I came home to my distressed children,
expecting that he would be murdered.

The excitement in town was up to white heat. On the street while I
faced the crowd, men's faces were livid & women stood in their door
relieved to see them pass with John living, as they expected to hear he
was killed. They told me not to be frightened; that he looked calm, & Mrs.
Rucker said he spoke to her very pleasantly. But I knew the hurricane
beneath the calmness. . . .

I learned afterward that the soldiers had been dreadfully excited at
John by Mr. ———'s representations, & for more than an hour after he
got to the Fair Ground he was taunted & insulted in every possible way.
But he kept apparently calm amid it all; said that he had no fear, that the
bullets would not have hurt him. Then gradually they began to find out

21. The name was deleted by Donald Riddle.

that many of them had been at our house & had been treated politely, & the last two that I had played for, who had been very abusive, found out who he was & apologized & they all got gradually calmed & every circumstance of the case was gradually made clear to them—for every man has a contempt for a cowardly, mean act.

It came out that it was only a personal quarrel between John & Mr. ————. . . . Mr. ———— & John were talking about the arrest of the ladies, & John said that the language used was disrespectful. Mr. ———— said it was not, & justified it. John read mine & told him he called it most damned disrespectful for a military officer to tell a lady in such a document that she did not attend to her household duties; that it was not in the province of the military, & how would they know if some neighbor did not report anything about ladies affairs. (119–24)

*John had used strong and "imprudent" language, which led "Mr. ————"
to report to the military that he had been threatened, that John Scott had used
treasonable language, calling Lieutenant Bax "a low-lived scoundrel."*

After sundown I went to Mr. ————, determined to leave no stone unturned, for I realized his [John's] danger. He expressed the greatest penitence, & said that he would do his utmost to get John out of the trouble. He offered to withdraw his charges. I asked him why he did not fight it out. I would have respected him more highly if he had. I talked to him until he was moved if ever a man was moved, & Mrs. ———— cried bitterly. The family was greatly troubled. We had been intimate friends for nearly eighteen years. They came home with me, to the gate. Old Charley stood at the stable door, neighing for his master to care for him. The white tents were gleaming in the distance where he was a prisoner. . . . I wrote a note to be sent to John in the morning in which I said that if anything I did or said could bring such danger & trouble to him I would rather stay a prisoner in my own house & never speak of the frightful war. I then laid down with both my children, but not to sleep. Such is the history of one day of sorrow & anguish. (125)

*John Scott was released on parole until his trial. Mrs. Scott voluntarily reported
to Lieutenant Bax along with several women who had been summoned.*

SATURDAY MORNING, [JULY] 12, 1862

. . . When I went into the parlor, the three culprits were sitting on one side of the room, also McHicklin & Bax, . . . leaning in what he no doubt thought was quite a graceful attitude with one elbow on the table & a white handkerchief spread out. . . . He did not wish, it seemed, to enter into any details or particulars of their cases, but simply wanted them to promise not to talk treason.

Mrs. Lewis insisted that he should define what treason was, but he would not, or was not able to do so. He brought nothing special against any one of them; only accused Mrs. Lewis's children of calling his soldiers abolitionists, etc. Mrs. Lewis said that he could not prove that they were her children, & if he could she did not see that he could hold her accountable for what little children of from seven to ten said. He told her that she must have taught them, & that she had talked more than any of the ladies. . . .

I put in here, & asked him what objections he had to his men being called abolitionists, when so many of them were. . . . The truth is that he did not know what an abolitionist was, but is a rank one himself. I then branched out a little about the different policies pursued by the Federal government; their inconsistencies; that it seemed torn into factions & atoms. He interrupted to say, "Madam, you be talking treason now, blaming the government & speaking against it." Mrs. Lewis remarked to him, "Now you are coming at what I asked you a while ago." I made some remarks about the South maintaining herself & the probability of it, & was told that all I was saying was treasonable; that this rebellion would soon be crushed out. I remarked that it did not have much appearance of that now at Richmond, Charleston and Vicksburg, where they were not only holding their own but defeating the Federals.

The ladies seemed alarmed at my temerity & said they did not wish to talk politics with him. He said that the women were at the bottom of this devilish rebellion—their influence. Mrs. Lewis told him he was very flattering, that he gave the ladies more credit than she thought they deserved. He was very complimentary just here, & said that he could never be rude or impolite to a lady, & acknowledged their influence & power. I referred to his treatment of me on the street the day of Mr. Scott's arrest. I told him I thought it very rough. He denied it altogether, but that was useless, for there were too many witnesses. I told him to understand that I was not afraid of him; that I did not come of a cowardly race; that my ancestors were those who fought the Indians in the wilderness, native born Americans for centuries. I intended this to hit on the subject of his nativity, when he spoke of the flag of his country. Perhaps he was too obtuse to take the hint. . . .

He had accused Mrs. Bell of Hurraing for Jeff Davis. She straightened herself up in her own peculiar style & said, "Sir, I profess to be a lady, & I do not hurra for anyone." . . .

He was all gladness to get rid of us. He found ladies to deal with who would not condescend to be abusive, but yet did not fear him in the least. He was hardly prepared, I think, for such womanly dignity &

fearlessness. He thought, I suppose, that we would come frightened & trembling, begging his mercy.

I told him that all I asked for John was justice. . . . [He said that] he respected John more for having the courage to speak out what he thought than many others who felt as he did but were afraid to speak. He got excessively polite, & insisted, as the bell was ringing, that I should remain to dinner. He bowed me out the front door after I refused with quite an air. He had told us during our interview that it was against the rules & entirely improper for soldiers to enter private houses, & that he would be obliged if we would inform on them. I had not been home more than a few minutes when three came in & called for dinner. They told us that they had been sent, & I concluded that it had been done to see what we would do, & I gave them their dinners. . . . Lt. Bax said that he never went to a private house without an invitation, when only two nights before he came to ours between nine & ten at night, with a dozen or more of his men—uninvited, of course. (127–31)

Lieutenant Bax disclaimed responsibility for the language used in Elvira Scott's arrest order, and her husband was acquitted and released. The "little Lieut.," Elvira wrote, "being very ignorant as to the consequences, became frightened" (131–32), and apologized to all the ladies. For a while John tried to continue running his business in Miami, but Elvira thought it would be better for him to stay away. She wrote on July 27, 1862, "I cannot breathe freely under such oppression, & if I were a man I would either be fighting against it or get away from it" (141).

Elvira was not the only woman with a fighting spirit. On July 29, she wrote about some brave women who had been "banished" from Independence. One woman had refused to make a flag, and the other was accused of taking ammunition to the guerrilla leader W. C. Quantrill.

JULY 29, 1862

. . . One, a Mrs. Tillery, refused to sew for the soldiers while in prison, & refused to furnish material to make a flag. She told Col. Penick that the materials were not to be had in the town, & that she did not have the money to buy them & therefore would not do it. He told her that if she failed to do it within five days he would put her in solitary confinement & oblige her to sleep in a cell with one blanket, with the roughest soldier in his command for a companion. She disguised herself that night & made her escape on foot & alone. (164)

Elvira had occasion again to show her bravery. One evening some drunken soldiers tried to take John hostage.

[JUNE 16, 1863]

. . . They seemed to be struggling together, or, rather, the soldier was shoving John before him with his gun.

In an instant I was between them, holding both of them apart as well as I could. I was too much excited to know what I was doing, only acting from impulse. I kept between them until we got around to the dining room door, when the man thrust me out from between them. But I got back. As I did so, I felt the gun come against my back, but I maintained my position. . . .

The emergency unloosed my tongue. If ever I was gifted with eloquence it was then brought out. I must have made an appeal, judging by the effects, for in a few minutes the man was softened, became obliging, even kind, & permitted John to go & get his horse. (199–200)

Along with five other prominent citizens, John was taken away, the soldiers "yelling like fiends" and one woman cheering from the crowd for Jefferson Davis.

After this episode it was evident that John would not be safe in Miami. He went to St. Louis, and eventually the family joined him for the remainder of the war.[22] After John found employment with the railroad, he sent Elvira to Miami in December 1863, to collect money from his debtors. She brought back $300, but the trip was exhausting because she "had to travel more than 50 miles in an open wagon, & had to take my things & cross the ice over the river on foot" (243). When they came home to Miami, Elvira wrote on June 21, 1865: "I hope I return a wiser and better woman" (242). She found bloodstains on the floors of her house, which had been used as a hospital, but John's finances were sound and he resumed management of his store. Elvira determined to manage the household well.

SEPTEMBER 23, 1866

I have formed some resolutions which, with God's help, I hope to carry out. First, to get up early in the morning, to seek God's guidance & help, & then try to get both of my children up, read from the Bible with them in our sitting room, & then attend to breakfast—& try through the day to

---

22. Elvira left Miami September 15, 1863, and returned June 21, 1865. The Scotts were away during the election of 1864, when Abraham Lincoln got the majority of votes in Saline County. "In 1860 it had been extremely perilous to vote for Lincoln. In 1864 it was dangerous not to vote for him" (Napton, *Past and Present*, 188). The experiences of Elvira and John Scott are comparable to those of Elizabeth and Peter Levengood, of Memphis, Missouri. Like John, Peter was a merchant. Like Elvira, Elizabeth was outspoken in expressing sympathy for the Confederates as well as support for Jefferson Davis. As a result Peter Levengood was jailed in 1862; when released, he went immediately to Iowa. Elizabeth joined him there for a while; then Peter went West by wagon train and Elizabeth moved with her five children to the home of relatives in Kentucky (Peavy and Smith, *Women in Waiting*, 16).

keep order & system in domestic affairs. Life seems to be frittered away in little unimportant calls on time that are very trying to my patience. (275)

Running an orderly house was not easy.

TUESDAY, JANUARY 14, [1867]

. . . It makes John cross to find things out of order. I try not to expect too much . . . , but I know it is not necessary to let children put us to so much trouble. I want them to play & enjoy themselves, but not wantonly put things out of place, get in drawers, throw shells & peelings & sticks over the floor. They can be taught politeness & neat habits. With Pet I succeeded better than with Hebe.

I have petty trials daily that are very annoying. I know that it is a woman's duty to have obedience & respect from all for whose comfort she has to provide. Had I always had courage to have claimed it & enforced it from all beneath my roof, I know that my children would have been different. (297)

Elvira lost her husband in 1888.[23] Then she, who had been so delicate, lived until 1910—helping her family when needed, appreciating the beauty of flowers and trees, cultivating her talent as a painter, enjoying travel, and reflecting on the meaning of her experiences: "I have sometimes wondered if ever a young girl had such a bounding, hopeful nature as I once had." Life had brought her many "days of darkness," and she realized that "were my blooming girlhood offered back, with the same path before me to tread, I would shrink back" (258). Instead, Elvira Scott, a "wiser and better woman," was grateful that she had found peace of mind.

23. Scott, "one of the old pioneers of Saline County," was praised for operating his store successfully for more than forty years and for the historical and political sketches he wrote using the pseudonym "Quince" (*Boonville Weekly Advertiser,* January 13, 1888). John Scott also wrote poems for family and friends. In 1871 Pet married Lewis William Miller, a lawyer, who died in 1874. Hebe married a doctor, Alexander Summerville McDaniel, son of John P. Scott's business partner, Reuben Ellis McDaniel. Hebe and Alexander had a daughter, Mary Margaret McDaniel Jones, whose son is Scott Jones, donor of the diary to WHMC-C (Diary transcript, 342, 347; materials at Marshall Public Library).

Elizabeth Hobbs Keckley (1818–1907)

"Slavery was the dominant economic and social system that shaped the experiences and lives of black women from the early seventeenth through the middle of the nineteenth century," writes historian Darlene Clark Hine.[1] Elizabeth Keckley was born into slavery in 1818. She shares her memories of humiliation and physical mistreatment in *Behind the Scenes, or Thirty Years a Slave and Four Years in the White House*, published by G. W. Carleton in 1868. Like other selections in this anthology, only part of the story takes place in Missouri. Some of her years as a slave were spent in St. Louis, but it was also in St. Louis that Mrs. Keckley became a self-sufficient seamstress and achieved her freedom.

Moving to Washington, D.C., in 1860, Keckley enjoyed success as a dressmaker and became a friend of Mary Todd Lincoln. Most of the book, published in 1868, tells about life "behind the scenes" at the White House and efforts to help the widowed Mrs. Lincoln. The book is difficult to classify. It is in part an example of the "slave narrative," because it tells about the injustice and suffering endured by Mrs. Keckley during the early part of her life. Conforming to the fashion of the period, she used the style of a sentimental novel. Whether Mrs. Keckley actually wrote the book by herself has been a question for speculation, but the authenticity of her story is accepted. Focusing more on external events and other people than on herself, she produced a memoir rather than an autobiography.[2] Despite considerable reticence and modesty, Elizabeth Keckley appears in her self-portrait as a proud, dignified, and self-confident woman.

Editor Henry Louis Gates, Jr., acknowledged the significance of Keckley's book when he chose it for the series "The Schomburg Library of Nineteenth-Century Black Women Writers." Reprinted by Oxford University Press in 1988, *Behind the Scenes* received critical attention and scholarly analysis. Suzanne Scafe expressed disappointment at finding little "insight" or "analysis" in the account, while Eric J. Sundquist grouped it with other "invaluable personal narratives," referring to the book as a "curious gem."[3] Hine has used it as evidence to support her thesis that

1. Hine, " 'In the Kingdom of Culture': Black Women and the Intersection of Race, Gender, and Class," 339.
2. James Olney, introduction to Elizabeth Keckley, *Behind the Scenes* (New York: Oxford University Press, 1988), xxxiii; Kathleen Thompson, "Keckley, Elizabeth (1818–1907)," in *Black Women in America*, 1:672–73. Page references to the first edition of Keckley's memoirs appear in parentheses within the text.
3. Scafe, *London Review of Books*, February 16, 1989, and Sundquist, *New York Times Book Review*, July 3, 1988.

"the ever present threat and reality of rape" is found in almost every nineteenth-century narrative by a female slave.[4] Like other women in her situation, Keckley was vulnerable and powerless; her son had a white father, the son of her former master. For William L. Andrews the Keckley narrative provides a vivid example of the "descent narrative," in which a former slave experiences an "emotionally charged" reunion with a former master or mistress. Keckley's visit with Anne Burwell Garland and her family was a happy and triumphant episode, affirming their mutual respect and the mood of optimism and desire for healing that followed the Civil War.[5]

Elizabeth Keckley was burdened with poverty when she wrote this book. "I have worked hard, but fortune, fickle dame, has not smiled upon me" (330). She selected highlights of her experiences intended to appeal to a contemporary audience and must have hoped that sale of the manuscript would ease her financial distress. Publication of the book led to estrangement from Mrs. Lincoln and negative reactions from many other people because of the "intimate disclosures" about the Lincolns. Later Mrs. Keckley obtained a teaching position at Wilberforce University in Ohio as "instructor in plain sewing and dressmaking." After retirement she was supported financially by a pension to which she was entitled because her son had been a Union soldier killed in action.[6] Elizabeth Keckley died in 1907.

Following the Civil War, black women in Missouri gradually began to achieve success in education, business, and the arts. Unfortunately the editors have not found private papers or a published autobiography by some of the most memorable women of the era, like Josephine Silone Yates (1859–1912) or Annie Turnbo Malone (1868–1957). Mrs. Yates enjoyed a career as a professor of chemistry, head of the Department of Natural Science, and Dean of Women at Lincoln Institute in Jefferson City, where she taught from 1879 to 1889. She returned to Lincoln in 1902, to serve until 1910 as head of the Department of English and History. An excellent essayist and public speaker, she was prominent in the women's club movement, serving as the founder in 1893 and first president of the Kansas City Women's League and as president of the National Association of Colored Women from 1901 to 1906. Yates understood that through their organizations women could accomplish a great deal, such as providing education for homeless and unemployed

4. Hine, "Rape and the Inner Lives of Black Women in the Middle West: Preliminary Thoughts on the Culture of Dissemblance," 912.

5. Andrews, "Reunion in the Postbellum Slave Narrative: Frederick Douglass and Elizabeth Keckley."

6. Adele Logan Alexander, "White House Confidante of Mrs. Lincoln." The Wilberforce University catalogs for 1893–1898 list Mrs. Keckley as a faculty member.

adolescents.[7] Malone lived and worked in St. Louis from 1902 to 1930, and achieved great success as a businesswoman by manufacturing and marketing her own line of cosmetics. "Poro College," her factory and store in St. Louis, was a large facility, making it appropriate for use as a community center and the headquarters of the National Negro Business League. Malone, who became a millionaire, was a philanthropist whose generosity benefited hospitals, orphanages, and other worthy causes.[8]

Yates and Malone gained remarkable prominence, and both did what they could to teach, help, and inspire others. Economic limitations and a lack of political power hampered African-American women; opportunities were particularly limited in rural areas and small towns.[9] Nevertheless, progress was made and, as Hine writes, "black women's culture reached a new height of self-awareness in the closing decades of the nineteenth century." Whether focusing on personal achievement or on agenda set by organizations, black women have found themselves at a unique meeting place of race, gender, and class.[10]

Articulate, assertive, and independent, Elizabeth Keckley was a fascinating individual whose life story reflects a typical configuration of race, gender, and class. Mrs. Keckley survived the oppressive effects of slavery, established a new identity, and became a witness to history and a backstage player in the drama of the Lincoln administration.

_____ *BEHIND THE SCENES, OR THIRTY YEARS A SLAVE* _____
AND FOUR YEARS IN THE WHITE HOUSE

I have often been asked to write my life, as those who know me know that it has been an eventful one. At last I have acceded to the importunities of my friends, and have hastily sketched some of the striking incidents that go to make up my history. My life, so full of romance, may sound like a dream to the matter-of-fact reader, nevertheless everything I have written is strictly true; much has been omitted, but nothing has been exaggerated. In writing as I have done, I am well aware that I have invited criticism; but before the critic judges harshly, let my explanation be carefully read and weighed. If I have portrayed the dark side of slavery, I also have painted the bright side. The good that I have said of human servitude should be

7. Information on Mrs. Yates may be found in Elizabeth Lindsay Davis, *Lifting as They Climb,* 166–68, 412–13; *Black Women in America,* 1:97–98; and Gary R. Kremer and Cindy M. Mackey, " 'Yours for the Race': The Life and Work of Josephine Silone Yates."

8. On Mrs. Malone, see *Show Me Missouri Women,* 1:81, and *Missouri Historical Review* 67 (July 1973): opp. 664.

9. Lorenzo J. Greene, Gary R. Kremer, and Antonio F. Holland, *Missouri's Black Heritage.* See chapter 7, "Separate and Unequal."

10. Hine, " 'In the Kingdom of Culture,' " 345, 351.

thrown into the scales with the evil that I have said of it. I have kind, true-hearted friends in the South as well as in the North, and I would not wound those Southern friends by sweeping condemnation, simply because I was once a slave. They were not so much responsible for the curse under which I was born, as the God of nature and the fathers who framed the Constitution for the United States. The law descended to them, and it was but natural that they should recognize it, since it manifestly was their interest to do so. And yet a wrong was inflicted upon me; a cruel custom deprived me of my liberty, and since I was robbed of my dearest right, I would not have been human had I not rebelled against the robbery. (xi–xiii)

It may be charged that I have written too freely on some questions, especially in regard to Mrs. Lincoln. I do not think so; at least I have been prompted by the purest motive. Mrs. Lincoln, by her own acts, forced herself into notoriety. She stepped beyond the formal lines which hedge about a private life, and invited public criticism. (xiii)

Keckley describes her early childhood in chapter 1, "Where I Was Born."

My life has been an eventful one. I was born a slave—was the child of slave parents—therefore I came upon the earth free in God-like thought, but fettered in action. My birthplace was Dinwiddie Court-House, in Virginia. My recollections of childhood are distinct, perhaps for the reason that many stirring incidents are associated with that period. I am now on the shady side of forty, and as I sit alone in my room the brain is busy, and a rapidly moving panorama brings scene after scene before me, some pleasant and others sad; and when I thus greet old familiar faces, I often find myself wondering if I am not living the past over again. The visions are so terribly distinct that I almost imagine them to be real. Hour after hour I sit while the scenes are being shifted; and as I gaze upon the panorama of the past, I realize how crowded with incidents my life has been. Every day seems like a romance within itself, and the years grow into ponderous volumes. As I cannot condense, I must omit many strange passages in my history. . . . I presume that I must have been four years old when I first began to remember; at least, I cannot now recall anything occurring previous to this period. My master, Col. A. Burwell, was somewhat unsettled in his business affairs, and while I was yet an infant he made several removals. While living at Hampton [Hampden] Sidney College, Prince Edward County, Va., Mrs. Burwell gave birth to a daughter, a sweet, black-eyed baby, my earliest and fondest pet. To take care of this baby was my first duty. True, I was a child myself—only four years old—but then I had been raised in a hardy school—had been taught to rely upon myself, and to prepare myself to render assistance to others. The lesson was not a bitter one, for I was too young to indulge in philosophy, and the precepts that I then treasured and practised I believe developed those principles of character which have enabled me to triumph over so many difficulties. Notwithstanding all the wrongs that slavery heaped upon me, I can bless it for one thing—youth's important lesson of self-reliance. The baby was named Elizabeth, and it was pleasant to me to be assigned a duty in connection with it, for the discharge of that duty transferred me from the rude cabin to the household of my master. My simple attire was a short dress and a little white apron. My old mistress encouraged me in rocking the cradle, by telling me that if I would watch over the baby well, keep the flies out of its face, and not let it cry, I should be its little maid. This was a golden promise, and I required no better inducement for the faithful performance of my task. I began to rock the cradle most industriously, when lo! out pitched little pet on the floor. I instantly cried out, "Oh! the baby is on the floor"; and, not knowing what to do, I seized the fire-shovel in my perplexity, and was trying to shovel up my tender charge, when my mistress called to me to let the child alone, and then ordered that I be taken out and lashed for my carelessness. The blows were not administered with a light hand, I assure you, and doubtless the severity of the lashing has made me remember the incident so well. This was the first time I was punished in this cruel way, but not the last. (17–21)

In the third chapter, "How I Gained My Freedom," Elizabeth describes the various types of work she did for the Burwells, assisting her own mother as much as possible. For a brief while her father was allowed to live with them, but he had to leave them permanently to accompany his master out west. After bearing a son to a white father, Elizabeth became the property of a Mr. Garland . . .

. . . who had married Miss Ann Burwell, one of my old master's daughters. His life was not a prosperous one, and after struggling with the world for several years he left his native State, a disappointed man. He moved to St. Louis, hoping to improve his fortune in the West; but ill luck followed him there, and he seemed to be unable to escape from the influence of the evil star of his destiny. When his family, myself included, joined him in his new home on the banks of the Mississippi, we found him so poor that he was unable to pay the dues on a letter advertised as in the post-office for him. The necessities of the family were so great, that it was proposed to place my mother out at service. The idea was shocking to me. Every gray hair in her old head was dear to me, and I could not bear the thought of her going to work for strangers. She had been raised in the family, had watched the growth of each child from infancy to maturity; they had been the objects of her kindest care, and she was wound round about them as the vine winds itself about the rugged oak. They had been the central figures in her dream of life—a dream beautiful to her, since she had basked in the sunshine of no other. And now they proposed to destroy each tendril of affection, to cloud the sunshine of her existence when the day was drawing to a close, when the shadows of solemn night were rapidly approaching. My mother, my poor aged mother, go among strangers to toil for a living! No, a thousand times no! I would rather work my fingers to the bone, bend over my sewing till the film of blindness gathered in my eyes; nay, even beg from street to street. I told Mr. Garland so, and he gave me permission to see what I could do. I was fortunate in obtaining work, and in a short time I had acquired something of a reputation as a seamstress and dress-maker. The best ladies in St. Louis were my patrons, and when my reputation was once established I never lacked for orders. With my needle I kept bread in the mouths of seventeen persons for two years and five months. While I was working so hard that others might live in comparative comfort, and move in those circles of society to which their birth gave them entrance, the thought often occurred to me whether I was really worth my salt or not; and then perhaps the lips curled with a bitter sneer. It may seem strange that I should place so much emphasis upon words thoughtlessly, idly spoken; but then we do many strange things in life, and cannot always explain the motives that actuate us. The heavy task was too much for me, and my health began to give way. About this time Mr. Keckley, whom I had met in Virginia, and learned to regard with more than friendship, came to St. Louis. He sought my hand in marriage, and for a long time I refused to consider his proposal; for I could not bear the thought of bringing children into slavery—of adding one single recruit to the millions bound to hopeless servitude, fettered and shackled with chains stronger and heavier than manacles of iron. I made a proposition to buy myself and son; the proposition was bluntly declined, and I was commanded never to broach the subject again. I would not be put off thus, for hope pointed to a freer, brighter life in the future. Why should my son be held in slavery? I often asked myself. He came into the world through no will of mine, and yet, God only knows how I loved him. The Anglo-Saxon blood as well as the African flowed in his veins; the two currents commingled— one singing of freedom, the other silent and sullen with generations of despair. Why should not the Anglo-Saxon triumph—why should it be weighed down with the rich blood typical of the tropics? Must the life-current of one race bind the other race in chains as strong and enduring as if there had been no Anglo-Saxon taint? By the laws of God and nature, as interpreted by man, one-half of my boy was free, and why should not this fair birthright of freedom remove the curse from the other half—raise it into the bright, joyous sunshine of liberty? I could not answer these questions of my heart that almost maddened me, and I learned to regard human philosophy with distrust. Much as I respected the authority of my master, I could not remain silent on a subject that so nearly concerned me. One day, when I insisted on knowing whether he would permit me to purchase myself, and what price I must pay for myself, he turned to me in a petulant manner, thrust his hand into his pocket, drew forth a bright silver quarter of a dollar, and proffering it to me, said:

"Lizzie, I have told you often not to trouble me with such a question. If you really wish to leave me, take this: it will pay the passage of yourself and boy on the ferry-boat, and when you are on the other side of the river you will be free. It is the cheapest way that I know of to accomplish what you desire."

I looked at him in astonishment, and earnestly replied: "No, master, I do not wish to be free in such a manner. If such had been my wish, I should never have troubled you about obtaining your consent to my purchasing myself. I can cross the river any day, as you well know, and have frequently done so, but will never leave you in such a manner. By the laws of the land I am your slave—you are my master, and I will only be free by such means as the laws of the country provide." He expected this answer, and I knew that he was pleased. Some time afterwards he told me that he had reconsidered the question; that I had served his family faithfully; that I deserved my freedom, and that he would take $1200 for myself and boy.

This was joyful intelligence for me, and the reflection of hope gave a silver lining to the dark cloud of my life—faint, it is true, but still a silver lining.

Taking a prospective glance at liberty, I consented to marry. The wedding was a great event in the family. The ceremony took place in the parlor, in the presence of the family and a number of guests. Mr. Garland gave me away, and the pastor, Bishop Hawks, performed the ceremony, who had solemnized the bridals of Mr. G.'s own children. The day was a happy one, but it faded all too soon. Mr. Keckley—let me speak kindly of his faults—proved dissipated, and a burden instead of a helpmate. More than all, I learned that he was a slave instead of a free man, as he represented himself to be. With the simple explanation that I lived with him eight years, let charity draw around him the mantle of silence.

I went to work in earnest to purchase my freedom, but the years passed, and I was still a slave. Mr. Garland's family claimed so much of my attention—in fact, I supported them—that I was not able to accumulate anything. In the mean time Mr. Garland died, and Mr. Burwell, a Mississippi planter, came to St. Louis to settle up the estate. He was a kind-hearted man, and said I should be free, and would afford me every facility to raise the necessary amount to pay the price of my liberty. Several schemes were urged upon me by my friends. At last I formed a resolution to go to New York, state my case, and appeal to the benevolence of the people. The plan seemed feasible, and I made preparations to carry it out.

When I was almost ready to turn my face northward, Mrs. Garland told me that she would require the names of six gentlemen who would vouch for my return, and become responsible for the amount at which I was valued. I had many friends in St. Louis, and as I believed that they had confidence in me, I felt that I could readily obtain the names desired. I started out, stated my case, and obtained five signatures to the paper, and my heart throbbed with pleasure, for I did not believe that the sixth would refuse me. I called, he listened patiently, then remarked:

"Yes, yes, Lizzie; the scheme is a fair one, and you shall have my name. But I shall bid you good-by when you start."

"Good-by for a short time," I ventured to add.

"No, good-by for all time," and he looked at me as if he would read my very soul with his eyes.

I was startled. "What do you mean, Mr. Farrow? Surely you do not think that I do not mean to come back?"

"No."

"No, what then?"

"Simply this: you *mean* to come back, that is, you *mean* so *now,* but you never will. When you reach New York the abolitionists will tell you what savages we are, and they will prevail on you to stay there; and we shall never see you again."

"But I assure you, Mr. Farrow, you are mistaken. I not only *mean* to come back, but *will* come back, and pay every cent of the twelve hundred dollars for myself and child."

I was beginning to feel sick at heart, for I could not accept the signature of this man when he had no faith in my pledges. No; slavery, eternal slavery rather than be regarded with distrust by those whose respect I esteemed.

"But—I am not mistaken," he persisted. "Time will show. When you start for the North I shall bid you good-by."

The heart grew heavy. Every ray of sunshine was eclipsed. With humbled pride, weary step, tearful face, and a dull, aching pain, I left the house. I walked along the street mechanically. The cloud had no silver lining now. The rosebuds of hope had withered and died without lifting up their heads to receive the dew kiss of morning. There was no morning for me—all was night, dark night.

I reached my own home, and weeping threw myself upon the bed. My trunk was packed, my luncheon was prepared by mother, the cars were ready to bear me where I would not hear the clank of chains, where I would breathe the free, invigorating breezes of the glorious North. I had dreamed such a happy dream, in imagination had drunk of the water, the pure, sweet crystal water of life, but now—now—the flowers had withered before my eyes; darkness had settled down upon me like a pall, and I was left alone with cruel mocking shadows.

The first paroxysm of grief was scarcely over, when a carriage stopped in front of the house; Mrs. Le Bourgois, one of my kind patrons, got out of it and entered the door. She seemed to bring sunshine with her handsome cheery face. She came to where I was, and in her sweet way said:

"Lizzie, I hear that you are going to New York to beg for money to buy your freedom. I have been thinking over the matter, and told Ma it would be a shame to allow you to go North to *beg* for what we should *give* you. You have many friends in St. Louis, and I am going to raise the twelve hundred dollars required among them. I have two hundred dollars put away for a present; am indebted to you one hundred dollars; mother owes you fifty dollars, and will add another fifty to it; and as I do not want the present, I will make the money a present to you. Don't start for New York now until I see what I can do among your friends."

Like a ray of sunshine she came, and like a ray of sunshine she went away. The flowers no longer were withered, drooping. Again they seemed to bud and grow in fragrance and beauty. Mrs. Le Bourgois, God bless her dear good heart, was more than successful. The twelve hundred dollars were raised, and at last my son and myself were free. Free, free! what a glorious ring to the word. Free! the bitter heart-struggle was over. Free! the soul could go out to heaven and to God with no chain to clog its flight or pull it down. Free! the earth wore a brighter look, and the very stars seemed to sing with joy. Yes, free! free by the laws of man and the smile of God—and Heaven bless them who made me so! (43–55)

Mrs. Keckley quotes from letters dated in 1855 that verify the financial and legal arrangements made to emancipate Lizzie Garland, "the wife of a yellow man named James, and called James Keckley" and her son, "a bright mulatto boy" called "Garland's George." Keckley's next chapter, "In the Family of Senator Jefferson Davis," begins the story of her new life in freedom.

The twelve hundred dollars with which I purchased the freedom of myself and son I consented to accept only as a loan. I went to work in earnest, and in a short time paid every cent that was so kindly advanced by my lady patrons of St. Louis. All this time my husband was a source of trouble to me, and a burden. Too close occupation with my needle had its effects upon my health, and feeling exhausted with work, I determined to make a change. I had a conversation with Mr. Keckley; informed him that since he persisted in dissipation we must separate; that I was going North, and that I should never live with him again, at least until I had good evidence of his reform. He was rapidly debasing himself, and although I was willing to work for him, I was not willing to share his degradation. Poor man; he had his faults, but over these faults death has drawn a veil. My husband is now sleeping in his grave, and in the silent grave I would bury all unpleasant memories of him.

I left St. Louis in the spring of 1860, taking the cars direct for Baltimore, where I stopped six weeks, attempting to realize a sum of money by forming classes of young colored women, and teaching them my system of cutting and fitting dresses. The scheme was not successful, for after six weeks of labor and vexation, I left Baltimore with scarcely money enough to pay my fare to Washington. (63–64)

Elizabeth Keckley uses the remaining pages of the book to tell about establishing herself as a successful seamstress, counting among her clients the wives of Jefferson Davis and Abraham Lincoln. Mrs. Keckley often came to the White House, where she observed the Lincolns at times of festivity, worry, and bereavement. Not only was she responsible for fashioning elegant gowns for Mary Lincoln, she became her confidante and friend. The book ends in 1868 in New York City, with Mrs. Keckley "toiling by day with my needle, and writing by night." While writing the book she has enjoyed recalling the past; now she faces the future with courage. "Though poor in worldly goods, I am rich in friendships, and friends are a recompense for all the woes of the darkest pages of life" (330).

PHOEBE WILSON COUZINS (1842–1913)

$\mathcal{D}$uring the Civil War job opportunities for women expanded, some in teaching, others in government clerical work and nursing. Less educated women were already employed in factories producing fabric or doing piecework at sewing machines. The educated had traditionally worked as teachers, governesses, companions, missionaries, or authors. A number of women worked as stenographers, law clerks, and bookkeepers in the offices of their fathers or husbands. In the second half of the nineteenth century women could be found competing with men for jobs in industry and gaining entry into professions.[1] In an article on January 29, 1893, headed "Lady Notaries," the *St. Louis Post-Dispatch* remarked:

> The multitude of women who have taken places formerly occupied by men in various lines of human endeavor is one of the wonders and problems of modern civilization. "What is the limit of the adaptability of women" the men ask themselves, but no one has the hardihood to draw the line, for every day girls and young ladies are taking up some branch of work new to the breadearners of their sex.

Phoebe Wilson Couzins entered a new "branch of work"—the field of law. Born in 1842,[2] Phoebe was the daughter of Major John E. D. Couzins. During the Civil War he served as chief of police and acting provost marshal in St. Louis, while his wife Adaline was a leading member of the Ladies' Union Aid Society. Sharing a home with a father who held responsible civic positions and a courageous mother who faced the dangers of battle to nurse soldiers during the Civil War helped her to develop confidence in her intellect and a zest for service in the public arena. While serving with the Western Sanitary Commission during the Civil War, the young woman was converted to the cause of pacifism and women's rights. In February 1869 she spoke to a joint meeting of the Missouri State Legislature on behalf of woman suffrage.[3]

With the encouragement of Professor Chester H. Krum, on December 1, 1868, Phoebe Couzins submitted an application to Dean Henry Hitchcock to join the junior class in the St. Louis Law School at Washington University. Hitchcock wrote to the Board of Directors of Washington University that the faculty could find no clear statement in the university's statutes as to whether it was permissible to admit female students. "If the question were left to them to decide, however, the Law Faculty

---

1. See Alice Kessler-Harris, *Out to Work: A History of Wage-Earning Women in the United States.*

2. Sources disagree on Phoebe Couzins's birth date. It is given variously as 1839, 1840, 1841, 1842, 1843, and 1845. Her tombstone in Bellefontaine Cemetery in St. Louis is engraved "1842–1913."

3. A. K. Koetting, "Four St. Louis Women: Precursors of Reform," 19.

see no reason why any young woman who in respect to character and acquirements fulfilled the Conditions applicable to male Students, and who chose to attend the Law Lectures in good faith for the purpose of becoming acquainted with the laws of her Country, should be denied that privilege."[4] Permission was granted, making the law school at Washington University the first in the nation to admit applicants regardless of sex. Phoebe was cordially received by her fellow students, who elected her secretary and treasurer of the Lyceum, the law school's first student organization. Later she was elected vice president of the school's first alumni association.[5] Passing a "severe and trying" examination, Phoebe Couzins earned the degree "Bachelor of Laws" in May 1871,[6] becoming the first woman law graduate in the state of Missouri and probably the third in the nation.

At about the same time that Phoebe Couzins was granted admission to the St. Louis Law School, Lemma Barkeloo came from New York to study law at Washington University, having been denied admission by Columbia and Harvard. She is acknowledged to have been the second woman lawyer actually practicing in the country and the first in Missouri. Barkeloo earned her place in the annals of women's history by passing the Missouri Bar examination in March 1870, without completing a degree. She began practicing with a St. Louis attorney and became the first woman lawyer in the United States to try a case in court. Her career was brief since she died in September 1870. Lemma Barkeloo had, however, "evinced to the world the intellectual power of woman," as W. H. H. Russell stated in his tribute presented to the St. Louis Bar.[7]

After earning a law degree, Phoebe Couzins actually handled very few cases. She was admitted to the Missouri Bar in 1871 and later was admitted to practice in Arkansas, Kansas, Utah, and the Dakota Territory and in the federal courts. For a while she devoted herself to the suffrage movement, as an early member of the Woman Suffrage Association of Missouri (W.S.A.M.) and a founder of the National Woman Suffrage Association, where she worked with Susan B. Anthony. In 1871 Couzins withdrew from the W.S.A.M. because of its conservative tendencies. At her best she was a stirring advocate, pleading the cause of women's rights at the Democratic National Convention in 1876 and on speaking tours in most major cities of the United States. Elizabeth Cady Stanton described

4. Report from Faculty of the Law Department to the Rev. Wm. G. Eliot, D.D., President of the Board of Directors, Law Faculty Records, Washington University, 1868, J. E. D. Couzins Papers, Missouri Historical Society, St. Louis.

5. Karen L. Tokarz, "A Tribute to the Nation's First Women Law Students," 95.

6. *Boonville Weekly Eagle*, May 12, 1871.

7. On Barkeloo, see Tokarz, "A Tribute"; Karen Berger Morello, *The Invisible Bar: The Woman Lawyer in America, 1638 to the Present;* and documents in the Missouri Historical Society, St. Louis.

her lecture on women as lawyers: "In a deep, rich voice, she told her audience what she had seen, and felt, and believed, with a calm, dignified, self-assertion that seemed to say the earth is the Lord's and the fulness thereof, and I am one of the rightful heirs to this inheritance."[8]

In her prime Phoebe Couzins could hold a crowd spellbound with not only her speaking but also her singing. One triumphant appearance took place in Whitewater, Wisconsin, in May 1878. In town to visit friends, Miss Couzins was invited to join a temperance campaign already underway. On Sunday evening she sang two solos "with a great deal of sweetness and power." The next evening "an immense crowd, the largest gathering of people ever witnessed in Whitewater—over 3,000— assembled in a tent to listen to a speech from her." Beginning with a read-ing from Scripture, Phoebe Couzins spoke for two hours while the "quiet and orderly" audience listened with "the deepest attention." Her success led to an invitation to return to Whitewater to give a commencement address at the Normal School, but first she would keep a commitment to speak at a county fair in Michigan.[9] Obviously audiences of that period liked her combination of intellectual content, elaborate style, intense conviction, and charisma.

When her father was appointed U.S. Marshal for the Eastern District of Missouri, Phoebe Couzins served as his chief clerk. Upon her father's death in 1887, President Grover Cleveland appointed Phoebe Couzins to complete the unexpired term. The first woman ever named a U.S. Marshal, she had a brief term of office and later went on to try a variety of work as an administrator with the United States Census Corps, a writer, a secretary for the Board of Lady Managers at the Chicago World's Fair in 1893, and a lobbyist for the United Brewers Association. Feeling unappreciated as a crusader for women's right to vote, Couzins became a bitter critic of young, wealthy suffragists. Couzins abandoned her support of both the temperance and suffrage movements and began to speak of motherhood and homemaking as the best way of life for women. In her lecture "Building the Temple," she glorified "the temple of sweet motherhood," while in a tribute to Nancy Hanks, the mother of Abraham Lincoln, she imagined his birth in an aura of divinity: "the arch of Heaven's blue dome ne'er reverberated to grander music, than the wail of that tiny infant in his enfolding mother's arms, or the stars in their vigil ne'er witnessed a more triumphal scene than the advent of that great spirit and heart. . . ."[10]

8. Morello, *The Invisible Bar,* 48.

9. "A St. Louis Lady Abroad," *St. Louis Republic,* May 10, 1878, J. E. D. Couzins Papers, Missouri Historical Society, St. Louis.

10. "Phoebe Couzins' Tribute to Nancy Hanks" and "Miss Couzins Talks: Her Theme, 'Building the Temple,'" manuscripts, J. E. D. Couzins Papers, Missouri Historical Society, St. Louis.

Once so capable and acclaimed, Phoebe Couzins became physically handicapped and emotionally unstable.[11] She died in poverty in 1913, and was buried wearing the U.S. Marshal star. In 1950, women lawyers of St. Louis and Kansas City erected a marker in Bellefontaine Cemetery at the grave of this pioneer who had led the way for other women to enter the field of law.[12]

The J. E. D. Couzins Papers in the archives of the Missouri Historical Society in St. Louis contain essays and speeches by Phoebe Couzins, but no private writings to help us understand how she regarded her achievements or why she became so bitter and eccentric. Included in the collection is an unidentified newspaper clipping headed, "The Graduation of Miss Couzins: Complimentary Dinner—A Speech by the Lady Bachelor at Law." The editors present these ornate and confident words of thanks Phoebe offered to the law faculty and friends who gathered on May 17, 1871, for an "elegant entertainment" at the home of Dr. and Mrs. G. S. Walker. After dinner the host made an impromptu speech, saying that he believed in women's rights and was pleased to see this "triumph of its principles." After Dr. Walker's toast to "Law—The great bulwark of civilization" and to "the recognized equality of men and women," Miss Couzins responded with the following speech. Not only industrious as a student of the law, she was skilled in the gracious manners of St. Louis society, eloquently expressing her appreciation for the enlightened attitude of Washington University and her hope for increased opportunities for women.

_____ A SPEECH BY THE LADY BACHELOR AT LAW _____

Two years ago I entered upon the study of the law with many forebodings, toned with many conflicts and doubts as to its expediency, yet, actuated solely by a desire to open new paths for woman, enlarge her usefulness, widen her responsibilities and to plead her cause in a struggle which I believed was surely coming. I have steadily pursued my way, encouraged by many and discouraged by not a few; feeling at every step, however, amply repaid for the struggles which it has occasioned, until, having

11. In 1898 friends in St. Louis were planning a benefit for Phoebe Couzins, to show their support after she had been publicly described as "crazy . . . for the past six years." Writing in defense of Couzins, V. C. Whitney praised her "birth, breeding, and brains" (Whitney, letter to Lillie D. Blake, January 18, 1898, Lillie Devereux Blake Papers, Missouri Historical Society, St. Louis). Couzins apparently suffered from arthritis; as a result she was confined to a wheelchair at times (Tokarz, "A Tribute," 99).

12. For further information on Phoebe Couzins, see Tokarz, "A Tribute"; Tokarz, "Opening the Way"; Morello, *The Invisible Bar;* Koetting, "Four St. Louis Women"; Paula Coalier, "Beyond Sympathy"; and *Show Me Missouri Women,* 1:173–74.

finished the cause and kept the faith, I stand ready to fight the good fight for justice and humanity.

Blackstone says: "For I think it an undeniable position that a competent knowledge of the laws of that society in which we live, [is] a proper accomplishment of every gentleman and scholar, and highly useful—I had almost said an essential—part of liberal and polite education."[13] Had the learned gentleman lived in our day, we should tell him that we deem it an essential part of woman's education, also; and it would seem as if, amid the swift changes of the present, when, perhaps, the unwelcome responsibility of a voice in framing her country's laws will be conferred upon her, woman should hasten to repair her ignorance of its laws and needs, by a thorough knowledge and acquaintance of those which govern her and affect humanity. Her moral and political irresponsibility seems one; she can no longer retain the lily's passive state in the world's field of action; henceforth, she must be a helper, not an idler; and, believing this, I am glad to welcome any and all movements which tend to lift woman out of her narrow, traditional life, and place her upon her feet, where she may think and act for herself. Hitherto, the doctrine of self-reliance, self-culture, personal responsibility, has never been taught to woman; she has been regarded as created for man's self-love, alone; with no soul to feel, no mind to expand, no brain to weigh argument, no individual accountability to render her Maker, and thus the race has slowly, painfully climbed the heights of progress, dragging a dead weight, securely manacled at feet and wrists, which its own hands have forged. This inert mass now threatens death and destruction unless released from bondage. Woman's irresponsibility and man's culpable negligence is working ruin to our social and political fabric; and, unless some power can galvanize the slumbering virtue of this people into new life, we, as a nation, are doomed to irresistible disaster.

But, I rejoice to-day that my native state, destined to be, I trust, a grand controlling power of the future, has broken one of the links of this chain, and bidden the captive live. Henceforth, on Missouri's banner shall be written, "Dared to do right—dared to be true." To the Washington university, which has thus conferred this honor upon her, let me return thanks for all true men and women. The law faculty and board of directors by unanimous action, signified their willingness to open the doors of this institution to woman, nobly declaring that sex should be no barrier to those who desire to acquaint themselves with the laws of their country, or to enlarge the mind and cultivate the judgment by a study of that science which furnishes the intellect with food at every step; and I think, gentlemen, that your university may become as celebrated in the future

13. Sir William Blackstone (1723–1780) is remembered for his *Commentaries on the Laws of England.*

as was the University of Bologna, Italy, in the past. It was long the chief glory and the most ancient of Italy's schools, famous for a lengthened period as the first law school of Europe. It has the peculiar honor of having had the professors' chair in almost every department filled at some period or other by learned ladies. Novella de Andrea was renowned as the learned professor of the canon law; Laura Bair [Bain?], a lady doctor of laws, had the chair of mathematics and natural philosophy. The beauty of Christiana de Pianu, another of these lady professors, is said to have been so fascinating that when she lectured it was necessary to have a curtain drawn before her in order that the students might not be distracted by her charming face from the clear study of the law. It was here the researches of medicine were extended by introducing human dissection, and it is probable we owe this important discovery to a woman, as Anna Marzelenu, noted for her dextrous handling of the scalpel, was one of the professors of surgery, and her wax preparations of every part of the human body become [*sic*] the pride of Bologna. Within its walls, originated the discovery of galvanism, and if the c[e]lebrity of that university is partly due to the influence of its learned and fascinating lady professors, I hope, gentlemen, that the fame of your institution is already established in the future.

To the law faculty I desire to tender my personal thanks for the many words of encouragement and the courtesies which have been extended to me during my two years of study. To Judge Krum I am especially indebted for my first introduction in the school, and substantial aid in the loan of legal works throughout the term. To Judge Reber I tender the gratitude of a sincere woman's heart for the words spoken in behalf of her sex at the graduating exercises. To one whose soul has been sadly torn and bruised by endless friction with the carping spirits and narrow minds of to-day, his kind and fatherly anointing fell as oil upon the troubled waters. In him and the faculty whom he represents I recognize the honor which Charlotte Wilborne tells us "is the finest sense of absolute justice tempered by the tenderness of the largest benevolence. The inborn patent of nobility drawn primarily for the basis of our own respect, it is benevolent, because it recognizes in the individual *ego* the universal humanity, and finding its own soul worthy of respect, confesses the in[n]ate worth of all souls. It is even more scrupulously considerate of another's rights than of its own, knowing how nobler it is to endure loss than to perpetuate." And in taking farewell of you, gentlemen, let me express the regret which I feel at the dissolution of the pleasant relations we have sustained. If, as a woman, I was not welcome in the class, the students have never manifested it by word, look or deed, and one of the delightful memories of my life will be my studentship in your college, and as in [the] past, so too in the future I trust there may be no cause for regret in the step taken, but one and all may congratulate ourselves that we were connected with an institution which led the vanguard to a higher civilization, where soul and mind is to be the only criterion of nobility and worth.

In responding especially to the spirit of the toast, let me say that I trust the day is not far distant, when men and women shall be recognized as equal administrators of that great bulwork [*sic*] of civilization, law. In this recognition we shall get back to first principles, for as I look ahead, I find that God in his formation of animate and inanimate nature created a duality.

Gentlemen, The sentinels of great ideas, which have kept lonely watch across the centuries, are calling to each other from mountain top and peak, "Watchman, what of the night?" The nineteenth century responds, "Traveller, the dawn usually breaks in the east, but, lo! the morning cometh from the west, and the star of Wyoming and Missouri proclaims the birth of freedom's daughter!"[14]

The newspaper account concludes, "The fair speaker was loudly applauded."

14. In 1869 women were granted the right to vote in the new Wyoming Territory.

MARIE WATKINS OLIVER (1854–1944)

$\mathcal{M}$issouri owes its flag to the vision and perseverance of Marie Watkins Oliver.[1] Working with a committee of the Daughters of the American Revolution, Mrs. Oliver discovered in 1908 that the state had no flag. She did research, planned a design with artist Mary Kochtitsky, and persuaded her husband and his nephews to introduce a Senate bill endorsing the flag. When the original paper version was destroyed in the 1911 fire at the Capitol, Mrs. Oliver made a new flag in silk, enlisting the help of another artist to paint the Great Seal in the center. The "Oliver flag" was adopted on March 22, 1913. Marie Watkins Oliver had earned her place in history books as "the Betsy Ross of Missouri."[2] Her granddaughter, Marguerite Oliver Dearmont Lewis, recalls that Mrs. Oliver kept the flag carefully folded in a bedroom drawer. "She would get it out very frequently and show my sisters and me and tell us of its importance and the story of how it was formed. . . . She kept it very, very carefully." Now on display at the Missouri State Information Center in Jefferson City, the delicate silk flag is a reminder of a woman who was devoted to public service and her family.[3]

The extensive Oliver family material at the Western Historical Manuscript Collection in Columbia includes records of the career of Marie's husband, Robert Burett Oliver (1850–1934) as a lawyer, a prosecuting attorney, and a member of the State House of Representatives, the Senate, and the University of Missouri Board of Curators. Documents tell of Marie's love of history and her leadership in various organizations, including the Colonial Dames of America, the Daughters of the American Revolution, the United Daughters of the Confederacy, and a Santa Fe Trail committee. Together, the Olivers established the Cape Girardeau County Historical Society. Public service, mutual interests, family life with five sons and a daughter, and membership in the Presbyterian Church were the substance of more than five decades of happy marriage. Before Marie

1. For biographical information, see Blanche S. Leach, *Missouri State History of the D.A.R.*, 162–68; and *Missouri Historical Review* 52 (October 1957): 35–39, and 63 (January 1969): [inside back cover].

2. The "Oliver flag" has three horizontal stripes—the blue standing for "vigilance, permanency, and justice," the red representing "valor," and the white symbolizing "purity." The coat of arms in the center of the flag signifies independence, and the surrounding twenty-four stars represent Missouri's place as the twenty-fourth state in the union (Pat Scott Van Hooser, "Marie Watkins Oliver," in *Show Me Missouri Women*, 2:258; "The Story of the Missouri Flag," bulletin from the office of Secretary of State Roy D. Blunt).

3. *Capper's*, cited in "Ozark Happenings Newsletter," Texas County Missouri Genealogical and Historical Society, vol. 9, no. 2 (April/May/June 1992): 36. The flag was presented to the State of Missouri by Allen L. Oliver in 1961. The flag was restored in 1988 at the initiative of then Secretary of State Roy Blunt and paid for by funds raised by Missouri schoolchildren.

Elizabeth Watkins and Robert Burett Oliver began their partnership, however, there was a cautious and proper courtship during which they exchanged gentle and intelligent letters, revealing courtesies and gender roles typical of the period, as well as the self-respect and individuality of the writers.[4]

Marie Elizabeth Watkins must have been an extraordinary individual. Born in Ray County, Missouri, in 1854, she was the sixth of eleven children born to Henrietta Rives Watkins (1824–1885) and Charles Allen Watkins (1820–1864). Although she called herself "a country girl," she observed a "ladylike" code of behavior and was intellectual, clever, and a skilled housekeeper. On April 28, 1876, she wrote: "My country home always proves a most delightful 'haven of *rest*' to me when I have spent several weeks with my City friends, in a whirl of gayety and pleasure. I like 'Society' but cannot help tiring of it, for in it there seems to me so much glitter and so little gold, and we so seldom meet with persons whose, face, manner and expressions, show forth their real character and feelings." Burett Oliver assured Marie on May 14 that he also found much "glitter" in society: "*I too*, you must bear in mind, am and have always been, a country boy." In letters to her beau, Marie provided testimony of her ability to work hard and administer a household. Sensitive to the beauties of nature as well as literature, she longed for something beyond the "sordid cares" of domestic tasks—poetry "inwoven" with her daily life.

Like many unmarried young women, Marie was expected to focus her attention on family life. She was educated by governesses, at private schools in Farmville, and at Richmond College. Her three younger brothers also attended the college, and she tutored them in preparation for admission to the University of Missouri.[5] Marie assumed more than the usual share of household responsibilities because of her mother's ill health. The relationship between mother and daughter was affectionate but sometimes strained.

Burett began writing to Marie's family because he knew her brother, Charles Allen Watkins, who died in 1874. Charlie, who received an A.B. degree from the University of Missouri, was Burett's roommate, best friend, and fraternity brother.[6] Burett and Marie exchanged many letters before they met in early October 1876, during a visit to St. Louis. The law student wrote from Columbia on October 7: "My studies have just been finished and as I looked out and saw the pale beams of moonlight

4. From the group of handwritten letters the editors present a selected number that tell the story of the courtship. They appear in this anthology with the permission of Marie Watkins Oliver's great-grandchildren, Penny Hawkins and John L. Oliver, Jr.

5. Folder 922, Oliver Family Papers, WHMC-C.

6. John L. Oliver, Jr., letter to Carla Waal, August 9, 1995. For more on the deaths of Charles and a younger brother, Benjamin Rives, see Marie Oliver Watkins and Helen (Hamacher) Watkins, *"Tearin' through the Wilderness": Missouri Pioneer Episodes* . . . , 107–8.

falling like threads of silver upon the limbs and leaves of a tree near my window, I remembered how faintly, yet how beautifully, it shown through the smoky clouds of St. Louis last Monday night as I walked and talked to you whom I was and am so glad to meet." In the next step of their courtship, he became a guest welcomed by the entire family to the Watkins country home, Westover,[7] in Ray County. When Burett visited in April 1877, he and Marie became engaged.

The courtship and lengthy engagement of this couple exemplifies the pattern recommended in advice books and domestic novels of the period, which have been studied by Frances B. Cogan for her book *All-American Girl: The Ideal of Real Womanhood in Mid-Nineteenth-Century America.* Marie Watkins, in fact, resembles the ideal of Real Womanhood presented by Cogan as a contrast to the True Woman described by Barbara Welter in *Dimity Convictions.* The Real Woman was intelligent, physically fit, well educated, and competent. Marie did not have to demonstrate that she could support herself financially; instead, a sense of duty to her family made her a typical Real Woman. She exercised careful judgment when choosing a marriage partner, using the years of courtship to verify that Burett was hardworking and reliable, that their interests and attitudes were compatible, and that their marriage would be characterized by warm emotions and shared responsibility.[8] A man also was expected to make a prudent choice. A friend wrote to encourage Burett to see "farther than the mere outward appearance" and appreciate "a pure and noble heart."[9]

To have her own home and family was Marie Watkins's dream, as it had been that of Susan Vanarsdale. Society was changing, and some women chose to train for careers. Marie reported to Burett that an older woman had urged her to consider becoming a doctor. That friend could envision a time when every town would have a woman physician. She had probably heard about some of Missouri's pioneer women doctors. The first to be licensed in the state was Margaret Schmidt, who started practicing in Hannibal in the 1860s and continued for almost forty years.[10] While a number of women were practicing midwifery, massage therapy, homeopathy, and other unorthodox medicine in the late 1860s, Nancy Leavell and other women physicians with "legitimate" training began to practice in St. Louis. One of the best known would be Dr. Mary Hancock McLean, a skillful surgeon, who graduated from the University of Michigan and established a practice in St. Louis in 1884. She became

7. Westover was the country home of Marie's mother, Henrietta Rives Watkins. Marie's father, Charles Allen Watkins, developed extensive property and businesses with his uncle, James R. Allen (*Show Me Missouri Women,* 2:258; Leach, *Missouri State History of the D.A.R.,* 162).

8. On courtship patterns, see chapters 3, 4, and 5 in Cogan, *All-American Girl.*

9. M. L. Alexander, letter, October 31, 1876, Oliver Family Papers.

10. Hagood and Hagood, *The Story of Hannibal,* 58–59.

the only woman to intern at a St. Louis city hospital until the 1940s and the first woman elected to membership in the St. Louis Medical Society.[11] Marie Watkins Oliver showed by her later leadership in organizations and public causes that she could have been a capable career woman, but she probably mentioned the possibility of becoming a doctor only to evoke an assurance of Burett's love.

Their correspondence chronicles the development of a stable, generous relationship that was carefully nurtured for several years. There were some misunderstandings, but dramatic conflicts were always resolved in favor of the warm friendship that grew into trust and commitment. Letters played an essential role in the success of the relationship. Writing frequently, expressing concern for each other's well-being, and sharing private thoughts were ways of strengthening their love. Burett wrote, "your *dear letters cheated me* of *fatigue, lighted up the future and made me really a better man*" [undated letter, ca. 1877]. They looked forward, however, to the day when they would no longer have to write letters and when, as Marie said, "none can dictate *to us—*we can do as we please."

After their wedding at Westover on December 10, 1879, Marie and Burett Oliver lived in Jackson, where their six children were born. In 1896 they moved to Cape Girardeau and built a beautiful home called "Oliver Heights." Here Marie lived the rest of her life. Following Burett's death in 1934, she was a widow for ten years, looking back on "a full, fruitful and very worthwhile life."[12]

──────────────── LETTERS OF MARIE WATKINS OLIVER ────────────────

Westover
MARCH 15, 1876

MR. OLIVER

Allow me to express, my most sincere thanks for the beautiful bouquet of which I was the delightfully surprised and happy recipient last Saturday morning. The flowers were so fresh bright and beautiful, the sight of them warmed the hearts of the whole household, and of course the genial feeling was extended to the kind friend who afforded us so much pleasure.[13]

11. Marion Hunt, "Woman's Place in Medicine: The Career of Dr. Mary Hancock McLean." See also Martha R. Clevenger, "From Lay Practitioner to Doctor of Medicine: Woman Physicians in St. Louis, 1860–1920."

12. Folder 922, Oliver Family Papers.

13. The editors have selected a number of letters exchanged by Marie Watkins and Robert Burett Oliver during their courtship. The letters appear in this anthology with the permission of their great-grandchildren, Penny Hawkins and John L. Oliver, Jr. The

Were I not naturally fond of flowers, poetry, and the like, I should long ago have cultivated a taste for them, for they constitute the principal charm of country life. I do in real earnest *love them* and therefore, do appreciate to the fullest extent your charming gift and pleasant letter.

Mama desires me to say, she received your kind letter last week, thanks you for your kind expressions of friendship and good wishes Should you find it convenient to visit us when you return to Columbia in July or at any other time, you will ever meet with a cordial reception at our home.

Enclosed you will find the picture of brother Charlie which you desired. Mama says she would be glad to have your Photo.

WITH KINDEST REGARD I AM SINCERELY YOUR FRIEND

MARIE E. WATKINS

Marie later writes to thank Mr. Oliver for a letter and his photograph.

APRIL 28, 1876

. . . We thank you most sincerely for the picture of yourself. I should not have been so impertinent as to ask you for it, had it not been Mama's earnest request, though I must confess I had some curiosity to know what manner of man you are. . . .

Hoping we will sometime *ere long* meet when I am sure we will be good friends if we are not already. . . .

JUNE 16, 1876

MY DEAREST FRIEND

Ten days have passed since your hastily written but dear good letter of 4th inst. [the current month] was recd, and I fear you think I have been a little neglectful, but I hope, yes I know *you* will believe *me* when I tell you this is *absolutely* the first half hour of leisure the very first time I could claim to write a letter *even to you*. Have hoped to hear from you again, but suppose you are waiting for me to write (which *I will* do this evening tho' I am not at all well and am tired) and then our mails have been so irregular and for several days we were entirely cut off from the mails by the *high waters*. [T]he [Missouri] river has been out of its banks and injured some of the farms besides stopping all travel but did not come out far enough to do *us* any damage. [O]ur farms you know are principally in the *"bottom."*

When I wrote you we were in the midst of the closing exercises of R[ichmond] College. It was my duty as well as my pleasure to attend, for

---

handwritten correspondence is in the Oliver Family Papers at WHMC-C. The editors have, on the whole, retained the original spelling, punctuation, and capitalization. A few exceptions have been made for ease in comprehension.

my brothers took part in the Exercises, and I must say we were very proud of them all and thought they were surpassed by none of the students, except perhaps the *Graduates*. [W]e had five this year and they are, *some of them* young men of more than ordinary *talent*. Then for two days I was housecleaning (by no means an enviable occupation) and since then we have had a *house full* of company, friends from St. Joseph, Lexington and Richmond, so our family or rather household have numbered from ten to twenty five all the time, and a portion of the time I had no cook *impossible to get one*. You may imagine how difficult it was for me [to] fill the places of hostess, housekeeper, and *cook* all at the same time, but our guests all expressed themselves *satisfied* and *I know* we have one and all spent the time happily. *I have enjoyed it so much,* and in truth I am winning a reputation as a *remarkable* girl. The last seven of our friends left us since supper this eve. Among our visitors were Mrs. Oliver *and her son Mordecai* (of St Joe.). Mrs. O. is an old friend of Mamas whom she had not seen for eleven years. [T]he first day she was here *Mama came down to dinner* and has every day since been down stairs and has been out riding once. It makes me so happy to see her better, think we must send for some more of her friends of former years. . . .

While in Richmond a few days since I called to see Mrs. King and *Mabel,* who returned home from Columbia last week. They both asked about you with much interest, but on comparing notes we found they had received as late news as I. "Mr. Oliver" was I assure you thoroughly discussed. Mrs. K. wanted to know "how and when our correspondence first commenced." I told her the story of the cigar case and gave the *dates.* "[H]ow often you wrote to me last winter." I told her as nearly as I could. Then she wanted to know "how often does he write now, is he in love with you." I answered laughing—"that would be right difficult to tell, perhaps he likes Mabel too well for that." Then in the most excited manner she asked *at least a dozen* times "has he courted you, has he talked love to you, has he addressed you, are you engaged." I answered all these questions evasively until at last Mrs. K. laid her hand on my shoulder, looked in my face and said tell me truly Marie *"yes or no."* [T]hen I said *no.* I could not say anything else even had I felt inclined to confide in her (which I didn't). I would not have done so under those circumstances. 'Twas clearly evident Mrs. K. asked all these questions through interested motives and I was sorry to see Mabel was even more interested than her mother. Remember you are not to tell Mabel I wrote all this.

. . . My remembrance of the Sunday evening you have mentioned is by no means *"faint"* but I had forgotten we had strawberries for lunch 'till you mentioned it. [W]ish we could have eaten them together fresh from the garden during the last two weeks, in other words I wish you could have been here to share all our fun as well as our feast of strawberries. [W]e've had *"considerable"* of both.

How very generous you are *to consent to listen* to anything I wish to say and at the same time coolly set aside my advice or rather admonition. . . . Thank you for the pretty little ferns. [T]hey are, some of them, different from any we have, I appreciate them from the circumstances under which they were culled and for the evidence they give of your refined and cultivated taste. It is getting quite late and I have already written more than I ought. Hoping to hear from you soon. I am always your

MARIE E. WATKINS

Marie has been prevented from replying to two letters from "my own darling Burett."

JUNE 18, 1876

[POSTSCRIPT] READ THIS FIRST

. . . [S]everal times I have tried to hide for a half hour and write but invariably some one found me out and said I was just then indispensable either in the parlor, dining room or kitchen. You will not censure me but sympathize with me in being deprived of *my greatest pleasure*. . . .

Westover

AUGUST 11, 1876

MR. R. B. OLIVER
KIND FRIEND,

Your letter of Aug 8th was recd yesterday evening. Its contents surprise me a little. Of your surmises in regard to the cause of your not receiving a reply to your letter before the last, that which you thought most improbable is in truth *right*. The *mails* were at fault.

After waiting a *reasonable* time, long enough to punish you a little, I answered your letter, and in that letter told you, that I thought our acquaintance scarcely sufficient to justify a correspondence, that being strangers I feared the correspondence might grow wearisome and had perhaps better be closed while we were such good friends. I regret exceedingly you did not receive the letter for I am sure that instead of entertaining unkind feelings toward me as you have done you would have liked me better. I'll tell you just here—*I never close a correspondence by simply neglecting the letters of a friend, that would be unladylike to say the least of it.*

In truth Mr. Oliver I felt that *I* had thoughtlessly been the *first cause* of its beginning, and that you would feel duty bound to keep it up until I saw fit to put an end to our exchange of letters. Though your letters were always interesting and very pleasant I did not wish to impose upon *your valuable time.*

Suppose you will return to Columbia this fall, hope sincerely we will meet sometime during the year, am very sure we will be good friends.

Am glad to tell you Mama's health is restored. She is quite well now and sends kind regards and good wishes to you.

Believe me always
Truly Your friend
Marie E. Watkins

Havana, New York
September 11, 1876

Mr. R. Burett Oliver
Jackson Mo.
My Kind Friend

Your letter of Aug 25th was forwarded me here and received only a day or two since. . . .

You do not expect a reply and would probably be quite satisfied without this effort of mine, and yet I write flattering myself it will not be unpleasant to you, for I shall believe just what you said, that our correspondence is pleasant and profitable—you remember I'm very credulous—

You must not think it is *womans contrariness* that prompts me to write, for 'tis with the best of good feeling, the truth is I cant resist the temptation, despite the romance (which like yourself I cant help liking sometimes).

[Marie tells about her trip to St. Louis, Chicago, and Buffalo, and how impressed she was by Niagara Falls.] . . . No American should die without viewing Niagara. Were I to attempt a description, am afraid I would only write as the little girl did to her Mother from that place "Oh! Oh!! Oh!!! Oh!!!! Oh!!!!!" and nothing more. . . .

From here we go to N. Y. City spend a few days there, then to Philadelphia (of course) to see the "Big Show" [the Centennial Exposition] on to Washington, Baltimore, Columbus, Ohio, and into St. Louis about the last of Sept. or first of Oct. *About which time you will be there, will you not?* If you should be, I would like to meet you and if you are equally anxious to see me, just send me a note care of, Jas. A. Watkins. 508 N. Sec. Str. and he (my brother) will deliver it as soon as I enter the City. [T]hen of course I'll write you where to call. What you term *"irksome duties"* shall henceforth be a *great pleasure*. [W]rite soon.

Your friend always.
Marie E. Watkins

At last the couple meet in St. Louis, and the friendship blossoms into romance.

Westover
DECEMBER [13], 1876

MR. R. B. OLIVER
COLUMBIA MO.
MY BEST OF FRIENDS,

I have just been out walking and watching the most glorious *sunrise*, the morning is so bright and pleasant, the air just cold enough to be right bracing. The scene would be the more enjoyable did I not know such brilliant hues in the morning clouds always presage bad weather. This morning I am more free than I have been for a week, since the receipt of your last good letter I have been so very very busy scarcely a moment I could call my own. [B]usy too with only the sordid cares of life, ordinary household duties. It is abominable to be compelled to live only to eat and sleep and to attend to the wants of the physical nature. If there is any poetry in life (and I'm sure there is) I like to get it out, to have it inwoven with every day experiences.

A life devoted to study, to the pursuit of knowledge, knowledge which deals Justice to all men and to each and every man the greatest good; such a life as *yours must be,* would, I think be *glorious.*

> What is [a] man
> If his chief good, and market of his time,
> Be but to sleep and feed? a beast, no more.
> Sure, he, that made us with such large discourse
> Looking before, and after, gave us not
> That capability and godlike reason
> To fust in us unused.[14]

One of my friends, rather an old lady and quite intelligent, has used all her influence, all her powers of persuasion, of late, trying to induce *me to study Medicine,* to become a Physician, a practitioner. What do you think of it? She says there should be a female physician in every community and I am better fitted for it than any young lady she knows. I begged leave to disagree with her, and think I am much better fitted for a quiet life than to assume the dignities and responsibilities of a *Profession.*

I send you a clipping from our paper a description of the marriage I have more than once mentioned to you. We did see our friend[s] safely launched upon the "sea of troubles" and left them with, "God bless you both." But I must tell you, we had so much *fun* while at Missouri City; there we had the benefit of some *real sure enough* "unsophisticated country gallantry." The place is very small, the people nearly all very very plain, in short—*country-fied,* but at the same time *very very good.*

14. *Hamlet,* 4.4.

> Abash'd I stood,
> And felt *how awful* goodness is—[15]

Mr. Schweick (my attendant) is an old school fellow and classmate of mine, neither he nor Mattie H. it seemed could adapt themselves to circumstances and were all the while ill at ease, I've no doubt they "laughed in their sleeves" at the manner in which I ingratiated myself into the good will of those *good people*, but I dont know when I ever enjoyed anything so much. Now I know 'tis unbecoming in a *country girl* to talk this way (I hav'nt, and would'nt to any one else) but I believe you can appreciate it, for I dare say you have sometime been placed in a like position. . . .

How inconsistent you are to even think of *scolding* when I do not reply promptly to your letters, when it is *so very difficult for you to spare a half hour* to ans. mine. I'll promise tho' to be as prompt as you, in truth I think a prompt correspondence so much more interesting than when letters are long neglected.

Most truly your friend
Marie E. Watkins

Burett replies on about December 17, 1876: "I have thought of you almost the entire day. . . . My stupid pen cannot find even the outline of the heart that thanks you a thousand times for what you have said in these two last. They are without doubt the best letters ever penned. Your sentences follow each other with the ease and grace that shadow does substance and you glide from one subject to another with the harmony of music! Truly you are the 'Queen of Hearts' and I hold you dont I in this game? Yes darling it is my lifes object now to 'shield you from the rough blasts' & to make you happy and cheerful. . . ."

In another letter Oliver comments on her studying medicine: "The idea is to [sic] ridiculous to be entertained for a single moment. So you can inform that old lady friend of yours that there is a diversity of opinion upon the subject. . . ." He concedes that it would be beneficial to gain some knowledge of medicine: "understanding of our anatomical structure, some of the primary laws of hygiene and pathology are not only absolutely necessary to our well being but to a polite education."

Westover
January 4, 1877

My Dear Friend

Never in all my life did I experience more pleasure from the receipt of a letter than your last has given me. . . .

---

15. *Paradise Lost*, 4.846: "Abash'd the devil stood, / And felt how awful goodness is, and saw / Virtue in her shape how lovely."

I have not had a "jolly jolly Christmas" (thank you for the kind wish) but it has passed quite pleasantly, except Christmas Eve, Mama being sick I had to act in the capacity of "Santa Claus." [W]hen my work was finished I looked around and there were only *five* stockings filled where *once there were eleven.* The many jolly happy Christmas times past and gone crowded upon my memory and I could not resist a hearty cry, here all alone in the still hour of the night thinking of the loved ones gone from us some of them never more to return, unless their blessed spirits gather with us round the fireside in our "fond old home" *and I firmly believe they do.* We have never had a merry Christmas since Brother Charlie died. I do not think we ever will again.

Richmond has been full of gayety, entertainments every evening, but I have participated in very few of the festivities. Several weeks ago the young ladies of R—— gave a *leap year* party, and on Friday evening last the gentlemen gave a return party. Though I did not take part in the former I attended the latter, 'twas an elegant party and I had so much fun. [H]ad a serious lecture from some *good* Presbyterian *Bretheren* for playing a few games of cards in a quiet corner. On that occasion I met Mr. Lovelock, a-n-d I think somebody else must surely "possess a peculiar power" of winning hearts. What have you done for that young man, assisted him in his studies or his *love affairs?* Such encomiums such praises I never heard bestowed, such admiration, such perfect devotion was never before expressed. [O]ne would think you a perfect Apollo that very deity himself decended from his high estate for a while to mingle with and benefit poor frail mortals. Long as I would to change the topic of conversation, 'twould *invariably* drift back to *Mr. Oliver.* I gave him a number of ridiculous messages for you, has he delivered them? . . . When I wrote you last we had just finished making near 600 lbs of lard which I superintended and *assisted with too.* I had been so deep in the mysteries of *Grease* that I had in *western phrase* "a huge disgust on." Do you wonder that I failed to discover any *poetry* in such duties? . . .

Your letters make me feel so sensibly my inability to write anything interesting, but if you are willing to be so cheated, write me again very soon,

AND BELIEVE ME ALWAYS
YOUR SINCERE FRIEND
MARIE WATKINS

[P.S.] Mama sends kind regards

During a visit in the spring of 1877 Burett proposes and Marie promises, as he writes, "to love me to overlook my errors and to make me happy and noble like yourself." Sometime later, however, Burett receives a letter that seems lacking in "confidence" *and* "unmixed faith." *He offers [in an undated letter] to release Marie from her commitment: "I would feel very miserable indeed if I thought our engagement did not have the full and unqualified assent both of your heart and sense of duty or judgment."* On May 17 Marie replies, admitting that Burett is not her *"first love,"* but never has she known such *"complete love, trust, confidence which now fills my heart to overflowing, and* of which heart you *are* sole possessor."

Westover

MAY 21, 1877

My Dear Dear Friend

The last letter I wrote you was by no means satisfactory to myself or to Mama (I read a *portion* of it to her) and I am sure 'twas not so to you. . . .

We have had occasion to observe that it is so difficult for the reader to catch the exact spirit of the writer. In the outset of this let me say, You must not feel hurt at anything I say, but know I never loved you more than at this moment, and want to write you with the same candor I would talk to you if you were here. It seems tho' that I have forgotten or never learned *to express my thoughts* just as I ought.

The letter I wrote you on the 11th inst. produced a very different impression from what I intended it should. . . . Above all things *we should* deal tenderly with the delicate sensitive fibres which even "a breath may break." [S]omehow from that letter you got it into your head that I thought or *imagined* you had in some thought word or deed wronged me. [Y]ou answered it on the impulse of the moment, trying to show me you had done nothing of the kind—which I knew full well before—and except in one instance believe I have dealt equally justly with you, and for that you are partly at fault. I refer to the fact that you have from my lips learned but little of my own history or that of our family, but remember *you were my guest* and of course I had to *listen* respectfully all the time while you talked. On this account I appreciate all the more your perfect trust in me. . . .

You thought I was not as confiding as I might have been, about that (*abominable* since it caused you pain) trouble of mine. There are in every household quick and even angry words spoken sometimes but their impression is fleeting as a flash of lightning seen at *a great distance;* and there is no malice in the heart. *There is no perfection in Humanity.* Well to tell you *the* whole truth, all the trouble arose from the fact that I refused to show or read to Mama your letters and showed but little inclination to tell her of them. Mama loves me devotedly, yes even with a more perfect pure disinterested love than *you* do or ever can, and it is perfectly natural for her to feel a deep interest in my welfare and to wish to know the character and *disposition* of the man to whom her daughter is betrothed. She felt that I treated her slightingly and with indifference. I thought she ought not to expect me to be very free with *my* affairs, finally we talked of the matter, both were excited, and each spoke unkindly to the other.

I was in the wrong for I should have been more respectful than to have resented *anything* my Mother might say. I have always confided in my Mother, *have tried* to humour her every caprice, and now that she is so weak, nervous, and entirely isolated from society should I not if possible redouble my kindness and attention to her. Now I have confessed my wrong both to you and to Mama. As I told you *the cloud is dissipated* there is no trace of it left. Mama loves, blesses, pets me every day as she has always done. And she desires me to say, "It is her wish to dispel from your mind all forebodings of an unhappy character, (if there be such) on her part. She does *esteem you highly,* and has for you the *kindest feeling,* which she hopes will *always* exist."

When she kissed me good night last night she said, "Let us not think of that any more. [Y]ou know I love you and that I like Burett better than most any body.["] and I was asleep in ten minutes, the happiest of mortals. . . .

LOVE ME ALWAYS AND BELIEVE ME
TRULY & SINCERELY YOURS
MARIE E. WATKINS

Westover
AUGUST [1879]

MY DEAR DEAR BURETT

You certainly are the most true and devoted lover living, . . .

Your letter of 24th and the flowers came yesterday afternoon and I thought, when I saw and read them, bless his dear life I'll write him a long letter tonight, but unfortunately I had *a severe sick headache*—the third time in my life I ever had it—I only suffered two or three hours—refused all medicines—and called loudly for *hot water,* which relieved me in ten minutes time. I slept soundly all night and am all right this morning. That you may know I am not sick I'll tell you the cause of my trouble. . . . We had melons and grapes in the parlor of which we all ate heartily. . . . *[Marie also ate preserves and pickles.]* [A]ll together was too much of "a mince pie" for my delicate stomach, and the headache in consequence. Sooner or later we suffer the penalty for every disobedience to *the law.* . . .

Let me *thank you* now for the confidence you gave me in regard to that unhappy Friday evening. . . . When you said "I felt that I would give all I possessed to be with you then." You expressed exactly the feeling that was in my heart, *at the very same time.* The words rose to my lips and if I had been in my room I should have uttered them—he is in some trouble

[and] is wishing for me. [O]h! if I could only fly to him this instant, how quickly and gladly would I go. Do you know *I almost felt frightened,* when you told me my presentiment was truth itself. Does it go to prove our souls are one? . . .

The flowers were just as fine and sweet as you are, were so fresh and pretty, perfumed the whole room. . . . Thank you a hundred times. [I]f you were here I would give you the rare jewel *of a kiss* (they are the richest I have) for them.

MUST STOP.
YOURS FAITHFULLY
MARIE E. WATKINS

During the fall Marie and Burett make plans for their wedding in December. She writes on November 29:

I sent you *our cards* Wednesday. [H]ope you have rec'd them and like them. I am all impatience now for the names and address' of your relatives and friends. [H]ope I will receive them today. I am anxious they should receive the cards in time to *find some business* in this part of the country *and come* if possible.

Your plan to be with me Sunday is a capital one. [B]less you. . . .

Since the breaking of the St. Charles bridge we have had only one train a day on the main line between St. L. and K.C. tho' I hope the trains will be running regularly when you come. . . . You shall be with us till Monday, tho' I fear the busy homefolks here will want to separate us then and send you into R. for a portion of the time. Mama says you may come every evening—ha ha. [W]e will submit to all orders then—for very soon—none can dictate *to us*—we will do as we please. . . .

You asked how my Mama's health is. She is trying very hard to be well, tho' is not by any means so. I am trying very hard to make her take care of herself. . . .

I must go to work. [W]e will finish most everything in sewing today.

ALWAYS YOUR OWN
MARIE W.

The courtship letters end with this one, written by Burett:

DECEMBER 1, 1879

How my hand trembles at the thought of this being my last *Monday letter* to you as your *lover.* . . . *Knowing* you were always glad to hear from me I have written you as promptly and as frequently as circumstances would permit though but few times have I said just what I would like to have said to you. . . . Bless your dear life you have invariably read what my *heart* said and not what was penned on paper. . . ."

The final item among the letters is a sales slip from Eugene Jaccard & Co. Watchmakers and Jewelers in St. Louis: "1 Plain Gold Ring $10.00 Engraving on one ring $1.00."

Henriette Geisberg Bruns (1813–1899)

"My life was very difficult, even though there were many happy days. I have always endeavored honestly to do my duty, and more if the opportunity was offered."[1] In 1886, Henriette (Jette) Geisberg Bruns was reflecting upon the balance of hardship and happiness in her life and how she had chosen to respond to her fate. The autobiography she wrote for her family and letters she sent over a period of seventy years, primarily to her brother Heinrich in Germany, constitute a valuable record, available in *Hold Dear, As Always: Jette, A German Immigrant Life in Letters.*

Jette is fascinating because of her individuality and courage; in addition she represents one of the ethnic immigrant groups who settled in Missouri. Jette and her husband, Dr. Bernhard Bruns, did not give up during the difficult months after they first arrived at the Westphalia Settlement on the Maries River in 1836.

Henriette Geisberg was born in 1813 in the Westphalian City of Oelde, where her father was mayor and tax collector. In 1831 she met Dr. Bernhard Bruns, whom she married the next year. Like many immigrant women, Jette had enjoyed a sheltered and comfortable life in her native land. When her husband decided to immigrate to America, she joined him in establishing a home in Missouri and struggling through years of hard work and anxiety. The Bruns family persevered despite harsh living conditions, financial worries, illness, and bereavement. They lived at Westphalia until 1851, then at Shipley's Ferry, and after 1853 in Jefferson City. There her husband ran a store, was a major in the Union Army, and served as mayor before his death in 1864. Jette's life had resembled that of other women of her era; she was sensitive to her husband's needs, devoted to their children, and responsible for the household. Upon her husband's death, she learned that he had mismanaged their finances and left her in debt. Jette dealt with the consequences and earned money by giving piano lessons, selling produce from her garden, and running a boarding house when the legislature was in session.

The lodgers at Jette Bruns's boarding house were politicians, pages, and others associated with the state government; most were also either natives of Germany or the children of German immigrants. Like her boarders Jette had a double identity as a German-American. She kept in close touch with her family in the Old World, yet when she visited them in 1856 and 1882, she realized that she no longer felt at home in

---

1. *Hold Dear, As Always: Jette, a German Immigrant Life in Letters,* ed. Adolf E. Schroeder and Carla Schulz-Geisberg, 260. Subsequent references to the book will be given in the text. Carla Schulz-Geisberg, granddaughter of Jette's brother Heinrich, has granted permission for use of the letters in this anthology.

Germany. The pattern of her life had been typical of many immigrants: arriving in the New World with hope, struggling with disillusionment and ordeals, working and enduring, and becoming assimilated into the American way of life. In contrast to Mother Philippine Duchesne, who came to Missouri to serve God as a teacher and missionary, the Bruns family had arrived seeking property and prosperity, a good life they envisioned partly because of the influence of a book published in 1829 by Gottfried Duden.[2] His book persuaded many German immigrants that Missouri would be a utopia. Bernhard Bruns visited the state in 1835 to choose where his family would live, seeing the new environment with the combination of practicality and romanticism typical of Duden's book (9). The Bruns family, as members of a German Catholic colony, felt pressured to become Americanized. Jette quickly realized that learning the English language was a necessity. By 1825 all the land in Missouri had been acquired from Native American tribes, primarily the Missouri and Osage,[3] and immigrants continued to arrive throughout the century. Many settlers were Americans, most of them from Tennessee, Virginia, and Kentucky, but there were various ethnic groups like the Germans who came directly from Europe. The Bruns family contributed to Missouri's German heritage, which is still honored in Missouri place names, architecture, festivals, and other cultural traditions.[4]

In some ways Jette represents the German-American women described by Linda S. Pickle as "strong, even heroic figures, and superior frontier homemakers,"[5] but she was also a woman who acknowledged her moods of loneliness, tension, and doubt. In 1849, twenty years after she met Bernhard Bruns, Jette pondered what their future would hold. "What will brighten my life's evening?" (149). She could not have imagined the wounding and deaths of her son Heinrich and her nephew Caspar Geisberg during Civil War battles, her children's problems, or the loss of independence as she grew old.

Following a selection of letters about her early experiences in Missouri, the editors present letters Jette wrote in the 1890s, when confronting old age. She faced aging with the intelligence, self-discipline, religious faith, and conflicting emotions that had always characterized her. She would let

2. Gottfried Duden, *Report on a Journey to the Western States of North America and a Stay of Several Years Along the Missouri. . . .*

3. See "The Missouri and Osage: Indians of History," in Carl H. Chapman and Eleanor F. Chapman, *Indians and Archaeology of Missouri,* 99–117.

4. On the immigrant experience, see Adolf E. Schroeder, "The Survival of German Traditions in Missouri"; Giovanni Schiavo, *The Italians in Missouri;* Russel L. Gerlach, *Immigrants in the Ozarks: A Study in Ethnic Geography; The German-American Experience in Missouri;* and William E. Foley, *A History of Missouri,* vol. 1.

5. Pickle, "Stereotypes and Reality: Nineteenth-Century German Women in Missouri," 297.

conversation "wash over" her because of deafness (280). When her son-in-law Carl Hess spoke, he would shout and frighten her. "To be blind, however, is worse," she wrote. "I distinguish the colors, but frequently I pull flowers instead of the weeds . . ." (289). Jette had remarkable willpower. Despite physical limitations, she spent her last years mentally active, usefully occupied, and concerned about her family. Jette Bruns died in 1899. Letters from the 1890s represent the closing chapter in her life, a time when she wished she could live near the "magnificent wilderness surrounded by the great water" of the Northwest, for she saw herself as "a pioneer by nature" (277).

———————————— Letters of Jette Bruns ————————————

Westphalia Settlement
Tuesday, November 14, 1836

Dear Heinrich:

We arrived here at eleven in the morning on All Souls Day. The log cabin was locked up, but Bruns broke the lock. It consists of one room the size of our living room with one window; in it there were a table, four chairs, and two bedsteads. So this was to be our home for the winter! I have to confess that I nevertheless felt good to have reached a safe asylum, and very uplifted by the firm knowledge that I want to stand everything with fortitude. The sun shone warmly and kindly through the leafless trees; soon a bright fire was burning, and for the noon meal we had some wonderful vegetables. . . .

Last Thursday and Friday we had Divine Service. A dignified young Jesuit . . . read the Mass, and all received Holy Communion. In counting the Catholic community we arrived at seventy members. Only Bruns and I could go to Mass on the second morning. The rain poured down from heaven in buckets; it was a hard walk. After confession Mr. Huber was married, and then the Mass began. We had coffee at the Hesses and started on our way back, but we almost got stuck. The water had gathered so much that we had trouble getting through. If by next summer we have a horse I shall certainly be able to use it; however, Bruns will probably have to buy one sooner because he has to get out almost every day. The Americans seem to have a great deal of confidence in him. If Bruns is not at home and an American comes, then, my dear Heinrich, it is a joy to see how beautifully we endeavor to speak English. It is really my greatest annoyance that I cannot use it. However, it will soon improve. (74–75)

Sunday, December 3, 1836

. . . During this time we all have been very busy. We have done our laundry, a hog was butchered, corn had to be harvested, etc. . . . Now today we have rainy weather again, the third time since we have arrived here; for two weeks we had a freeze. It froze pretty heavily during the night, but during the daytime it always turned very pleasant and the sun shone warmly as it probably never did in Westphalia so late in the year. When it rains, it is just too sad in these log cabins; the one in which we live lies on a slope, and thus a little ditch had to be made so that the water would not run into the shed and even into the house. In cold weather one is a little hesitant to get up in the morning, and I frequently think back to our comfortable living room. However, here we just have to live through it.

There is one situation that makes me very cross. It is that Jenne is not at all adaptable.[6] The thought that I will have to get along for years with this disorderly, clumsy person can discourage me any moment. Too often I am vexed about this, and I believe that she is a hopeless case. Thus it happens that I myself have to do most of the cooking and have to try to find work for her outside the house if possible. I shall commend this cross to Heaven!

You cannot believe how satisfying it is to work. I probably have had few days in which I was ever as busy as I am here, that is, having to do hard work, but I'm quite happy in doing it, and like all the others I have a tremendous appetite and sleep soundly. (It is strange, but almost every night now I dream of our father, and then I am still a child with him and spend beautiful hours in my dream.) . . .

. . . Greetings to all, especially to the brothers and sisters, to the uncles and aunts a thousand times; also the brothers and sisters Geisberg, the Boners, Lena, Trude, and all our acquaintances! So many times I think of you back home! (75–77)

Westphalia Settlement
AUGUST 1837

DEAR HEINRICH:

Today I was alone all day long with my little ones.[7] And I thought that I would write you a lot. I talked with you in my thoughts all morning. But here comes an American on horseback, and I have to try to speak English with him. He is waiting for Bruns, who will not return until this evening. I have progressed with my English speaking so far that I can understand occasionally a few common little sentences and can reproduce them. I must really learn more, for it annoys me tremendously when I stand there like a blockhead and cannot answer. . . .

We have had very little luck with anything that we have tackled this year, and it takes a great deal of perseverance and patience not to lose

---

6. Jenne is the maid who accompanied them from Germany.

7. Hermann was born in Oelde in 1833, and Max was born in Westphalia in 1837. Henriette and Bernhard Bruns would have eleven children, five of whom died in childhood.

courage. You know that we believed we would be able to occupy our house soon after our arrival. But still only the skeleton is standing, and a few shingles have been attached to indicate how the roof will be. Our carpenter, to be sure, has done his work well, but has proceeded so very slowly that the entire world is amazed. . . . The few things that have been planted have been destroyed by the flood. Here on Franzen's farm we planted two-thirds in corn and one-third in wheat. The corn stand is good, so we hope the corn will ripen, although it has received very little care. In the spring our horses suddenly got sick and we could not plow, and the weeds got out of hand, and so the corn had to be hoed, which was very troublesome and was not completed. The wheat grew very poorly and had to be stacked in a big pile since we still have no shelter for it. We could plant only very few vegetables because the little fellow [Max] took too much of my time. The few things on the stiff upper land did not succeed very well. Now we have many people and little to eat. . . . Well, what else should I complain about? That I am very often vexed? That I feel doubly annoyed with all these misfortunes and the domestic annoyance with Jenne etc. etc.? That it is no fun to represent cook, nursemaid, and housewife in one person? Away, away, with further song concerning these things. To say it in brief, I wish and hope that things will improve!

My boys sweeten many a disagreeable thing for me; unfortunately the big one [Hermann] has already begun to be quite unruly, but when that is past I really love him very, very much. And the little one is a complete little angel. All day long he is friendly, but he does not want to sit or lie down, and I always have to hold him. With his bare little head with the golden brown hair shining, lightly dressed, often wearing only a little shirt, he mumbles loudly with a strong voice and approaches Hermann, then looks at him cheerfully, and the latter jumps in front of him and makes him laugh loudly. Bruns also pays a great deal more attention to Max than he did earlier to Hermann; he is probably now used to them. Also, the good man has far more consideration for me; he probably thinks that I am now in greater need of it. When I express a wish, he seeks to fulfill it. . . .

And now farewell! Write frequently, even if it is only small details of what you do on this or that day, and then embellish it a little bit because I like that so much. . . .

Hold dear, as always, your faithful sister Jette. (77–80)

Westphalia Settlement
SEPTEMBER 7, 1837

DEAR HEINRICH:

. . . A quarter of a year ago now a very beautiful piece of furniture, which outshines all other items, a piano, found its way into our log cabin. . . . How could I have imagined that just such an instrument as I had denied myself would be made available to me in America! Until a few days before the departure of the Hesses we had not thought of it; then the Hesses offered it. German price, German work, without the cost of transportation! Thus we agreed. However, I have to confess that the beautiful piano neither has a suitable place nor is it being properly used. Both will be taken care of better in the new house. It has a beautiful full sound, and the outside has brown finish; there is nothing lacking. The Swede, Mr. Blumenthal, was recently kind enough to tune it. The guitar kept very well on the trip. . . . [8]

. . . Do you know that I also ride a horse? On the 4th of July I rode on a brand new side saddle to the Scheulens. Max was sitting very happily in my lap. There were several Americans and Germans there, and the noon meal took place in accordance with the American way. At first all ladies sat down, and several gentlemen served us. Soon after the meal there was some dancing. But there was only one fiddle there. American dancing is really quite boring, without a beginning and without an end, almost like contre dances but with no different couples. Finally they figured out that one could also waltz to the tune; and I even danced around a few times. In the end it almost turned too dark for us. . . .

. . . Twice already Indians have been nearby. At first there was a group in Lisletown, where a Mr. Williams speaks their language. They drank mightily until someone finally thought it wise to show them the door. A little while ago some forty Indians with wives and children appeared in the Swedes' store on the Osage; they love whiskey very, very much. The women simply are told to go into the woods, where they make a fire and prepare their food until the men feel like eating or lying down. The men swam through the Osage on top of or alongside their horses, shouting wildly; all who saw it were amazed at their skill in guiding their canoes very quickly. There is no thought of danger or attack. They obey as soon as they are told. Unfortunately I heard of their stay at the Osage too late; otherwise I would have ridden over there because I have not seen any yet. (80–82)

APRIL 21, [1838]

. . . Spring is as beautiful, I almost believe, as it is with you; I welcome it much more than I did last year; it is much prettier. Our farm is getting more friendly every day. From the bedroom where I am writing the yard forms the foreground, the red blossoms of the Judas tree and the white of dogwoods, the sprouting green between the rocks—then straight in

---

8. Jette had enjoyed singing and playing the piano as a young girl in Germany. In 1842 she decided to sell the piano bought from the Hesses because she no longer played it (121).

front of me, approximately fifty paces gently down hill, is the little gate to the bottom field. Here is the garden where Mrs. Bruns[9] has been busily occupied during the past two weeks and enjoys the sprouting peas, beans, and other plants by the hour. (85)

Westphalia
JUNE 14, 1840

DEAR HEINRICH:

. . . Johanna had been sick for two weeks and constantly demanded my care, but now she is improving and begins by being quite ill-humored.[10] Once I sat down at the piano for recreation and found "Easter Morning," the last piece we practiced in the club [in Germany] before Wenner's death.[11] He was already sickly at the time, and it touched me when he sang to me two very appropriate solos. I keep thinking farther back to his first wife, an angel, and the second one, no less one. How they liked us, how we liked them! They are all, all gone! I shall never forget them all the days of my life! —Here, how lonely I am; there is not another congenial female being with whom I could exchange now and then my feelings when I need some relief and would forget the daily worries and cares and set these aside for a short time. —Yet what difference does it make, for I tell Bruns everything and he listens patiently even though he cannot get so deeply involved.

I rarely get to go out of the house. Business does not permit it; if, however, the mill is finished, then I will have to catch up on my visits. (105)

Westphalia
FEBRUARY 15, 1841

DEAR HEINRICH!

First let me report for myself that I once again, in spite of all the fear that I would lose my life, have a stout boy on my lap, who drinks mightily, screams, and sleeps, is named Rudolph, and has blond hair, blue eyes, and a snub nose.[12] My health is returning gradually, and next week I shall again take over the cares of the household.

. . . On 5 November, Franz was married to Trude Stievermann.[13] The wedding took place here in the house. . . . The young woman did not

---

9. Jette often refers to herself in the third person as "Mrs. Bruns."
10. Johanna, Jette's daughter, was born on March 3, 1839.
11. Ludwig Wenner was a doctor of law and director of the music club in Oelde.
12. Rudolph was born January 26, 1841.
13. Franz Geisberg was Jette's oldest brother.

bring anything along; what she has earned she left with her parents and did well in doing so. Franz knew this and has already asked me to take care of some things that otherwise make the beginning of a trousseau. You may keep what I am chattering here to yourself; and otherwise you will agree with Franz that if he can live with his wife beside him that is the best trousseau. She has a good heart and more feeling than one could expect. I also hope that she will do well in the house. . . . I live on very friendly terms with her; however, I want to confess to you that the changed relationship is still somewhat strange to me, and she has probably gotten a very critical relative. But I would be sorry if she notices this in the slightest. She will probably have no cause, for she is always equally modest and friendly and helps wherever it is necessary, asks for advice, etc. Mrs. Bruns likes to help now and again and assists with all kinds of things that they are lacking, and thus I think this will turn into a very beautiful relationship. . . .

BEST REGARDS.

P.S. . . . Send some little gift as a souvenir for the young sister-in-law; here everything is valued even though it is of no great value otherwise. Perhaps a bow or a little kerchief. However, you must know best. (106–8)

Westphalia
JULY 11, 1841

DEAR HEINRICH!

. . . Now our family is limited to Bernhard and one [servant] girl, which pleases me immensely. Never before in America have I had such a small household. Now I would be satisfied if I were not so lonely. Foolish soul! Often I think I don't want to write anymore and don't like to think of you all anymore, but that is not possible. You all always stand before me, fresh and alive, and always there is the ocean and the world between us. There can never be hope for a reunion. You are constantly growing deeper into the situation over there and we into the situation here. Do you know anything that could silence the raging emotions? Can no harmony come to my heart? I would think it would work out, but I don't know how to undo the knot no matter how I think about it and brood about it recently. If I were living with the Clarenbachs I would surely become melancholic. The house stands high on top of the hill. The fields lie down the slope and in the valley. The bottom stretches to Lisle and over the Maries. In the far distance the eye sees the steep rocky banks of the Osage. Recently I spent the night there with Rudolph. It made a very strange impression on me in the glow of the moonlight and in the splendor of the rising sun. The far-reaching view! I thought the faraway hills with the forests on top would reveal something precious to me. If longing could have wings and could jump over trees and rivers! But when the sun rose higher I no longer dreamed, but I quietly smiled and asked myself: what do you find there? Desolation, emptiness! No, here in our neighborhood it's better! (110)

October 17, [1841]

Dear Heinrich!

We all had dysentery. Hermann was the first to become sick. On the 8th of September Max and Johanna were afflicted by it. The latter was indescribably sick and died on the 13th of September at 2:30 in the morning. "Mother, mother!" she cried loudly. I still believe I can hear her. On Tuesday Rudolph became sick, then I on Thursday, then Bernhard and Bruns. On Sunday the 19th, at 1:30 during the night, Max died. It was the third night that I had feared his end almost any hour. He quietly fell asleep and passed away. It was God's will to also take Rudolph from me. He died on Sunday, the 2d of October, at 7:30 in the morning. To the very last minute, I had the strength to endure. And then his breath was failing, his eyes closed. He was buried at 5 o'clock on Sunday. All three of them rest side by side now. In the next letter I shall give you a few more details about my angel children. Only when everything was quiet, when everything was over, I began to feel that I also was in need of rest. (111)

November 15, 1841

Now all wishes, all striving have been quieted! I even no longer wish to go back to you, to Germany! It is so painful to me. Up there where the angels live and where the Almighty is enthroned, it's probably singularly beautiful. There I will also find you all again! Until then we shall postpone our reunion. There it will be happier. —How I wish I could have said farewell to the world six weeks ago, if only the Good Lord would have considered it my time. I had been provided with the last sacrament. Even though my life, full of sin and weakness, made me fear, yet the hope was strong to find a gracious judge. I believe I could have been able to take leave of my husband and son. It really hit me too hard that I also had to lose little Rudolph. It had been twelve days since his dysentery had been over. I had already tried again to breast-feed him. I could only cry when (I had the little one in my lap) the neighbor entered with Franz's newly born child and announced that I was the godmother and asked me to select a name. The next day Rudolph died. The little one resembled his father and his deceased little sister so much. I myself sewed him his shroud. A lock from his curly head is all that is left of him for me. Oh, how lovely he was, how dear. Johanna always played so nicely with him. She was the pride of her father, an angel on earth. If Bruns had been out and she saw him, she would call, "Mother, Father!" and run quickly to meet him. Max followed a little more clumsily. If Bruns gave her an apple or something like that, she always said, "Hermann, Max!" and brought the gift to them joyfully. Twice she had a little doll (a rarity here), which everybody had to admire, and at night she held her in her arms. She was vain but easy to satisfy. A clean apron, a little kerchief pleased her. . . .

You see, dear Heinrich, that I do not tire of talking about the little ones. But you like to hear me pour out my heart. (112)

The years passed, and Jette bore seven more children. At times she felt "at odds with the entire world" (141), but she coped with challenges and bereavements. By the time she wrote the following letters, Jette had lost seven children, her husband, and other close relatives. Finally she faced the challenges and limitations of old age.

Jefferson City
APRIL 16, 1893

DEAR HEINRICH:

First I want to tell you that you really know how to appreciate a picture. While sitting for it I thought only of you, and I sat once more for you. What do the young people know of that? They think I would look this way at age ninety. The eye speaks to you although wrinkles and seriousness are probably frequently also there. In general I maintain a cheerful attitude, much of which can be explained by my generally good health. I really should be much more serious, and I tell myself every day that in the late fall I shall be eighty years old. In the morning I begin by singing the school song: "Mein erst Gefühl sei Preis und Dank" ["Let my first feeling be praise and thanks"]. But soon thereafter all kinds of gay and worldly thoughts occur. I live for the present, but I still enjoy reminiscing. I often tell myself that it could suddenly be that I will have finished my earthly career, and what good would I then have to show for the dark beyond?

It is true that what I have accomplished in earlier years, when I struggled and strove to fulfill my tasks, must be credited to me. Today I live quietly and in seclusion, for myself, and I have and seek no opportunity to do much good for mankind except for those nearest me. Every morning after breakfast I take the Thomas à Kempis (following the example of our dear father, who after church always first took *Philotea* and other devotional books in hand), and I try to remember something for the day. I would like to know whether St. Hieronymus and other hermits did not also find pleasure in contemplation of nature? For me, my thoughts immediately fly outside and far into the world. My reading does not only treat science and progress; I then make comparisons, and I find a lot is true, and I drop silly things. I really do not like to read a lot. It strains my eyes and in general does not give me much pleasure. I am becoming so indifferent. I would like to be able to look toward the future calmly. I cannot understand how many people, even quite pious people, have such a great fear of death. . . .

Best regards, soon more. I remain always with sincere love, your sister, Jette. (281–82)

Jefferson City
JULY 22, 1893

DEAR AUGUSTE:[14]

. . . Now we are in the middle of summer, and since spring was late and brought with it a long period of wet weather, there was an extraordinary amount of work to be done, of which Tillie particularly got her share.[15] I became stronger with moderate exercise outside. We are now both tired of it and threaten to do nothing. But the reward for our effort already shows in the great abundance in the garden. Several gallons of cauliflower were put into vinegar, as well as beans and cucumbers, and masses of raspberries were converted to jelly, even six quart jars for her sister. And then Tillie says I really did myself honor with raspberry vinegar, which is refreshing for the sick and cooling for the healthy. There is little fruit this year. Tillie bought a new horse, and so she can call for her husband daily at noon in the city. And in the evening we can go for a ride. (283)

Jefferson City, Mo.
NOVEMBER 25, 1893

DEAR HEINRICH:

It has been almost four weeks now since I celebrated my birthday, showered with attention. For three days I have been back here again where . . . my home is. And so I am sitting again in my own room, with everything so clean and orderly. My own bed, my own desk, many memories that have been guarded, my books, and a few dear pictures. . . .

A few weeks ago I was at the eye doctor's. He explained that my eyes were suffering, caused by something, and that he could not heal them, but that by treating them they probably would become somewhat strengthened. Thus I was discharged, to report back three months later. I must say that I still cannot get used to this. I am only permitted to read and write a little, but especially not in the evening. Also I am not allowed to do needlework. I am primarily to avoid things that would strain the eyes.

Many thanks for your congratulations on my birthday. You took the eightieth so seriously that I myself did too, and even though I did not get

14. Auguste was the wife of Jette's brother Heinrich.
15. Tillie (Ottilie), Jette's youngest daughter, had been a teacher before her marriage to Carl E. Hess.

to go to church, I still allowed for some serious meditation, a conclusion of times past, which lie behind me with their joy and sorrow and lead perhaps, of late, a short distance downhill to the end of my earthly career. Well, that is all right, if only I could tear myself gradually, peaceably, and quietly away. However, there is still much that pleases me greatly and much that worries me. After all, I need not be indifferent to the fate of my fellow men, my beloved ones. . . . Farewell, my dear faithful brother. If only I could do something good for you to raise your spirits, to make it easier for you.

FROM THE BOTTOM OF MY HEART,
YOUR SISTER JETTE (286–87)

Jefferson City, Mo.
JUNE 10, 1894

DEAR HEINRICH:

. . . You still go out for rides, and at night you always have a nurse, and you have very crooked legs. I am after all much better off, and I should console myself with that, and yet I cannot be resigned that my eyesight is so weak that I am permitted to read so little. I have to let everything be done for me. However, every morning I look gratefully at the trees outside, I look at the tapestry and the pictures to see whether they are clear, and then I have my meditation for the day, as our father did, and then if possible I go outside.

At the request of the eye doctor I was recently in St. Louis again, the third time. He now gives no hope for special improvement. (And, after all, how should that be, at my age?) However, I again got some drops, and I am to report back to him later. The worst thing is that I lack something to do. Here in the house it is very quiet. Ottilie only rarely allows me to assist her in the household. In the evening there is some reading for recreation or the two of us talk. When Carl is there, he listens quietly or he speaks in English with his wife. The hard times have brought him losses, and so he cannot control his moods. . . .

The bad times continue. Great numbers of unemployed (mostly tramps) move about and force the railroads to carry them. The military should really interfere. No groups have yet passed here. Daily, however, hungry people pass, and they always receive something here. You do not know such things. In all bigger cities here, organizations have been created to give the fathers of families work and bread. . . .

A postscript to this letter is addressed to her sister-in-law Auguste:

. . . Ottilie is too lonesome here. She admits it herself. Gradually she is getting to be just like her husband. They lead the lives of real hermits. To be sure, besides us two people she has two cows and a calf, approximately one hundred fifty chickens, eight cats, and a flock of singing birds in addition to three canaries. And then the place is so beautiful. A big catalpa tree is in full blossom. There are bushes, flowers, and vegetables, which are arranged between fresh stretches of grass. Only there is no fruit this year except some berries. Should this not be sufficient, and should not one be able to live without worries? (287–89)

St. Louis
JANUARY 4, 1895

DEAR HEINRICH:

So now we have entered the new year, and in spite of my resolution to send you greetings before that time, it was not done. You will have got together for Christmas and New Year's, and in spirit I was with you!

In person I have been here with Effie for over a month and am quite satisfied with the change.[16] Mother and sons are very considerate and are constantly thinking of entertaining me since the loss of my sight takes away all my pastimes. Usually I knit with closed eyes, I occupy myself in the house, and that is all. People read to me, they play for me. In the evening they play cards. Recently I contracted a cold, had rheumatism, and was quite impatient with that. I think less of your long-lasting suffering than of my Wilhelm.[17] You have a wife, children, little nuns, who surround you, who console you and seek to give you relief. He, however, was struggling for months by himself, was starving, and was only barely supported by Louis until he was confined to a hospital for two months and recuperated. It is not astonishing that I would have liked to venture on a trip. Now he writes that he is employed on a range and hopes for better times and hopes that he can visit me in another year. I thank God for the consoling news. . . .

God protect you and bless you with relief and many good things that are unforeseen for the New Year. For myself, I wish that I may have patience and humility for that which may befall me. All here send their greetings with those of your sister Jette. (293–94)

St. Louis
JUNE 6, 1895

DEAR, DEAR AUGUSTE:

So, suddenly the inescapable has happened, and you stand alone. In spite of the many troubles your dear husband brought you, he was also

16. "Effie" was Jette's daughter Euphemia, the widow of Ernest William Decker II.
17. Jette's sons Wilhelm and Louis (Ludwig) were living in the Northwest. She visited them in Seattle in 1891.

a support to you. I have to put myself in your position; you do not at all know what is to be done and are completely lost. In the beginning the news of his death shook me very much.

Now I am calm, and I do not begrudge him relief from his misery and eternal rest—or you the freedom and the end to the many troubles and worries you had for him for so many years, and during which you relieved his pain so very much. I have to tell you that I shall always be grateful to you for this. (296)

One of Jette's final letters was to her sister-in-law Auguste, written in 1897. She described her daily routine, which began with prayer and the Ave Maria.

JUNE 10, 1897

. . . My vase is filled with the most beautiful roses, a smaller one with carnations and heliotrope. I frequently put my nose into them with pleasure. Then I put my hands in my lap and think. Involuntarily the melody of a hymn or a worldly song comes to mind and I drum the beat with my hands or feet. (298)

On November 8, 1899, Ottilie wrote to her aunt that at 6:45 the preceding evening, "our dear mother closed her eyes forever" (300).

Margaret Gilmore Kelso (1855–1948)

*M*ost of the early settlers of Greene County, Missouri, came from Tennessee, prepared to work hard establishing farms and towns. "They were poor but honest," writes an early historian. The undulating landscape, the clear streams, and the woods filled with game had been enjoyed by Delaware, Kickapoo, and Osage Indians. As settlers from the East cultivated the land, the Indians migrated, returning each fall to hunt and fish. By the mid-1840s "improvements finally became so numerous and the pale faces so thick that they no longer found pleasure in their woodland and prairie life in their old haunts, and their visits ceased."[1]

The name Boone figures prominently in Missouri history, including that of Greene County. Nathan Boone brought his large family to Ash Grove, west of Springfield. Others who settled nearby in the 1830s were the grandparents and parents of Margaret Gilmore Kelso. Her father, James Kannon Gilmore (1827–1923), born in Tennessee, settled east of Ash Grove. He and his wife, Sophronia Edmonson (1831–1920), had twelve children, of whom Margaret was the fourth.[2] All the places Margaret mentions in her memoirs are close to each other, north and west of Springfield: Walnut Grove, where her mother's family lived; Clear Creek, where Margaret was born in a log cabin in 1855; Ebenezer, where the family lived in the early 1860s; Hackney Mills, where her husband took his grain; and Mount Pleasant, where she was a faithful member of the Baptist Church.[3]

As a child, Margaret saw her father labor in the fields by day and in the gleam of a grease lamp by night. Her mother, grandmothers, and aunts labored no less with their traditional work. Children had their chores also, as the family made do with limited means. Margaret's playfulness and love of mimicry sometimes got her into trouble, but discipline was swift and expectations of proper behavior were unequivocal. Living in a cabin with a dirt floor, extracting dye from nuts and stones, going barefoot in every season but winter, and making coffee from corn, wheat, and rye were all conditions of a way of life—not causes for complaint.

On February 9, 1873, in the same log cabin where she had been born, Margaret married Jacob Thomas Kelso. Jake's family, like hers, had come to the county from Tennessee in the 1830s. Born in 1848, Jake became a farmer. He and Margaret had twelve children, of whom daughters Flora and Grace died in the flu epidemic during World War I, while Mollie died

1. *An Illustrated Historical Atlas Map of Greene County, Mo.,* 18.
2. Two of the children were stillborn.
3. Organized in 1836, the Mount Pleasant Baptist Church was one of the first Baptist churches in southwestern Missouri. The name Gilmore appears among the list of original members (*History of Greene County, Missouri,* 715).

in 1922. The other five daughters and four sons outlived their mother.[4] Although she did occasional work as a practical nurse, Margaret spent most of her life at home with her family. The two unmarried daughters, Pearl and Frances, kept house for their mother. Margaret was a cheerful, friendly, and strong-willed woman. Eventually she became deaf and unable to walk, but as long as possible before her death in 1948 she relished her role as family storyteller.

After years of telling about the old days, Margaret Gilmore Kelso decided to write her memoirs. In contrast to the immediacy, spontaneity, and privacy of diaries and of letters written to one person, memoirs offer an interpretation of the past intended for a group of readers. Mrs. Kelso wrote hers as a family history, not an autobiography. Rich in descriptions of material details of rural life, character sketches of family members, and colorful anecdotes, this document is also a valuable source of historical information.[5] Writing with pencil in a Big Chief tablet, Mrs. Kelso spent about three years on this project, beginning at the age of eighty-three. She added a final entry nine years later.

Family, home, work—these are the themes of Margaret's life story. She states that she always lived within four miles of her birthplace.[6] The story may have a narrow focus geographically, but Margaret Gilmore Kelso held a broad view of history and social change. She recalled the abundant natural resources of the Ozarks in her youth, and felt proud of her pioneer ancestors. Although she enjoyed a happy childhood, she witnessed the tragic consequences of war. Margaret recalled the past fondly, but she lived in the present, content with the progress that made life comfortable in her old age. The editors present this selection as an example of the emotional balance and perspective of an older woman, who drew upon her remarkable memory and dramatic flair to leave a vivid record of life in the Ozarks.

4. At the time of her death, Mrs. Kelso was survived by nine children, two sisters, twenty-four grandchildren, twenty-two great-grandchildren, and one great-great-grandchild (Obituary, *Springfield Leader-Press*, August 4, 1948). For additional information on the family we thank Robert K. Gilmore, Fern Nance Shumate, and Paul Jones.

5. Quotations appear in the exhibit of the History Museum for Springfield–Greene County. Excerpts have been published in *Ozarks Watch* for fall 1990, and spring/summer 1991. Fern Nance Shumate, wife of Mrs. Kelso's grandson Ronald Shumate, made a number of typed transcripts of the memoirs in 1958. She normalized the punctuation, which consisted of only commas. One of the transcripts, entitled "Family History," was donated to the History Museum for Springfield–Greene County by Professor Robert K. Gilmore, Mrs. Kelso's great-nephew. This copy is the source of selected passages presented here, with the permission of the Museum and Mrs. Kelso's descendants. Page numbers refer to this typescript.

6. Actually the Kelsos lived in Kansas for a while in 1879, near the town of Lazette. They staked a claim close to the farm of John Kelso, Jake's brother, but returned to Missouri because Jake was seriously injured when a horse kicked him in the face and hip.

Often I have been asked to write a memory story of my life and have hesitated to do so because I have had so little schooling. I grew up in the time of the Civil War.

Eighty-three years ago, I was born on May 6, 1855, in the old log cabin home on Clear Creek. I was married in that same log cabin on Feb. 9, 1872 [1873], to Jacob Thomas Kelso. Uncle Jack Justice read the ceremony. He came from the preaching service at Mt. Pleasant.

The school houses were few and far between and we had to walk three and four miles. In the wintertime, through mud, slush and snow to a one room, poorly equipped school house. We used slabs for benches. There was a little square opening in one of the side walls of the building to furnish light. There was no blackboard and we used slates.

I was too young to do much figuring, but I used to beg to borrow a slate at noontime from the older pupils and drew pictures of men, women and animals. I admired my work very much, but I don't think anyone but myself could have decided what my drawings were intended to represent.

This story, I know, will have many mistakes in spelling, phrasing and punctuation, but it is true, every word. We lived in what we called the "Ozarks," which is the garden spot of Missouri, called the "Land of Smiles." Fine fertile land, beautiful scenery, many fine springs of cold sparkling water, rivers and lakes in which fish abound. . . .

Our first settlers in the Ozarks were almost all from Tennessee. Many of them came from the same county and the same neighborhood, and they settled and lived near each other here in Greene County. When I first remember, almost every family lived in a log cabin. Our pioneer fathers looked for a spring first, and then homesteaded the land. Almost all of them settled in the timbered area. Later settlers came from Ohio and Kentucky and settled the prairies.

I have heard my mother say that when she and father went to housekeeping they moved into an unfinished log cabin, on a dirt floor and built a fire in the wash kettle, until father could make a fireplace and build a stick chimney and daub it with mud. She made her beds on the dirt floor until he could get time to bore holes in the log walls and put in poles, with the bark on, to make a frame for her beds.

When she got her beds made up on these pole frames and spread on her clean covers that she had made by hand in blue and white patterns, woven from wool; washed, carded and spun into yarn by herself, she stood off and admi[r]ed her room and beds and thought they were so pretty. She was so proud of it . . . (1)

When I was a child and my father had occasion to go to Springfield, he went on horseback. Sometimes I begged to go with him. He would spread a blanket on behind his saddle and put me up behind him and take me along. We traveled about four miles through timber, winding along the rocky road, then we came into "Grand Prairie." From there we just traveled in the general direction, through the tall prairie grass toward Springfield. I don't recall a field, a fence or a house until we were in what would be the suburbs of what is now Springfield. There was one house there at the time, on what is now the public square. . . .

My father led me around by the hand until his errand[s] were finished then he would buy a little "poke" of cheese and crackers and we would eat it on the way home. We started in the early morning and were back home at about sundown. The trip was about twenty-five miles each way. . . .

I think the first remembrance I have of my mother was of waking one night and seeing her sewing . . . by the light of a grease lamp, stuck in a crack in the chimney wall. The stem turned [u]p at the end to hang it by. It held about two tablespoons full of grease. Sometimes we tore a strip of cloth, doubled it back, then twisting it, pushed it down in the grease for a wick. It made a light, but a very poor one. My father sat nearby making shoes for the family by the same poor light. We wore those home-made shoes until I was a big girl, about twelve years old before I ever had a pair of "store-bought" shoes.

One day my father went to Springfield and bought all of us a pair of shoes. He tried them on our feet. He felt my foot over and said he thought they were a little too small. He thought he had better take them back. I told him, "No, they are a good fit." He let me keep them, but they were too small and almost ruined my feet. I was afraid that if they went back I would never get another pair of store-bought shoes.

We went barefooted until about Christmas. We had to make one pair of shoe[s] last until it was warm enough to go barefooted in the Spring. Our feet would chap and crack open and bleed, and mother would make a salve of mutton tallow and turpentine and bind it over our feet and heal them overnight.

I remember so clearly, seeing my father make fire. He made a little nest of cotton on the fire shovel and put about a teaspoon of gunpowder on it. He then made fine shavings from a piece of pine and stacked it around the cotton. He then took two pieces of flint and struck the edges together over the powder until the sparks caught and made a flame. He then built the shavings around it and soon had a fire going. We had no matches at that time, and everyone tried to keep a little fire covered in the fireplace. If it happened to go out, then we either had to make a fire again or go to a neighbors. We called it borrowing fire.

I remember one morning when mother got up the fire was out. She wakened me and I started on the run to borrow fire. I went to Uncle George Thomas's place. On the way, the wild turkeys were coming off the roost and running out into the road ahead of me. . . . I went on to

Mr. Thomas's place, got my fire between two long pieces of bark and ran all the way home. When I reached home, mother was standing at the door waiting for the fire, which was blazing and soon had breakfast ready. . . .

Passenger pigeons had a roost on our place. We had a strip of young timber, about three or four acres, I suppose, and the pigeons came over to roost there of evenings. They came from the west and the noise of their wings was like distant thunder. They came in such numbers it was like a dark cloud. I liked to stand in the doorway and watch them. They were flying low as they neared the roost. I often went down to the roost after they had settled. They were so thick on the limbs that they bent the trees almost to the ground. I could have picked them off by the hundreds if I had wanted to. I would stroke their wings and they would coo and let me pet them. They sat on limbs as close as grapes on the vine, and at times would break the young trees and limbs down with their weight.

When they cleared away in the morning, there would be crippled pigeons, some with broken wings, others with broken legs. We would take them to the house to use for meat. They were so good. . . .

I have s[e]en father walk on his knees to cut wheat with the reaphook. Mother quilted pads for his knees, and when he threshed our grain, he tossed it onto a big canvas threshing floor and started the horses round and round to tramp out the grain. He would pour the grain into the old fanning mill and blow the chaff away. One evening father was building a rail pen and lining it with straw to store the wheat in, and when he reached down to pick up a rail that was on the ground, there was a big rattlesnake stretched along the side of the rail. Father killed it with a pitchfork. He then skinned it, and its hide was covered with fat. Mother fried out the oil and saved it in a bottle for rheumatism. A man from Illinois wanted to buy it for his wife, who had rhe[u]matism. Father gave it to him. The skin of the snake was stuffed with bran and kept on the mantle for a long time. It measured the full length of the mantle. . . .

Snakes surely were plentiful. . . . One morning I went to the spring to get the milk for breakfast. We had a little well built where we dipped the water. It was covered by boards and we kept our milk there. I got down on my knees and reached my hand in to get the bucket of milk and a great big old moccasin slid down over my hand into the water. It had been coiled under the boards. If you ever have a snake touch you, you will never forget the feel of it. It is like an icicle sliding over you.

A long time afterwards we were staying all night with Henry and Gusty [Augusta] Kelso. The weather was hot and I had my feet outside the covers. Toward morning I felt a snake crawl over my foot. I lay perfectly still, trying not to move until Henry got up. When he passed through the room, I said, "Henry, be careful, there is a snake in the house . . . one crawled over my foot last night." Gusta said, "Margaret, what do you mean, a snake in the house?" I said, "Yes, a snake crawled over my foot." They began to search, and found the snake lying stretched along the wall at the foot of the bed. I knew it was a snake for I had never forgotten the feel of the old moccasin that had crawled over my hand. . . .

One time I was going to take father a drink. He was making rails in the timber, and I met a deer in the road. It was crippled. Some hunters had shot it and broke one of its forelegs. Poor thing, it had such a hunted sad look. Its tongue was out, and it looked almost human out of its eyes. I never think about that little deer but I feel sad. It was a doe and not very large. It had run to the creek and stood in the deep water. The hounds bayed, and the hunters followed on and shot it. One of the men was Mr. Jim Grantham. He sent us a quarter of venison. . . .

Before the Civil War my father moved to Ebenezer. There was a good school there that he wanted to send us children to. We were not there very long until the war broke out and he moved back to the farm, but we were there long enough to get a little bit of schooling. We had a big house and mother kept regular boarders and overnigh[t] travelers. There was one man stayed overnight by the name of Scott. He slept upstairs and made a terrible noise snoring. That noise scared me so bad I cried and cried. My father took me in his arms and walked about with me. I kept crying, and he finally took me up the stairs and showed the man to me. He was lying on his back with his mouth wide open, sno[r]ing until he could have been heard a block away. I was not scared anymore after I saw what made the noise.

A Mr. and Mrs. Avery taught the school and boarded with us. They made a pet of me, and Mrs. Avery taught me a little piece to speak. She had me make gestures, but I can only remember two lines of the piece now. She had me say, "These little hands, no work can do," and place my hands together. "This little mind is feeble, too," and place my hand on my forehead. There was quite a bit more of it, but I can't remember it. I did it just as she taught me, when she took me to school, and had me stand up and speak the piece. The grown-ups stomped their feet, clapped their hands and laughed until they were red in the face. I stood there after I had finished, wondering what in the world was the matter with them, until the teacher came and led me to my seat.

After we went home, father had me stand and say it for him. But he wanted me to say, "These little hands, some work can do." I stood there a long time while he tried to get me to change it. I kept telling him that was not the way, and I never did say it the way he wanted me to. I don't know when I learned to read, but he used to have me stand and read the newspapers to people. I think he must have been real proud of me. (3–7)

The first piece of money I ever owned was a $5.00 gold piece. I found it while we lived at Ebenezer. Grandfather and Grandmother Edmonson came from Walnut Grove to visit us in a borrowed buggy. A buggy was a very rare thing then, and we children were sitting in it looking it over and making the seat spring up and down. We picked up a piece of covering from the floor. I saw something bright and p[i]cked it up and ran into the house to show it. Grandfather looked at it and told me it was a $5.00 gold piece, and asked me where I found it. I told him and he said it was not his, but he would take it and show it to the man who owned the buggy. If it was not his then it would be mine. Nobody claimed it, and he said he would give me a $5.00 greenback for it. I looked at both pieces of money for quite a while, and finally decided that the paper money was so much larger, I would be making a good trade. So I gave grandfather the gold piece, and he gave me the greenback. I felt richer than I have ever felt since, or ever will. . . .

The first oath I ever heard, was while we lived at Ebenezer. There was a man stayed overnight, and in the morning he was grooming his horse. He was wiping down his front feet when his watch fell out of his vest pocket, and the horse stepped on it, breaking the crystal. He picked the watch up, looked at it and said, "God damn it." I didn't know it was wrong. I just thought it was something to say when I was mad. So the first thing that went wrong with me, I said, "God damn it." Mother heard me and got a little switch, and cured me completely of wanting to say words like that when I was mad. I don't think I ever said the word again, or ever wanted to. . . .

. . . There was an old woman by the name of Bristow. She was short and fat and always had a bundle of some sort on her hip when she came, and carried one when she went away, half bent as she limped along. I was always a kind of mimic and made the other children laugh. One day I got a bundle on my hip, bent over, and went limping off and said, "Here goes old Mrs. Bristow." Mother heard me, and called me to her, and she certainly gave me a good switching. I can almost feel the sting yet on my legs. That cured me of ever making fun of old people. . . .

. . . I was at Ebenezer when Francis and Pa and mother lived there, and saw the old place where we used to live. The house had burned down years ago, but there were two big trees standing in the yard. I went to the old spring and took a drink from it. It looked so desolate and alone. The place where we went to school was made over into a church. When we lived there, one night an old negro man preached at the school house. My father went with us to hear him preach. While he talked he made gestures with his hands, and I noticed that his hands were white inside and black outside. I asked father why his hands were white. That was a hard question to answer. (7–9)

When we moved back to the old home on Clear Creek, at the beginning of the war, in 1861, my father joined the "Home Guard" and was a staunch

Union man.[7] We suffered from the raiding of what we called the "Secesh" [Confederate sympathizers]. I remember one time when father was away, there was a forage train of I don't know how many wagons. They took all the corn we had in the crib and all the hay we had. They also went into the smoke house and filled one wagon box full of meat. . . . The foragemaster paid mother in Confederate money. It was perfectly worthless, he knew, but he put up a good show of being honest.

While General Price occupied Springfield, after the Battle of Wilson Creek,[8] two men came to our place, went to the barn lot and caught a horse we all loved. He was a fine dapple gray that we called old Jim. . . . How we children hated to see Old Jim go. . . .

The bushwhackers also raided our house.[9] They were men who did not belong to either army, and kept themselves hid away in caves and in the deep woods, and were mostly Union sympathizers. They went on raiding parties when they knew the women would be at home alone. They had their lookouts and their get-together signals, and we could hear their whistles and horns when they were planning a raid. They usually disguised themselves and dressed in Union uniform.

One evening, in the fall, we were at the barn lot milking. Four men came riding up to the gate, dressed in blue uniforms of the Union soldiers. We thought they were soldiers coming to spend the night, until one of them jerked the gate off its hinges and rode right over it. Three of them rode in and one kept watch at the gate. Mother stopped milking, and when we reached the house they were tearing up the beds, emptying trunks and boxes on the floor and taking everything they happened to want. . . . Then one of them cocked his pistol in mother's face and shoved her about the room, saying, "Tell me where your money is!," but mother kept insisting there was no money in the house.

One of them threw a shovel of fire from the fireplace onto the floor, scattering it all over. Mother very carefully swept it up. They scattered another shovelful, which she swept back into the fireplace. She was so mad at the scattered fire she would not let them see that she was badly frightened. . . .

7. James K. Gilmore was commissioned in Company I of the 72d regiment of the Missouri Militia in February 1863, and left the regiment in 1864 (*History of Greene County, Missouri*, 427).

8. On August 10, 1861, General Nathaniel Lyon, leading the Union troops, made a surprise attack on Confederate forces near Wilson's Creek. During the battle Lyon was mortally wounded. By afternoon the Confederates, with their superior numbers, were in control. The Union troops retreated to Springfield, and two days later the Confederates, led by General Sterling Price, occupied that city.

9. Mrs. Kelso says that "bushwhackers" were usually Union sympathizers, but it is more common to use that term for Southern sympathizers. Antislavery raiders who crossed into Missouri from Kansas were called "jayhawkers," and gradually that term was applied to any group of Union sympathizers who robbed and terrorized private citizens.

They took their plunder, stopped at the door and cursed mother and told her if she reported them before morning they "would come back and burn the damn house down over our damn heads." They said they didn't care what she did the next morning as they would be in Arkansas by then.

Sister Melissa was crying and one of the men stuck his head back into the house and said, "What you crying about, Sissie?" She said, "I want my new shoes back." All of the shoes had been hanging on the wall, and they had taken every pair of them. He said, he couldn't give them back to her as number fourteens would just fit his wife in Arkansas.

They had gone [no] further than the gate when mother had a big lump of brown sugar, about the size of a teacup in each hand, holding it out to my brother Jimmie and myself, telling us she would give them to us if we would go by the path, the short way over the hill, to our nearest neighbors and tell them the "Bushwhackers" were coming. Money was scarce then, and sugar was high. Scared as we were, the BIG lump of sugar was a great temptation to us, so we took it and ran through the dark as fast as we could go to warn our neighbors. . . . They began loading their pistols, and the women began to hide things, and we started on our way home.

We crossed the lot, and were just about to climb the fence into the road when we heard the robbers coming. They were riding slow and talking low. We dropped down into the fence corner and hardly breathed until they had passed. They went a little ways past us, then stopped and talked low for quite a while, then rode on and passed the corner, turned toward the house and stopped and talked again. Then they turned back past the place where we were hiding. At the corner, they took another road and went to Aunt Lucinda Gilmore's home and robbed her. She was alone. Uncle John had not been dead very long, and she kept his clothes in a little side room. They were taking his clothing, his hat, and his gun. She clung to his gun and begged them to let her keep her husband's things. They knocked her down and kicked her, breaking her ribs, and beat her over the head with the butt of the gun. When Aunt Lucinda heard the bushwhackers had been to our place, she came over to see us. I can see her yet, as she sat there in the chimney corner, crying and telling us how they had abused her, and how bruised and battered she was. How black her poor face was! It was just as black as flesh can be. She died a few days after she visited me, from the terrible beating they had given her. . . .

The day the Wilson Creek Battle was fought, on August 10, 1861, my mother walked the floor all day, and wrung her hands and cried, until the noise of the big guns ceased. It must have been five o'clock in the evening before she got us anything to eat. We children were too young to understand, and followed her around and begged her to tell us why she cried. She would place her hands on our heads and say, "Oh, children,

Oh, children!" My brother and I would lay our heads on the ground, and we could hear the guns and feel the earth tremble.

In later years we could understand mother's grief, as her relatives and friends were divided in ideals and politics. . . .

Mother always thought she knew the hooded men who came to raid us time after time. She thought they were men who lived in the neighborhood, as we could hear unexplained signals and they were always just before raids. What they took from us on these occasions represented much hard work, and many times was the difference between us being able to eat, and starving.

They wanted money, but never did find any. The money was in a big, green jug-shaped bottle with a large neck and mouth, and it was nearly full of gold and silver coins. Mother always told the raiders, "There is no money in the house," and that was true . . . there was no money in the house. It was hid in the ash-hopper. I saw the bottle, with the money in it, after the war was over. . . .

After General Lyon was killed at Wilson Creek, his soldiers passed the Uncle Hope Skeen place on a forced march. The neighborhood gathered to see them pass by, and to serve them coffee and a bit of something to eat. The we[a]ther was hot, and the poor, tired soldiers were black in the face with dust and sweat. . . . Now and then one would drop out of the ranks and fall down under the shade of a big tree that stood in the yard near the road. The women would run with cups of coffee and pie or ginger cakes, or whatever they had, and the poor soldiers would rest on their elbows while they ate. After they rested a bit, they would fall in line again. They marched four abreast all day and were still going by when we went home about sundown. I never pass that place now, but I think of those poor tired soldiers, black with dust and sweat. (9–12)

Before the war some of the slaves had a hard time. I have heard the cries of the poor slaves from three miles away, when their masters were plying the whip. "Oh Lordy, Massa, don't kill me, please don't kill me, Massa!"

After the war was over, a colony of negroes settled on some railroad land near where we lived at Cave Springs. The old mammy colored women worked for my mother; washed for her or helped her with any kind of work, when she needed them. We did our washing at the spring, and I helped Mammy Cinda. I dipped water, kept the fire going under the wash kettle, and helped her hang out the clothes and things like that.

One day, she sat down to rest and smoke her pipe, and I noticed a big cord-like scar below the back of her neck, where her dress pulled down. I said, "Aunt Cinda, what made those terrible scars?" and she said, "Oh law, chile, I could show you sights." She unbuttoned her dress and pulled it down to her waist. Her back had literally been cut to pieces. It had healed in rope-like cords all over her back. I said, "What made that, Aunt Cinda?" and she said, "It's whar ole Massa whipped me." Well, I said, "He just about killed you, didn't he?" She said, "They turned me on a sheet for weeks." I often think now of the poor slaves. It is no wonder they followed Abraham in the streets, crying, "God bless Massa Linkum, God bless Massa Linkum." . . .

I attended a Baptist Association as a delegate a few years ago. There was a colored preacher present, soliciting funds for a negro school. . . . When the time came for him to make his talk, one of the white preachers asked him if he would sing for us, while the voluntary offering was taken up. He said, "Yes, I will be delighted to sing. We colored folk all know you white folks can't sing." He stepped down from the rostrum and sang, "Swing Low, Sweet Chariot," and I don't think there was a dry eye in the house when he had finished. What strides this race has made since they were set free—it seems almost like a miracle. When I remember them as they were when I was a child—so poor, so pitifully ignorant, and now they are keeping pace with the best of them.

In those early days, the women were brave and helped each other in every way that they could. The night was never too dark, or too cold for them to go to a neighbor in distress. We would hear a "Hello" at the gate, and some neighbor would be there with a horse for mother to ride, and many times she would be gone for several days at a time helping a neighbor woman as midwife.

Everyone worked in the fields, women and children too, and helped to plant and gather in the crops. Often I have looked across the fields in the evenings, when the day's work was done, and wondered if I could possibly get back to the house, I would be so tired.

My little brother, who was two years younger, and I plowed with the old ox team. We plowed with Old Lamb and Brandy, our faithful old oxen. The plow was heavy and hard for me to handle at the corners, and brother walked along beside with a long switch in his hand, to keep the oxen going. They moved so slow, but one hot day our old ox team ran away with us. We begged and pleaded with them to stop, but they paid no attention to us. We drove them by the "gee, whoa, and haw" method. That day they paid no attention to our "whoa" and ran right on, bolted right through the bats at the gate, plow and all, right on into the creek, and stood in the deep water clear up their sides. We stood on the bank and begged and pleaded with them to come out of the water. But they stood there until they were all cooled off, and were good and ready to come out. After they got cool, and drank their fill, they finally decided it was time to go back to work, so out they came, dragging the plow with them. . . .

. . . My little b[ro]ther was about six, and I was about eight and a half years old. That sort of work was cruelly hard on little children of our age, but it was war-time, and there was no other way to get the work done. . . .

My mother gave me wool rolls to spin, and let me have thread to knit socks and mittens for the soldiers. She taught me to shape them and let me have the money I sold them for. We knit of night, and kept the spinning wheel going, too. We could spin a nicer, more even thread when the doors were closed and the room warm. (12–14)

Mrs. Kelso provides information about her marriage to Jake Kelso and their children: Erna, Arthur, Victor, Eddie, Pearl, Frances, Lester, Jennie, Flora, Gracie, Mollie, and Rosa.

Rosa and Jennie used to keep me in hot water. They had a habit of wandering away. Once I missed Rosa and walked and ran in every direction all over the pastures and fields. . . . [Willies Barker] found her up near the Neaves place, over two miles away. He asked her where she was going, and she said she was going to find Jake. She always called her father Jake, and I had to start calling him "Pa" myself to break her of the habit. . . .

They would go and rob my hen's nests, and if I set a hen they would break all the eggs to see if they were hatching. One time, for ever so long, I could find no eggs when I would go to gather them of an evening. Then I decided the hens had stolen their nests out somewhere, so began to search for the nests. I found a place where four trees had branched out from the roots of a stump, and there was a large hollow place in between where the trees had grown around it. It would hold a bushel or more, and it was almost full of egg batter. The sticks Rosa and Jennie had stirred it with were in it. They had been making "custard" and having a fine time. (8)

While we lived on the Thompson place, one hot evening in the summer, an old woman came to the door. She didn't offer to come in, but told me she was selling medicine, and that it was a dollar a bottle, and it would cure rheumatism. The weather was so hot, and I saw she was very tired, and asked her to come in and stay with us over Sunday. She said, "Ye are very kind," and came in, put aside her little sailor hat and satchel, and wiped the sweat from her face. When supper was ready, she sat down at the table, folded her hands and gave thanks. When she finished eating, she patted my shoulder and thanked me for the supper, and that night she knelt down to pray at her bedside. . . .

When she was preparing to leave on Sunday morning, I said to her, "This is the 4th of July, you won't find anyone at home today. Just stay over with me until tomorrow, and I will give you some soap and you can start a fire down by the spring, and wash all the clothes you have on. I will give you a change of clothing to put on while you do it, and you can have a bath and nice clean clothing to start out again with."

She was so pleased, and ironed all her clothing so nice. Her skin was so clear and smooth. I touched her arm and said, "What pretty skin you have." She said, "Ye have been kind to me—I believe I will tell you the story of my life." . . .

The woman told that she and her husband emigrated from Denmark. After her husband's death, she and her son settled in Nebraska. During a plague of grasshoppers she sent the little boy for help, but he disappeared. She spent the rest of her life on the road, selling rheumatism medicine and searching for her son.

When she started away the next morning, she kissed my face, my neck, and my hands, and said, "Ye have been kind to me, and I have prayed for ye, that when ye come to Heaven's Gate, an Angel will open and let you in." Poor woman, I have always felt that was one time when I entertained an angel unawares. A few months afterward, I read of her death. A train had run over her at Verona. . . . It was supposed that she had sat down to rest and had fallen asleep on the railroad tracks.

Wishing that we would never have to live through another war had nothing to do with the actual state of things. We did have to see another— World War I. Lester [her son] went away to that war, and it [s]eemed to me if he was just going somewhere else, I could stand it, while he was away, but not going to war! The terrible suspense of it! I think the mothers who were left at home must have suffered as much as the boys who went away. I knit sox, sweaters, scarves and mitts for the soldiers. The Red Cross furnished the wool, and every mother knit as fast as fingers could fly. . . .

I had a dream during the World War, or it was more of a vision, as I saw it. I was standing in the yard looking toward the west, and I saw white doves coming over in great numbers, and flying low. They seemed low enough I could almost touch them. I reached up both hands and they just eluded me, and I said, "I do believe they are going to roost right here." I heard a voice say, "No, they will roost further on," and I stood watching until they had gone from sight, flying toward the east. After they had all gone on, I saw a dark object far in the west. I stood watching, trying to make out what it was. It came nearer, and hung suspended over me. It was an American Eagle, stripped of all flesh and feathers, except a few ragged feathers in the tip of each wing. There was a big, black, gaunt, hungry wolf sitting on its haunches, snapping and biting at those ragged feathers.

I have always felt that the vision meant something, and have tried to interpret it. I have it figured like this. The white dove is the emblem of peace; the American Eagle the emblem of our nation; the wolf the emblem of hunger. I believe I am living to see my dream interpreted.

When we thought peace was here, we had no peace. Peace seems further on. Our nation is being stripped to the bone, and men are walking the streets today, jobless and hungry. We can only pray for peace.

I am now eighty-five years of age. When I decided to write my story, I was eighty-three. Then I hardly knew where to begin. Now I can hardly find a place to stop. So many dear pioneer faces keep asking to be remembered. So many things keep crowding in, clamoring for expression, filling my mind with early day history, bringing loads and loads of "food for thought" to fill the later years of my life. . . .

I have lived a long time, and I consider this a wonderful period of progress. It is a far cry from the ox team to the automobile, and the flying machine; from the Indian trails to the paved highway; from the log schoolhouse to the well-equipped consolidated school; from the weekly mail delivered to the postoffice on horseback, to the daily mail delivered to our door; from the grease lamp used by our pioneer ancestors, hung from a crack in the chimney wall, to the incandescent light.

The improvement over the old ways is so great, I certainly am not among those who are crying for the "good old days." I have had more comfort in my latter days than I ever had before. I do not yearn for the inconveniences of past years.

My greatest disappointment has been that I could not do more for my children. My greatest [s]orrow was to see some of them die. I do not think of death now, as I did. I have come to feel it is a good thing we can die. I have seen so terribly much suffering, and only death can set us free.

We bought this place here, and received the deed the day of the armistice, November 11, 1918. I named it "PEACE VALLEY." I have always loved it here. It has been nearer what I wanted from life than anything we ever had before—more room, and more comfort. . . .

My father, James Kannon Gilmore, was ninety-six years of age when he died. My mother, Sophronia Edmonson Gilmore, was eighty-nine. Those dear old pioneer fathers and mothers . . . how wonderful they were! What a splendid heritage they have left us. How I wish my pen could do justice to their memory.

Our mail, in the early years, after the postoffice in Springfield was established in 1833, was brought in once a month from Harrison's place on the Little Piney River. . . . Uncle Joe Goodin kept the postoffice about four miles from where we lived. We went about once a week to get our mail. It was delivered there on horseback, in saddle pouches. We seldom received a letter. Sometimes we would get a newspaper. Grandma Goodin saved any reading matter for us that she could. We would get it through Aunt Mary Woodard, her daughter. Sometimes she would send us a paper from New York, all full of pictures and crime stories. We had to hide it from father, as he would not allow us to read it, if he knew it. I don't suppose it was very choice reading matter for children, but we were so hungry for the colored pictures and anything to read, I guess it was good for us anyway. At least it was better than having nothing at all to read.

I have often thought, in my earlier years, that I wished the time would come when I could read all I wanted to. It has come now, and so much of everything good to read, and so cheap. But now I can't see, only the plainest print. Most of it is too fine for my eyes, and what a disappointment that is, I am so hungry to read. My hearing is not so good either, now. I am soon to follow father, mother, brothers, sisters, husband and some children to the grave.

I won a silver and gold medal, after my hair was gray, in a "Matron's W.C.T.U." contest at Springfield by giving a "Temperance" reading. I am now in my ninety-second year and living on borrowed time. I was born, grew up and lived within four miles of where I now live. I have suffered every bereavement a woman could suffer, and still live on. . . .

When I look back over my life, I can truly say that I have tried to do my best, but I have made many, many mistakes. But with intelligence, the means, and the strength I had I don't see where I could have done much differently. I wish, with all my heart, that I could recall every impatient act, every unkind word, thought and deed of my life. I am holding naught in my heart against human kind. My last breath will be a prayer that we may be one unbroken family in the "Home Where Many Mansions Be." (22–26)

Margaret Gilmore Kelso died on August 3, 1948, at the age of ninety-three, and was buried at Mount Pleasant Cemetery.

GENEVIEVE BENNETT CLARK (1856–1937)

$\mathcal{S}$ome Missourians have led quiet lives, focused on home or farm or family or local politics. Their days echoed with the sounds of children playing, of printing presses clattering, of choral societies singing, of train whistles blowing. Like Carry Nation, Genevieve Bennett Clark found that her early focus on domestic bliss and wifely duties broadened, and she moved on to election campaigns, decision-making in Jefferson City, and the corridors of power in Washington, D.C. Marriage to an ambitious and admirable man shaped her life, but the demands of politics and public service did not prevent her from pursuing an interest in historical research and developing her skill as a writer. Although there is no extended memoir among the Clark family papers, many essays and speeches combine to give a picture of Genevieve's experiences in Missouri and Washington, D.C.[1]

Born in 1856, the youngest child and the pet of the Bennett family, Genevieve had fond memories of her childhood in Callaway County. She went to live with her married sister, Annie Pitzer, while attending school in Clarksville in Pike County. Later Genevieve obtained teaching positions in the public school at nearby Louisiana and at Pike College in Bowling Green. Genevieve was in demand as an elocutionist. She recalled later her popularity as an elocutionist: "At that time I used to love to make people cry when I recited for I was young and liked to exercise my power."[2] One of her recitations impressed a young lawyer, James Beauchamp ("Champ") Clark (1850–1921), who invited her "buggy riding." On December 14, 1881, at a ceremony in Auxvasse, they were married. In addition to practicing law Champ worked as a schoolteacher and newspaper editor. An early biographer wrote, "Mrs. Clark is a bright woman, in whom Champ Clark's life, since his marriage, has centered."[3] Considering herself a "full fledged professional" performer of declamation, Genevieve gave lessons in elocution for a brief time after she married in order to earn money. Then she established a literary society for which she presented a series of lectures.

After serving as Prosecuting Attorney for Pike County and as a member of the Missouri State Legislature, Champ Clark served in the U.S. House of

1. Among the manuscripts that have provided information for the biographical sketch of Genevieve Bennett Clark are such essays as "The Real Champ Clark," "My First Valentine," "The Last Funeral of President McKinley," "I Married a Politician," "The Field-Mouse Fear," and "The Burden of an Honor"; all are included in the Champ and Bennett Champ Clark Papers, WHMC-C.

2. "Address to the Honeyshuck Club," manuscript, Clark Papers, WHMC-C.

3. Wilfred R. Hollister and Harry Norman, *Five Famous Missourians* (Kansas City: Hudson-Kimberly Publishing Co., 1900), 289–90. See also Ray Stannard Baker, *Woodrow Wilson: Life and Letters (Governor 1910–1913)* (New York: Charles Scribners' Sons, 1931, 1946), and Champ Clark, *My Quarter Century of American Politics*.

Representatives from 1893 to 1895 and 1897 to 1921. He became known nationally as Speaker of the House and as a serious contender for the Democratic Presidential candidacy in 1912. After his death in 1921 Clark was recalled as "the idol of his district, and the most popular man in Missouri." His widow pursued her interests in public issues, history, and genealogy, continuing to write for newspapers and for her family.[4] Her busy life included travel to Europe and membership in the Presbyterian (U.S.) Church and the D.A.R. Genevieve offered advice and support to her son in his political career, during which he was a Democratic U.S. Senator from 1933 to 1945.[5] Genevieve Bennett Clark died in 1937. The Clark family is still honored in Bowling Green, where their home Honey Shuck,[6] located on Champ Clark Drive, has been restored by the local chapter of the D.A.R.

As a young bride Genevieve kept a diary in which she described the delights of domestic bliss and her distress when struggling with the duties of homemaking and the discomfort of pregnancy. The Clarks had four children. The first two, Champ and Anne Hamilton, died when very young. Bennett Champ Clark, born in 1890, and Genevieve Clark Thomson, born in 1894, were always in the public eye—and so was their mother. Mrs. Clark learned that being the wife of a politician involved her in the stress of campaigning, the issues of state and national government, and encounters with prominent public figures such as Theodore Roosevelt, Woodrow Wilson, Oliver Wendell Holmes, and Thomas Edison. She admired capable and courageous women, including those leading the ardent suffrage campaign. Genevieve wrote essays about her experiences, a number of which were published in the *St. Louis Globe-Democrat*. In her role as a journalist she traveled to Dayton without her husband to report on the funeral of President McKinley in 1901. Further evidence of professionalism is her affiliation with the Woman's News Association.[7]

On the campaign trail Genevieve Bennett Clark would listen to her husband "with rapt attention." She had chosen the traditional role of

4. Topics of extant essays include Thomas Jefferson, the Civil War in Missouri, pacifism ("Father and Sons"), lives of privilege contrasted to those of poverty ("The Field-Mouse Fear"), the history of New Orleans, George Whitfield and the Calvinist Methodist Church, Eugene Debs, William Jennings Bryan as an orator, the Democratic Party ("The Hotspur of Democracy"), African-Americans ("Missouri Sappho"), and woman suffrage ("Our Fathers! Where Are They?"). The essays are with the Clark Papers, WHMC-C.

5. In 1945 President Harry S. Truman appointed Bennett Champ Clark to the U.S. Court of Appeals, where he served until his death in 1954. His sister Genevieve married a newspaper editor, James M. Thomson, with whom she lived in Virginia and Louisiana.

6. In the Clark papers the home and a political club are referred to as "Honeyshuck." The name is now spelled as two words.

7. The Woman's News Association seems to have been a syndicate to which newspapers sent payment at "space rates." Note on manuscript, "My First Valentine," Clark Papers, WHMC-C.

helpmate and mother, but could imagine herself pursuing a higher education and a career. Eager to improve her mind, she wished she could have attended the University of Missouri. Having seen politicians in action, she felt, "If I were a man, I would begin running for President as soon as I was born and keep on running till I died or was elected."[8] In her more traditional role as the wife of a public servant, she was proud of establishing the Servants' Club in Washington, D.C., in 1912, an organization that aimed to find "self-supporting labor" for people in need.

Excerpts of two manuscripts by Genevieve Bennett Clark are presented here. One is the diary she kept during the first year of her marriage;[9] the other is an essay entitled "I Married a Politician." They show a marked contrast in style and attitude, for the private diary of a naive bride is very different from the entertaining reminiscences of a poised and mature woman accustomed to the public gaze and the sometimes cynical world of politics. Looking back on her determination to excel at elocution, Genevieve Clark wrote, "I was not an ordinary person. . . ." No, she was not.

DIARY OF GENEVIEVE BENNETT CLARK

JANUARY 23, 1882

I am convinced that a diary is a good thing to keep so I am resolved to keep one. Champ keeps one; he doesn't write his up every night . . . but collects a great many ideas & then records them all "at one fell swoop." Champ is my husband, his surname is Clark, and we have been married one month and nine days today. We married the 14th of December. I was afraid Champ was a kind of a [word crossed out] but I am glad to say he isn't at all; the more I see of Champ the better I love him. We live at Bowling Green and I am very very happy. Every body says, or at least a great many, that we will get over all this & will grow indifferent to each other just like other people but Champ says that is a big story & I have to think Champ ought to know, leastwise I will ask him every night if he loves me as much as ever and if he don't answer [yes?] I will just precipitate myself from the window and then he can marry again if he wants to but if he does I hope he will be the most miserable fellow alive. I just wrote that to make Champ laugh for he sees me writing and

8. "A Family Row," manuscript, Clark Papers, WHMC-C.
9. The handwritten diary and typewritten essay are with the Clark Papers, WHMC-C. To make these excerpts more readable, we have altered punctuation slightly, generally adding commas and periods where Clark had often just used a dash.

I know he will ask me to let him see this. He may see *this* one entry, if he likes. . . .

JANUARY 26, 1882

. . . Champ scolded me about loaning F. G. some books, says I will never see them again. I will take good care that I do get them back and then I will let him lend his own books. . . .

MARCH 14, 1882

Didn't do much; had a good many visitors. . . . I was rather cross & disagreeable to Champ tonight.

MARCH 15, 1882

Was cross & disagreeable. Said some hateful things before breakfast because C. said something good about the Norris's—was ashamed and resolved never to say anything bad about anybody else. . . . Have picked up a book to help me through an attack of ennui—*Heart's Ease*. . . . Champ came home this morning to tell me that Mrs. Birkhead [?] had a daughter. He sent them a postal saying, Compliments & congratulations of Champ & Genevieve to Dr. & Laura. The Baby may she live long and rival Martha Washington Cleopatra & the Queen of Sheba rolled into one. . . . C. has gone over to the court house to argue a case and, though it is nearly 10 o'clock, he hasn't returned.

MARCH 19, 1882

Rained all day. Spent the day very pleasantly. I tried to get Champ to listen to Jean Ingelow but he would not do it or listened only long enough to ridicule, said she never wrote a line that was any account,[10] that poetry was "beautiful thoughts expressed in beautiful language" and where was the poetry in

> There is no dew left on the blossoms & clover
> There is no rain left in Heaven

surely that was very common place and

10. Jean Ingelow (1820–1897) was the author of *Mopsa the Fairy,* the novel *Off the Skelligs,* and numerous poems, which appeared in collected editions in 1866, 1876, and 1894. In the 1870s women students at the University of Missouri organized two literary societies, calling one of them the Jean Ingelow Literary Society.

I have said my seven times seven times over
Seven times one is seven

What was that but the multiplication table? I was very very sullen and said some things that I could have killed myself for saying but I can't bear to hear my favorite poet disparaged. . . . I won't ever discuss poetry with him again. We can never agree and I ought to let him think as he likes. There is not so very much in common between us after all. Our tastes are so different. There are other people that could have made him happy as I have.

MARCH 20, 1882

. . . I have turned over a new leaf & made a new resolve. See if I keep it.

MARCH 21, 1882

. . . It has been a very windy, disagreeable day. I have had so much trouble with my fire, the house has been full of smoke. . . .

AUGUST 19, 1882

I had dinner nearly ready today and it lacked 15 minutes to twelve when a boy brought a basket [of peaches] and a note from Champ saying in the note that Eugene Pearson and Wm. Rowley would be here to dinner. I was a good deal frustrated because it was already so late but I thought I would do the best I could. . . . I always hate to see a man made to feel bad because his wife is put out about company. I had dinner about half past twelve. Had hot rolls, broiled steak, sweet potatoes, irish potatoes, cucumbers, & tomatoes. I had a pie left from yesterday which I used as dessert. Then we had the peaches and got through very well. The rolls were very nice inside but crust a little too hard. I will try to improve next time.

AUGUST 20, 1882

Champ had last night in the *Republican* an account of poor Mittie M———'s attempt at suicide by jumping from a second story window. Poor girl. I pity her. She is now but a mark for the finger of scorn while the man who ruined her is uninjured and unblamable in the eyes of the virtuous world. This is a bad world we live in I think. . . .

AUGUST 22, 1882

Fearfully warm. I can hardly keep my clothes on. . . .

August 24, 1882

I got up at one o'clock this morning & worked my bread & set it to rise. Was up at half past five & worked it again and made rolls for breakfast. . . .

October 23, 1882

It has been a long time since I made an entry here. I hardly know why except that I did not feel like it. It has been nearly two months since Tish [her sister?] came. Staid two weeks and resigned her place to go home and stay with Ma and George [her brother].[11] I looked forward to her coming with much joy but she seemed to be so very much dissatisfied and they all seemed to be in such a bad way at home that I was glad she concluded to go home but I think the rest of us ought not to let her lose anything by it for she is beyond all doubt the most unselfish person I ever saw. She writes me that she is coming to wait on me when I am sick which will be the 1st of December but I wrote her that I did not want her to come. Of course I feel safer and more comfortable when I am sick to have some of the home folks at hand but for various reasons I have concluded that it would be best for none of them to come. Champ said he was going to have Dr. Campbell to attend me but I was so much opposed to it and begged him not till he at last let me have my way . . . . I am sad sometimes though I try not [to] be, but I cannot help being afraid that all will not turn out well. My health is good now as it can be. It is not *myself* so much that I think of. If my baby is born alive and healthy I will be the happiest woman in the world. . . . I would be blue this evening if I would let myself. Champ brought me a pair of beautiful shoes from Mexico; they fit me nicely. He wrote to his father not to come before the 1st of January. . . .

October 24, 1882

Much to my surprise Champ came home at 2 o'clock this morning. We had a late breakfast. I worked on my gown all my spare time. When we get up so late I do not get cleaned up till it is dinner time so that I don't get to sew any in the forenoon. I can hardly walk. My back aches and my legs feel queer. . . .

11. In the 1870 census, the family, living in Liberty Township, Callaway County, is listed as: Joel D. Bennett (65), and his wife Mary M. (56), both born in Kentucky. Five of their children, all born in Missouri, were living at home: John M. (27), Sadosia [sp.?] B. (25), Joel A. (20), George L. (18), Mary C. (15), and Genevieve (14). John, Joel A., and George are listed as "laborer on farm." Tish may have been a nickname for Sadosia.

NOVEMBER 1, 1882

I feel very well today but will have to look out for someone to stay with me tonight. Abbie McLean has her hands full at home and I can't ask anything of her. Her sister is quite insane, tried to drown herself in the pond today, and they are afraid for her to be a moment alone. . . .

NOVEMBER 2, 1882

I feel badly, am all unstrung and feel like going to bed. I don't know what makes me so nervous. Perhaps the fire last night had something to do with it. Perhaps I have taken cold. I feel darting pains all through me and I am sick at the stomach. McLeans store, the butcher shop, the bakers and the Livery stable were burnt last night. Every body was excited. I thought if I had Champ around the neck he would not get away from me very easy. . . .

NOVEMBER 24, 1882

We have finished *Vanity Fair* and Champ is now reading *Pendennis* to me.[12] I am looking for Ma. She is coming to stay with me. If she don't hurry Miss Clark will be here before she is.

This is the last entry in the diary. The baby was a boy, Champ, who died at the age of eighteen months.

The Clark papers include many other manuscripts by Genevieve, some intended for publication and others to be delivered as speeches. The following is one of two essays with the same title, in which Genevieve recalls her husband's first campaign for the U.S. Congress in 1892.

I MARRIED A POLITICIAN

Thomas Brackett Reed, that masterful man from Maine, once defined a statesman as "a dead politician"; that being the case, and as my husband is, at present, alive and doing well, it is no harm to admit that I married a politician. . . .

When I first met the young man who afterward became my husband, he had set his heart upon a political career; up to that time I had not felt specially attracted toward politics. I had been taught to believe that the

---

12. *The History of Pendennis: His Fortunes and Misfortunes, His Friends and His Greatest Enemy,* by William Makepeace Thackeray, published in London in 1849–1850.

political "Jord[a]n is a hard road to travel," especially for the politician's wife. [This view of the case was largely due to a] poem called "Hannah Jane," which had a barn storming popularity throughout the country; and appeared in all the recitation books. Hannah Jane, the born-of-man heroine of the ballad, thought it no hardship to stay at home and drudge, (her picture represented her engaged in making soft soap in the back yard) while her husband made big speeches in Congress and received the congratulations of admiring lady friends. "I know," (says Hannah Jane's husband in the poem),

> there is a difference
> At reception and levee
> The fairest, wittiest, and most famed
> Of women smile on me
> And everywhere I take my place
> Among the greatest men
> And sometimes sigh with Whittier's Judge
> Alas, it might have been.

Now the role of Hannah Jane didn't appeal to me at that time any more than did that other heroine of fiction, the Lord of Burleigh's bride, who pined away and died "with the burden of an honor, unto which she was not born." I felt that I was able to live up to any honor or other good thing that fate had in store for me.

Fate decreed that I should marry a politician and as I was very much in love with him and he with me, I have always considered it the luckiest thing that ever happened to me. Having married a politician, I was determined it should never be said of him that his career was spoiled by a fool wife. To tell the truth, I have observed that the men who fail on account of fool wives are slack-twisted fellows themselves and unable to command the situation. . . .

I believe I have said that I hadn't any appreciation for the role of Hannah Jane—the aforesaid lady of the poem who fell from the estate wherein she was created by minding too closely her own business. Perhaps in my anxiety not to fall into her error I may have gone to the other extreme. Certain it is that I took a lively interest in everything that concerned my husband, while my own affairs were of secondary importance. (1–3)

At first it was smooth sailing and I had a royal good time; the offices of Presidential Elector, Prosecuting Attorney, and member of the State Legislature were given him without a struggle—almost by acclamation, but when he announced himself a candidate for Congress, "Then came the tug of war" which made the whole country sit up and take notice. . . .

The campaign which followed was wild and woolly. . . .

In the inspiration of the moment, I composed a campaign song which if it served no other purpose was a great relief to my pent up feelings. . . . Our song, after recounting in bold numbers the valiant services that our candidate had rendered to his party and to the country at large, appealed to the Powers that Be to hear the voice of the People before it was everlastingly too late: and wound up with a brave chorus in which all lovers of liberty, and good government every where, were supposed to join:

> Hear the people speak;
> Hear the people cry.
> We'll have him for our Congressman
> Or know the reason why.

I hummed the tune, and a country newspaper editor wrote out the music and taught it to the boys and they made the welkin ring with it.

The editor praised my work and I felt greatly flattered. He said it was the most inspiring campaign song that was ever written. With it, he said, we would storm the citadel of the Opposition and put the whole garrison to the sword. We did storm the citadel but it was the stubbornest garrison that ever resisted an onslaught.

Finally, however, our side won out and my husband was declared the nominee; then our side came out strong on Brotherly Love and preached Harmony with a big H. (4–6)

. . . I suppose I have heard more political speeches than any other woman in this country, and I can say with truth, as an all around stump speaker, I have never heard his [Champ's] equal. He was now making a whirl-wind campaign speaking three or four times a day: I usually accompanied him to rub him down and keep him from taking cold, but about a week before the election I was detained at home on account of the indisposition of our little boy [Bennett Champ]. The child was as well known everywhere as was my husband, and was a great pet and favorite with his father's friends. I had been writing very flattering accounts of the boy's progress to my husband, for I feared lest his anxiety on that account would unfit him for speechmaking; but when he telegraphed me to bring the child to meet him at a certain town where he had an appointment to speak, I had to tell him the plain truth with the result that he cancelled his engagement and came home as fast as the train could bring him . . . .

. . . [T]he enemy started a tale to the effect that the whole thing was a ruse of mine to get possession of my husband who "had put an enemy into his mouth to steal away his brains" . . . ; so a few days before the election I received a letter from a friend of ours telling me that the opposition was making great headway with the story and that something must be done to offset it. Now there lived in our town a man [Captain Flemming] who was personally a friend of mine but who was known far and near as a bitter, vindictive partisan of the opposing party. . . .

And now when I received our friend's letter, I went to see my fellow-townsman and asked him if he believed it. "Why no, of course not," he replied, "it is absurd." "Then," said I, "I want you to give me a written statement to that effect over your official signature." "O come now"; he said, "I couldn't do that; you cannot expect me to give my own side away." "But," said I, "you said yourself that it was a campaign lie." "What if I did?" he replied. "It isn't my business to straighten out all the campaign lies. . . ." I looked at him contemptuously. "I thought you were a man," I said; with that he jumped up in great excitement. "Madam," he cried, "it ill becomes you to disparage the campaign liar. His natural habitat is in your husband's party. No Madam, personally, I would do anything to oblige you but as an official I would cut off my right arm before I would write a line or give out a statement that would make a single vote for your husband."

"If that's the way you feel, Sir, I have nothing further to say," I retorted as I walked out and slammed the door.

But in truth if he had studied night and day for six months, he couldn't have done, said or written a thing that would have helped us half as much as that unguarded speech. Befo[re] night a score or more of stern visaged men had called to see me to hear the story from my own lips. I hope I didn't improve upon it every time I told it but I think I may claim that it lost nothing in my report. (7–9)

After the election in which my husband received a rousing majority and our party in the state and nation carried everything that wasn't nailed down, I met Capt. Flemming on the street. "I suppose," said he, extending his hand, "that you are out for congratulations, will you accept mine?" "Ah, my friend," I cried, "How can I thank you for your courage and self abnegation in coming to the rescue of our party! And to think that I, in my shortsightedness, was angry with you for not writing my husband a certificate of good character; pray forgive me."

"Receive my blessing," he replied. "Since it seems I was foreordained to make a fool of myself, I am glad that you were the beneficiary."

All this was quite a while ago. My husband has kept the place he won in the confidence and affections of the people. For the people love above all things courage in a public man; and next to courage, honesty, and he has both.

As for myself, when people ask me, as they often do, if I enjoy Politics, I might answer as I did the other day when a lady asked me if I used the broad A in conversation and I replied, "Sometimes I do and sometimes I don't." (9–10)

LAURA INGALLS WILDER (1867–1957)

*P*ictures of apple orchards and rich farmland near Mansfield, Missouri, persuaded Laura Ingalls Wilder and her husband Almanzo to seek a better life in "The Gem City of the Ozarks." They had lived for some years near De Smet, South Dakota, struggling to make a living on a homestead. Years of drought and other natural disasters, Almanzo's ill health, high-interest debts, and the Panic of 1893 forced them to leave. After a brief stay in Florida they had returned in 1892 to De Smet, where Laura worked as a seamstress and Almanzo as a carpenter. They then decided, along with the Cooley family, to head south. In 1894, when they had saved enough money, they started out for "The Land of the Big Red Apple"—Missouri.[1]

Unlike most of the women represented in this anthology, Wilder is an international figure. She was born in Pepin, Wisconsin, in 1867. With her family she later lived in Minnesota and the Dakota Territories. Laura married Almanzo Wilder in 1885. They had two children: a daughter, who became a writer, and a son, who died as an infant. After moving to Mansfield in 1894, the Wilders established Rocky Ridge Farm. At the age of sixty-five Laura began to write the "Little House" series of children's books based on her childhood. Having received many awards for her autobiographical novels, Laura Ingalls Wilder died in 1957. The availability of both her private papers and those of her daughter has led researchers to conclude that the daughter, Rose Wilder Lane, did extensive editing and collaborating on the final versions of the "Little House" books.[2]

The "Little House" books end with *These Happy Golden Years* and the marriage of Laura and Almanzo. The series, according to biographer and critic William Holtz, represents "the archetypal romantic story of the young lovers whose union marks the triumphant end of struggle and the establishment of a fruitful order on the land."[3] But *The First Four Years*, the diary of her early married life, tells a different story. This diary remained unpublished until after her death. Comparisons between *The*

---

1. Rose Wilder Lane, introduction to Laura Ingalls Wilder, *On the Way Home: The Diary of a Trip* . . . , 8. Subsequent page references will be noted in the text. The original manuscript may be found in the Wilder museum in Mansfield, and a microfilm copy is at WHMC-C.

2. See William Holtz, *The Ghost in the Little House: A Life of Rose Wilder Lane.* Holtz presents evidence that Lane exerted a much more pervasive role as her mother's editor than was previously assumed. In the appendix, he compares Wilder's passages with Lane's to prove his point that "one must simply read her mother's fair-copy manuscripts in comparison with the final published versions. What Rose accomplished was nothing less than a line-by-line rewriting of labored and underdeveloped narratives" (379). See also Rosa Ann Moore, "Laura Ingalls Wilder and Rose Wilder Lane: The Chemistry of Collaboration." Moore calls the Little House books "the legacy of a unique mother-daughter team, one providing the objectivity and the craft, the other bringing the life and the perspective" (108).

3. Holtz, "Closing the Circle: The American Optimism of Laura Ingalls Wilder," 80.

First Four Years and her children's fiction have revealed important aspects of Wilder's character that also appear in her travel diary, *On The Way Home*.

The First Four Years account of Laura's reaction to Almanzo's proposal to marry and join him on the farm is very different from the account of the same events in *These Happy Golden Years*. There is no hesitancy on Laura's part in the latter, but in the former, she is not sure what to do. The reader has a glimpse of the very practical nature of the real-life Laura Ingalls, not as romanticized as her fictional persona. She demurs because "a farm is such a hard place for a woman. There are so many chores for her to do. . . . Besides a farmer never has any money. He can never make any because the people in towns tell him what they will pay for what he has to sell and then they charge him what they please for what he has to buy. It is not fair." She has other reservations, but decides to marry Almanzo. Rosa Ann Moore labels Laura's hesitancy as "practical, cautious, doubtful . . . one might say 'modern.'"[4] Her practical concern for economics also comes through in the travel diary.

As Laura and Almanzo Wilder traveled for fifty-five days from De Smet to Mansfield, Laura recorded her impressions in pencil in a memorandum book. Harper and Row published the diary, edited by Rose Wilder Lane, with the title *On the Way Home*, in 1962.

On the Way Home is a straightforward, realistic portrait of a family forced to create a new life because there is no more hope in their present circumstances. Along the trail they met many settlers, some coming from Missouri, some going to it, some traveling to other places along the way. People affected by the hard economic times seemed to feel that if they could just start over somewhere else, all would be better. That proved to be the case for the Wilder family, but Manly's careful hunt for just the right section of land to buy once they reached Missouri confirms that their past experience had bred caution. Laura's description of land they passed through on their way shows her sharp eye for good farmland and her preoccupation with how much land cost, as she recorded prices in her notes. Her enthusiasm for Missouri was rewarded when they enjoyed the scenic views, found their land, recovered a lost $100 bill, and Manly sold his first load of wood for fifty cents. They were on the way to a more successful life. Wilder's diary reminds us that even at the turn of the century, many women were still on the road with their families, continuing the search for the "American dream" of acquiring a parcel of rich land that would allow them to prosper and raise their families in a place of their own.

Laura Ingalls Wilder's sturdiness and spirit come through in both her private and fictional writing. Moore notes that in personal letters

---

4. Wilder, *The First Four Years*, 4; Moore, "Laura Ingalls Wilder's Orange Notebooks and the Art of the Little House Books," 106–8.

she wrote in 1937, Wilder explains her explicit purpose in writing the historical novels for children: to pass on the "spirit of the West," to describe a way of life that "could never be again for modern children." Wilder defined this spirit as one "of humor and cheerfulness no matter what happened. . . . My parents possessed this frontier spirit to a marked degree. . . . They looked ahead to better things."[5]

Wilder learned from her parents to look ahead. Many young wives and mothers might have exhibited less stamina after the difficult years in South Dakota. The Wilders departed from De Smet with only $100.00, which they would use for the down payment on a new place. They left behind a buried infant. Almanzo's health was permanently broken, and he would always suffer a limp as the result of diphtheria and a stroke afterwards.

In a newspaper article written in 1911, Almanzo, likely with a great deal of assistance from Laura, wrote about their first look at Rocky Ridge Farm, which they purchased near Mansfield. It was named that because there were several ridges on the land, covered with rocks and brush. "It needed the eye of faith . . . to see that in time it could be made very beautiful."[6] But the rocks and timber were cleared to make room for apple orchards and pastures for cows to graze. With hard work, a head for details and, in later years, a daughter who was willing to help both with financial resources and editorial skills, Laura Ingalls Wilder realized her goal to share, with generations of children to come, the story of her faith in the pioneer dream that built America.

On the Way Home

July 17, 1894

Started at 8:40. Three miles out, Russian thistles. Harvesters in poor wheat. . . . Grain about 8 inches high, will go about 1 1/2 bushels to the acre. Hot wind.

July 18, 1894

. . . At 11:30 we left Howard [South Dakota] one mile east. . . . Worst crops we have seen yet. No grass. Standing grain 3 inches high, burned brown and dead. (15)

5. Moore, "Laura Ingalls Wilder and Rose Wilder Lane," 105.

6. A. J. Wilder, "Rocky Ridge Farm July 1911," in Wilder, *Little House in the Ozarks: A Laura Ingalls Wilder Sampler, The Rediscovered Writings,* ed. Stephen W. Hines, 39. Hines notes that although "A. J. Wilder" is the byline, the article was likely written by Laura Ingalls Wilder.

JULY 20, 1894

. . . We left Bridgewater half a mile to the east. . . . [W]e came to the first piece of oats worth cutting that we have seen since we left De Smet, and they are not very good.

. . . All through McCook [County], this year is the first crop failure in 16 years. . . .

Mr. Cooley overtook us at 12 o'clock when we came to a Russian settlement. He had not been able to get grain or any feed in Bridgewater though there are three mills in the town.

. . . We can see timber along the Jim [James] River. . . . This is nice country but as one Russian said, "Nix good this year, nix good last year." . . .

Land here is priced from $2,500 to $3,000 a quarter section [160 acres]. (17–19)

SUNDAY, JULY 22, 1894

. . . The Russians have hung around us all day, children and grown folks both. They cannot talk and they understand only a little. They are very kind, they brought milk and a pan of biscuits, and gave them to us, showing us that they were presents. The biscuits are light and very good. We got to feel a little acquainted with the folks, told them all our names and asked theirs and let them swing in the hammock and sit in the chairs. They are very curious and want to examine everything, talking about it to each other.

They wanted us to come to their houses, so Manly and I went. They showed us the geese and we watched the milkmaids milk. They look like the pictures of German and Russian milkmaids and peasants. Their yellow hair is combed smooth down each side of their faces and hangs in long braids behind and they wear handkerchiefs over their heads. They are all dressed alike. There are no sleeves in the women's long blue calico dresses but under them they wear white shirts with long white sleeves. The men have whiskered cheeks and long golden beards. They wear blue blouses that hang down long, to their knees almost, with belts around their waists. They were all very polite and smiling, seeming to try to say they were glad we came. . . .

When we were leaving a woman opened the front of her dress and took out a baking of cold biscuits from right against her bare skin and gave them to me. The man told me to put them in my *shirt*, but I carried them in Manly's clean handkerchief instead. The man said it was hard for people to cook when traveling. They are very kind people. A pity to waste the biscuits but we could not eat them. (21–23)

JULY 23, 1894

We started at 8. Hated to leave our camping place, it seems quite like home. We crossed the James River and in 20 minutes we reached the top of the bluffs on the other side. We all stopped and looked back at the scene and I wished for an artist's hand or a poet's brain or even to be able to tell in good plain prose how beautiful it was. If I had been the Indians I would have scalped more white folks before I ever would have left it. . . .

We reached Yankton at 4 o'clock. . . .

I am greatly disappointed in Yankton, it is a stick in the mud. We drove all over the town to find a little feed for the teams, went to the mill and the elevator and the feed stores, and finally found a couple of sacks of ground feed. . . . There were no green vegetables, nor any figs nor dates in the grocery stores. . . .

I got my revolver fixed, then we had to spend so much time hunting for feed all over town that Mr. Cooley got to the ferry first. (23–27)

JULY 24, 1894

. . . We were all tired from being up so late last night, and did not get started until 9 o'clock. We had taken the wrong road, so we had to go back to the river and start again on the right one. For a little way we followed the river and could see down it, four or five miles across the water. It was a grand sight, though the scenery on the banks is nothing.

What is it about water that always affects a person? I never see a great river or lake but I think how I would like to see a world made and watch it through all its changes. (28)

JULY 28, 1894

We washed this morning, or rather Mrs. Cooley did out a washing and I washed 4 garments. I wash out the most of the clothes in a pail as they get dirty so I do not have washings. The neighbors sent us a pailful of delicious cold milk, out of the water where they keep it for the creamery. (34)

AUGUST 7, 1894

On the road at 7:30, we crossed the line into Kansas at 10:28¼ exactly. Judging from what we have seen and heard of Nebraska, the south east corner is quite a good country, but taken as a whole it is "nix good." I don't like Nebraska. (43)

SUNDAY, AUGUST 12, 1894

Today was not as monotonous as common. Three emigrant wagons passed us going south, and one going north. . . .

We had a good camping place on a little headland by the river. I rode Little Pet awhile, bareback, not going anywhere—she was turned loose to feed. Two emigrants talked to me, a young man and his mother in their wagon. They used to live in Missouri, went to Colorado, are now going back to Missouri to stay. (48)

AUGUST 13, 1894

. . . At noon we went through Rossville [Kansas], a small place, but just as we were going by the depot the train came in. The engine frightened Prince [the horse] and he went through a barb-wire fence. He struck it straight and went right through it, end over end, jumped up, ran against a clothesline and broke that and ran back to the fence. He stopped when Manly said, "Whoa, Prince," and Manly helped him through the wire. He had only one mark, a cut about an inch long where a barb had struck him. How he ever got through so well is a wonder.

Watermelons are ripe and plentiful. Manly and Mr. Cooley bought big ones for 5 cents. We stopped by the road in the shade of trees and all of us had all the watermelon we could eat. . . .

It is *terribly* dusty. We breathe dust all day and everything is covered thick with it. (49–50)

AUGUST 22, 1894

A good start at 7:15 and this morning we are driving through pretty country. Crops look good. Oats are running 30 to 60 bushels to the acre, wheat from 10 to 30. All the wood you want can be had for the hauling and coal is delivered at the house for $1.25 a ton. Land is worth from $10. an acre up, unimproved, and $15. to $25. when well improved, 12 miles from Fort Scott [Kansas].

Exactly at 2:24¾ P.M. we crossed the line into Missouri. And the very first cornfield we saw beat even those Kansas cornfields.

We met 7 emigrant wagons leaving Missouri. One family had a red bird, a mockingbird, and a lot of canaries in cages hung under the canvas in the wagon with them. We had quite a chat and heard the mockingbird sing. We camped by a house in the woods. (62–63)

AUGUST 25, 1894

. . . Well, we are in the Ozarks at last, just in the beginning of them, and they are beautiful. We passed along the foot of some hills and could look up their sides. The trees and rocks are lovely. Manly says we could almost live on the looks of them. (65)

AUGUST 28, 1894

. . . Arrived in Springfield at 9:25. It is a thriving city with fine houses and four business blocks stand around a town square. The stores are well stocked and busy. . . . [W]e bought shoes for Rose and myself, a calico dress for me, and a new hat for Manly. . . . We were out of [the city] before noon. It has 21,850 inhabitants, and is the nicest city we have seen yet. It is simply grand. (67)

AUGUST 29, 1894

Left camp at 7:10. We are driving along a lively road through the woods, we are shaded by oak trees. The farther we go, the more we like this country. Parts of Nebraska and Kansas are well enough but Missouri is simply glorious. There Manly interrupted me to say, "This is beautiful country."

The road . . . is rutted and dusty and stony but every turn of the wheels changes our view of the woods and the hills. The sky seems lower here, and it is the softest blue. The distances and the valleys are blue whenever you can see them. It is a drowsy country that makes you feel wide awake and alive but somehow contented.

We went through a little station on the railroad and a few miles farther on we came to a fruit farm of 400 acres. A company owns it. There are 26,000 little young trees already set out in rows striping the curves of the land, and the whole 400 acres will be planted as soon as possible. Acres of strawberries and other small fruit are in bearing. We stopped to look our fill of the sight and Manly fell into conversation with some of the company's men. They told him of a 40 he can buy for $400., all cleared and into grass except five acres of woods, and with a good ever-flowing spring, a comfortable log house and a barn.

We drove through Seymour in the late afternoon. . . . A man spoke to us, who had lived 14 years in Dakota. . . . [Now] he is farming near Seymour. He said the climate here can't be beat, we never will want to leave these hills, but it will take us some time to get used to the stones.

Oh no, we are not out of the world nor behind the times here in the Ozarks. Why, even the cows know "the latest." Two of them feeding along the road were playing Ta-ra-ra *Boom!* de-ay! The little cow's bell rang Ta-ra-ra, then the bigger cow's bell clanged, *Boom!* de-ay. I said, "What is that tune they are playing?" and we listened. It was as plain as could be, tones and time and all, and so comical. We drove on singing "Ta-ra-ra *Boom!* de-ay!" along the road.

We passed several springs and crossed some little brooks. The fences are snake fences of split logs and all along them, in the corners, fruit grows wild. There are masses of blackberries, and seedling peaches and plum and cherries, and luscious-looking fruits ripening in little trees . . . , a lavishness of fruit growing wild. It seems to be free for the taking.(68–70)

In 1911, writing under Almanzo's byline, Laura described the farmland they bought and the new life they carved out together in the Ozark hills.

It was hard work and sometimes short rations at the first, but gradually the difficulties were overcome. Land was cleared and prepared by heroic effort in time to set out all the apple trees, and in a few years the orchard came into bearing. Fields were cleared and brought to a good state of fertility. The timber around the buildings was thinned out enough so that grass would grow between the trees, and each tree would grow in good shape, which has made a beautiful park of the grounds. The rocks have been picked up and grass seed sown so that the pastures and meadows are in fine condition and support quite a little herd of cows. . . .

We are not by any means through with making improvements on Rocky Ridge Farm. . . .

When I look around the farm now and see the smooth, green, rolling meadows and pastures, the good fields of corn and wheat and oats, when I see the orchard and strawberry field like huge bouquets in the spring or full of fruit later in the season, when I see the grapevines hanging full of luscious grapes, I can hardly bring back to my mind the rough, rocky, brushy, ugly place that we first called Rocky Ridge Farm. The name given it then serves to remind us of the battles we have fought and won and gives a touch of sentiment and an added value to the place.[7]

7. Wilder, *Little House in the Ozarks*, 39–40.

KATE CHOPIN (1850–1904)

"*A*St. Louis Woman Who Has Won Fame in Literature" was a head-line in the *St. Louis Post-Dispatch* for Sunday, November 26, 1899. Work, achievement, sophistication, discernment, motherhood, celebrity these are the terms in which Kate Chopin was presented. Although most of the selections in the anthology are private writings by women not known to the general public, this essay is by an ambitious author who received na-tional and international recognition at the turn of the century. Recently, Chopin's bold treatment of women's experiences and the artistry of her fiction have received more serious critical treatment and appreciation than they garnered during her lifetime.[1]

Born in St. Louis in 1850, Kate was the daughter of Eliza and Thomas O'Flaherty. After her father was killed in 1855 when a train fell from the collapsing Gasconade Bridge, Kate was reared in a household of women, of whom the most influential was her great-grandmother, Victoire Verdon Charleville. She was educated at the St. Louis Academy of the Sacred Heart, and in that regard benefited from the work of Philippine Duchesne. After two seasons as a debutante and "belle" of society, Kate married her cousin Oscar Chopin in 1870. The Chopins lived in New Orleans until his business failed; then they moved to a plantation in Natchitoches Parish, Louisiana. They had five sons and a daughter.[2] Widowed in 1882, Kate Chopin managed the business affairs of the plantation before returning to St. Louis in 1883. She retained property in Louisiana and owned real estate in St. Louis, proving to be an excellent businesswoman. In 1889 she began to write fiction, having her first story appear in the *St. Louis Post-Dispatch*. She continued to write fiction, poetry, and essays, maturing artistically as she drew primarily upon her experiences and observations in Louisiana.

Kate Chopin's famous and significant novel *The Awakening* was pub-lished in 1899. Some contemporary critics and general readers found the book shocking; the *Post-Dispatch* warned that it should be labeled "poison." Men tended to object to the book, while women more often admired it. In fact, seven months after its publication, the Wednesday Club, a women's group in St. Louis, put on a program honoring Chopin.[3] About sixty years later *The Awakening* was rediscovered and began to be

---

1. Harold Bloom, ed., *Kate Chopin; Perspectives on Kate Chopin: Proceedings from the Kate Chopin International Conference, April 6, 7, 8, 1989;* Mary E. Papke, *Verging on the Abyss: The Social Fiction of Kate Chopin and Edith Wharton;* Lynda S. Boren and Sara de Saussure Davis, eds., *Kate Chopin Reconsidered: Beyond the Bayou.*

2. The sons were Jean, Oscar, Jr., George, Fredrick, and Felix, born between 1871 and 1878. The daughter, Lelia, was born in 1879.

3. Emily Toth, *Kate Chopin,* 21.

highly regarded for its intense portrayal of a woman's ill-fated effort to experience passion and freedom. It has been part of the myth of Chopin's life to visualize her as depressed and "mute" because of the reception of *The Awakening*. Actually she continued to make public appearances and to write short stories for several years, but health problems necessitated periods of rest and she had trouble with her eyesight. Migraine headaches had plagued her for decades and may be related to the illness which caused her death in August 1904, after a day spent at the World's Fair— the Louisiana Purchase Exposition.[4]

A variety of personal observations about her sense of identity, wedding, honeymoon trip, and literary efforts may be found in diary passages published in *A Kate Chopin Miscellany*.[5] Although she would later write for an audience, in 1869, the year before her marriage, she confined herself to the private pages of the diary: "What a dear good confidant my book is. If it does not clear my doubts it at least does not contradict and oppose my opinions—You are the only one, my book, with whom I take the liberty of talking about myself." Thirty years followed in which Kate Chopin experienced a happy marriage, the birth and nurturing of six children, the loss of her husband, the development of her literary gifts, the management of a career, bereavements, and disappointments. Then late in 1899 she published the following article, which was included by Per Seyersted in *The Complete Works of Kate Chopin*.[6] The tone of the essay is light and witty, belying the assumption that the author was still dejected about the response to *The Awakening*. Instead, she reveals a sense of humor which her daughter Lelia said was characteristic. Chopin reveals facets of her charming personality, the irritations of her situation as a celebrity, and the way in which work as an author was interwoven with the pattern of domestic routine.

Chopin presents herself to readers of the *St. Louis Post-Dispatch* in the image of a mother fond of her children and an author worthy of respect, frank in expressing opinions and vigilant in guarding her privacy. The essay is introduced with a brief biographical sketch and critical comments that give no hint of the controversial reaction to *The Awakening* that spring. Her novel is compared to that of another St. Louis writer, a young man named Winston Churchill, who wrote a historical novel entitled *Richard Carval*. Chopin's *The Awakening* has not enjoyed the "vogue" of *Richard Carval*, the *Post-Dispatch* asserts, but it has aroused "more discussion and probably deeper interest." One gets the impression that *The Awakening* is admired without reservation: "The perfection of its art is

4. For additional biographical information, see Toth, *Kate Chopin*; Per Seyersted, *Kate Chopin*; and Bonnie Stepenoff, "Kate Chopin in 'Out-At-The-Elbows' St. Louis."

5. Ed. Per Seyersted, asst. Emily Toth, 63.

6. 2:721–23.

acknowledged in this country and even more cordially in England." Accompanied by a photograph of Chopin and a sketch of the house in which she was born, the article praises the author as a woman of dignity and an artist of renown. Rather than suggesting that Chopin went beyond the bounds of good taste and morality in her fiction, the *Post-Dispatch* says that she appealed "to the finer taste" and remained true to her "artistic conscience."

Kate Chopin was often the center of a lively scene—writing while surrounded by friends and children, playing the witty hostess of a salon attended by avant-garde intellectuals, and promoting her writing with an assertive flair. She also valued solitude and quiet. In "A Reflection," Chopin describes life as a colorful moving procession, in which many people march, unheeding of those "souls and bodies" which fall and are trampled. She cannot hear "the rhythm of the march" or risk being crushed and stifled; instead she chooses to "be still and wait by the roadside."[7]

ON CERTAIN BRISK, BRIGHT DAYS

On certain brisk, bright days I like to walk from my home, near Thirty-fourth street, down to the shopping district. After a few such experiments I begin to fancy that I have the walking habit. Doubtless I convey the same impression to acquaintances who see me from the car window "hot-footing" it down Olive street or Washington avenue. But in my sub-consciousness, as my friend Mrs. R——— would say, I know that I have not the walking habit.

Eight or nine years ago I began to write stories—short stories which appeared in the magazines, and I forthwith began to suspect I had the writing habit. The public shared this impression, and called me an author. Since then, though I have written many short stories and a novel or two, I am forced to admit that I have not the writing habit. But it is hard to make people with the questioning habit believe this.

"Now, where, when, why, what do you write?" are some of the questions that I remember. How do I write? On a lapboard with a block of paper, a stub pen and a bottle of ink bought at the corner grocery, which keeps the best in town.

Where do I write? In a Morris chair beside the window, where I can see a few trees and a patch of sky, more or less blue.

When do I write? I am greatly tempted here to use slang and reply "any old time," but that would lend a tone of levity to this bit of confidence,

7. *The Complete Works of Kate Chopin,* 2:622.

whose seriousness I want to keep intact if possible. So I shall say I write in the morning, when not too strongly drawn to struggle with the intricacies of a pattern, and in the afternoon, if the temptation to try a new furniture polish on an old table leg is not too powerful to be denied; sometimes at night, though as I grow older I am more and more inclined to believe that night was made for sleep.

"Why do I write?" is a question which I have often asked myself and never very satisfactorily answered. Story-writing—at least with me—is the spontaneous expression of impressions gathered goodness knows where. To seek the source, the impulse of a story is like tearing a flower to pieces for wantonness.

What do I write? Well, not everything that comes into my head, but much of what I have written lies between the covers of my books.

There are stories that seem to write themselves, and others which positively refuse to be written—which no amount of coaxing can bring to anything. I do not believe any writer has ever made a "portrait" in fiction. A trick, a mannerism, a physical trait or mental characteristic go a very short way towards portraying the complete individual in real life who suggests the individual in the writer's imagination. The "material" of a writer is to the last degree uncertain and I fear not marketable. I have been told stories which were looked upon as veritable gold mines by the generous narrators who placed them at my disposal. I have been taken to spots supposed to be alive with local color. I have been introduced to excruciating characters with frank permission to use them as I liked, but never, in a single instance, has such material been of the slightest service. I am completely at the mercy of unconscious selection. To such an extent is this true, that what is called the polishing up process has always proved disastrous to my work, and I avoid it, preferring the integrity of crudities to artificialities.

How hard it is for one's acquaintances and friends to realize that one's books are to be taken seriously, and that they are subject to the same laws which govern the existence of others' books! I have a son who is growing wroth over the question: "Where can I find your mother's books, or latest book?"

"The very next time anyone asks me that question, " he exclaimed excitedly, "I'm going to tell them to try the stock yards!"

I hope he won't. He might thus offend a possible buyer. Politeness, besides being a virtue, is sometimes an art. I am often met with the same question, and I always try to be polite. "My latest book? Why, you will find it, no doubt, at the bookseller's or the libraries."

"The libraries! Oh, no, they don't keep it." She hadn't thought of the bookseller's. It's real hard to think of everything! Sometimes I feel as if I should like to get a good, remunerative job to do the thinking for some people. This may sound conceited, but it isn't. If I had space (I have plenty of time; time is my own, but space belongs to the *Post-Dispatch*), I should like to demonstrate satisfactorily that it is not conceited.

I trust it will not be giving away professional secrets to say that many readers would be surprised, perhaps shocked, at the questions which some newspaper editors will put to a defenseless woman under the guise of flattery.

For instance: "How many children have you?" This form is subtle and greatly to be commended in dealing with women of shy and retiring propensities. A woman's reluctance to speak of her children has not yet been chronicled. I have a good many, but they'd be simply wild if I dragged them into this. I might say something of those who are at a safe distance—the idol of my soul in Kentucky; the light of my eye off in Colorado; the treasure of his mother's heart in Louisiana—but I mistrust the form of their displeasure with poisoned candy going through the mails.

"Do you smoke cigarettes?" is a question which I consider impertinent and I think most women will agree with me. Suppose I do smoke cigarettes? Am I going to tell it out in meeting? Suppose I don't smoke cigarettes. Am I going to admit such a reflection upon my artistic integrity, and thereby bring upon myself the contempt of the guild?

In answering questions in which an editor believes his readers to be interested, the victim cannot take herself too seriously.

Perhaps later scholars have taken Chopin more seriously than she did herself. Per Seyersted wrote of her as "petrified into the silent, but proud 'White Eagle,'" a realist ahead of her time. Chopin published a number of essays and stories in her later years, some intended for children and youth. She continued to manage her financial affairs; the census of 1900 identifies her as a "capitalist." She visited and corresponded with relatives in Louisiana, and helped her children at times of illness and bereavement. Actually the balance of her life may be its finest feature. As Billy Reedy wrote in her obituary: "She was a remarkably talented woman, who knew how to be a genius without sacrificing the comradeship of her children."[8]

8. Seyersted, *Kate Chopin*, 199, and Toth, *Kate Chopin*, 379, 386, 391, 395.

CARRY A. NATION (1846–1911)

"*My* life beyond dispute has been marvelous and no one that will stop to consider but will know and must admit that an unseen power, one super-human, has upheld me. . . ." Looking back on a life of heartbreak, hard work, protest, and fame, Carry Nation saw a pattern: she had responded to God's call and God had protected her. "I have had visions and dreams that I know were sent to me by my Heavenly Father to warn or comfort or instruct me."[1] With assurance and zeal she defied civic authority and mobilized her followers to oppose the sale of liquor. The nineteenth and early twentieth centuries witnessed various reform movements—abolition of slavery, temperance, peace, labor reform, women's rights. Although her tactics were outrageous, Carry Nation represents the many women who worked in the service of good causes, motivated by personal experience, religious conviction, and dedication to the welfare of families.

In *Creating a Female Dominion in American Reform: 1890–1935*, Robyn Muncy studies the evolution of reform activism. Much reform work was led by middle-class white women during the nineteenth century. Directing their efforts through voluntary organizations, preferably separate women's societies, they became active in the public sphere, working with mission societies, Sunday schools, and temperance organizations. After the Civil War, women built large voluntary organizations, not only because they believed in the causes but because reform work allowed them to use their education and channel their ambition. The reform movement extended the female dominion beyond the home, but emphasized family issues such as child welfare, food labeling, and sobriety. However, when women reformers became professional, demanded an end to discrimination against women in hiring and salaries, or agitated for the vote, they were often criticized as being "unfeminine."[2] Carry Nation exemplifies the reform movement in her unique way: active for a while in the Woman's Christian Temperance Union (W.C.T.U.), forming her own organization, pursuing a career, yet idealizing woman as wife and mother in a happy family.

The life story of the woman whose emblems were a hatchet and the W.C.T.U.'s white ribbon presents a mixture of sincere confessions about painful private experiences and a proud recounting of her success in working for temperance, interwoven with theories on the evils of liquor and tobacco. There are three editions of Nation's autobiography. The first

1. Carry Nation, *The Use and Need of the Life of Carry A. Nation*, [1904], 37, 39; [1908, 1909], 82, 86.
2. Muncy, *Creating a Female Dominion*, xi-xvii, 4–5.

184

was published in 1904. The second was published in 1908, and a third in 1909. The three versions differ primarily as to the length and contents of the final chapters.[3]

Carry Amelia Moore[4] was born in Garrard County, Kentucky, on November 25, 1846, to a kind, admirable father and a mother whose eccentricities were not far removed from the legal insanity of other family members. George Moore moved his family to Belton in Cass County, Missouri, in 1855. When the Civil War threatened, he took his slaves to the South. After a stay in Texas, the Moore family returned to Cass County. Carry did some nursing of wounded soldiers, and took over much of the housework from her ailing mother. Mrs. Moore may have been in ill health, but she was vigorous in her opposition to Carry's marriage to Dr. Charles Gloyd in 1867. That unhappy marriage was a decisive event in Carry's life; its significance is revealed in the section of chapter 4 of the autobiography that the editors have chosen to present. Although Carry was writing almost forty years later, she described vividly her longing for love and the shock of discovering the destructive power of alcohol. After supporting herself as a teacher, Carry married David Nation in 1877. Disappointment about this marriage, too, which ended in divorce in 1901, anxiety about her daughter Charlien's illnesses and alcoholism, and backbreaking labor filled her life until she clearly heard God call her to "smash" the "joints" in Kansas where liquor was sold illegally.

Carry Nation entered the temperance movement comparatively late. She moved with her family to Medicine Lodge, Kansas, in 1890, and began her temperance work there in 1899 with members of the local W.C.T.U. chapter. The national organization was founded in Ohio in the early 1870s. With temperance as their primary focus, members worked closely with churches and schools, attracting thousands of women from all levels of society. State and local organizations might differ in their policies and actions, but they shared the commitment expressed in this typical pledge of the Columbia, Missouri, chapter: "I hereby declare my resolution, God helping me, to abstain from all distilled, fermented and malt liquors, including wine, beer, and cider, as a beverage, and to employ all proper means to discourage the use of and traffic in the same."[5] One

3. The passages we quote, describing Nation's marriages, may be found in the following editions and pages: [1904], 28–34, and [1908, 1909], 61–74. The reflections on her retirement are found only in the third [1909] edition, 402–3.

4. "Mrs. Nation's whole name is Carrie Amelia Nation, but having noticed from old records that her father wrote the first name 'Carry,' she now does the same, and considers the name portentous, as concerns what she is trying and means to do. She believes, she says, that it is her mission to 'carry a nation' from the darkness of drunken bestiality into the light of purity and sobriety . . ." (Nation, Use and Need [1908], 301).

5. "Constitution and By-Laws," Woman's Christian Temperance Union, Columbia, WHMC-C.

issue over which chapters disagreed was whether or not the W.C.T.U. should be identified with the struggle for suffrage. Carry Nation came to believe that it was important for women to gain the vote. In remarks to the Kansas legislature in 1901, she said, "You refused me the vote and I had to use a rock."[6]

Carry led her first violent attack on saloons in 1900, in the town of Kiowa, Kansas. At first she threw rocks, but later a hatchet became her favorite weapon and the symbol of her crusade. Carry's actions in mobilizing demonstrators and engaging in destruction of property were extreme, her uninhibited public statements were provocative, and her physical appearance lent itself to caricature. Eventually Carry Nation became a figure of ridicule, to which she made herself vulnerable by appearances on stage in plays and as a lecturer in burlesque theatres. After her retirement from reform work in 1909, Carry lived peacefully in Arkansas. She died in 1911. Many thought she had done the temperance cause more harm than good, an evaluation perpetuated by a number of biographers,[7] but a revisionist view of Mrs. Nation credits her with persuasive wit, generosity, and courage.[8]

The temperance movement is part of women's history, for the stereotypical drunkard was a man whose wife and children waited at home for his return from the saloon. Those who sold liquor and politicians who condoned such sale were usually men. By battling for prohibition, Carry Nation believed that family life would be restored—and that others might enjoy the happiness she never knew.

_____ THE USE AND NEED OF THE LIFE OF CARRY A. NATION _____

In the fall of 1865, Dr. Gloyd,[9] a young physician, called to see my father to secure the country school, saying he wished to locate in our section of the country, and wanted to take a school [teach] that winter, and then he could decide where he would like to practice his profession.

This man was a thorough student, spoke, and read, several different languages. He boarded with us. I liked him, and stood in awe of him because of his superior education, never thinking that he loved me, until he astonished me one evening by kissing me. I had never had a gentleman

---

6. Robert Smith Bader, *Prohibition in Kansas: A History,* 147.

7. Herbert Asbury, *Carry Nation;* Carleton Beals, *Cyclone Carry: The Story of Carry Nation;* Robert Lewis Taylor, *Vessel of Wrath: The Life and Times of Carry Nation;* Arnold Madison, *Carry Nation.* See also J. C. Furnas, *The Life and Times of the Late Demon Rum.*

8. See Bader, *Prohibition in Kansas,* 133–55.

9. Charles Gloyd, who was originally from Vermont, had been a captain in the Union Army.

to take such a privilege and felt shocked, threw up my hands to my face, saying several times: "I am ruined." My aunt and mother had instilled great reserve in my actions, when in company of gentlemen, so much that I had never allowed one to sit near or hold my hand. This was not because I did not like their society, but I had been taught that to inspire respect or love from a man, you must keep him at a distance. This often made we [me] awkward and reserved, but it did me no harm. When I learned that Dr. Gloyd loved me, I began to love him. He was an only child. His parents had but a modest living. My mother was not pleased with seeing a growing attachment between us, for there was another match she had planned for me. When she saw this she would not allow me to sit alone in the room with him, so our communication was mostly by writing letters. I never knew Shakespeare until he read it to me, and I became an ardent admirer of the greatest poet. The volume of Shakespeare on his table was our postoffice. In the morning at breakfast he would manage to call the name "Shakespeare"; then I would know there was a letter for me in its leaves. After teaching three months he went to Holden, Missouri, and located; sent for his father and mother and in two years we were married.

My father and mother warned me that the doctor was addicted to drink, but I had no idea of the curse of rum. I did not fear anything, for I was in love, and doubted in him nothing. When Dr. Gloyd came up to marry me the 21st of November, 1867, I noticed with pain, that his countenance was not bright, he was changed. The day was one of the gloomiest I ever saw, a mist fell, and not a ray of sunshine. I felt a foreboding on the day I had looked forward to, as being one of the happiest. I did not find Dr. Gloyd the lover I expected. He was kind but seemed to want to be away from me; used to sit and read, when I was so hungry for his caresses and love. I have heard that this is the experience of many other young married women. They are so disappointed that their husbands change so after marriage. . . .

About five days after we were married, Dr. Gloyd came in, threw himself on the bed and fell asleep. I was in the next room and saw his mother bow down over his face. She did not know I saw her. When she left, I did the same thing, and the fumes of liquor came in my face. I was terror stricken, and from that time on, I knew why he was so changed. Not one happy moment did I see! I cried most all the time. My husband seemed to understand that I knew his condition. Twice, with tears in his eyes, he remarked: "Oh! Pet, I would give my right arm to make you happy." He would be out until late every night. I never closed my eyes. His sign in front of the door on the street would creak in the wind, and I would sit by the window waiting to hear his footsteps. I never saw him stagger. He would lock himself up in the "Masonic Lodge" and allow no one to see him. People would call for him in case of sickness, but he could not be found.

My anguish was unspeakable. I was comparatively a child. I wanted some one to help me. He was a mason [Freemason]. I talked to a Mr. Hulitt, a brother mason. I begged of him to help me save my precious husband. I talked to a dear friend, Mrs. Clara Mize, a Christian, hoping to get some help in that direction, but all they could say was, "Oh, what pity, to see a man like Dr. Gloyd throw himself away!" The world was all at once changed to me, it was like a place of torture. I thought certainly, there must be a way to prevent this suicide and murder. I now know, that the impulse was born in me then to combat to the death this inhumanity to man.

I believe the masons were a great curse to Dr. Gloyd. These men would drink with him. There is no society or business that separates man and wife, or calls men from their homes at night, that produces any good results. I believe that secret societies are unscriptural, and that the Masonic Lodge has been the ruin of many a home and character.

I was so ignorant I did not know that I owed a duty to myself to avoid gloomy thoughts; did not know a mother could entail a curse on her offspring before it was born. Oh, the curse that comes through heredity, and this liquor evil, a disease that entails more depravity on children unborn, than all else, unless it be tobacco. There is an object lesson taught in the Bible. The mother of Samson was told by an angel to "drink neither wine nor strong drink," Judges 13:4, before her child was born. God shows by this, that these things are injurious. Mothers often make drunkards of their own children, before they are born. My parents heard that Dr. Gloyd was drinking. My father came down to visit us, and I went home with him. My mother told me I must never go back to my husband again. I knew time was near at hand, when I would be helpless, with a drunken husband, and no means of support. What could I do? I kept writing to "Charlie," as I called him. He came to see me once; my mother treated him as a stranger. He expressed much anxiety about my confinement in September; got a party to agree to come for him at the time; but my mother would not allow it. In six weeks after my little girl was born, my mother sent my brother with me to Holden to get my trunk and other things to bring them home. Her words to me were: "If you stay in Holden, never return home again." My husband begged me to stay with him; he said: "Pet, if you leave me, I will be a dead man in six months." I wanted to stay with him, but dared not disobey my mother and be thrown out of shelter, for I saw I could not depend on my husband. I did not know then that drinking men were drugged men, diseased men. His mother told me that when he was growing up to manhood, his father, Harry Gloyd, was Justice of the Peace in Newport, Ohio, twelve years, and that Charlie was so disgusted with the drink cases, that he would go in a room and lock himself in, to get out of their hearing; that he never touched a drop until he went in the army. . . . He was fighting to free others from slavery, and he became a worse slave than those he fought to free. In a little less than six months from the day my child was born, I got a telegram telling of his death. His father died a few months before he did, and Mother Gloyd was left entirely alone.

Mother Gloyd was a true type of a New England housewife, and I had always lived in the south. I could not say at this time that I loved her, although I respected her very highly. But I wanted to be with the mother of the man I loved more than my own life; I wanted to supply his place if possible. My father gave me several lots; by selling one of these and Dr. Gloyd's library and instruments, I built a house of three rooms on one of the lots and rented the house we lived in, which brought us in a little income, but not sufficient to support us. I wanted to prepare myself to teach, and I attended the Normal Institute of Warrensburg. . . . I got a certificate and was given the primary room in the Public School at Holden. Mother Gloyd kept house and took care of Charlien, my little girl, and I made the living. This continued for four years. I lost my position as teacher in that school this way: A Dr. Moore was a member of the board, he criticised me for the way I had the little ones read; for instance, in the sentence, "I saw a man," I had them use the short a instead of the long a . . . ; having them read it as we would speak it naturally. He made this serious objection, and I lost my place and Dr. Moore's niece got my room as teacher. This was a severe blow to me, for I could not leave mother Gloyd and Charlien to teach in another place, and I knew of no other way of making a living except by teaching. I resolved then to get married. I made it a subject of prayer and went to the Lord explaining things about this way. I said: "My Lord, you see the situation[.] I cannot take care of mother and Charlien. I want you to help me. If it be best for me to marry I will do so. I have no one picked out, but I want you to select the one that you think best. I want to give you my life, and I want by marrying to glorify and serve you, as well as to take care of mother and Charlien and be a good wife." I have always been a literalist. I find out that it is the only way to interpret the Bible. When God says: "Commit thy way unto the Lord; trust also in him he shall bring it to pass," Ps. 37:5, I believe that to be the way to act. . . .

In about ten days from that time I made this a subject of prayer, I was walking down the street in Holden and passed a place where Mr. Nation was standing, who had come up from Warrensburg, where he was then editing the "Warrensburg Journal." He was standing in the door with his back to me, but turned and spoke. There was a peculiar thrill which passed through my heart which made me start. The next day I got a letter from him, asking me to correspond with him. I was not surprised; [I] had been expecting something like it. I knew that this was in answer to my prayer, and David Nation was to be the husband God selected for me. He was nineteen years older than I, was very good looking, and was a well-informed, successful lawyer, also a minister in the Christian Church. My friends in Holden opposed this because of the difference in our ages and of his large family.[10] I gave him the loving confidence of a true wife and he was often very kind to me. We were married within six weeks from the time I got the letter from him. Mother Gloyd went to live with us and continued to do so for fifteen years, until she died. My married life with Mr. Nation was not a happy one. I found out that he deceived me in so many things. I can remember the first time I found this out. I felt that something was broken that could never be mended. What a shattered thing is betrayed confidence! Oh, husbands and wives, do not lie to each other, even though you should do a vile act; confess to the truth of the matter! . . .

I shall not in this book give to the public the details of my life as a wife of David Nation any more than possible.[11] He and I agreed in but few things, and still we did not have the outbreaks many husbands and wives have. The most serious trouble that ever rose between us was in regard to Christianity. My Christian life was an offence unto him, and I found out if I yielded to his ideas and views that I would be false to every true motive. He saw that I resented this influence and it caused him to be suspicious and jealous. I think my combative nature was largely developed by living with him, for I had to fight for everything that I kept. About two years after we were married we exchanged our mutual properties for seventeen hundred acres of land on the San Bernard river in Texas, part of which was a cotton plantation. We knew nothing of the cultivation of cotton or of plantation life. . . .

While Carry struggled to manage the cotton crop, her husband went to Brazoria, the county seat, to try his luck at practicing law. When it became clear that life on the plantation was hopeless, Carry took over management of a hotel in the small town of Columbia, Texas.

. . . I borrowed of Mr. Dunn three dollars and fifty cents, and with this money began the hotel business. The house was a rattle trap, plastering off, and a regular bed-bug nest. I fumigated, pasted the walls over with cloth and newspapers, where the plastering was off, and made curtains out of old sheets. . . . The transients at one meal would give me something to spend for the next. I assisted about the cooking and helped in the dining-room. Mother Gloyd and Lola attended to the chamber work, and little Charlien was the one who did the buying for the house. I

10. It is not clear why Carry refers to a large family, since Nation had only one child, Lola, who was eight years old when Carry married for the second time in 1877.

11. The Nations were married for twenty-four years. Supposedly because she was away from home so often doing temperance work, Mr. Nation divorced Carry on the grounds of desertion (Nation, *Use and Need,* [1908], 187).

would often wash out my tablecloths at night myself and iron them in the morning before breakfast. I would take boarders' washing, hire a woman to wash, then do the ironing myself. . . . I can never put on paper the struggles of this life. I would not know one day how we would get along the next.

The bitterest sorrows of my life have come from not having the love of a husband. I must here say that I have had, at times, in the society of those I love, a foretaste of what this could be. For years I never saw a loving husband that I did not envy the wife; it was a cry of my heart for love. I used to ask God why He denied me this. I can see now why it was. I know it was God's will for me to marry Mr. Nation. Had I married a man I could have loved, God could never have used me. Phrenologists who have examined my head have said: "How can you, who are such a lover of home be without one?" The very thing that I was denied caused me to have a desire to secure it for others. Payne who wrote "Home Sweet Home" never had one. There is in my life a cause of sadness and bitter sorrow that God only knows. I shall not write it here. Oh! how the heart will break almost for a loving word! I believe the great want of the world is love. Jesus came to bring love to earth.

Through years of backbreaking work managing hotels and boarding houses, anxiety about her daughter's health, and fervent religious faith, Carry Nation grew resolute and fearless. At last she saw that she could serve God and help countless others through dramatic confrontations and public appearances as a temperance campaigner. Starting in 1900 she traveled widely from her home in Medicine Lodge, Kansas, to lead demonstrations that attracted thousands of supporters. Despite her violent tactics and controversial behavior, Nation deserves to be honored for her courageous crusade against the sale of liquor and her belief in the "rights and dignity of women." [12]

After living for a while in Topeka, the Oklahoma Territory, and Washington, D.C., and campaigning in Scotland and England, Carry Nation moved to Alpena Pass, Boone County, Arkansas. She closes her life story with a hopeful view of the future.

I feel now that this great wave of Prohibition that is sweeping over the whole land propelled by a mighty power of public sentiment will go on and on, until national Prohibition will be the ultimate outcome, and seeing that younger people are taking up the work, I can, with a good conscience, retire for the winter to my mountain home, where we have the old fashion fire places, where the simple life, the delightful life, the country life, is there in all its fullness with tame fruit in abundance, and

12. Bader, *Prohibition in Kansas*, 153–55.

wild grapes hanging in myriads of clusters in the gorgeous colored forest trees. . . .

And now in closing this last chapter of my book I can say to humanity, that I feel grateful for their many kind words and deeds, expressions of gratitude for the imperfect way in which I have served you. I can see where I have made grievous mistakes, they were of the head and not of the heart. Yet exceeding all this is the gratitude I owe to God for using me on behalf of the motherhood to rescue the boy.

Carry Nation died in 1911 and was buried in Belton, Missouri, next to her mother. In 1924 a monument was placed at her grave with the inscription "Faithful to the Cause of Prohibition. 'She Hath Done What She Could.' "[13]

13. Madison reports that Carry Nation collapsed during her final public appearance at Eureka Springs. While being carried from the stage, she is supposed to have said, "I have done what I could" (*Carry Nation*, 151–52). She stated in the preface of *Use and Need* [1909], "Some day I will lie under the shade of a tree, and I want these words on the marble above my dust, 'She hath done what she could.' "

Emma J. Ray (1859–1930)

*A*lthough she was born a slave, Emma J. Ray's life proved more fortunate than many. All her family members were purchased by one owner and allowed to stay together. Lloyd P. Ray, her husband, was born in Texas in 1860. His mother was a slave and he never knew his father, reported to be a white man.

Because of their race and economic class, the Rays represent an important voice in this anthology. Although Missouri, admitted to the Union as a slave state in 1821, had the highest concentration of black people among the prairie states, it is difficult to obtain personal writings from black women who lived during the nineteenth and early twentieth century in Missouri.[1]

Emma Smith and Lloyd Ray met in 1881 and were married in 1887. In 1889 they moved to Seattle, where rebuilding in the city after a devastating fire meant work for Mr. Ray, a stonecutter and mason. Both experienced a spiritual conversion in the African Methodist Episcopal Church. Afterward they committed themselves to evangelical work among the lower classes. *Twice Sold, Twice Ransomed: Autobiography of Mr. and Mrs. L. P. Ray*, published in 1926, weaves together the religious and social threads that helped create the fabric of the lives of former slaves and the poor during the late nineteenth and early twentieth centuries.

Attention to the spiritual and social needs of common laborers and the unemployed finds its roots in the ministry of John Wesley in England and America during the latter half of the eighteenth century. Wesley reached the working classes with a simple and understandable message. His methods of personal devotional growth enlivened the rituals of the Anglican Church and struck a harmonious chord among the uneducated and downtrodden. He was firm in his commitment to "free" churches that were not dependent upon pew rental by the middle and upper classes to raise funds and reserve seats. He denounced slavery as "that execrable sum of all villainies," and in the 1743 General Rules of the Church he prohibited "buying or selling the bodies and souls of men, women, and children, with an intention to enslave them."[2] In the early days of the American Methodist Church, itinerant preachers had to agree to emancipate slaves, as did church members. This requirement was eased considerably in 1785, in order to accommodate the political and economic forces of the southern churches. When the American Methodist Church

1. Cf. Glenda Riley, *The Female Frontier*, 25–28.
2. William B. McClain, *Black People in the Methodist Church: Whither Thou Goest?*, 55, 10. See also Warren Thomas Smith, *John Wesley and Slavery* (Nashville: Abingbon Press, 1986), which contains a reprint of John Wesley, *Thoughts on Slavery*, 3d ed. (London: R. Hawes, 1774).

split in 1844 over the issue of slavery, the northern conferences still compromised on the issue in order to hold onto their members from the border states and those whose livelihood depended on cheap cotton from the South.

Methodism had a strong appeal among slaves prior to the Civil War. John Thompson, a slave in Maryland, born in 1812, gives some idea why in his diary:

> My mistress and her family were all Episcopalians. The nearest church was five miles from our plantation and there was no Methodist church nearer than ten miles. So we went to the Episcopal Church, but always came home as we went, for the preaching was above our comprehension, so we could understand but little that was said. But soon the Methodist religion was brought among us, and preached in a manner so plain that the wayfaring man, though a fool, could not err therein. This new doctrine produced great consternation among the slaveholders. It was something which they could not understand. It brought glad tidings to the poor bondsman; it bound up the broken-hearted; it opened the prison doors to them that were bound, and let the captives go free. As soon as it got among the slaves, it spread from plantation to plantation, until it reached ours, where there were but few who did not experience religion.[3]

The Methodist Church appealed to the slaves and other poorer classes for several reasons: the simplicity of its message, lack of emphasis on ritual, a tradition of hearty congregational hymn-singing, opposition to slavery, organization into small societies for study and learning of Scripture, strong emotional appeal in preaching, and allowing African Americans and women to serve as lay preachers.[4] In spite of Wesley's focus on inclusion of all races and classes in the church, as early as 1796 African Americans separated from the John Street Church in New York and established the African Methodist Episcopal Zion Church. In 1816, a Philadelphia congregation formed the African Methodist Episcopal Church. The black congregations remained in close fellowship with their white counterparts, but developed their own distinctive cultural features.

Besides its appeal to former slaves, Methodism beckoned the working poor and those displaced by industrial and economic changes. Believing that spiritual and physical needs went hand in hand, John Wesley engaged in active social work among the poor.[5] William and Catherine Booth carried on this tradition as Methodists, then left that denomination in 1861 to found the Salvation Army. Meanwhile, in America, several Methodist pastors deplored the church's straying from the original

---

3. John Thompson, *The Life of John Thompson, A Fugitive Slave*, 18–19.
4. Cf. McClain, *Black People in the Methodist Church*, 21–35, and Earl Kent Brown, *Women of Mr. Wesley's Methodism*, 15–25.
5. Leslie R. Marston, *From Age to Age A Living Witness*, 106–7.

dictates of Wesley, both in doctrine and practice. Many of these "Reformers" lamented the church turning away from its antislavery stance and racially integrated churches. Also, there were more and more Methodist churches renting pews, thus leaving fewer free spaces for the poor, especially in urban areas. In 1860, several Reformers were expelled by the General Conference of the Methodist church. They founded the Free Methodist denomination, returning to the older General Rules of Wesley as their guidelines. They stressed antislavery and free pews as well as adherence to doctrinal and behavior standards of the early Methodist *Discipline*.[6]

The Rays, like many freedmen, found solace in the Methodist experience and delivery from what they considered to be destructive social habits such as drinking and dancing. They soon, however, found themselves in doctrinal disagreement with the Methodists and joined the Free Methodist Church in Seattle, although they continued to do evangelistic work for several denominations. Influenced by the Wesleyan tradition of social work, particularly the model of the Salvation Army's work in cities, the Rays worked among the urban poor, reaching out to their own race. Emma Ray exemplifies the important role played by religious women who responded to God's call and became leaders in their communities.[7]

Twice Sold, Twice Ransomed gives a glimpse of life from a post-slavery African American perspective. Mrs. Ray dedicated herself to pioneering work among her "own people." She confronts the realities of racism while also noting that class played an equally important role in perceptions and prejudices: "I want to say right here that many of the white people think that the colored people are all alike. . . . However, there are different classes of us. . . ." Mrs. Ray acknowledges "that the better class of our people had no idea of the conditions as they existed among the unfortunates. . . ."[8]

Mrs. Ray's life demonstrates that hope persists no matter what the hardship. Unlike many of the women quoted in this text, she had few material possessions and little money throughout her life, and what she had she gave away. Because her husband was a common laborer, she

6. The *Book of Discipline* was the official document—always revisable and often revised—in which the Methodist way of life is spelled out. During the 1730s Methodist revival, Wesley composed a short document known as "The Nature, Design, and General Rules of the United Societies" (1738, published in 1743). This document became the basis of what later Wesleyan denominations called the *Book of Discipline*. Professor Richard Steele, Department of Religion, Seattle Pacific University, interview by Barbara Oliver Korner, January 10, 1997.

7. Cf. Carolyn De Swarte Gifford, "Women in Social Reform Movements," in Rosemary Ruether and Rosemary Keller, eds., *Women and Religion in America: The Nineteenth Century*, 296–97.

8. Emma J. Ray, *Twice Sold, Twice Ransomed: Autobiography of Mr. and Mrs. L. P. Ray*, 287–88. All passages are from the 1926 edition. Page references will be identified in the text.

saw herself not only as a black, but as a member of the lower classes along with poor whites and other ethnic groups. She found guidance in the Christian message, experienced firsthand through the change in her own life after her conversion. The road was not easy for anyone, but there was help available through faith in an omnipotent God. She lived out the resolution adopted by the 1866 General Conference of the Free Methodist Church and approved by subsequent general conferences: "To civilized and savage, bond and free, black and white, the ignorant and the learned, is freely offered the great salvation."

While her husband earned a living in the construction industry, Emma Ray worked in Seattle jails and slums. He would join her in the evenings, on the streets. On a visit to Missouri in 1900 to visit family and friends, Emma felt called to establish a mission in one of the most destitute areas of Kansas City. Her husband joined her. Unlike many middle and upper class women who engaged in such work, she chose to live among the people she served. Two years later the Rays returned to Seattle and again took up mission work in the slum areas. They conducted Sunday evening meetings for the Olive Branch Mission run by the Free Methodists and became popular as evangelistic speakers throughout Washington and Oregon and in California. Letters of support included in her autobiography describe Mrs. Ray as "a stirring preacher." She died at her Seattle home on November 25, 1930, survived by her husband.[9]

Although there are no records describing Emma Ray's speaking style, from her writing style and other testimony, we can imagine her as part of two traditions of the nineteenth century: 1) those passionate voices among African American women reformers including Sojourner Truth, Anna Haywood Cooper, Ida Wells, Victoria Earle Matthews, and others;[10] and 2) the tradition of the Methodist Church and later the Free Methodist Church of incorporating both African American and female lay preachers. Many biblical allusions are woven into her writing, as one can imagine they were in her speaking. Also, one gets a sense of the deep emotion she was capable of imparting as she spoke. In later life, one man recalled the Rays' impact on Pleasant Valley, Washington:

> When the news spread through the community that 'colored preachers' were going to tell the 'white folks' where they were going, the frolicking crowd of young people (of whom I was one) planned a time of great fun. No doubt you remember how the young folk swarmed into the church, chewing gum, cracking peanuts, lighting matches, etc., but, Sister Ray, we knew not what we were doing. Your patience and kindness and love for us young folk, demonstrated from the pulpit, began to be felt, and Holy Ghost conviction seized the

9. Obituary, *Seattle Times*, November 28, 1930.

10. Cf. Shirley Wilson Logan, ed., *With Pen and Voice: A Critical Anthology of Nineteenth-Century African-American Women*.

crowd, until one young person after another said he didn't know what was wrong with him, but he didn't feel like disturbing the meeting any more.[11]

We have selected passages from Emma Ray's autobiography that highlight her years growing up, first as a slave and then in the family of a poor freedman in Missouri, along with sections describing her work in "Hick's Hollow" in the slums of Kansas City. Mrs. Ray's effectiveness as a minister of the gospel to a wide range of people, poor and rich, black and white, is captured in an undated letter written by the Rev. Harry E. Kreider, District Elder of the Washington Conference of Free Methodist Church:

> I was reminded of a discussion I had with a fair-faced man from southern Missouri. He was of the opinion that the Negro did not have a soul. If he had been present and had seen Brother and Sister Ray, and had heard them sing, testify, preach and pray, under the blessing of God, he would have been thoroughly convinced that the Negro had a soul in which God deigned to dwell. . . .
>
> They have proven themselves capable, under the grace of God, of rescuing precious souls from the cesspool of sin in the slums. Their ability and adaptability to labor for the salvation of all men make them successful evangelists to all classes.[12]

TWICE SOLD, TWICE RANSOMED

Autobiography of Mr. and Mrs. L. P. Ray

I was born twice, bought twice, sold twice, and set free twice. Born of woman, born of God; sold in slavery, sold to the devil; freed by Lincoln, set free by God.

I was born in the State of Missouri, January 7, 1859, in a little town called Springfield. I was born of slave parents. My great grandfather was brought from Africa and sold as a slave in the State of Virginia. My father's name was John Smith, that being the name of his master. My mother's name was Jennie Boyd.

When I was one month old, I, my sister, who was one and one-half years old, and my mother, who held me in her arms, were sold at the auction block to the highest bidder. Two of my father's young masters bid us in, so our names became Smith.

My father was never sold, but lived in the same family where he was born until he became free. He was very much troubled at the prospect of

11. Ray, *Twice Sold,* 287–88.
12. Ibid., 284–85.

seeing his wife, my mother, sold, and became restless, consequently his young master bought us in just to please my father, as he threatened to run away.

Every slave, after being made free, had the privilege of choosing a name for himself, but my father kept the name of Smith until his death. He was much loved by his owners. They moved to the State of Missouri when he was but a child. He was really the property of the young mistress, who refused to sell him, but kept him as chore boy in the big house and the whole family loved him. This explains why they so readily bought us in at the auction. (15–16)

When the glad tidings came that we were freed, and the war was over, such rejoicing and weeping and shouting among the slaves was never heard before, unless it was the time that the Ark of the Covenant was brought back to the children of Israel.[13] Great numbers of the slaves left their masters immediately. They had no shelter, but they dug holes in the ground, made dug-outs, brush houses, with a piece of board here and there, wherever they could find one, until finally they had a little village called "dink-town," looking more like an Indian village than anything else. There they sang and prayed and rejoiced. Later on, the soldiers began to come through, returning from the war. They brought many negroes with them who were searching for members of their families. I remember my mother, with me holding on to her skirts, standing watching the soldiers as they passed in their blue suits, and the colored people all shouting "hurrah for Marse Abe," and cheering the Union boys as they passed. That was a glad day. That certainly was a year of jubilee for the poor black slave.[14] They had heard about the Liberation from Bondage of the Children of Israel from the Egyptians and their prayers were always to the Almighty God, and the God of Abraham, Isaac and Jacob that they too some day might be delivered, and now it had actually come. Oh! what joy!

My father was the only colored man [in the community] that could write. Slaves were not allowed to learn to read and write, under penalty of flogging, but my father was a house servant and had stolen his education from the young masters as they said over their lessons. He was kept up for hours at night, and sometimes almost all night, writing letters trying to find out where loved ones were. Some had been run south, some were sold away, and they could not tell their names, only the first names. Mothers were hunting children, and husbands hunting wives; they kept my father very busy.

13. II Samuel 6:12–21. The Ark of the Covenant was a sacred object for the Hebrews, representing God's Presence, Holiness, and Mercy.

14. Leviticus 25:8–55. Every fiftieth year the Hebrews were supposed to celebrate the "Year of Jubilee." All debts were cancelled, slaves were set free, and lands that had been sold were returned.

It was also very hard upon the slave owners, as there were none of the white women that knew anything about work, and they were left without a single servant. It was hard for both blacks and whites to become used to the change, for the slaves had no idea how to earn a living. Some of the slaves that had good masters never left, but stayed on the plantations the rest of their lives.

. . . Soon after that came the assassination of Abraham Lincoln. That brought great sorrow over all the land, and especially to the blacks. I remember the village of huts where the negroes lived; every one would have a little piece of black cloth hung on it. They could not afford crepe, but it was merely a piece of old black pants, or coat, or anything in order to show their bereavement and their sorrow, that one so great had been taken from them. . . . I heard them speak so much about "Marse Abraham" in their prayers, and sermons, and talk, and about "resting in Abraham's bosom" that I thought for a long time that Abraham Lincoln, and Abraham in the Bible, were the same man, until I began to go to Sunday-school and learned the difference. (20–22)

Emma's mother died in 1868, leaving nine children, the youngest "not over a year old." Determined to keep the family together, the father allowed the children to "work out" for local families.

In the fall of the year, after working in the summer time, the children that were old enough were sent to school. Two of us girls were old enough; our three brothers and oldest sister had no chance to go; they had to work. Our white school-teachers, sent from the North, were devout Christians and missionaries. They taught us not only to read, but also to study the Bible and to learn the ways of God. . . . I did not go very steadily. I worked out in the summer and went to school in the winter.

I soon got to the place where I wanted pretty clothes, and I was ashamed of my dresses, but father could not give us any better.

Part of the time I did not have enough to eat. I have gone to school many a day without having anything to eat until night, with the exception of a piece of cold corn bread. When I saw other girls, who had mothers, have good things to eat in their dinner pails, I would hide mine. I thought then as much of a white-flour biscuit as I would of the finest fruit-cake now. Everybody ate corn bread, and, if we had that and bacon, we fared well. This was also the fare of many of the poor whites. I ofttimes took my little sister and went off by myself and ate my corn bread with sorghum molasses, if I was fortunate to have that, and I would never let them know but that I had dined sumptuously. One time when I saw the white girls coming home from school I called to them and asked what they had left in their dinner pails. One girl gave me a biscuit with peach preserves on it. It was made of white flour and I think it was the best biscuit I ever tasted. I am sure it was, for I have never forgotten the taste of it, and as I write it almost seems that I can taste it now; old-fashioned peach preserves, made as only a Southerner can make them.

As poor as we were, our father did not allow us to beg, especially for something to eat. He told us it was a disgrace to beg. He thought it better to go hungry than to beg, and if he saw a person, especially a white person who had been free all his life, begging, he would say, "I can't see how persons that have had their liberty all their lives need to come to such want." He told us to wait. He would get it for us . . . [and] he would be sure to come in with a little meal, and ofttimes with bacon, at night.

I went to school until I entered the fourth grade. Of course our privileges were not such as they are now, but I learned to read, and write, and spell, and that was considered among our people a pretty good education. My father wanted me to keep up my studies, but I soon got to the age when I wanted to work and buy some clothes, as I would ofttimes have to go to school with the sole of my shoe all loose and tied on with a string, through deep snows and zero weather. When I look back now and see how other girls who were clothed so much better than I, sickened and died from catching cold from exposure, I realize it was only the mercy of God that I lived through it, and that He had a purpose in it all. I can see plainly that it was all in answer to my mother's prayer. (26–28)

Later on, the Christmas holidays arrived. Everyone was making presents for the Christmas tree in the church and I knew we would have no presents because we were poor, and I hated to see my little sisters left out, so I began to plan some way to have our names called. Right here I practised my first church deception. We got together and said, "We'll put something on for you if you'll put something on for us, and we will just wrap up wooden chips in paper and put them on as though they were presents. We won't open them in the church, but we will have our names called." So we each did this, our names were called; and we received our presents, and yet there was a consciousness of guilt on us, but we never told it. We watched the other children get their presents and, as we started away, one said to the other, "It's better than any." We meant it was better than none. (34–35)

I met my future husband, L. P. Ray, in Carthage, Missouri, in '81. He was young like myself and had not been from home very long. Mr. Ray's home was in Emporia, Kansas. We were married in Fredonia, Kansas, in '87. He learned the trade of stonecutter and mason. We were very happy for a short time. Later, my husband began to drink, not so very heavily at first. I knew that he drank when we were married, but I didn't think much of it at that time. I thought so long as he could take a drink or let it alone when he liked, it was all right. I thought it looked manly for him to smoke a cigar. I didn't give it much thought, until it began to come so often—then our trouble began. When I woke up I found that he had become a drunkard. The class of men that he worked with was made up of drinking men, and he always said that he felt he had to be a man among men. When they got their pay they would all take a drink around. It soon came to pass that he began to lie about his wages. He got despondent afterwards, and declared that he would never take another drink, but it would not be very long—a space of possibly a week—until he would be at it again and I got to the place where I had no confidence in him. And he would say, "I'll prove to you that I will be a man yet," and then he would get morbid and say, "I'll leave this town. If I can get away I'll go where I am not so well acquainted, and I will do better." He went ahead, as we never had money enough left to go together, but he would always send for me as soon as he could, and then we would start again to live a new life. It would not be very long before it would be the same old drink, the same old devil, the same old sin. I had a temper equal to a tigress. And a drinking man and a woman with a high temper make a home a hell. (37–38)

The Rays moved to Seattle in 1889. The rebuilding of the city after a recent fire meant work for Mr. Ray as a stonecutter. Shortly after arriving, the Rays were converted during revival services at the African Methodist Church. The Woman's Christian Temperance Union visited ladies at her church, and Mrs. Ray was elected President of the first "colored" W.C.T.U. in Seattle. Soon the Rays began a jail ministry, often taking released prisoners into their home. Their work expanded into hospitals and street ministry, especially in slum areas in Seattle. Mrs. Ray's autobiography gives a poignant account of work among drug addicts. After a decade, she returned to Missouri for a visit.

On the first day of May, 1900, I started from Seattle to go east. I had been praying for a long time that God would open the way that I might go back and tell the good news, to my relatives and friends, as to what the Lord had done for me. When I left there I was in sin and darkness. I had been in great expectation, waiting for the time to come to start back to my old home. I . . . bade good-bye to my friends in Seattle. Brother Ray remained behind, as he had a job of work to finish. He planned on coming a couple of months later. As I left Seattle, . . . I looked out on the old County Hospital where I had seen so many poor souls saved and started for heaven. I couldn't help but shed a few tears. After I got out of the city, my mind turned toward the old state of Missouri, where I was born. My joy was so great I could hardly sit still in the train. I would ride for about an hour, and then I would go back into the dressing room and get down upon my knees, right while the train was moving, and thank God for every mile-stone along the way.

When I came west and would cross a canyon or high bridge, or any dangerous place, I would become frightened. . . . [But now going back] I was saved and could pass the rough and smooth places with great peace of mind and soul. There was one song especially that I was singing in my heart,

> Leaning on Jesus, leaning on Jesus,
> Safe and secure from all alarm,
> Leaning on Jesus, leaning on Jesus,
> Leaning on the Everlasting Arm.

I had no fear of a train wreck or anything else. I was thinking of the time when I should look into the face of my dear old father once more and tell him of the joy I had in serving the Lord. . . . It seemed as though the blessing of God was upon the fields, and mountains, and the cattle. I could see God in the rivers, in the little streams and in the flowers, and it all made me think of heaven. . . . It seemed as though the very wheels of the train were saying, "Praise the Lord, praise the Lord!" When the engine would scream it seemed to say, "Glory to God! Glory to God!" I shouted for joy all the way from Seattle to Kansas City, Missouri, over two thousand miles.

When I arrived in Kansas City, my sister and husband met me at the train. I had not seen her for thirteen years. . . . When we got to their home in the city . . . we talked almost all night. I told them of what the Lord had wrought in the lives of my husband and me.

On the following Sabbath she took me with her to church. It was a very large, fashionable church, and the people were dressed in the latest styles. The choir sang well, but I missed that old-fashioned spirituality and hand-shake that they used to have when I was a girl. Things had changed with the times, and while they had progressed wonderfully, financially and intellectually, I was sorry to see that in many of them the old-fashioned spirituality had died out, and a new era of things had set in. I was with my sister a couple of weeks. . . . She took me to look over some parts of the slums, and we found the slum work much different from what it was in Seattle. There was no work being done among our own people in the slums. There was Salvation Army work among the whites and lots of missions, but no rescue work of any kind in the slums where the colored people were. We could see sin and vice on every hand. I began to cry as I looked around and saw so many of my own race in sin, drunkenness, and misery. Among the better classes of our race they had schools, and we found just as cultured people as we had ever met among the whites in the north. We had an opportunity to speak to the pastor of one of the leading churches and he told us that there was not a work of the kind in the city. My sister said that I had better stop over and work, as there was plenty to be done among our own people. I wrote to my husband and told him of the conditions as I had found them. The saloons down among the lower classes were one to every block. Men, women, and children carried beer by the pail. I saw children from four years up with buckets of beer and, oh, how my heart bled for them. I began to hope that some way the Lord would redeem some of these poor souls from their debauchery and shame. "Sin is a reproach to any people, but righteousness exalteth a nation."[15] I had seen sin of a different type and slums of a different type, but both were caused by the same principle, that of sin. My sister begged me to come there, with my husband, and work. These people of my race had come to this city from the farms and plantations of the south. Being illiterate and helpless, they had drifted down into this part of Kansas City. Some of the people of the better classes told me that if these people down in this low section wanted to make anything of themselves, they should come up from there. They did not think it right to go down and mix with them. We saw some of the same conditions among some of the poor whites, and Italians. I would cry everywhere I went, as I looked out on these awful sights and I saw that there was no one to rescue them, only as they came up to the churches. This they scarcely ever did. I wrote to my husband about it and wished he were with me to hold street meetings. (103–8)

Mrs. Ray left Kansas City to visit family and friends in Springfield, where her husband joined her from Seattle. In Springfield, she found "no slums among our people there" and enjoyed visiting places and people from her past and sharing with many of them her conversion experience. Mrs. Ray attended a Presbyterian Church service.

As it happened, it was an Old Folk's Day, and they had sent out carriages to bring all the old people, who were not able to walk, to church. Some came who were nearly a hundred years old . . . most all of whom I had known when a child. . . . After prayer and reading of the Bible, the meeting was open for testimonies before preaching . . . and then I rose and told them of what the Lord had done for me. How I thanked them for their prayers for me when I was young and couldn't realize what it meant, although I belonged to the church. I didn't know then what vital salvation was. I thanked them for their godly lives, and they began to shout and it seemed like old times when I was a child. Well, it really seemed like getting into heaven. . . . It was a pleasure to me to go to some of their homes, although there were great changes. Instead of some of the old log cabins there were cottages and beautiful yards, and I could see a wonderful improvement intellectually and financially, for which I was very thankful. I also visited an old spring near the old home from which I had at times carried many a [pail] of water upon my head [and at the same time one in my hands] for about a quarter of a mile. (109)

15. Proverbs 14:34.

Armed with a letter from the Seattle Woman's Christian Temperance Union, where Emma Ray had been County Superintendent of Jail and Prison Work, the Rays decided to heed her sister's recommendation and work in Kansas City for awhile.

This Union was a white one, as there were no colored W.C.T.U.'s in Kansas City. They greeted me quite heartily. After bringing them greetings from the W.C.T.U. of Seattle, I told them that we had decided to stop over in Kansas City and work among our own people in the slums, jails, and workhouses. They were very glad to help us in any way they could. We saw the need of it, and we hoped to get up an interest among the colored people along this line. They voted to give me a recommendation to the sheriff, so that I could immediately begin my work. . . . [The sheriff] gladly consented to have us come in and work among our own people. There was only one colored woman in Kansas City who had done any special work along this line. She had been working with the whites. Her name was Mrs. Moore. She had quit this work and was a matron at the Old People's Home, so we were the first band of colored people to organize themselves for work in the jails and workhouses of Kansas City, Missouri. The Lord graciously rewarded our labors. (113–14)

Their first work was in the prisons, where they were received gladly. They found terrible conditions, but through prayers, singing, and Bible lessons, worked to lift the morale of the prisoners and convert them to a better way of life upon their release. While writing her book twenty-five years later, Mrs. Ray notes that the prison work they started in Kansas City was still being carried on by Elder A. B. Ross. Due to cold weather, Mr. Ray had difficulty finding work as a stonecutter, and they struggled for awhile to make ends meet. Their meals were often corned beef boiled with rutabagas or other vegetables. They saved the juice to cook with for the next day's meals and skimmed off grease for frying an occasional egg given to them by others. Once the cold spell lifted, Mr. Ray found work that continued until they left Kansas City two years later.

Moving from more comfortable quarters, they established a mission at 590 Lydia Street, "Hick's Hollow," which Mrs. Ray describes as "one of the roughest and most notorious corners." Here they shared meals and household goods with the children and adults of the neighborhood. They took the children on outings to parks in the summer, for in that area "there was not a sprig of grass growing around there . . . for them to play on." Mrs. Ray writes with pride that when the children from her mission were taken to join the "better classes" for the exercises at a church Children's Day, they were "the best behaved children of all. They knew the Scriptures better than those children who had had better experiences" (120).

The people that came to the meetings, in their testimonies, would frequently say, "Sister Ray's Mission," as they always found me there and

Brother Ray out working. I did not feel that it was fair, because Brother Ray made it possible for me to get out to the day meetings to work with the children, by going out and making the means of our living. I always said, "Don't say Sister Ray's Mission and work. It is Brother and Sister Ray's work. Husband works through heat and cold and never seems to tire. He is always willing to put in every cent for the salvation of souls or to help them." I would ofttimes say, "I'm preaching the gospel and he is working to pay expenses," which was a real truth. I heard a sister tell of once taking a voyage across the sea on a large liner. She said the most prominent man on the ship was the captain. Every one was saying, . . . "I will talk with the Captain. He is running the ship." This woman said she would like to see the stoker and asked some one to take her down in the hold of the ship to see him. When she got in the engine room there was the man with his face all dirty from the coal and perspiration. He was poking the coal in the furnace and keeping the fire going to keep the steam up to run the engine. The woman said, "That's the man I feel like praising. If he failed at his job, the Captain would not get very far." I got a lesson from this story and from that time on I didn't want anyone to say "Sister Ray's" for by the help of the Lord and by the backing and cooperation of my husband I was able to do the work and felt that we were workers together. To God be all the glory. (122–23)

The Rays had the upper part of the mission building completely to themselves, but the carousing, which often led to violence, in the rooms below and in the street outside their windows, worried Mrs. Ray terribly. They often were in fear for their own safety, so much so that Mr. Ray thought they should return to Seattle. Inspired by a sermon, however, they decided to stay. Upon returning to the mission from the inspirational church service,

. . . we could see that the doors were open down stairs. Thank the Lord, our disturbers had all moved away while we were at the meeting. . . . We rented the vacant rooms in the lower part of the building. We had some extra Sunday-school rooms. Of course it meant much for us to have to pay the rent, but we did not tell any one of our needs. There was one brother and sister who gave us a dollar or two occasionally. We did not take up any collection, except to let the children bring their pennies to Sunday-school, as they wanted to do it. However, this was never enough to meet the expenses of their literature, but we were only too glad to pay the balance ourselves.

Husband worked this summer and the Lord helped us to get a little money ahead. This was one of the hottest summers they had had in years. People were dying all over the city from the heat. Horses were dropping on the streets. They had to cover the horses' heads. The Lord gave Brother Ray the strength to go right on with his work. He never lost a day while making a stone foundation. (129)

The last winter we were there the smallpox was very prevalent all over the city and more so in this place on account of the insanitary conditions. We had read the promises of God in the ninety-first psalm, "He that dwelleth in the secret place of the most high shall abide under the shadow of the Almighty." It says that no plague shall come nigh thy dwelling. The health officers did not pay much attention to the people down there.

The children came into the Mission all broken out. When we were in the meetings in the fall several cases broke out. Brother Ray was working every day. We had saved a little bit for the winter and I felt that he should stop his work and help me in the work, but the man he worked for insisted on his taking another building so he continued his work. Then he took the smallpox. . . . We felt so sorry, as we had held meeting all day Sunday and had had a great many visitors, and we thought of the little children, and cried mightily to our Father to not let any of them catch it, as they had all been exposed. We sent word around to the houses for none to come in, and sent for an officer to come and quarantine us. We quarantined ourselves. We did not go outside or let any one come in. The officers failed to come. We sent for them every day for over a week. This shows how indifferent they are with those poor neglected people. Finally they came after Brother Ray, when he was getting better. . . . For the first time I became somewhat discouraged and wished that we were in Seattle. I wondered at first why he should have the smallpox. When we were having our prayer for the night, I knelt on the floor and wept bitterly, and husband said, "Sing, don't weep." I told him I couldn't sing, that I had to cry it out. Finally we prayed again and went to bed and way in the night it seemed as though I heard a voice say, "Look to Jesus." From that moment I became reconciled. We had with us a book called, "Christian's Secret of a Happy Life." We read this book through and got such an uplift to our souls. I was a very tired woman. The children all had to stay home. We had no mission and this gave us a chance to rest, as Brother Ray was very tired himself. Our trial turned out to be a blessing and we had such sweet communion with the Lord while we were closed in. We were glad after all that it happened. We didn't know we were so tired. It was a blessing in disguise. We never needed a rest so badly in our lives. . . . Just as Brother Ray was on his feet again and it was time for the scabs to fall off, the officers came for him and took him to the pesthouse. We had decided that if we got the smallpox we would go to the pesthouse together, but we heard of the awfully insanitary conditions there, and that they used blankets from one patient's bed for another, so I thought that as long as I did not have it I had better not go and get it. Brother Ray decided to leave me home. They took the mattress that he was on. They did that with most of the poor people as it saved the county something. After the mattresses got good and dirty they would burn them up. We only had one in the Mission, but I was glad to have him take it as I had heard how filthy it was at the pesthouse. (130–33)

Mr. Ray received a grateful welcome as a preacher at the "pesthouse," and the other patients dubbed him "Elder Ray." After a few days, convinced that she had safely escaped taking the smallpox, Mrs. Ray went to visit her husband.

The pesthouse was two miles from the city limits. There was a deep snow on the ground and it was very cold. After I got the house fumigated I took a basket of apples, oranges, tracts, and other things I thought he would need. I rode as far as I could on the street car and walked two miles out there. The place was fenced in with a high fence. It was like a stockade with guards on the outside of the place. I called and some colored women came and looked out the door, and I asked them if there was a Mr. Ray there and they said, "No, he died the other night." You can imagine how I felt. I said it couldn't be he, so they described him and I saw that it wasn't he. . . . [Then they called for "Elder Ray" to come out.] I wasn't allowed to go near where he was, but I could call to him from the distance. I hung the basket on the fence and walked away about one hundred feet. He told me he was doing fine. I thanked God and came away and praised Him all the way home for the experience. I felt that I would be a better woman, and that I would have more faith in Him after I had had such a good opportunity to prove Him out, like Job, in a time of testing and trial.

It certainly did not take long to discover that my dream was verified. Of all the dirty places I ever got into, this place was the limit, and this "Hollow" was the black stream of my dream. Our having to live among them and see their sins, and praying for them, was the swimming in the water. The Lord certainly helped us in getting some of them pulled out of the muck and mire. Many of them have moved out of the place and have lived better lives. (134–35)

Mr. Ray recovered and returned to work as both a stonecutter and partner in the mission work.

We would hold our meetings within a block or so of the Mission. In fact, all of our work was in this neighborhood. We did not have to go beyond the block to get a congregation. We usually held our meetings right between two saloons. We started out from the Mission, singing like the [Salvation] Army, marched down to the corner and formed a ring. By the time we got our ring formed and started to pray there would be a band of men, women, and children around us. We stayed for an hour and then marched back to the Mission. Ofttimes there were a few white people who stood listening, but usually it was all our people. Now and then one or two whites came into the Mission. The butcher from that neighborhood, an habitual drunkard, usually came out with his wife to listen to our testimonies and songs. One night he stood and wept and followed us into the Mission. He came to the altar and found the Lord. He went up into the city to the white people's Mission and told what the Lord had done for him, and was not ashamed to tell where the Lord found him.

One Saturday night as we walked down the street we started to pass the saloons and go up the street one block farther, but looked down the alley and saw a crowd of men and women standing at the side door of a saloon and drinking beer. A crap game was going on in the alley on the ground. We turned right in where they were playing dice and forming a ring, began to sing. They backed away. We sang a song and began to pray. Some one had a couple of bulldogs and they got to fighting. We kept right on with our prayer, although they were right around us. It was an exciting time for them and the onlookers. By the time we had finished praying, they were quiet. Sister Clayton, who was filled with the Holy Spirit, stepped into the ring and began to testify. It seemed to grip their attention and we had a splendid audience. The Lord helped us to tell them of their sinfulness and how badly they were bringing up their children, and that it was no wonder they were having so much trouble as a people. They believed us. We came away believing that those testimonies would have a lasting effect on those people. (143–44)

I am sorry to say that the better class of our people had no idea of the conditions as they existed among the unfortunates, as they had nothing to do with one another. I want to say right here that many of the white people think that the colored people are all alike. Human nature is the same the world over. However, there are different classes of us people the same as in other nations, and some just as refined, considering opportunities. They have their societies, churches, doctrines and ideas just as other people. The Lord gave us a few of the best colored Christian characters from the best churches to help us. As we had visited these churches and tent meetings through these we got an opportunity to lecture in a few of the churches. They were very much surprised when we told them of the conditions in the slums among our own people. I will mention here a couple of school teachers of Kansas City, Kansas, Mrs. Lizzie Bullett and Mrs. Mollie Harrison. There was also a Sister Woodford and a Sister Smith, and many others I have not space to mention. When they heard of the conditions they came down and rendered us all the assistance they could, going with us to the jails and on the streets. I will never fail to praise the Lord as long as I live for the assistance of those consecrated women, and some of the men. The first time that any of them came they said they went home and couldn't sleep of nights. Some said

Reverend and Sister Ray live in hell. They didn't know there was such a place on earth. We thanked the Lord for helping us to blaze the way. By doing this work there have been great results obtained in that place today. While we did not see all that we wanted to see done, as most of their hearts were hardened, and the light was new to them, but we did see a great change. We expect to see it when the Lord calls the roll on the other side. For we know that He is a prayer-hearing God, and He answers according to our faith. Lord, I believe!

When the first year of our stay in this place was up, husband took a week off. We fasted and prayed and wanted to get the mind of the Lord about coming home. But we couldn't find any one to take our places; although it was a good work, no one wanted the job. We couldn't get the mind of the Lord, and the children were so afraid we would leave, they would ask the Father not to let us leave them, saying, "What would us little children do?" We decided to stay.

The second year conditions were much better. The policemen walked through, one at a time, and they acknowledged a great change. We prayed over it. We had stayed over two years. One day after much prayer we both seemed to feel that it was the will of the Lord that we should leave. While we felt sorry for the children, there was a Baptist preacher who said he would take the work up, and the Lord lifted the burden of them off us. We knew that our work was done and I got so blessed in thinking of what the Lord had done for us. When I knew that we were going to Seattle and that this Baptist preacher was willing to undertake the work, I said to my husband, "How do you know but what the Lord will let us go back together?" We had decided that Brother Ray should go first, as we did not have the means for both of us to leave, as we had had such a hard winter. He said, "You have faith for it and ask Him to give us the means for both of us to go." I prayed over it. There was a Christian man who was the treasurer of the Armour stock-yards, whose acquaintance we had made while there. He consented to get us half fare. We belonged to a Faith Missionary Society while there, and they also gave us a half fare apiece. The Lord gave us more than we asked for. I became so blessed thinking of it that I said one day to some of the sisters when they were saying they hated to see us leave, "I believe that the Lord has said go and I feel the go in my heart." (146–48)

We left Kansas City, Missouri, August 4, 1902. It had been two years and three months since we had left Seattle to go east. We had fulfilled our mission with our kindred, finished our work in these parts and had done with our might what our hands found to do, and were now on our way back home with a greater love for our Savior, a deeper consecration, and a greater vision of things eternal. I had gone east alone, but on the homeward trip husband was with me. The journey was a happy one. We sang and rejoiced together all the way back. (150)

Upon their return to Seattle, the Rays became active again in mission work and street preaching, and also became popular as evangelists. Demand was high for them to hold revival services in small towns in Washington and Oregon, often where there were high populations of mill workers.

Mrs. Ray maintained her involvement in the prohibition movement and was part of a rally and parade in Seattle in 1914.

I had witnessed such a sight once before when but a child, and that was when the Negro race celebrated its first national independence. I felt just such a thrill then as I did when in the parade. Every one that could walk marched in the parade. Mothers with small children holding on to their skirts, and with babies in their arms, some of the returned soldiers from the war, and old ex-slave men.

We had no paved streets to march on at that time, but dirty rock roads, but we expressed the gladness in our hearts that we were free. Abraham Lincoln, under God had set us free.

This same joy of freedom was in the hearts of some of the men in the prohibition parade. Had not they, too, been slaves, and had not the Lord delivered them? (243)

In the last chapter of the autobiography, entitled "Dorothy Herald's Question," Emma Ray explains her satisfaction in her racial heritage and her service to God. She recounts an event when a young child approached her after a camp meeting and asked why she was black.

I took Dorothy by the hand and we went into a tent alone. She looked me right in the face as I told her the story of Jesus. Then I told her about the creation and how God made everything of its own kind, and that He loved variety. I told her of the different kinds of animals, birds, and flowers, and that He also made different colored people—some white, some black, some red, and some yellow, and that He loved them all, and that it was His choice to make me black and her white. She seemed perfectly satisfied with the explanation. I wish every one was as simple and childlike. I was glad to explain to her what I believe is the reason for my color, and if He has another purpose I can gladly say, "Good is the will of the Lord." I am perfectly satisfied with my color, and I would be almost frightened to death if I should turn white. I can truly say that I have never seen any one with whom I would change faces or places. I am satisfied with the way God made me. I want to be just myself in the Lord, because it pleases Him to have it so. The only thing I covet above everything, is to have a pure, white heart. (316–17)

MARGARET NELSON STEPHENS (1859–1929)

$\mathcal{D}$uring the nineteenth century women usually remained on the side-lines of politics and public service, but a few assumed the duties of an office and demonstrated administrative ability. Anne Hawkins Gentry was the second woman in American history to be appointed postmaster, serving Columbia, Missouri, from 1838 to 1865. Annie White Baxter of Carthage, the first woman in Missouri elected to a public office, assumed office as clerk of Jasper County in 1890. Later she worked as registrar of lands for the State of Missouri. The elegant and fashionable Margaret Nelson Stephens played a more traditional public role, motivated by devotion to her husband and sympathy for unfortunate people who turned to her for help.

Margaret Nelson was born in Boonville in 1859. Lon Vest Stephens, her future husband, was also born in Boonville, in 1858. Their romance began early. Margaret described a party in her diary: "Lon Stephens was my partner and he got me a plate of chicken salad and pickles. I noticed his hand and it is so large and strong for 14 years of age. Lon complimented me for being pretty and I got as red as a beet." Soon Margaret mused in her diary: "All day I've been wondering who I'll marry. Lon I hope."[1] That hope was fulfilled in 1880.

A banker and editor, Lon Vest Stephens became active in Democratic politics and served as state treasurer from 1889 to 1897. In Jefferson City he and his wife lived in an attractive home called Ivy Terrace. After his election as governor, they resided in the Executive Mansion from 1897 to 1901. After living at Ivy Terrace another two years, they moved to St. Louis. Governor Stephens died in 1923. Margaret Nelson Stephens built a home in St. Petersburg, Florida, where she met John W. Johnson, who was thirty-nine years her junior. They were married in 1928; Margaret died the next year. She was buried in the Walnut Grove Cemetery in Boonville next to her first husband, her tombstone reading "Margaret Nelson Stephens."[2]

Margaret Nelson, known to family and close friends as Maggie, began to keep a diary in 1869; she continued for the rest of her life. Each evening she wrote an entry, unless very busy or distressed, as during her bereavement after the death of Lon Vest Stephens. Mrs. Stephens kept a detailed record of her social life. Although inspired by Christian teachings, she did not meditate or philosophize in the diary. Her comments were mostly kept confidential, but she occasionally read entries to family

1. Cited in Nadine Mills Coleman, *Mistress of Ravenswood*, 14, 17.
2. Charles W. Leonard, interview with Carla Waal, February 20, 1988.

members or friends.[3] The many volumes are owned by the Leonard family of Ravenswood, except for the last two, which were given to her second husband.[4]

What is a "first lady"? As with the presidents' wives living in the White House, the role of First Lady of the State of Missouri has varied according to the individuality of each woman serving as hostess at the mansion and to changes in society. Mary Clarissa Honey Fletcher, whose husband was governor from 1865 to 1869, was a gracious, serene hostess noted for her work with temperance organizations. Mary Barr Jenkins Hardin, First Lady from 1875 to 1877, was a poet, painter, and Bible scholar with a knowledge of Greek and Latin. Serving as hostess for her father, who was the governor from 1877 to 1881, Mary Phelps Montgomery became noted for her kindness and charity to the poor of Jefferson City. A handsome woman with the "bearing of a queen," Jane Perry Francis was dedicated to raising her six sons, but she was also credited with renovating the mansion and persuading legislators to keep the state university in Columbia during her husband's administration from 1889 to 1893.[5]

As the last first lady of the nineteenth century and the first to reside in the mansion in the twentieth century, Margaret Nelson Stephens had her own distinctive style. Enjoying the good fortune of private wealth and a happy marriage, she was devoted to her family, fond of friends, and sympathetic to less fortunate people whom she called "lower class." While responsible for hospitality at the Executive Mansion, she took delight in decorating the house, planning parties, and dressing fashionably. Her existence was not carefree, for she worried about her husband's well-being, did work for the Methodist Church, visited inmates of the penitentiary and received supplications from their relatives. She must have had a warm and endearing manner that put everyone at ease. Despite her taste for propriety in manners, she sympathized with convicts and

3. Mrs. Stephens suffered great distress when portions of her childhood diary were made public by a friend. An editorial in the *St. Louis Post-Dispatch* defended the diary as "free from personal vanity" and characterized by "pure and gentle womanhood" (cited in Coleman, *Mistress of Ravenswood,* 59).

4. Ravenswood, located near Bunceton in Cooper County, was the home of Margaret's sister Nadine and her husband Captain Charles E. Leonard. The 2,000-acre farm was established in 1825; the mansion was built in 1880.

A number of diary entries have been quoted by Nadine Mills Coleman in *Mistress of Ravenswood.* The selections presented here, with the permission of Charles E. Leonard, covering only the years in the governor's mansion, are found in typescript at WHMC-C. The transcript by Micca M. Ruffin was presented to the archive by the Missouri Mansion Preservation in 1977. While maintaining characteristics of Mrs. Stephens's style, the present editors have corrected an occasional spelling or typographical error and added capitalization and punctuation for clarity. The omitted passages report on family members, pet dogs, social visits, arrangements for entertainment at the mansion, health, weather, vacation trips, and political appointments.

5. Eleanora G. Park and Kate S. Morrow, *Women of the Mansion,* 159, 202, 206, 235–39.

their families and others in need. Some idolized Mrs. Stephens, and she appeared to enjoy her image as a generous, saintly benefactor.

The following pages give an impression of Margaret Nelson Stephens's gifts as a gracious hostess, dismay at her husband's imbibing of liquor, and contentment with her role as helpmate. It was a role Lon Vest Stephens described in a commencement address at the School of Mines in Rolla in 1897:

> We have come to the period when all see the necessity for educated women. The intellectual and moral tone of the women of the country determines the tone and spirit of the men of a country. It is women's office to assist men to live as they ought.[6]

Her diary reveals Margaret Nelson Stephens's efforts to play exactly that role, assisting her husband to "live as he ought." He was a competent businessman rather than a skillful politician or distinguished statesman.[7] Mrs. Stephens may have been a more gifted politician than her husband; in fact, the Republicans thought she had undue influence on the governor and others in regard to political appointments, pardons, and certain legislation. Referring to the governor and his first lady, the Republicans suggested that the Democrats had elected "the lesser man of the two."[8] Mrs. Stephens would not have described herself as a politician. The diary reveals that the political was only a thread interwoven in the fabric of a life of marital devotion and social grace.

DIARY OF MARGARET NELSON STEPHENS

Executive Mansion
JULY 1, 1897

The beginning of another book—my last book (diary) is well filled, and is now locked in my writing desk drawer and the key lost.

How I regret that I have not written in my journal during the past year. While . . . my life has been sad at times, and [with] many rough places, yet there were many epochs I would like to have noted down! To think Lon has gone through a campaign and [been] *elected governor* of this *great state!* To say he has gone through a political campaign means I have

---

6. Cited in Coleman, *Mistress of Ravenswood,* 55.

7. A Republican review of his administration summarizes Stephens's term as "clean" and "businesslike" but "a disappointment to the whole state," whereas a Democratic evaluation praises his work in bringing the World's Fair to St. Louis in 1903 and his support of higher education and charitable institutions (*Jefferson City Republican,* January 7, 1901; William Rufus Jackson, *Missouri Democracy* [Chicago: S. J. Clarke, 1925], 1:249).

8. *The St. Louis Star,* July 8, 1897.

gone through it and [am] still alive—and that accounts for the ups and downs. . . .

Just think we have lived six months in the Mansion! We have had it greatly improved, painted, carpeted, &c.[9] Everyone greatly admires the drawing rooms with the green carpet and rose colored buds in it and furniture and hangings of that beautiful rich deep pink. The dining room is blue, deep blue. The library is papered in tapestry silk. The velour portieres [are] of tan, and tan figure[s] in the reddish purple tapestry. The hall is green. Our room is light blue. . . .

Tuesday night I had eight girls to spend the night with me. . . . Most of them dressed up in Male attire and had a jolly time. No young men were expected! How pretty Winnie [Pope] looked in Nelson's old military suit. Minnie [Crafton] looked too funny and stuffed. Bessie Miller and Edna [Gordon] were typical summer boys! . . .

JULY 3, 1897

I have spent most of the morning with Wilson the train robber's wife, who was here with her three children. He is the man who held up the Mo. Pac. [Missouri Pacific] train when Lon and I were passengers several years ago.

She seems a nice plain little woman. She says whiskey caused him to do it—and that is the cause of most of the suffering in this world.

I have to see so many heartbroken mothers and wives every day or two. Lon fears it will break my health down. But I don't think so. If I can lighten their burdened hearts it is a pleasure to me. . . .

JULY 5, 1897

Today, we breakfasted *early*—and were out at the prison by eight o'clock.[10] . . . After the convicts were through late breakfast we all went down in the dining room where Lon addressed them. After his speech he pardoned two white men and a negro.[11] When he called each up such

9. On the decor of the mansion, see *Past & Repast: The History and Hospitality of the Missouri Governor's Mansion,* 30.

10. The state penitentiary had an average population of 2,200 prisoners at this time. Because of labor performed by the inmates for private manufacturers, the prison was self-supporting and earned money for the state. *State Tribune* [Jefferson City], November 24, 1900. Contract labor continued and disciplinary practices were still "archaic" when Kate Richards O'Hare entered the prison in April 1919. For a description of conditions in the penitentiary, see Sally M. Miller, *From Prairie to Prison: The Life of Social Activist Kate Richards O'Hare,* 160–66.

11. It was customary for the governor to pardon two convicts on the holidays observed at the prison—the Fourth of July and Christmas Day. Stephens departed from tradition by pardoning three men on July 4, 1897 (*The Republican Courier* [Jefferson City], July 9, 1897).

a shout as went up. He was cheered often throughout his speech. This was an innovation. Peg and I became nervous and left the dining room, going up on the balcony that looks down on the yard. They were all turned loose there. Lon spent most of the morning in the office window shaking hands with the poor unfortunates. Lon introduced me to them— a crowd—as the Lieutenant Governor—and told them if I had my way I would turn them all loose.[12] I then listened to many who came to me with heavy hearts. . . .

JULY 8, 1897

Yesterday July the Seventh in the morning was one of the hottest days I ever experienced. I was completely *prostrated*—and never suffered as much in *my life*. My head was dizzy, and the perspiration dropped off of me in streams. . . . I laid down and had a wet cloth to my head and took a lemon and was greatly helped. Lemons always help me. At noon yesterday a carriage stopped here and I looked out and it was Mrs. Forster of St. Louis, with the old Gypsy woman, the mother of the condemned man that was to have hung today; also another gypsy woman. I did not see them then, was too nervous—but when Lon came a few moments later and told me he had commuted the sentence to fifty years I sent over to the hotel for them. When they came they had heard the news—and seemed very happy. They said they would always pray for Lon and myself. The poor old woman said she never could have lived if he had hung. He killed his unfaithful wife.[13] . . . That is two souls Lon has saved—*lives* I mean. John Smidt the young man is the other. I often see him. . . .

JULY 15, 1897

We had a very enjoyable trip to Fulton—in spite of the intense heat. . . . That night we attended a large reception given at the Deaf and Dumb asylum. Lon and I were handshaking most of the time we were there. We stopped at the Lunatic Asylum with Dr. and Mrs. Coombs.[14] . . . We went all over the institution—and talked to many patients. It is a sad place.

12. See *The Republican Courier,* July 9, 1897.

13. The day before his scheduled hanging Andrew (or André) Worten received a telegram announcing the commutation of his sentence to fifty years in prison. "His gratitude knew no bounds" (*The Daily Tribune* [Jefferson City] and *The St. Louis Star,* July 8, 1897).

14. At their national meeting in Buffalo, New York, 2,000 homeopaths paid tribute to Governor Stephens for his "honest courage" in "placing under homeopathic control the large insane asylum at Fulton" (*The Republican Courier,* July 9, 1897).

When I returned home I noticed in the *Courier* where Stella Gordon, one of my Sabbath School Scholars, a lovely girl, too, was ill with appendicitis. Dr. Mudd performed the operation Tuesday successfully. I have been out daily to see how she was. She died at 12:30 today—and I am saddened by her death—! . . .

. . . [There was] a long piece in the *St. Louis Star* of Saturday or Sunday, headed with these words: "Is Missouri Run by a Governess"—[with] my picture—and saying I was the cause of the different pardons, of the veto of The Peers hanging bill &c—[15] Sunday a reporter from St. Louis came to see me, a representative of the *Chronicle*. . . . Finally in Lon's presence [I] had a talk with him. He had a long article refuting that piece of the *Star*. Several of the Country papers have had complimentary pieces in answer to that "black sheet."

Lon just handed me the *Hannibal Journal*. In its article it says the Republican papers and their gold bug brothers are not "mashed" on Governor Stephens—&c—and says "they have even become desperate enough to charge the Governor's excellent wife is the power behind the throne in the present administration. Mrs. Stephens is a model woman and the state would not suffer should her splendid judgement prevail in matters of state—" but goes on to deny it, says I prefer the *retirement of home* rather than the vexations of politics. I think I share the latter with my husband! In all of his trials and joys I have been his confidential friend and shared them—even before he was governor. . . .

AUGUST 11, 1897

. . . Yesterday was a rather busy day. Mrs. Green called with her sisters to have me show them through the house. When she came, a poor old mother was in the library with me—wanted me to intercede for her boy. Then while she was here, Mrs. Martin, another convict's mother, called— she had been here the day before. Her only child is in the prison. Her second husband recently beat her, and she is without a home or means and is so anxious for her boy to come to her and give her a home. She appealed to me more than usual—seems a *good* woman.

15. Until 1938 executions in Missouri took place by hanging in the county of the conviction of the crime. The law proposed by Senator Charles E. Peers would have required that all executions be held at the state penitentiary. Mrs. Stephens protested that "Jefferson City would become a human slaughter house." By mobilizing "her young lady guests" and exercising her own "feminine arts," she presumably brought about a veto of the hanging bill, prevented reduction of appropriations for improvement of the Executive Mansion, and played a role in removing a clause from a bill that would have prohibited employing homeopathic doctors in state institutions. The series of incidents led to a charge that the governor "is under petticoat rule" and "that pretty and persuasive Mrs. Stephens is our chief executive" (*The St. Louis Star,* July 8, 1897; Harriet C. Frazier, telephone conversation with Carla Waal, January 7, 1997).

Just now an old mother was here, so intelligent and overflowing. Her son is a government prisoner and she wants Lon to give him a letter for McKinley. She is going herself to Washington to see the president. She said she was so afraid I was haughty, but she was so glad she called to see me—! . . .

The Stephenses traveled to New York City via Niagara Falls in August. Their vacation included some days in Boston and at beaches in Massachusetts, New Hampshire, and Virginia.

AUGUST 26, 1897

We are still in New York City. . . .

. . . There is a crowd of Missourians here. . . . Yesterday Lon had me go down and meet them. I was so unhappy about this "treating custom"—it almost kills me for my husband to take anything intoxicating.[16] Brother Lewis tells me I am a "crank" &c—and that Lon is the *best* governor Missouri ever had and all that but that is no reason to take a drink; I want him kept pure and undefiled. *He says* he has taken nothing intoxicating, but he is with the crowd that takes it and takes something. Yesterday we laughed so much over "Gin Fizz." That is what Lon says *he* takes! Mr. Scullin was talking to us last night and something was said about drinking, and he said his wife was very much opposed to anything of the kind. How I wish there were more wives like her—and may God help me to keep my husband out of the evil temptations. . . .

THURSDAY AFTERNOON, SEPTEMBER 23, [?, 1897?]

"Prince" and I have just had a nap.[17] I go presently to Maud Hoggs for tea. . . . Last night I went to tea to Mrs. Crafton's. . . . It is really comical how I am counted in with the girls—but am really more congenial with them than most married ladies my own age. . . .

. . . I must say I like *Mrs. Clarke.* . . . She said I was so popular because I treated everybody with kind consideration—the meek and lowly &c. She gave me a bottle of her "catsup" before I left.

. . . When I came home at noon, the fattest, prettiest baby named Lon V. Stephens Rose awaited me—the little fellow's parents are poor people here in town. . . .

16. Mrs. Stephens's anxiety about drinking may relate to having seen her father, James Nelson, drink to excess. An entry in her mother's diary reads: "[Papa] is about over his last spree. Will he never cease. He says he will try again. Oh I pray that he may hold out" (cited in Coleman, *Mistress of Ravenswood*, 5).

17. Prince was one of Mrs. Stephens's many pet dogs.

THURSDAY, SEPTEMBER 28, 1897

. . . I bought me a beautiful pattern hat—and it came today . . . brown and tan filled with wings and an owl head. When the girls left about noon I put my hat in the bandbox in my closet and said I was afraid Lon might lie on it. I went over to Miss Emma Terrel's a few moments. When I returned Lon met me at the top of the steps with my fifteen dollar hat in his hands *ruined*—he found it torn to pieces on the stairway—the owl head and wings scattered over my room—imagine my feelings! "Dot," that mean Fox Terrier, did it. I had told sister I was going to give him to her because he runs off so much and now I told Billie to ship him *at once*![18] My dear sweetheart felt so for me [that] he handed me ten dollars and begged me not to worry. . . .

NOVEMBER 1, 1897

. . . We had such a delightful visit to Nashville—were there two days. The sixteenth was Missouri Day! So many Missourians went. . . . We were beautifully entertained. The only thing that was objectionable was the drinking—oh! When will the day come that "treating" will not be so universally popular! No one seems to realize the sin, the heartaches, and ruined homes it is making! . . . Governor Taylor made the first speech,[19] then Lon. I was real nervous at first but never heard him do as creditably. I can just see the audience now that greeted him with applause and so often interrupted him by their enthusiasm. I never was as proud that I *was* a *Missourian*. . . .

NOVEMBER 12, 1897

I have been doing nicely and feel real well again—some one said yesterday it was because I had a new doctor—the homeopathic—Dr. Antrobus. For the past week or two he has had me bathe in cool sea salt water to my waist and then practice with dumb bells. I have gotten into a bad habit of waking every night at two and remaining wakeful and nervous for an hour or two. . . .

. . . [*Because her sister was involved in a squabble with friends*] Lon said yesterday when we were driving he was going to write sister to come

18. Billie had been the family butler for the Nelsons, but when Margaret married, Mr. Nelson sent Billie to manage his daughter's household (Charles W. Leonard, interview, February 20, 1988).

19. Tennessee's Bob (Robert Love) Taylor, like Lon Vest Stephens, was a "free silver" Democrat (Robert E. Corlew, *Tennessee: A Short History* [Knoxville: University of Tennessee Press, 1981], 409). Many Democrats advocated the free coinage of silver, while a majority of Republicans supported the gold standard.

down and spend the winter *here*—he says such *persecutions* are disgusting to him and instead of influencing him against sister, he loves her more than ever. Bless his dear heart—! How could I *love* him more—he is so just and *true*. The longer I live with him the more good I see in him. . . .

DECEMBER 31, 1897

The last of 1897—! What a busy woman I have been for the past few weeks!! . . .

. . . The teachers association met here this week. There were twelve hundred in attendance. Lon delivered an address to them Tuesday. I was so nervous—because he had been suffering with his head, and had difficulty in seeing the written speech to read—everyone, though, speaks so highly of it. We gave the teachers a reception Wednesday night, and such a jam was rarely ever witnessed—like the *inaugural* ball.

JANUARY 19, 1898

I can't tell exactly why I am up here alone now. . . . I came up to put on my hat to go to prayer meeting but Lon said it was raining and too bad for me to go out; so I am still up here and seeing my diary untouched still; all of these busy gay weeks have gone by and not a line have I written—!

. . . On the first of this month we gave the regular military reception—and the military band was here and I had the house decorated in flags, [and] bunting [of] red, white, and blue. . . . Everyone says it was the prettiest reception and [the] most enjoyable we have had in town this winter. I had sherbet and cake passed all evening in the dining room—and coffee and bonbons. I wore my yellow satin—ruffled to the waist—and waist trimmed in fur and lace. . . .

JANUARY 31, 1898

Everyone was so enthusiastic over the reception. Many old residents saying it was the prettiest affair that was ever given in the Mansion. . . . The library was a perfect garden scene. The fruit frapp[é] was delicious—. . . and the little fairies too sweet serving it. . . . The decorations and programs were pink. . . . The mantels [were] banked—and the receiving party stood behind a lattice of smilax. We did not retire that night until about three. . . . I wore my pink rose reception dress. Everyone admires it so much. I had it last winter, but many here had never seen it before and were admiring it so much. . . .

. . . Saturday evening we all went to a spelling match at music hall given for the benefit of our church. It was lots of fun. Lon called the words out from the old blue[-]back speller. Anna and John spelt: and Anna almost won the pri[z]e—she had to go down on Guin*ea*. . . .

Jennie, sister and I drove out to the prison . . . and heard the negro women sing. Most of them shook hands with me and called me "Miss Maggie."[20] . . .

FEBRUARY 1, 1898

. . . We . . . went down and met Mr. Williams, whom Lon has appointed supreme [court] judge in Judge Barclay's place.[21] He lunched with us and at 2:30 I could persuade none of our crowd but Jennie to go over to the supreme court building and see Mr. Williams take the oath. Judge Sherwood did it in a few seconds.[22] I then went to the dentist for a short while—another tooth is troubling me.

Lon came home at four—he was nervous and could not sleep but rested a little while. He was unhappy because I told him I believed he had resorted to *something* to quiet his nerves. I am so opposed to him taking intoxicants—it makes me *ill* when I suspect it. I can't help it!

FEBRUARY 4, 1898

MASQUERADE—!

Well, we had a good time last night at the Masquerade. . . . Sister crimped my hair all over, and braided it in two plaits down my back. . . . I was late; they were marching when I went in, and such a crowd. The only soul I recognized was Jennie. I took the arm of a woode[n] shoed little Dutchman and marched around and actually waltzed a little with him—we did not speak—and my curiosity was great to know who my "beau" was. . . . [Lon] was a *terrible* looking old "Lone Fisherman" with his camp stool, basket &c—and a grey beard. He did not know me at once, but when he saw my hair plaited down, recognized me. I surprised everybody when the mask was taken off. I never saw people so surprised at my identity. I looked like a girl everyone said, and the blue satin came to my shoe tops—trimmed in bands of black velvet and gold braid. . . .

20. The women prisoners were housed separately and had their own dining room, chapel, laundry, and a work room equipped with sewing machines, according to the *Appendix to Senate and House Journals of the Thirty-Ninth General Assembly of the State of Missouri, 1897*, vol. 39 (Jefferson City: Tribune Printing Company, 1897), 179–80.

21. William Muir Williams replaced Shepard Barclay, who resigned in January 1898 after serving for ten years (Gerald T. Dunne, *The Missouri Supreme Court: From Dred Scott to Nancy Cruzan*, 210).

22. Thomas Adiel Sherwood, who served on the Missouri Supreme Court from 1872 to 1902. Dunne, *Supreme Court*, 93, 203–6, 210.

. . . Mrs. Morrow's [costume] was excellent—as Free Silver. She had bands, sixteen of silver around the skirt and one gold, a crown of thorns on her head, and carried a large cross of gold. Picture of Lon on her back and Bryan on her chest.

Anne Ewing represented *me*. She wore my violet dress—and my earrings and some of my pins—and looked well, too

FEBRUARY 17, 1898

Well the musicale is over! and such a *grand* success it was. I did so thoroughly enjoy every moment of it all. . . .

Mr. Snider was tuning the pianos all day; when night came [he] was barely through. . . . I staid with the crowd in the hall for quite a [while] listening [to] Robyn, Mrs. Van Studdiford (oh! her voice is divine), and the quartette. . . .

. . . We had a nice lunch at five. Bouillon, then cold turkey, ham, sweet bread croquettes, oyster patties, beaten biscuits—then chicken salad and tomatoes on lettuce leaf on our plate, coffee, orange ice and cake. . . . Had a harp centerpiece of flowers and lilies at each end—and stuffed dates, salted almonds, and musical instrument cakes. . . .

FEBRUARY 21, 1898

Boone the mind-reader and hypnotist is here—and how interesting it is. . . . On our way [to the Church's] Peg, Anna and I watched him blindfolded in a carriage driving to find a key &c. The key had been hid at the Church's so we were right there and witnessed it all. When he found it, we were all breathless. . . .

. . . He had me open a book, Lon marked a word—*record*—then closed it, and he then had me to put my finger on his temple and think of the word. He turned to the correct page and then took a sheet of paper and wrote the word on it, blind-folded as he was! . . .

. . . The papers are now *filled* with the destruction of the *Maine*—our vessel—and there is much talk of war. Lon is receiving letters daily from men volunteering their services in case war is declared. . . .

MARCH 1, 1898

During "exciting times" I fail to write in my diary—for lack of time—and therefore the *sensational interesting* events are not recorded until they are things of the past—! Monday and Tuesday nights of last week we attended the entertainment at the opera house by Boone. It was so exciting. . . . The morning of the 22nd the cannon fired and I was sure it meant news from the war—just after saying I was afraid of nothing

&c—but the cannon frightened me and I telephoned 48 to know what it was when Arthur Willis said it was Washington's birthday. Anna has teased me about it since—! . . .

March 20, 1898

It is a rainy, gloomy Sabbath afternoon. I went to Sunday School but not to church. . . .

Well, my entertainment of the girls was so successful. Vena and Mrs. Crafton helped me with the game. The names of the governors were transposed and they wrote them out. Bessie Clark received the prize, a cut glass and silver top puff box. I gave each a china bon bon box, some round and some square. The girls were so enthusiastic over them! And [they] voted me an honorary member of their club. . . .

We leave tomorrow for our California trip. I hope and pray it will be a safe and happy one. I had a letter just now from my dear mama—not feeling well, was blue—and cried like the baby I am! . . .

April 25, 1898

We are right in the midst of the greatest excitement over war with Spain. The destruction of the *Maine* at Cuba by Spaniards on the sixteenth of February when so many lives were lost is the ground for hostilities. The past week many trainloads of soldiers have passed through going south—and the entire city of Jefferson, it does seem, goes down to greet them at every train.

War was practically declared a week ago—but is expected to be formally declared today when the president will send a message to congress recommending that a declaration be made that a state of war exists between this country and Spain.[23] I do hope it will be brief and settled as quickly as possible. It never occurs to me that anyone near or dear will go and participate. How I do pray very few lives will be sacrificed! . . .

April 27, 1898

. . . [Poor Brother Givens] had Dr. Antrobus to examine him thoroughly today and says he told him he was in a critical condition—he has been complaining for some weeks. He does not care for Dr. Young to know he has been to the homeopathic doctor—but my! the practice and success that doctor is getting is marvelous. . . .

23. War was declared by Congress, as requested by President William McKinley.

AUGUST 1, 1898

My birthday—! and such a happy day it has been. When we first awoke early this morning Lon kissed me, but I told him not to attempt to give me the same number as my years—as he used to do—on former birthdays. . . . The first thing I did before breakfast was to open sister's gift—such a lovely one it was—a miniature of dear mama painted by Edith Leonard. It was taken from a picture of her years ago with curls &c. . . . My dear Lon brought home at noon a package—and came up here and said it was my gift from him; he had come by town and selected it himself. It is so sweet, and really very pretty—a jewel case, brass with bevel glass above it. . . . I have felt so lighthearted and happy today. May I continue to serve my Master and do more for Him than ever before—is my prayer tonight—! . . .

WEDNESDAY, SEPTEMBER 21, 1898

It has rained continuously this entire day. It was a fine time to *work* and accomplished so much. Pauline and I cleaned out the old Mansion linen closet—so many old curtains, flags, rags &c stored away that I over hauled. Then I marked some new Mansion pillow slips—wrote letters— and accomplished much. . . .

Mama wrote me my dear papa had fallen in the sitting room at home while pushing the gas up and, she feared, fractured his hip. I read her letter yesterday and was almost ill from its contents. . . . Today we received invitations from Mr. and Mrs. R. E. Mills in Adjutant General's office to accompany them to Sedalia Friday to see Cody's Wild West show. [A] congenial crowd is going and I anticipate a good time. . . . Lon is taking a bath and called me in to see Prince—he was teasing him—he [Prince] is so afraid of water. . . .

Mrs. Stephens did not write in her diary in 1899, but at the beginning of 1900 she recalled major events of the previous year. Her cousin Anna Birch wrote part of the account.

JANUARY 4, 1900

. . . We gave a large Masquerade on the twenty-fourth of February [1899]. . . . Anna was a nun. I was [a] Gibson Military girl. When I went down the steps I was met by a Russian military officer—we led the march. . . . I remember how ridiculous Tom Hennings looked as a ballet girl and when we all unmasked, Anna sent him to the hotel the back way—to change his suit—! . . .

My birthday the first of August [1899] was spent at Ravenswood. The girls and sister surprised me that night by a ballet dance—! And [a] cake walk. Their costumes were very striking and pretty—home made! That morning on the dot when I went down to breakfast all of them were dressed in male attire and arose and saluted me. The presents were piled at my plates. . . .

I gave Mrs. D'Oench a lovely evening entertainment—*violet.* A violet guessing game. The first prize Mrs. Fox won, a lamoge [Limoges] compote decorated in handpainted violets—and the first gentlemen's prize a stick pin—violet. . . . After the supper of oyster cutlets, chicken salad, and orange ice violet shaded—Anna pinned a bunch of violets on each. Then coffee and delicious violet cake. . . . It was one of the prettiest informal parties I ever gave. Everything decorated in lavender and purple. . . .

Our church gave an old folks concert here at the Mansion on November tenth. I suggested it and worked very hard for it. Anna and myself went to the prison and sold a number of tickets. . . .

. . . [At our Christmas party] before we had gotten up from the table the children commenced pouring in. . . . The band was playing in the side hall. The tree was lit with electricity and was immense, touching the sealing [ceiling]. Anna had bought the presents for me at a wholesale toy store. Pretty dressed dolls, little toy sweepers, coffee mills, dust pans, drawing slates, balls, horns &c. We first commenced calling the names so each child would respond—but the crowd was too great so we had them to pass around the tree and get a gift. . . . Lon crawled under the tree to reach the articles. Some received several—and all received a toy, orange and candy. Some poor mothers were here and I sent by them things to the sick at home.

It was such a happy Christmas!

I never enjoyed one more. . . .

FEBRUARY 27, 1900

Our trip to Boonville and especially Ravenswood was ideal. . . . We went to church Sunday morning and heard Brother Farris—he is very much liked. I had quite an ovation after church. Mama commented on it and said it was the highest compliment that could be paid me to see the poor and all classes *kiss* me and beg me to return to Boonville—! . . .

. . . I brought with me from Boonville the sweetest little black woolly dog. . . . paid ten dollars for it—and it is still the dearest little thing—we all love it. . . .

MARCH 5, 1900

The musicale last Thursday night was quite a success considering the weather—a very nice crowd was here—and $58.00 was taken in—we had to give Mrs. Cole half of it. Every one here was convulsed at her—she is so vain and not much of a harpist. Thursday morning Edna and I walked up town but the temptation to sleigh was so great I sent York for one and how we enjoyed it. . . .

MARCH 9, 1900

Tuesday morning Mrs. Hanes spent the morning with Anna and I—while Mrs. Crow invited her guests for that afternoon to meet Mrs. Hanes. Anna and I went—about twenty ladies there—a game, as usual—cards were passed with the first line of a rhyme from Mother Goose—we had to finish the verse and illustrate it. Mine was "Little Jack Horner Sat in the Corner" &c. I almost received the booby so comical was my little Jack—! . . .

Wednesday I went to see Dr. Antrobus twice. He helps me just to talk to him! Gave me electricity. I have no rheumatism now. . . .

Peg came over this morning—and talked of the great amount of drinking this week in Kansas City. My objection to politics. I hope my husband will be spared before it is too late. If prayers can do it, he is safe—only ten more months of politics!

THURSDAY, MARCH 15, 1900

. . . Purchased dresses for the penitentiary babies—and a comfort for the mother who has just had triplets. Edna ordered the Victoria [carriage] and we went out to see them. Such cute little fat yellow girl babies they are! She wants me to name them. Then we went to the prison. Edna enjoyed the morning so much. . . .

MARCH 20, 1900

My eye is still inflamed—the day we drove out to see the triplets, I must have caught cold in it for it soon after became worse. . . . I sent Vera out Saturday afternoon to tell Martha Price I had named the babies—Ethel, Edna and Katharine, for the three young lady friends. She was very much pleased. . . .

SEPTEMBER 26, 1900

. . . My life is a happy one here in J.C. and now I am so attached to this dear old Executive Mansion and the yard (more especially) that I sigh to think of so soon leaving it—! About two weeks ago (the thirteenth) our new church workers and Sunday School class gave a Baby show and at night a musicale auction &c. Mr. Vance added electric lights in the yard and I had the tent put up in front and with the new fountain going (we have had put up recently)—the yard was a beauty. . . .

OCTOBER 29, 1900

. . . One of the happiest days I have spent for a long time was October the nineteenth. Lon myself with Billie and York and the bunch went in the Victoria to the Gordon farm. . . . The house is an old fashioned structure. . . . There were two violins and a bass viol there belonging to the work hands. After we eat [ate] in the yard, cooked bacon on charcoals, and made coffee, we went across to the barn lot and climbed hay stacks, gathered persimmons, &c. When we returned to the house, two farm hands [were] there and they with Claud played on the instruments sitting on a bench against the wall—and such dancing as we did! Real country quadrill[e]s and waltzes &c. I actually waltzed with Charlie Winston—did I ever think I *would*—! He was the most undignified one in our party—think *of it!* He and Lon pulled off coats in the heat of the quadrille of six. . . . The day was more than medicine for me. The artist is here from St. Louis, Mr. Cunningham—[he is] painting my oil portrait, [which] the ladies of the state are presenting to the Executive Mansion.[24] He commenced about a week ago. I sat for a photograph just to get the position the day before we spent in the country. . . . This house is infected with moths. We are constantly fighting them.

NOVEMBER 1, 1900

Well last night we had a telegram from Mr. Dockery (who was recently elected Governor) saying he and his wife would be here today.[25] She is delicate and the *girls* are hoping the weather is too bad for her to come—so we may go yet [to St. Louis]. . . .

NOVEMBER 20, 1900

Well, Mr. and Mrs. Dockery did come at 2:40 the afternoon of the above day Friday—and of course we could not go to St. Louis. They

24. John Wilton Cunningham painted the first portrait of a first lady for the mansion. Since then it has been customary for a portrait of each first lady to be presented for permanent display in the home.

25. Alexander M. Dockery had been a physician and, for sixteen years, a member of the U.S. Congress. Before being elected governor he and his wife Mary Bird Dockery had lost six children in infancy and two at a young age. Mrs. Dockery was "a devoted wife," who combined "fragility and strength." She died in the governor's mansion on January 1, 1903, and was buried in Chillicothe among her eight children. Park and Morrow, *Women of the Mansion*, 276–85.

had not had lunch so I ordered it after they arrived. . . . Mrs. Dockery was shockingly delicate looking but contended she was well—and really seemed stronger than I—for . . . when they left I was almost ready to collapse—after entertaining and showing her all over the Mansion— telling her a thousand and one things. I liked her very much, though. She seems so sincere. I asked Mr. Dockery as a personal favour to retain Will McMahan as Chief Clerk at the prison—and he promised he would. . . . They wanted all of our servants—engaged *York.* Lon offered them two of our horses and trap (as they have *no* horses). I told Mrs. Dockery she could have all of the servants but Billie and Pauline. . . .

December 4, 1900

. . . Yesterday sister drove up rather unexpected. We went out to the prison soon after dinner to see *Johnston* the criminal who has been in the prison for over eighteen years—the Governor pardons him tomorrow— he wrote me a letter to come to see him.[26] He told me he owed his freedom to Dr. Williams and myself. I have been so busy seeing criminals and penitentiary inmates of late. Just the day before Thanksgiving, a week ago tomorrow, Lon told me I could go out to tell Jennie Todd (who is there for killing her daughter) she could go home the next day—Thanksgiving.[27] I found her in the sewing room alone—and when I told her she hung on my neck and cried and *so* did *I.* She shouted for five minutes "I'm going home tomorrow, blessed God!" I went out on Thanksgiving Day just before church with Lon to give the holiday pardons. Jennie was one. So many, many are now appealing for pardons before my Governor leaves. . . . The oil painting of myself is at last completed—! Yesterday Mr. Cunningham finished it. Everyone thinks it perfect—and a fine piece of art. I sat about a week for it and read "When Knighthood was in Flower" while I posed.[28]

Last week and [the] week before [were busy]. I attended Mrs. Kirtley's reception one afternoon winning the prize—a book—and everybody was so sweet—throwing bo[u]quets at me. . . .

26. J. B. Hunt, alias "Firebug" Johnson, was considered "the most notorious criminal in the Missouri penitentiary." Having entered prison at the age of twenty-six, he was now forty-four years old and in ill health. Before leaving for El Paso, he requested to see Mrs. Stephens "to ask you for your blessing and to forgive me for the deeds of the past" (*State Tribune,* December 5, 1900).

27. Virginia B. Todd was sentenced in 1898 to twenty-five years in prison for murder in the second degree. Although she was charged with killing her daughter-in-law, "there was grave doubt about her guilt" (*Jefferson City Daily Press,* December 1, 1900).

28. Charles Major, *When Knighthood Was in Flower* (Indianapolis: Bowen-Merrill Company, 1899).

DECEMBER 27, 1900

What a happy Christmas I have had—just did as I pleased. Went to the prison and had [friends] for six o'clock dinner. Such lovely presents—and so many—[I] could not wish for more happiness—! . . .

JANUARY 4, 1901

Just a few more days at this dear old mansion. My attachments are so strong. I now dislike to leave this home as I did Ivy Terrace when I came here. Well, we will be moved in a week. The carpets are most all down—and so many repairs I have had done. . . .

Tuesday we went to Boonville—on account of Martha Stephens Rolwing's death. Oh! It was *sad*—sad. We went up with her husband who was in Charleston during the latter part of her illness—poor man! How my heart bled for him. Speed and Jennie were overcome with grief.[29] Jennie said, "Oh! Maggie, you should be thankful you have no children." I have *always* regretted God did not give me children but He knows best. I do not believe I could live through such grief. . . .

. . . Lon pardoned Maud Lewis yesterday. He came by "Ivy Terrace" to tell me. I of course went out to see her. . . . She was hysterical and happy—hugged and almost kissed me on the mouth. Poor woman promised me she would lead a pure life &c.[30] . . .

JANUARY 12, 1901

We are just ready to take the last of our goods to Ivy Terrace—this is the last day this dear old Mansion will be home. . . .

29. W. Speed Stephens, brother of the governor, and his wife Jennie had three daughters, Marie, Rilye, and Martha. Martha married Edward G. Rolwing of Charleston, Missouri, on April 18, 1900; she died in January 1901 at the age of nineteen (Robert L. Dyer, interview with Carla Waal, November 24, 1993; *Boonville Weekly Advertiser*, April 6, 1900 and January 11, 1901).

30. Maud Lewis had been sentenced in 1895 to fifteen years in prison for shooting and killing State Senator Peter R. Morrissey. Having denied a petition for pardon in 1898, Governor Stephens yielded to the persuasion of supporters of Lewis just before leaving office (*The Evening Courier* [Jefferson City], February 4, 1898; *Jefferson City Republican*, January 4, 1901).

MARIAN WRIGHT POWERS (1880–1969)

*A*n artist intent upon achievement or a wife and mother devoted to her family—Marian Wright Powers struggled to be both, but the conflict between these two roles was difficult to reconcile. In 1888 her family moved from Connersville, Indiana, where Marian was born in 1880, to the southwest Missouri town of Carthage. Her father, Curtis Wright, was president of the Carthage Stone Company; her mother, Nira Koogler Wright, was active as a speaker on history, temperance, and church missions. The Wright home was filled with music, for the mother was an accomplished musician and teacher of singing. Many of her eight children sang and played: "It was a musical family in which singing was a pleasure and chief entertainment."[1]

In 1903 Marian married Everett Powers (1869–1954), a Missourian who studied medicine in Cincinnati, Philadelphia, New York, and Germany. An eye, ear, nose, and throat specialist, Dr. Powers served in the U.S. Army Medical Corps during World War I and was active in medical societies and Masonic groups. He generously supported his wife's efforts to study voice and to perform on the concert stage, but her options were limited because she always considered him and their daughter Marian, nicknamed "Toots," when charting her course. It was not easy for Powers to be away from home, for the little girl would write to her: "Last Sunday, while Aunty Florence was reading your long . . . letter . . . , I was crying for you" (March 3, 1911), or, "If you dont come home I will pack up my trunk and come and get you I want you so bad" (ca. 1913–1914). This daughter, Marian Louisa Powers Winchester (1905–1981) left a bequest to the city of Carthage establishing the Powers Museum, which pays tribute to her parents and showcases the history of Carthage and the surrounding region in the late nineteenth and early twentieth centuries.

Marian Wright Powers recorded her thoughts by hand in a school composition binder with the printed title, "Exercises," to which she added, "Talks on Self, 1908 Marian Wright Powers."[2] The journal provides insight into the longing and tension of Marian Wright Powers's life as the intensity of her ambition clashed with family love and responsibilities. How could Marian stop dreaming of a career when she received encouragement from her teachers? In a letter of June 10, 1909, after Marian had returned to her family from months of study in New York, Madame Guilia Valda predicted a "great future" for her pupil, closing with the advice, "Remember you will do great great things if you will work." Madame

---

1. *Genealogical and Biographical Notices of Descendants of Sir John Wright of Kelvedon Hall, Essex, England* (Carthage, Mo., 1915), 235.

2. With permission from the board of the Powers Museum a major portion of the journal is presented here.

Valda also encouraged Marian's unmarried older sister Nira, who studied and taught at the Lamperti-Valda School in Paris and had some success as a performer.

The numerous programs and flyers in the archives of the Powers Museum in Carthage indicate the range of Marian's repertory. She would sing art songs by Schubert, Brahms, and Cadman, and arias from *Romeo and Juliet* by Gounod, *Madam Butterfly* by Puccini, and *Hamlet* by Thomas. Sometimes she and her accompanist would dress in costumes of the 1860s to present a program of "Old-fashioned Songs" dedicated to the memory of her mother. The songs, usually grouped by origin—English, Scottish, Irish, for example—included popular favorites such as "Believe Me if All Those Endearing Young Charms" and "Swing Low, Sweet Chariot."

Marian Wright Powers sang countless times in and near Carthage throughout her lifetime, but opportunities to perform elsewhere were difficult to find and conditions sometimes far from attractive. After a successful concert in Fayetteville, where the piano was out of tune and covered with dust, Powers reported the audience's enthusiasm and her own reservations: "As usual I sang some things well, and others not so well. I always want to do it right over again, to show them how much better I can sing!"[3] Finding engagements required self-promotion. Powers usually managed her own career, but she was listed with the Haensel and Jones agency in New York, and for a time she sent out Ella Harrison from Carthage as a booking agent. In 1920 Powers placed an ad in *Musical America* and received sisterly advice from Margie A. McLeod, the newspaper's manager in Chicago: "Now, don't you know that nothing is better for a voice than exercise, so why complain about watering the flowers and peeling the potatoes, etc. Just think of the breath control you get from work of this kind!"

Archival publicity material, which is evidence of her self-confidence and determination and her husband's willingness to provide financial support, shows how Powers tried to build her professional image and promote herself. Having presented a debut recital at Aeolian Hall in New York City, Powers is described in a typical flyer as "a young American singer who is rapidly making her way in the musical world today, and taking rank with the best known artists of the concert stage." Her voice is called "a clear, bell-like coloratura soprano, with phenomenal range," and a quotation from the *St. Louis Times* praises its "exceeding sweetness and clarity" and "perfect control." The limited venue in which she toured can be deduced from the location of the newspapers cited—Oklahoma City and Muskogee, Oklahoma; Dallas, Houston, and Taylor, Texas; and Carthage. Powers did, however, also appear in Chicago and with the symphony orchestras of St. Louis, Kansas City, and Minneapolis. She

3. Undated letter to Ella [Harrison], Powers Museum.

never became nationally or internationally known, but throughout her life she continued to sing—at club meetings, church services, weddings, and funerals. Sometimes she felt that she had "married and buried half of Jasper County." Dr. Everett Powers died in 1954, after having practiced in Carthage for more than fifty years. Marian Wright Powers died in 1969.[4] In her closets she had kept the collection of splendid gowns and costumes she had worn on stage. In her memory she kept the echoes of her inner voice saying, "I want to be . . . *a great singer.*"

TALKS ON SELF

Journal of Marian Wright Powers

Carthage Missouri
JULY 21, 1908

. . . Often have I planned to write something of my life, not for the delectation of others, but for my own perusal in other and later years that I may look back, and realize the trials and difficulties through which I passed. Always one sees the past thru rosy glasses and the present and future only thru blue goggles. Never can we see it as it really was, unless we have written it down, and can read with our own eyes that *"That was the worst time of our lives"!!* However, when I compare my life with those of so many many others who have had greater burdens to bear, it seems that mine has indeed been a very happy and fortunate life. It is quite true, I have never had poor health, or dire poverty; *merely my ambitions thwarted!* But to an extremely ambitious person could anything be more galling?

Unfortunate I, to be born in the *middle* of a big family of eight children. . . . When it came my year for a college education after finishing High School, it was during the panic, and no funds could be spared for me. My father held a scholarship in our town college,[5] however, and I took advantage of that. There I began my first study of the modern languages (French and German)—though I had already had a very good foundation of Latin. Always I was working toward my future career as *"prima donna,"* for such I had decided upon even as a young child. In fact it led me to many foolish sayings as well as doings. For instance, my mother wished me to give instrumental music a thorough study—realizing the

---

4. Brochure, Powers Museum. Obituaries, *Joplin Globe* and *Springfield Leader-Press,* July 26, 1969.

5. The Carthage Collegiate Institute, from which Marian Wright graduated in 1900.

vast benefit it would be to me later. To her arguments, I answered "I did not care to play the *piano*." "But for your accompaniments?" "I shall not need to play my accompaniments. *I* shall have an *orchestra!*" . . .

After I finished at College, each year there was a promise of better things, real study away from home, but they never came. . . . [E]very night some boy or other came to the house or we attended parties and entertainments, till my family felt I was only a "society butterfly" after all. *But always I wanted to sing.* . . . As for my voice, it was always clear and high, a decided lyric soprano, with range of three octaves. As a child it was more, as there was scarcely any limit to my upper range. One winter I went to Chicago with my sister Nira and we had lessons there under Prof. Burritt[6]—a man and teacher of excellent worth, but he did not have the great *principle* of voice production which we believe we have now found. I only had eight lessons with him, but worked *very hard,* and gained a great deal.

My life drifted on in this unsettled manner until I was twenty-three. I then met the man I loved and married him the fall of '03. We went abroad for a year where we both studied in Berlin; he, his specialty profession, (eye, ear, nose and throat) and I my vocal work under Frau Kornatius.[7] . . . She marvelled over my voice, and almost wept when I told her I would never do operatic work, as I had given up all hope of a public career when I married. I had never done coloratura work, scales, trills, and runs, but she gave me a heavy song, containing much cadenza work. I told her it was too difficult. I couldn't even *read* the little high notes!! She laughed, and insisted. When I returned in three days, I had conquered it somewhat. She threw up her hands. "Mein Gott im Himmel! You sing like the birds in Heaven, because you cannot help it, and you know not how you do it?" . . . [I]t was no *miracle,* I had *worked very hard on* it, all day long, as you can well guess. I loved her but realized that she did not build my voice much further, only gave me repertoire.

After our return to Carthage, we settled down to housekeeping, and at the expiration of another year, our dear little daughter came to stay at our house (à la Little Orphan Annie). For two years she kept me busy, *very* busy indeed, as she is the kind who is always doing something. I still sang, in fact had the leading (for me) role in two small operas, "The Dr. of Alcantara" and "Patience." In both I seemed to be successful. We had no one to train us at all, no one even to make suggestions, in these home talent affairs, but each did his or her own way. But several times later I heard of strangers asking "who was the *professional* and from what city," meaning my humble self. . . . In the meantime my sister Nira had been

6. William Nelson Burritt.
7. Powers studied with Marie Kornatius in Berlin, which she and her husband visited shortly after their marriage, during a year abroad.

studying in New York for two years with Mde. Giulia Valda, a pupil of the elder Lamperti,[8] and the direct exponent of his method. . . .

In the Spring of '07 I heard the Metropolitan Opera Company in St. Louis thru its entire program—Caruso, Eames, Farrar, Fremstad, Scotti![9] How happy I was! What thrills of delight went over me! I wanted to weep, and, turning to my sister said, "I would give *all* I own to be down there *helping!*" My old ambitions, which I had thought safely dead and buried, with my girlhood days, arose from their long trance as strong and decided as ever. I could not settle down to anything. I returned to my home, husband and baby, all of whom I dearly loved, but I felt again that I *must* sing. I would not *live* without it. . . . I tried to keep all these feelings from my husband, who was so good to me, and spoiled me constantly as tho I were a small child. However, when I sang for strangers and they said beautiful things of my voice, demanding of my father "what he meant by keeping that voice from the world," telling me I had "a fortune in my throat"—praising in extravagant fashion—I nearly went wild. Always I would come home to weep when alone. I realized only too well how little I knew, how far from being a great singer, and yet I wanted my "try." . . .

At last Mme. Schumann Heink came to a nearby town, and it was suggested to me that I sing for her.[10] I did so, and she was most gracious to me, she told me I had a "Wunderschön" voice, that I could do what I chose with it, but said I could not realize how hard it was for a wife and mother. [Of] my voice she said, I pushed too much in the middle and lower register, but its high tones were "ganz" perfect. We talked in German, and she said, I would go to many teachers and they would have me begin all over again in a new method but that she could make it "ganz schön" in six months. I told her I did not want to be mediocre but that I was married and twenty-six years old, and I wanted to be *only* a *great singer.* She said I could "be what I chose." I appreciated it all very much but knew too well how little she could judge of my ability. In the first place, I was really frightened, for the first time in my life, and so sang poorly, hard and unnatural and decidedly pushed. In the second place, I had had a hard trip over there in the rain (and in rainy day attire, in all its unattractiveness) and I sang in a very difficult place, on the closed stage

---

8. Francesco Lamperti (1813–1892), a teacher of singing in Milan, published a treatise on the art of singing. His younger son, Giovanni Battista Lamperti (1839–1910), also a teacher of singing in Italy and Germany, counted Ernestine Schumann-Heink and Marcella Sembrich among his pupils.

9. The soloists to whom Powers refers are Enrico Caruso, Emma Eames, Geraldine Farrar, Olive Fremstad, and Antonio Scotti.

10. Ernestine Schumann-Heink (1861–1936) was an Austrian-born contralto/mezzo soprano, who became a naturalized American citizen. After a debut in Dresden in 1878, she enjoyed an international career, appearing often in Bayreuth, Germany, and at the Metropolitan Opera in New York.

against the wall, which was only a few feet in front of me. She could tell nothing of my histrionic ability or mental capacity. She thought I had studied much more than I had, and there was no time to disillusion her. Also she had no idea of my study of languages and history of music, preparatory to a singing career. And above all, she had no idea how hard I could work! . . .

Needless to say I came home *determined to sing.* That means a great deal—determination! My dear husband agreed that what I wanted should be mine, in as far as he could give it me. He did not want me to have a great musical career, as he feared it would separate us more or less, but *if I wanted* it, he would help me all he could. Not many men would be willing to do what he has done, and says he will do, and no one, not even he, can realize my deep appreciation of his unselfishness. Never shall I allow ought to come between us if I can help it. My idea is that, if I am ever able to make anything financially, we can travel together as we have so longed to do, and see and visit the places we have so long adored from afar. If one could only read the future—Perhaps we would be too much discouraged—to live to meet it!

My sister Nira arrived home again from New York with voice much improved, and high enthusiasm for the "old Lamperti method." She expressed her willingness to give me the lessons as they had been given to her. Now for one year she has struggled with me in the most unselfish way. . . . I wish I could express on paper the discouragements and trials of this year's work, but it is impossible. Pen cannot express it, but they are registered forever on my heart. In the first place I had never known *how* I sang, I always had sung, and always expected to, but did not realize the art of it. Around the lawn and in the house, I sang continuously, often without knowing I did it. I trilled and ran scales, high and low, with never a thought of throat or breath or body. I sang as naturally as I talked, and almost as much, and I must admit, I talk *a great* deal. . . . I discovered one cannot learn to sing in a day. One's muscles must be hardened and strengthened by daily practice. I only injured myself by my hard work at first. My throat hurt me day and night, I pictured to myself the horrible nightmare of the possibility of never singing *easily* again—of eventually losing my voice! I wondered if I could live thru it, or if I did, could I ever be happy again? Down into the "Slough of Despond" I sank, but *I kept right on,* never *ceasing my practice!* My one hope [was] that assurance which my sister gave me, that "it was all right, only I had tried too hard. It would all come right in the end." . . .

I must have Italian, and cannot get it here, as no one speaks it in these inland towns, but I shall work on it in New York. I am now twenty-eight. I must work hard and sing ere my youth is departed. My husband had planned to study his profession in Berlin again, when I did, but now all is upset. He does not want me to take the three-year-old "Toots" to

New York's cold winter climate and to such close city quarters. But his sister, Mrs. Haden, wants her in her delightful winter home in Florida, and I suppose I should let her go. . . . I shall hate to give up my dear little house, for I am so fond of my pretty things. My pictures, books, piano and even my linens are dear to me. . . . So this summer I have embroidered and sewed constantly. All of my linen supplies are once more complete, and on all I have embroidered at least my initial. . . . A little later I will have to begin making my fall and winter clothes as well as Marian's. I have "put up" more fruit this year than ever before, preserves, jellies, and pickles, beside grape juice which I am making today. I have just received my new Italian dictionary, which looks fine. Will send for a grammar immediately, and try to do a little with it myself. I have sung it enough to know the pronunciation. Have been reading several books lately. . . . How I wish I could study astronomy, for the heavens have always interested me greatly, and have been my greatest solace when I am nervous and irritable. Every evening we drive, and I see my beloved sunsets and later my beautiful stars. Of course I know many of the constellations, but should enjoy a deeper study of the heavens. Some day I trust I may go across the equator and see the lovely Southern Cross and Crown. But I long to travel, and read many books on it, as I expect to need such information some day. I want to see the "Garden of Allah," the desert, which is "God's Garden" because man cannot go into the desert and return an unbeliever. I want to see its wonderful colorings, and those equally marvellous ones of the Arctic circle.

I believe that my most prominent characteristic is my intense interest in everything. Few things bore me, for everywhere one looks, something interesting is to be found, if he only trains his eyes, material and mental, to see them. . . . I trust if I ever sing and receive its worth in "filthy lucre," I shall make it not quite as *filthy* by raising it from its many sordid uses and using it to buy happiness for others and myself. To let it help people find their ideal. However I suppose that is impossible—for one's ideal is always in the distance alluring and beckoning, but advancing as we advance. The luxury of today is our necessity of tomorrow, as tomorrow we demand greater perfection than we do today. . . . I have Dr. Powers' books to finish for this month, as I am his *bookkeeper,* and while I have them practically finished for the month, have still a little work to do. Also have a party on for this afternoon, and [my things] need pressing. . . .

SEPTEMBER 7, [1908]

Sang two arias from "The Creation" yesterday at church. It is wonderful music. I did not sing as well as I could or as I have, but my voice shows improvement which is encouraging. Always after I sing, I have an intense desire to get up and do it again, for I feel sure I could improve very much

on the first rendition. Wish I could hear myself sing perfectly just once . . .
I could then be satisfied, but know it would only mean greater discontent,
as I should then be striving to reach that standard each time I sang, and be
miserable when I could not. Hear Toots howling, must depart on a run.

November 14, 1908

It seems to me to have been a long time since I last wrote in this little
book, but the calendar only shows a couple of months. Yet a great deal
can often take place in a shorter length of time. It has been one long
uncertainty to me, for my going away to study, my flight to New York
and Mde. Valda are plans which seem to have suddenly grown weak in
the legs. Everett has been so absolutely sure that I might study when we
first discussed it a year and a half ago, that I felt so certain I could go.
I was almost miserable because *I felt* I could go, and *Nira* might have to
stay at home, as father seemed to be unable to send her again. Now she
has taught and made her money, so that *she* is absolutely certain that *she*
can go and *I* am *"on the fence."* Mrs. Haden wanted to take Marian with
her south to Florida where all would be so ideal for her, and I had finally
brought myself to the point of allowing her to leave me the middle of
this month tho I felt I could not bear Christmas without her, when here
comes a letter from the good sister announcing her illness and fearing
she should not add to her cares by taking Marian now, *"but perhaps later,"*
etc. . . . . She really wants the baby, but I realize it is too heavy a task for a
sick person, and feel she is wise not to attempt it. I am *so glad* she felt free
to say what she did. Never-the-less my dreams of New York are vanishing
into dim air and if they never materialize, I feel I cannot endure it. If I
take her to New York with me, I could not study or go to any operas,
unless I had a competent nurse which would be a greater expense than
I could stand. It is really a dreadful question and I do not know how to
solve it. I simply know God takes care of his children and "whatsoever
ye ask, that shall ye receive," and I pray it may be enabled to study and
reach my heart's desire. . . .

December 20, 1908

Another long lapse since I have written a word in this book, but I have
had every minute full, and should not be writing now, if it were not that
it is night, and I am all alone, all the magazines for the month read, and
most of my Christmas letters written. Nira leaves for New York and Mde.
Valda in two or three weeks now, and I am still uncertain as to my own
going. . . . We now have a plan formulated for a housekeeper to keep the
house and baby for Everett while I go for a few months, until Mde. goes
abroad. Then, if our quarry deal goes through, Everett and Toots can join

me, and we all go abroad for a year. If he cannot come and bring her, I will return to them. At least I can have met Mde. and worked with her a while, I can hear the great singers, especially my beloved Melba whom I shall hear for the first time, as well as Tetrazzini.[11] In a hundred ways I believe it would be beneficial to me, but I cannot bear the thought of leaving Everett and the Baby. And leaving him to work and sacrifice for me, that I may stay in New York. I feel this keenly, and appreciate what he is doing. Never can I thank him enough for it, or love him enough to pay for all he does. I have plenty to worry me just now. But I refuse to worry. It is foolish. I put it in the Lord's hands—if it is right and best that I should go, it will come to me. If it is not right, then I do not want to go. . . .

JANUARY 11, 1909

At last my dreams are to come true and I am to study! For it is decided that I am to accompany Nira. What joy—and yet what pain! Truly it is a case of "bittersweet" with me, for I feel I cannot leave my darlings—Everett and Toots, and yet I *must sing!* As I am constantly saying and thinking, "Ambition is a queer thing." A beautiful letter from Madame Valda came yesterday in response to one from me. I am so anxious to see and know her. We were to start tonight, but after having the balmiest weather one could imagine for winter, a dreadful snowstorm has come down upon us, and we poor southern people are paralyzed. The home folks will not permit us to go off tonight, with the possibility of delays and even wrecks occurring on account of this storm. So we will wait until tomorrow. Miss Foor has come to care for baby, and she is fine—so serene in disposition, so conscientious and so really capable.[12] I am very fortunate in procuring her. . . .

New York City
JANUARY 24, 1909

"At last my dream has come true!" . . . I am here, after a delightful trip, and am beautifully situated, all ready to begin lessons—and—*have lost my voice!* Could anything be more discouraging? We stopped, en route to New York, at Connersville with Helen, at Toledo with Edna, and then at Niagara Falls. How sublime it is! Could anything be more wonderful, more awe inspiring than that great volume of water in its many exciting

---

11. Dame Nellie Melba (1861–1931) was an accomplished Australian soprano who made her debut in Brussels in 1887. Her most popular role was Mimi; she was also outstanding as Lucia, Gilda, Juliet, and Marguerite. Luisa Tetrazzini (1871–1940) made her debut in Italy in 1890. She had an international career that included appearances in London and Chicago and at the Metropolitan Opera.

12. Lucy Brown Foor (1857–1944).

gymnastics? . . . The day was all a dream of beauty to me, and after seeing it in its icy covering, I trust I may go another time when I can see it dressed in its wonderful shades of green, and again in its fall dress of gorgeous coloring. We stopped in Albany and saw its beautiful Capitol building, and then followed the Hudson down to Manhattan City. All along its course were men, horses and saws at work cutting ice and packing it for the hot days next summer. . . . Our first days in New York were busy ones, for we were hunting some place to stay, and have now found it in 60 W. 94th St. where we are just settled, and beginning to feel at home. Our first evening here we *stood* in the Metropolitan Opera house in order to hear a wonderful production of "Le Nozze di Figaro." . . .

MARCH 22, 1909

Some time has elapsed since I last wrote in this little book of mine, but busy indeed have I been, each day full with its various duties and pleasures. After I regained my speaking voice, Mde. Valda began work with me, the same foundation work Nira has given me, but from a more advanced viewpoint. I find her a delightful teacher. Always has been pleasant to us, for she realizes that we really work diligently, but I know that she pounces down hard on those who do not work. She feels that if anyone is willing to give plenty of hard work founded on the right principle of whatsoever branch they may be studying, that person will surely advance. . . . Mde. told me that I had a "beautiful voice," but did not hear me sing any songs until today when she asked me to bring something down for her to hear. . . . She said she was amazed that I could put into practice, in my song work, as much of the method as I did, and that I "had a wonderful future ahead of me," that my "voice would be more brilliant than Melba's" and Nira says that she said "and larger." . . . [O]f course all of us realize how much more work is ahead of me before I am *really great*. Oh! If I can only do it! If I can only continue my study. I am so anxious for it, so willing to give my time and energy. It seems a pity for one who loves it so, who is so intensely ambitious, to be unable to follow the loved profession. Sometimes I feel I *must* go on, I cannot give it up, but in my heart of hearts I know that when the time comes for me to go home, and give up my study, I shall go. . . . [T]he great Protector guards us all, and guides us into the proper path. My chosen profession may not be the right one for me in His eyes; in that case, I only pray it may slip by me and leave me *content*. Contentment is the greatest factor in the world's happiness. . . .

I am deeply grateful to my dearest husband for this great opportunity. How much this year will always mean to me. . . . But I have missed my two loved ones terribly, my husband and baby. Sometimes my heart has grown faint in me, for its continual hungering for them but I knew it was

a wonderful opportunity for me. . . . Then, too, I know so well, I could
not be satisfied in Carthage, if I did return. . . . What a dreadful thing it is
for one not to attempt the scaling of the ladder of fame before he marries.
If one is ambitious, every effort should be made to fulfill that ambition
while he is young. Should he wait until after marriage, the ambition is
still there, and the heart necessarily divided between the home ties and
the ambition. It is a serious matter to attempt to curb one's ambitions,
and the parents usually make a mistake when they do it. I cannot give up
my dear, self sacrificing, devoted husband and my darling little daughter,
but neither can I, with content, give up my music. They must henceforth
go hand in hand.

Mde. Valda is a wonderful teacher. Her knowledge of voice building
is profound, and her power of imparting it to others wonderful. . . . We
have met Mde. Francesco Lamperti, wife of the old maestro, who is here
visiting Mde. and we find her most charming. She is a regal-looking
woman with a queenly graciousness to all around her. We have been
privileged to attend two receptions given for her, through the kindness of
Mde. Valda. Altogether everything has been charming for us this winter
and we are and have been quite happy with our environment. Mde.
gives a little "Afternoon" this week for her girls to meet Mde. Lamperti,
and we are to attend and also to sing, which is very nice for us. We
heard the "Farewell Performance" given for Sembrich on the night of her
retirement from the Metropolitan stage,[13] and it was a most wonderful
affair. We were wild with excitement, and few could enjoy her triumphs
more than we did. The operatic stage has lost a beautiful singer and
charming personality, and all the world mourns with us the passing of
such a remarkable career. There is no city in the world which can be
compared to New York City. It is remarkable in many ways, and stands
alone in its class. The best of anything and everything can be procured
here, I firmly believe, if one has the wherewithal. . . .

JULY 23, 1909

And here it is mid-summer, and the book still waiting for another line
from me. I have been so busy having experiences, making incidents to
inscribe herein that I have had no time for the penning of them. We sang
for Mde. Lamperti, and heard the others sing, and beautifully too. What a
surprise they were to me, for I had heard them doing only this foundation

13. Mercella Sembrich (1858–1935) was a Polish coloratura soprano who became a
naturalized American citizen. A student of both G. B. Lamperti and his father, she made
her debut at the Metropolitan Opera in 1883 as Lucia. Her farewell performance was
on February 6, 1909, an occasion on which she was greeted with great affection and
enthusiasm. Sembrich continued to give concerts until 1917 and taught at Curtis and
Juilliard.

work, making foolish-looking grimaces and singing horrid sounding "ahs"
and did not dream they could really sing. What an amazement they were,
for all had beautiful voices, and were trained singers, with beautiful style
and rendition. . . . We sang and both teachers were quite gracious to us,
saying that we were the *best* of the pupils. Afterwards, when we were
alone, Mde. Lamperti kissed me, and told me that "Mde. Valda had said
that I had a fine voice but she did not dream it was so wonderful." That
I "had a wonderful career ahead of me." Many other lovely things were
said to me, but I know they all mean *nothing* unless I can work. . . . [I]n
May I had to leave. Miss Foor had to go to take care of three children,
whose mother (her dear friend) had died, leaving a request that Miss
Foor might care for her children. . . . I hated to leave Mde., but I could
hardly wait to see the baby and Everett. Before I left, I had daily lessons
and much hard work. . . .

My trip home was a pleasant one, with an afternoon off in St. Louis,
and Everett to meet me at this end. All seemed well and happy to be all
together again. The baby had not sorrowed much for me, as mother says
children of that age seldom do if they have the necessary wants attended
to. She seemed twice as *little* and sweet. Ah! but we are a happy family. My
summer has been most busy, for visitors, and sewing, music and friends
have kept me bustling. But the practice! Oh! it seems *impossible* to do
some practice, with all the demands which are made of a housekeeper's
time. Each day I hope to do a long day's practice, but only get in an
hour or so. However I still hope, and we are hoping we can further
study this winter. Mde. Valda could not go abroad this Spring, but sails in
October (this fall). Mde. Lamperti came to offer her the name, library and
manuscripts, and all that is left of the Francesco Lamperti School, and to
connect his name with Mde. Valda's in a school which shall be formed
in Paris, The Lamperti-Valda School of Music. She considers Mde. Valda
the greatest living exponent of the Lamperti Method. And we hope to
go. . . . Everett wants to study in Berlin, but I expect to go to Mde. It is
awful to be separated, but he does not know the French language, and
would be lost in a French clinic whereas he is at home in a German
one. I will take the small Marian Louisa who will be 4½ years old then.
Mde. V. expects Nira to "come out" in Europe next Spring, and wants me
to make my debut in the fall, a year hence. But I must go *with her* and
sweat blood a year. She says that "she and Mde. Lamperti" decided that I
have every requisite for a great singer "and that I can knock Tetrazzini sky
high," if I do as she wishes for my "voice is one which will astound the
world" and make them say when they hear it that "they do not believe
it!" All this sounds well, but will *not happen at my debut*, I fancy! I well
understand that it takes years to make an *artist*. But I want to try! And I
will work for it.

108 Avenue du Rossle, Neuilly, Paris, France
DECEMBER 14, 1909

Another dream come true.

Marian Wright Powers and her daughter spent the winter of 1909–1910 in Paris, where Marian studied at the Lamperti-Valda School. The following winter she studied in New York with Alfred Giraudet, and received further instruction from Louis Victor Rousseau and Anna E. Ziegler. Although Marian sang frequently, she had started her serious study of music too late, when her heart was divided between "home ties" and ambition. How often she must have wished she could have followed her own advice: "If one is ambitious, every effort should be made to fulfill that ambition while he is young."

ELIZABETH FLORA ANNA DIERSSEN (1884–1969)

"*My* childhood ambition, inspired by a cousinly example, was to become a teacher and wear a gold watch attached to a long chain that went around my neck." Anna Dierssen fulfilled her childhood ambition, teaching English in several southeast Missouri high schools. She was serving as the superintendent of a "tiny consolidated district [Lowndes in Wayne County] when the retirement system rang the last bell."[1]

A native of Wayne County, Anna was born at Gravelton in 1884. Her father, John August Dierssen, was a German immigrant, naturalized in 1879. His wife, Catherine Fox, came with her parents from North Carolina to Missouri after the Civil War. The Dierssen family moved to Cape Girardeau when Anna was eleven. There was an older brother, Fredrick Herman, and a younger sister, Freda, whose nickname was Fritzie.[2] After earning her degree at the Normal (teachers') college in Cape Girardeau and teaching for two years, Anna saved her money and went to Columbia in 1907 to "the University of Missouri where I revelled in modern languages and English higher composition for one year." Returning home, Anna assumed the role of "mother" in the household, since Catherine Dierssen suffered from ill health.[3]

At the request of Harriet Marston, who had been one of her favorite teachers at the Normal School, Anna joined the Wednesday Club in Cape Girardeau. Her diary, "Wednesday Club in Person," reflects the changing social roles of women in the period before World War I. In miniature and from a personal perspective, the diary shows what was happening throughout the United States. In the nineteenth century, literary clubs, along with the Sunday School movement, had helped women develop the communication, organizational, and leadership skills that would carry them into social campaigns, civic activities, and new professional pursuits.

1. Dierssen, "The Wednesday Club in Person: A Diary," 211, 313. Further references to pages in the diary are indicated in the text. This bound transcript of her original handwritten diary may now be found at WHMC-C. It is used with the permission of Miss Dierssen's great-niece, G. Delany Dean.

2. Information about the family has been provided by Alice R. Spillman of the Cape Girardeau County Genealogy Association and the late Colonel John C. Dean, nephew of Anna Dierssen. See also *Southeast Missourian,* December 30, 1968, and March 20, 1969.

3. In "Missouri University and I: 1907–1908," 95, Dierssen comments, "Mamma is not well, although her trouble is nervous and my being at home would be of little help for that. . . . I long to do something for my little sister. Maybe I can sometime." Dierssen notes that her mother could not live with the family because of the climate ("Wednesday Club," 312). Dierssen completed her B.S. in Education at Southeast Missouri State Teachers' College in 1933.

Historians have recently examined the significant role clubs played in creating influential political networks among women.[4]

By the time Dierssen became active in the Cape Girardeau Wednesday Club, the literary clubs that provided a cultural outlet for women had grown into a strong national federation. The General Federation of Women's Clubs was started by Jane Cunningham Croly in 1890, and out of it grew a network of state and local federations created with a specific mission: to spread woman's sphere of influence. What was good for the family could benefit society at large. Croly, who founded the influential Sorosis Club in 1868, after she and other women were excluded from a New York Press Club dinner for Charles Dickens, initiated the General Federation to advance reform work. She explains why:

> The eagerness with which the women's clubs all over the country have taken up history, literature and art studies, striving to make up for the absence of opportunity and the absorption in household cares of their young womanhood, has in it something almost pathetic. But this ground will soon have been covered. Is there not room in the clubs for out-look committees, whose business it should be to investigate township affairs, educational, sanitary, reformatory, . . . and report what is being done, might be done, or needs to be done, for decency and order in the jails, in the schools, in the streets, in the planting of trees, in the disposition of refuse, and in the provision for light which is the best protection for life and property.[5]

Many local clubs resisted affiliation with the suffragist movement and the community activism urged by state and national federations. Numerous clubs, especially in the early days, were racially, socially, and economically elite. This elitism comes through in Dierssen's record of Wednesday Club conversations. Gradually, clubs developed more open policies and moved from continuing or supplementing women's educational experiences into the realm of social and political activities. Unlike certain early feminists, many women involved in the club movement were not trying to change their role as moral caretaker; instead, they just wanted to enlarge it. Dubbed "Municipal Housekeeping," the expansion was encouraged by both the General Federation, an almost exclusively white organization, and the National Association of Colored Women, founded in 1896. Women were urged to extend their homemaking and mothering instincts into the arena of civic usefulness and

---

4. In 1980 Karen Blair, *The Clubwoman as Feminist: True Womanhood Redefined, 1868–1914,* called attention to the influence of women's literary clubs of the nineteenth century. Anne Firor Scott, *Natural Allies: Women's Associations in American History* (1991), reiterated their political importance throughout American history.

5. Croly, *The History of the Woman's Club Movement in America,* 112, cited in Blair, *Clubwoman as Feminist,* 98.

to take up the banner for public health, education, libraries, restricting child labor, and in the case of the NACW, human rights for African-Americans.[6]

Helen Hooven Santmyer's 1982 novel " . . . *And Ladies of the Club*" traces the lives of two charter members of a women's literary society in small-town Ohio from the club's inception in 1868 until their deaths in the 1930s. The novel vividly captures the essence of changing times through the long-lasting tradition of a women's club. Dierssen's diary is not so epic, but it tells how a young woman comes of age and develops confidence through the influence of other women, who gather to pursue mutual interests and solve problems, unhampered by household chores for a few hours. The Wednesday Club diary also shows a young woman's growing awareness of social issues. Dierssen's concern about a range of issues, fostered in her encounter with civic matters at the Wednesday Club, continued to the end of her life. Anna Dierssen, who never married, died in Cape Girardeau in 1969.[7]

The Cape Girardeau Wednesday Club Constitution and By-Laws, Article II, states its purpose: "The object of this club shall be to form an organized center for the intellectual, social, and moral development of the members to strengthen their individual efforts for humanity." A theme was selected each year, and women were assigned a topic for the biweekly meetings, which ran from October to May. In 1911–1912, the topic was England. On December 6, 1911, for example, the presentations included "Life and Work of Milton," "Milton's London," "Political and Economic Conditions of 17th Century England," and "The Extension of Government Control." Dierssen notes the papers presented at each meeting and often comments on the dress of club members and decor of their homes. Dierssen did library research to prepare her papers, but some women simply read articles from the *General Federation Magazine* or the Chautauqua magazine. After each program there was time for a "Round Table" discussion of civic or social issues, followed by a business meeting and refreshments. Dierssen's reports on the planning of annual themes show the tension between those members who saw the club as a cultural organization offering respite from the

6. Scott, *Natural Allies,* 141–58.

7. In the 1950s and 1960s, Dierssen expressed her opinion on legislative and civic matters to Tenth District Congressman Paul C. Jones. She urged him not to support easing immigration laws and advocated more stringent regulation of the Food and Drug Administration testing of food additives. She argued against required prayers in public schools: "The school is the place for teachers and pupils to live their religion, not preach it." Dierssen opposed the Vietnam War and the "unconstitutional and immoral public accommodation clause" of the Civil Rights Bill. She even expressed disapproval of Patrick Nugent, Luci Baines Johnson's husband, avoiding duty in Vietnam by attending the University of Texas (Paul C. Jones Correspondence, WHMC-C).

pressures of daily life, and others who wanted to effect change in their community.

Rarely daring to voice an opinion during her first year in the club, by the end of the second, Dierssen was elected secretary and became active on the program committee. She wrote about her experiences and set the diary aside. In 1963 she typed and edited the three-hundred-page manuscript, and gave a copy to the University of Missouri-Columbia. The editors have chosen passages that reveal Dierssen as an acute observer of humanity and a talented writer. More than her personal story, she tells about a society in transition.

With this "Backdrop," Anna Dierssen sets the stage for the story of the Wednesday Club:

> The period, 1911–1916, was the end of an era. It was pre-entangling alliances, pre-prohibition, pre-women's suffrage, and antedated many succeeding ways of carrying on daily existence. It was tapering down to lose itself in the ensuing cycle. . . .
>
> Money, not at all plentiful, had buying value in proportion to its rarity. Milk was delivered on the front porch for a nickel a pint. The ice man deposited in the box the desired amount, often a dime's worth. . . .
>
> As a general servant electricity had not been put to work. There was no electric washer, no iron, no sewing machine, no toaster, no heat pad, no vacuum cleaner. . . .
>
> Walking was still the prevailing way of getting to work, to church, to schools, downtown for shopping, to organization meetings, and to social functions both afternoon and evening, unless one happened to live in the limited orbit of the electric trolley which made a loop around the heart of town. Only the doctor pursued his calling in a vehicle, usually the iron-tired top-buggy. So far as other residents of towns were concerned, vehicles were for recreation and courting, on Sundays and other holidays. . . .
>
> For women . . . most clothes were still made on the treadle machine . . . . Since wearing apparel was far less plentiful than at present but of the finest silk, wool, or cotton, the life of a garment was usually prolonged by remodelling and sometimes turned inside out.
>
> Hats were bought at millinery stores, often trimmed to order with ribbon, flowers, or feathers; and last year's chapeau was frequently taken to the milliner for re-trimming, or this might be done at home by the clever fingers of the owner.
>
> Educationally all were grounded in United States History and general geography in addition to the three r's—at least that was the aim of teachers. Those who made it to Normals and colleges were given the prescribed course in Latin, mathematics, history, literature, and science, rounded out by electives. . . .
>
> Since radio and television did not exist, in addition to the printed page, the lecture platform and the pulpit provided spiritual and intellectual monitoring for the eager.
>
> In short, this was a rather quiet evening among home folks before the dawn of a day that would usher in with resounding drums the rest of the world. (319–21)

A Diary

OCTOBER 5, 1911

Yesterday I attended my first meeting as one of the Wednesday Club. . . .

[T]he pleasure of my going depended largely upon clothes, which in turn depended upon the weather. If it rained, I should have nothing suitable to wear. If it was merely cooler, my tan linen suit would do. If the sun would be so good as to shine, I could go comfortably in snowy linen.

Rain was pattering the windows when I awoke. By nine it had quit, but the skies were leaden grey. By noon, however, the sun shone splendidly, positively. October warmth was in prospect.

While the weather was wavering uncertainly, another matter occupied me. I almost had to have a pair of new gloves. My white silk ones had been washed so many times they were yellowish, beside having a few little mends in the fingers. Yet if I spent fifty cents for gloves, I should not have enough left to pay my dues; and being by nature a pay-as-you-go person, I did not want to put that off until the next meeting. I made up my mind to wear the old gloves. (1)

At her first meeting Anna encounters a discussion about "unappreciated charity."

"It has come to this with me," said Mrs. Himmelberger [wife of a prosperous timber mill owner]. "Unless it is a case of sickness, I'm afraid I don't respond to charity any more. I've tried it and been deceived too many times." She spoke with utter good humor.

"Let me tell you what happened to Mother when we lived in Ohio," Mrs. Duckworth, the brown-eyed French looking lady [who lived with her husband in a fine pressed brick mansion on College Hill], took it up. All animation and rocking back and forth, she told how her mother and some friends had fitted up a house with all sorts of furniture, good furniture. The small stove her mother gave was good enough to cook on for years. "We had a new range and just did not need it any more."

Others had furnished dishes, beds, chairs, tables—a complete outfit.

"Well, they took all that out there," she continued. "They even scrubbed the house and put up scrim curtains. A few days later some of them drove out to see how the family was getting along, and what do you think? Not a soul was there, not a soul. And not a thing in the house. They had sold everything and gone away on the money."

Mrs. Hawkins had a story to match. Her mother-in-law had done a lot of things for a poor woman, and she herself had given among other things a coat, a good warm coat.

"Of course, it was one I didn't want to wear any more. It had those tight sleeves, . . . but it would have kept her warm all winter. She told the next person who came in that Mrs. Hawkins wouldn't wear that coat herself, so she needn't expect her to wear it." . . .

The sad subject changed to fall fashions and to the lovely October day. Not obliged to contribute, I was enjoying the sight and sound of them all. The talk was light and good-humored and in no way touched with animus. As for the ladies themselves, they were engaging to behold.

Without staring, I was usually seeing Mrs. Himmelberger, her airy panama hat with its drooping sash, the pink rose at her belt, her large hands and arms comfortably bare, and the petticoat lace that would sag below a skirt which style made too narrow for women of her size. . . .

[Anna turns to her favorite.] It was of Miss Marston, however, of whom I was especially aware, for wherever she is that is always the center of the room for me. She has such a superabundance of intellect, such outreaching warmth of heart, and such complete lack of all snobbery that other kinds of distinctness give way in her presence. . . . I was seeing her tiny brown-shod feet, her little brown-gloved hands, the yellow chrysanthemum merging into the tan of her drooping hat, and the brilliant smile in her grey-blue eyes. . . . All afternoon I was feeling that protecting, encouraging smile, feeling it and appreciating it, but trying to slip away from it. I did not want to be an obligation. (36–37)

OCTOBER 19, 1911

Dierssen records her trials in reworking an old pin-striped suit to wear to a meeting.

. . . My suit was only approaching its fourth birthday at Christmas, but the skirt had been shorn of voluminous fullness and new faced; the back had been altered and the sleeves recut; and a couple of weeks ago I had decided to lighten considerably the expenditure for clothes this winter by turning it inside out and reshaping the coat to present lines. . . .

The Club meets every two weeks. I told myself I must have the garb ready for the second session in October. . . . The fall house cleaning was imminent. And I wanted to make hats, my special forte since I had constructed them of [pawpaw] leaves in play time long ago. I started a delectable chapeau for Fritzie [her thirteen-year-old sister] and a smart one for myself. The suit kept being shoved back, and time kept slipping away.

Fritzie, who is definite and practical, asked the evening before Club, "Will your suit be done?"

I nodded toward the leaden sky. "It has to be," I said and went on whipping the new velveteen collar.

She persisted. . . . "You've got the skirt done, haven't you?"

"Nearly. It has to have hooks and eyes. If you have time to peel the potatoes, I can finish this whipping before I stop." . . .

Grey dawn found me awake with a sense of eager hurry.

I swished through household tasks. The hat needed the feather tacked on and must be made to sit a trifle higher. By half past eight I could lay that creation on the couch beside my new kid gloves. By ten the skirt had its fastening and was pressed. I caught up the coat whose lining was only basted in, flew at it and kept at it . . . until I must stop at eleven to get dinner. The coat needed pressing. I shoved the smoothing irons on.

In the meantime the sun had come out beautifully. . . . *[Fritzie came in at noon.]* "Is it warmer?" I asked, catching at the possibility of resting from the suit until another occasion.

"I didn't need my coat coming home."

"I might be able to wear my linen suit."

Her grey eyes widened. "Didn't you get done?"

"All except pressing. But I'm not satisfied with the collar. It doesn't set quite right."

If I only had another day! I felt a strain in my neck and heaviness in my head. To hide the mist of pure weariness that stung my eyes, I hurried out with the empty dishes.

The sun grew still more delightfully warm. The chill air was gone, leaving one of those filmy golden days, one of those tenderly cheerful farewells of summer that are about the most precious of all the year. What I had an impulse to do was to start out and walk and walk down a white road past woods barely beginning to feel the breath of autumn. So restful that would be, and I was tempted, but I knew I should be disappointed in myself as well as being sorry to have disappointed Fritzie . . . [and] Miss Marston.

In the new hat and the linen suit, I fared forth [to attend the meeting]. (18–20)

NOVEMBER 1, 1911

"I don't see why we should be so rushed as we are. I don't see any reason for it," Mrs. Himmelberger had remarked with easy pleasantry at the last meeting. . . .

Some days later as I sat sewing, the question drifted back through my mind. Was it the hurry of fear? After long years of careless, adventuresome waste of the splendid opportunities and resources of the new world, were we Americans realizing in a panic that in trying to grasp too much, we were in a fair way to see everything slip through our fingers? . . .

On Monday afternoon before the third Wednesday Club meeting, the question was back with me, this time personally and specifically. Why was I so rushed for the next forty-eight hours? (34–35)

Miss Marston drops by to ask her to prepare a paper on Thomas à Becket for the next meeting.

. . . "I think what was wanted is [Becket's death] scene in the Cathedral more than anything else." . . .

Taking down our own old *Brockhaus,* and hunting a German novel that featured Becket, the martyr, I seated myself in the big oak rocker with a foot stool and put my modern language major to work.

As I read, I tried composedly to plan and select, but already my thoughts were rushing to the climax of agony, not Becket's, but my own as I faced the Club. I could see myself opening the hastily written paper, hear my voice half fail in the middle of sentences, and feel the hot flush of embarrassment in my cheeks. . . .

[Finally,] it occurred to me I had better give over imagining and get on with the deed before me.

After briefly outlining my findings in the *Brockhaus,* I wrote a translation of the death scene in Myer's *Der Heilige,* more to get into a Becket state of mind than for any use it would be, feeling it odd to be digging for an English martyr in German soil. (36–38)

Fritzie reminds Anna that she had promised to help her write twenty couplets to go on cards for a Halloween party.

"Wait a little," I begged, "I'll think while I get supper." . . .

. . . The rhymes came easy. While I worked with my hands, my mind flung them off as if from a whizzing wheel, twenty couplets maybe less clever than they might have been, but complete, ready to be copied from the sheet upon which each had been jotted as it came. Back to the Becket I rushed, and having made a tentative plan for the paper, I dropped into bed at the usual time, but I was so keyed up it took some extra time to persuade sleep.

Waking a half hour too early . . . [m]y plan was to go to the Normal a little after eight, dip into histories until ten, sign up for the Tennyson, come home, prepare dinner, skim the Becket drama, and settle down to write the paper. . . .

In the library, resisting an impulse to tarry at windows for the magnificent views, I took only one look downward across the town and

[Mississippi] river to the smoke-blue hills of Illinois beyond. Surrounded by the Britannica and Encyclopedia of Biography, a couple of histories, and the Tennyson, I sat down to work. My face was indeed to a window, but the tops of black-limbed, golden-leaved maples made a lovely tapestry enclosing me from all other sights.

Two accounts I read carefully, making notes. The others I skimmed for any personal and human touches that may have escaped the obliteration of time. The Tennyson I pushed to one side to be taken home. . . .

I read on, pushing back one book after another, and bringing from the shelves another to which I had found a reference.

A gong sounded and there was a general upheaval, closing of books and pushing back of chairs. . . .

Ten after ten and a half hour more would be twenty of eleven. . . .

Clutching the Tennyson, I hurried to the librarian's desk. "Miss Kent, may I check this out?"

Her smile was regretful. "All books of poetry are held as reference during the day. They can be taken out only after the sixth hour and returned before eight in the morning."

The sixth hour ends at three ten. . . .

Tennyson at three ten would be Tennyson too late. By that time I should be in the thick of writing the paper. Relinquishing him, I came away.

Why Tennyson anyway? Why should I borrow his imagination? Didn't I have an overdose of my own? . . .

Right after noon I scribbled the outline and fell to work. I was soon lost and racing along in a bit of a glow. Five o'clock found me rounding out the sixteenth page, closing the tablet, and laying it up until morning. (40–44)

Meantime I was worrying Mrs. Himmelberger's problem like a puppy with an old hat or shoe. I did see why we were rushed. It was our slipshod negligence in some things which made us so hurried in others. We wanted results that took time and effort and were unwilling to pay their proper value. Instead of spending effort to clear a road to our ideals, we dashed heedlessly into the brambles of a strange, new path. That was why we arrived so incoherent, breathless, tattered, and torn. (45–46)

NOVEMBER 1, 1911

I was approaching Miss Amy's house, and at the curb sat Mrs. Himmelberger's little, lady-of-leisure electric motor which has just appeared among our several odorous, honking, dust-flinging automobiles. . . . I admired it, although with a tinge of regret, for while she rides with her family in a big car, she has heretofore kept for her own use a horse and surrey, driving it with strong, skillful hands on the reins. Now she handles this sleek object with gloved fingers and has a holder of artificial flowers instead of the whip in its socket. . . .

[The program begins.] Mrs. Duckworth . . . had the first number, "Economic Conditions in England in the Sixteenth Century." . . .

Mrs. Hinchey gave a sketch of Chaucer's life and read interesting commentaries. . . .

For her "Chaucer's London" Mrs. Himmelberger . . . read us an extract from the Chautauqua Magazine. . . .

[Mrs. Hawkin's] paper, "Canterbury Cathedral," opened with a breath of sentiment. . . .

[Miss Knepper's] paper ["Canterbury Pilgrims"] was the most considerable and comprehensive I have heard as yet at the Wednesday Club. . . .

When Mrs. Albert called my name, I gathered my papers and rose. . . .

Once I was started, I had no difficulty. My findings I had thrown together in a narrative form, which I found readable as a story as I proceeded. . . . At the same time I took confidence from the close attention of the listeners . . . [and] I felt that my King and martyr were boring no one. . . .

In the rustle of applause [at the end] I subsided against my chair back, so glad it was over. (52–56)

The round table talk was to follow my paper. As the other leaders had so far, Mrs. Albert announced that she had not prepared anything. She had meant to have a discussion on the local milk question but had not had time to work it up.[8]

The ladies took up the subject and shook it about a bit. Mrs. Himmelberger had opened a couple of bottles with a lovely rich cream but a most unbearable smell. Mrs. Duckworth had sent two bottles to the Normal laboratory . . . to be tested, but samples had gotten mixed, and she did not know whether or not it was hers that contained the drug. . . . Mrs. Hawkins remarked that where ignorance is bliss 'tis folly to be wise, and we all laughed. (58–59)

After the meeting, Anna walks with some of the other women.

Turning at Independence [Street], we went up the slope toward Lorimier School. Mrs. Himmelberger, her motor full of smiling College Hill neighbors, passed us, everybody waving. Our admiring gaze followed the elegant equipage nearly to the top but changed to dismay when it came rolling backward down past us, nobody smiling.

"The brakes!" Miss Knepper gasped, turning to run into the street. . . .

---

8. According to Scott, *Natural Allies,* 151–52, "cleaning up the milk supply was a favorite enterprise" for women's clubs within the general area of public health. Clubs in some cities opened their own "pure milk stations to sell clean milk at cost."

Fortunately the driver got control, and the machine took the hill under its own power.

Leaving the last of my companions at the Pott home two blocks from here, I came on alone, feeling relieved and pleased. For the first time—this third meeting—I had become a member, not a visitor glad to get away after adjournment.

"Yes, a good meeting," I told Fritzie at home. "Yes, I survived the paper. I'll never mind so much again." (61–62)

NOVEMBER 15, 1911

. . . At the last meeting it had been decided that we should respond to roll call with a description of some portion of Norman architecture. The President, Miss Marston, and Mrs. Bell were the only ones who remembered. . . .

There was some discussion as to whether or not this should be a regular feature of roll call. Miss Knepper suggested that as we should soon run out of material we might take up the nomenclature of architecture and for a few meetings let each member answer with a definition of some term. . . .

Mrs. Hawkins did a quick twist in her chair. . . . "[W]hy couldn't we answer to roll call by some happy thought, a quotation"[?] . . .

Shades of school literary societies! "An honest man's the noblest work of God." . . . " 'Tis distance lends enchantment to the view." Repetition would be inevitable. Were we going back to this sort of treadmill?

A little silence fell. (69–70)

They decide to use architectural definitions since that is more in keeping with the year's theme.

[After the day's program], Mrs. McGhee was called upon for the Round Table on "Our Associated Charities." She . . . wanted to read a paper sent out to the different clubs by Dr. Bishop of St. Louis. It pointed out that club women were no longer working for self culture but were beginning to be a power in the community, and it outlined what was being done and what should be taken up.

The paper was interesting in itself and likewise because of the way the Wednesday Club, after a year or so of garbage cans and vacant lot beautifying have settled back to self-culture.

"How does this man know so much about it?" Mrs. Waters asked.

"Dr. Bishop is a woman," Mrs. McGhee elucidated.[9]

9. Frances Lewis Bishop began a practice of internal medicine in St. Louis in the late 1890s. She was the first public school health examiner in St. Louis, and the first physician to do "welfare work" for a large manufacturing company. Her activities included serving

It happened that I had a pleasing recollection of her. The year I taught in St. Louis she was a physician for the school system. . . .

Altogether I got such a favorable impression of her that I was now keenly interested in what she wrote, although not convinced that our ladies should throw culture overboard.

When Mrs. McGhee had finished the reading, she turned the discussion over to the club in general, to which no one contributed much. It went limping from one to another, not really taken in anywhere. Finally Madame President turned to Miss Marston . . . "Can you tell us something about our Associated Charities?" . . .

. . . [Miss Marston] told of her Springfield experiences, asked questions about the Associations of Cape Girardeau and drew responses, dealt generously with what was given her, and at the conclusion had the members warmly asking each other who our poor were and how they could be reached.

Mrs. Himmelberger repeated her opinion that we had no poor except in cases of sickness; then she was ready and willing to help.

Mrs. Albert had heard of poor people through school teachers. In that way we might find out who needed books and warm coats in order to keep in school. (74–75)

[After the meeting] the full joy of the afternoon came over me. As I stepped along through the cool twilight, the air flowing over me like a refreshing stream of water after the hours of being housed up, I was pervaded by a feeling of delight in all that had gone on. . . . [I]t was as if I were carrying, filched from a feast, a merry red apple, nuts to be munched by the fireside, and grapes to be nibbled in the morning. The fragrance of flowers, too, I should be sniffing for hours to come.

In short, I loved the Club. (79–80)

FEBRUARY 7, 1912

Miss Marston, head of the programme committee for the coming club year, [had a proposal]. . . . "You have had England this year. I wonder if you would like Scotland?"

A thrill was in the atmosphere. . . .

[There was mention of American History, but Scotland continued to prevail until] Mrs. Himmelberger, her big figure encased in a modish blue suit, and her eyes shining benevolently, rose. She wore her wide hat with its circle and standard of white ostrich feathers. She held a mink muff in one hand. Her curving nose was unusually earnest and purposeful. She was altogether in fine form.

---

on the Pure Milk Commission, the St. Louis Society of Social Hygiene, and as Chairman of the Health Department of the Women's Clubs of Missouri (*Notable Women of St. Louis, 1914*, ed. Anne André-Johnson [Mrs. Charles P. Johnson], 25–27).

"I should, of course, be delighted to have a programme on Scotland, but . . . what I want most of all is for the Club to do something for this town. It's time we were. Why, this body of women can do anything they make up their minds to—anything at all!" She sat down flushed.

"Splendid!" Mrs. Hawkins cheered, just as feet skip to a band as it passes. "Let's put our shoulder to the wheel."

"We might put our energies upon the Y.M.C.A. building that the men want," Mrs. John Kochtitzky suggested in her soft voice.

Mrs. Ivy [head of a boys' dormitory] spoke up . . . , "That's the greatest criticism of this town. There is no place for the young men to go except to the saloons. A few go to the Elks Club. Otherwise there is no place."

"What a creature a young man is!" Mrs. Hunt remarked in an aside. "I am glad I have only a girl."

Mrs. Himmelberger endorsed the Y.M.C.A. or any other good cause. . . .

Mrs. Bell squared her shoulders. "I agree perfectly. It is time this Club was doing something about this town. I've felt it for some time. I am not especially interested in a Y.M.C.A., not that I have any objection, but we ought to do something besides just for ourselves. Up to now we've been just a study club. It is time we add something else." . . .

One felt the atmosphere of transition from culture to crusading, lady-like, a shade militant, and maybe Quixotic. . . .

Miss Marston and several faculty members as well as a number of ladies of the town were silent, although doubtless thoughtful and wise within. All of them worked hard in their professions and in running their homes and were entitled to the stretch of soul and relaxation of the beloved study programme, but it was not the thing to advocate, merely to let the group realize. . . .

Members discuss having one group "work on a city problem" and another "follow a culture programme," but few want to divide the club.

[Finally], Miss Marston released us in her adept way. "On the subject of helpful interest in people, we might remember that this is Ruskin's birth month, and that February seventh is the one hundredth anniversary of Dickens's birth. No two men were more actively interested in their fellow men."

"And we have Dickens at our next meeting," Mrs. Johnson said happily. . . . A quite harmonious adjournment, no change decided upon, nothing iconoclastic predictable. (102–6)

MARCH 6, 1912

Anna's observations reveal how a woman's role was still identified by marriage and family.

One of our new members, Mrs. Ivan Lee Holt, was again present. Since her husband is so active, lecturing on Wagner, acting as toastmaster on state occasions, and taking part in political primaries, as well as belonging to the Commercial Club and the Provident Association, it is considered that she will be a valuable addition to the Club, particularly from a musical standpoint. A lady who can illustrate upon the piano those learned disquisitions of Dr. Holt should be an authority upon things musical. . . .

Miss Knepper then delivered a paper, but Anna did not hear much of it.

While listening with both ears, inside I was having a foolish fancy. It was the lines in Miss Knepper's neck that brought it on. She is an excellent mathematics teacher. She has many friends. She has travelled abroad, storing up interesting knowledge and experiences. She has a wide interest in matters cultural—except music. In brief, she is a well-rounded personality as-is. But how good if she were married. Or going to be.

I did not envisage the man, except that he would probably be fair, even-tempered, and a gentleman who maybe needed a bit of managing for his own good, about taking his umbrella or wearing his overcoat, for example. It was Miss Knepper as a grand mom that I was seeing, the ideal mom for two or three boys, maybe a little girl thrown in for good measure. As I considered her, here in her golden thirties, I felt an ache of regret, to think that this decisive, intelligent, adaptable, congenial expounder of the binomial theorem was day by day, year by year, slipping away from her manifest destiny. (116–17)

[There is discussion about the program for the next year.] I had an impulse to make a motion, my first since joining the club. A few days ago I told Fritzie I thought I should find my voice pretty soon. It had taken me several months in the Normal Clio Literary [Society], but thereafter I had enjoyed surpassingly furthering my ideas in the business meeting. . . .

. . . I let the impulse subside. I am busy listening and absorbing, revelling in everything, even the meaningful silences from which a few ideas break and play peek-a-boo with the outside world. I have only feelings, eyes, ears, not voice as yet, but it began to whisper inside today. (119–20)

The Wednesday Club decides on Scotland for the next year's theme, and there is no further mention of the Y.M.C.A. project. On March 20, 1912, Dierssen wrote, "I may be wrong, but I believe the members were glad to leave that project to the men" (124).

October 16, 1912

The period considered in today's meeting was from 80 to 1057. We have each bought a Scotch history and can keep ourselves in logical order and prepared to understand the speakers if we give a little time to preliminary reading. . . .

Miss Tyler, I thought, rather played down the "Historical Setting and Synopsis of Macbeth." It was all there, even rather comprehensive, but her manner emphasized the impression I have that she is not interested in cultural programmes. There seems to be a difference of opinion between two groups of Faculty women, one led by Miss Marston, the other by Miss Tyler. I may imagine it but do not think so. (134–45)

NOVEMBER 6, 1912

Mrs. R. B. Oliver was present as a visitor, accompanying [her daughter] Marguerite. They moved farther front, but Mrs. Oliver could not see too well there, so they moved back to the middle. And would Miss Knepper please speak a little louder, the older lady requested. Her hearing was not too good. This reminded me of a delightful party I had attended in her home during my last year at the Normal. I hoped she too would join us and add to the already varied personalities.[10] . . .

JANUARY 15, 1913

A large crowd gathered today. Nearly all members were present and some of them accompanied by guests. The reason for this was an interesting visitor, Miss Mary Helen Fee, a former Normal faculty woman who has been teaching in the Philippine Islands. . . .

When the call came for teachers to go out to our recently acquired Philippine Islands, she volunteered and sailed away. As a result she wrote *A Woman's Experiences in the Philippines*, and a novel, *The Locust Years*, which also had an island setting. Both of these books were mentioned in our local paper, and I read them avidly, especially the *Experiences*, which I have perused more than once, vicariously going out to the Islands myself to teach.

To see and hear the author in person was going to be a real treat. . . .

Madame President, impressive herself, clothed in native dignity and close-fitting grey cloth, called us to order. After the reading of the minutes, . . . she made a short speech. Maybe suspecting that we might be criticised by a forward looking woman for still being in the self-culture stages of clubdom, she spoke of the possibility of the organization at some future time dividing into sections, so that each member could follow her particular bent toward worthwhile achievement. She was very earnest,

10. Marie Watkins (Mrs. R. B.) Oliver, whose letters are included in this anthology, joined the Wednesday Club, along with her daughter and daughter-in-law.

indeed, [and] seemed almost to be throwing down the gauntlet to us of change. (161–62)

[FEBRUARY 19, 1913]

As a member of the program committee for 1913–1914, Dierssen plays a key role in the controversy, leading the discussion on behalf of the program committee.

The President turned to me. "We will now hear from the committee on suggestions for next year's programme." . . .

The committee's survey was on the board before them.

1. MODERN DRAMA
2. STUDY THROUGH HISTORY AND LITERATURE OF—
    A. FRANCE
OR   B. HOLLAND
OR   C. SPAIN
3. EMPLOYMENT OF WOMEN; FROM THE BEGINNING OF TIME—
    a. WOMAN IN THE HOME
    b. WOMAN IN BUSINESS
4. QUESTIONS OF THE DAY
5. OUR OWN COUNTRY

For a culture programme the committee thought we might spend a pleasant and worthwhile year studying Modern Drama, taking up Ibsen, Maeterlinck, Shaw, and others. . . .

"Study Through History and Literature" I did not discuss, merely stating that an informing and interesting programme could be made on either of the three countries mentioned. . . .

Number 3, the "Employment of Women," I spoke of as looking toward the active stage of club life. . . . "We are not able to equip and carry on public libraries, operate street sprinklers, or plant miles of highway with trees, but we can find out all that women have done and are doing." . . .

Number 4 I amplified by naming some of the "Questions of the Day"— cities and their causes of congestion, problems of country life, natural resources, schools, conveniences, culture, and woman's suffrage. . . .

Number 5, "Our Own Country," was rather my favorite subject. I gave it a bit of a peroration, which, however, barely grazed my inner enthusiasm.

. . . We should evaluate the ancestral way of living and draw a comparison with our own. For example, how could a man some generations ago live to be eighty-five and carry on his usual occupation to the end . . . while people today have nervous breakdowns in the forties or apoplexy around sixty?

. . . Let our aim be to study Americanism, the blessing under which we all live. If we are soon to step into the active stages of club life, we can not choose a better transition subject than this. It will be a useful background for any present day subjects we may undertake later. To know the causes behind our modern problems is the best approach to their solution. Such a study is far from being mere self culture. (189–92)

Following heated discussion, the ladies vote for "Number 4, Questions of the Day."

After adjournment several congratulated me upon the unwonted interest I had aroused and the lively discussion precipitated. (197)

March 5, 1913

Anna feels that she, Miss Tyler, and Miss Shilling as the new program committee can never live up to the standards set by the current committee led by Miss Marston.

. . . I cast a glance back over the Club as I have known it. I thought of the various minds and conflicting interests. I thought of Miss Marston who has been a power for unity among the changing group for seven years. And yet how little the members are united in one purpose. They— all of us—are in a state of individualism, which is, after all, a salutary condition for human beings.

No programme will reach all equally.

What Miss Marston with valiant Miss Knepper beside her has been unable to accomplish, can not be expected of the present committee. (213)

March 19, 1913

Anna delivers a paper on Sir Walter Scott.

I had about six thousand words, but I knew them so well it was more talking than reading. I had elected to tell the fascinating saga of Scott's life. So thrilled I was that when the end came I was as sorry as if a friend was gone. . . .

I began gathering my papers from the desk.

A hand clapping started back of me, the President. It went over the room, a surprising outburst. . . .

Mrs. Dearmont shook my hand. "Congratulations! How *do* you do it?"

"She learned it in Clio, reading papers, talking, running the business meetings, being president and all," my fellow Clio, Carrie Woodburn Johnson, laid claim.

"And don't forget those oratorical contests I egged Annie on to entering." Miss Marston reminded her.

"Which I never won."

"Except in thought and writing. And you were competing with young men. Judges expect an orator to roar."

"You have it in you," Miss Knepper said, "the real spark." . . .

The handshaking was going on. I liked the bit of an ovation although it was somewhat embarrassing. (223–25)

MARCH 30, 1913

The committee of Tyler, Shilling, and Dierssen meets to work on the program for the next year. Anna finds herself torn between the new agenda supported by Miss Tyler and her loyalty to Miss Marston and others who prefer a "cultural" program.

"You know, we never dreamed this subject would be chosen," I felt compelled to confess. . . . "[W]e . . . threw in 'Questions of the Day' for good measure."

[Miss Tyler's] friendly eyes widened. . . . "But it was nearly unanimous for this one!" she exclaimed. "Women are waking up. They are beginning to feel that there is something more than just study."

They might be waking up, but the blinds were still down, I thought, recalling how those round table discussions attached to last year's programmes had been Quaker meetings although they were upon current problems of importance.

Miss Tyler had a Federation book which outlined the nine departments. . . . We went through it rapidly for gleanings we might be able to use.[11]

"And conservation—" she paused to comment on one of the nine. "I don't think women are much interested in anything under that—except perhaps birds."

Birds, of course. But what about forests, water-power sites, mines, soil, country life, parks, natural wonders—everything that the word America covers? Birds, to be sure, for their beauty and companionship as well as being the foe of man's enemy, the insect, but all the rest should interest women. . . .

Opening up some papers, Miss Tyler showed me a sort of outline. "I thought we ought to narrow it down to some one thing. . . . Miss Shilling

---

11. Blair, *Clubwoman as Feminist*, 96–100, discusses the periodicals and methods used by the General Federation of Women's Clubs to disseminate information that would foster cooperation among clubs to carry out reform projects.

thought we might take as a subject 'Woman's Place in Progress.' What do you think?"

"Well, that is an important question, I am sure, if it covers what the ladies voted for."

"It covers everything. And nobody knows what they meant, with all that talk of combining. . . ."

"And I thought we might have on each programme some modern drama that would apply." (229–30)

The three women "hammered out the fifteen programmes: eight on 'Questions of the Day' and seven on 'Woman's Place in Progress.' "

Of the eight [programs] on "Questions of the Day" this is a sample [program for one meeting]:

1. THE CITY: A FACTOR IN SOCIAL, ECONOMIC, AND POLITICAL LIFE
2. THE PROBLEMS OF CITY GROWTH—ESPECIALLY THE MORAL EFFECTS OF ENVIRONMENT.
3. THREE-MINUTE DISCUSSIONS
4. [DISCUSSION OF PERTINENT DRAMA OR NOVEL]: EDWARD SHELDON—*THE BOSS*

Of the seven on "Woman's Place in Progress" the following is a sample:

1. WOMAN AN UNRECOGNIZED FACTOR IN ECONOMIC LIFE
2. WOMAN'S ENTRANCE INTO AND POSITION IN INDUSTRIAL COMPETITION
3. THREE-MINUTE DISCUSSIONS
4. [DISCUSSION OF] OLIVE SCHREINER—*WOMAN AND LABOR* . . .

"I don't suppose Miss Marston will take to it," Miss Shilling said. "She may want it made over her way." The tone was disparaging.

A pink flush spread over Miss Tyler's face. She spoke without looking up, "No, I think she'll take it all right. I—think Miss Marston is waking up. She's beginning to see."

Miss Marston waking up! The widest awake teacher that was ever on the faculty! And these girls speaking of her beginning to see!

"Miss Marston is wonderful," I said. "You can always expect the finest and best of her and not be disappointed."

"Yes, I'm sure," Miss Tyler agreed. "She'll be nice about it."

We concluded the session amiably enough. . . .

On the way home I was still smarting under the affront to Miss Marston. To hear her spoken of as "waking up"! She that is more wide awake in her little finger than her critics are in their whole bodies. Why can they not accept her success and superiority as a teacher as do her contemporaries? (238–40)

APRIL 2, 1913

The Club temper is a trifle uncertain these days. We thresh about in the toils of transition. Some are dragging a crippled wing and sorrowing. Others are pecking impatiently at seeming barriers. The rest are flitting this way and that uncertainly. . . .

The matter [of next year's program] came first in the business meeting. . . . The whole outline followed.

"The Civic Awakening, Public Works, Sanitation, The Rural Problem, The Good Roads Movement, Present Day Organization of Counties, State Aid and Supervision of County Problems, The State: Its Relations to General Government." Some of those topics must be catching like cockleburs in the hair of some of the ladies. . . . Was not this just another study programme but of a different flavor? . . .

Miss Marston, coming in while we were focussed upon this, followed our eyes and nodded with a pleased smile. As her eyes ranged further, her face went politely sober. She was sitting across from me, and I could see that she kept this non-committal attitude during the whole procedure. Irreproachable it was but to me sad.

"And at the end of each of these programmes," Miss Tyler said in conclusion, "there is to be a synopsis and discussion of some modern drama or other piece of literature that will apply and bring out the point of the two main topics. . . .

Of this sop to the culture people Mrs. Hawkins said with a laugh, "Well, be sure you find room in the yearbook. Some of that heavy diet will need seasoning."

A general laugh relieved the solemnity. (241–43)

The club votes unanimously to accept the program.

. . . Regrets I had about the coming programme, but Miss Marston had accepted the situation nobly [seconding the motion to accept], and those who had been asking for a change would have their chance. Also, those who so ardently wished to keep the Club as a unit had been spared the breaking up into sections. (258)

OCTOBER 2, 1913

At this meeting the two papers are "The State: Its Relation to the General Government" and "Duties of Citizenship: As Women Should Know Them." Miss Marston's mantle seems to be passing to Anna, who is now secretary of the club.

Special dismay the sight of the first page [of the new yearbook] was giving me. There I was, spread over it in all three places—as an officer, a member of the executive committee, and a member of the programme committee. And Miss Marston's name absent entirely! My eyes went to her involuntarily.

She gave me her brilliant smile, as if to say, "Don't you care. It doesn't matter in the least." . . .

Concerning suffrage for women, Mrs. Houck quoted the learned Austrian, Dr. Gonzalos, "When women vote, there will be no more social evil, liquor traffic, or war." Some questioned. The millennium? Or Utopia? If so, then let's have it. Opinions pro and con were given on the suffrage subject and illustrative incidents of the struggle. (279–80)

. . . From now on my diary entries of the Club will be few and far between, if any at all. After concentrating on note-taking at the meetings and going over the same ground writing the minutes at home, I shall have neither the right time nor the fresh inclination to record my personal reflections. It is an interesting phase of the Club which is practically at an end. (282)

January 22, 1914

Mrs. Himmelberger's paper yesterday on "Cape Girardeau Problems" precipitated heated discussion [about the problem of lack of supervision of young girls who worked at the local shirt factory]. . . . *[The members come to no resolution about how to help, but determine that the management of the factory should do something.]*

I think we all came away somewhat disturbed and confused as to our mission in contrast to the relaxed aftermath of the culture programmes, disturbed and confused but far from hopeless of recovery. (282–85)

March 6, 1914

Dierssen quotes an article that appeared in the local paper.

"The Wednesday Club began its session on Wednesday afternoon with the reading of that section of the revised Missouri statutes defining the property rights of married women. This was followed by a most interesting talk by Miss Marston on 'The Shifting of the Ideals of Home Authority.' . . . She spoke of the ideal home as being the one in which both parents agreed as to measures of authority and insisted upon prompt obedience from their children. She considers the lax government of the home and the general disobedience of children one of the dangerous features of present-day society.

"Miss Annie Dierssen then read a paper on 'The Child in Industry.' The paper was a most excellent one, giving fully the history of the child labor movement and bringing the discussion quite up to date by announcing the bill just introduced in Congress outlawing child labor just as the Mann Act outlaws white slavery. . . .

"The club is planning to continue its study of social problems next year, as this year's programme has proved so vitally interesting and helpful to the entire membership." (286–88)

OCTOBER 8, 1914

On the surface the first meeting of the Wednesday Club for the year was very much as always, yet there was something under the surface, a sort of undertow that kept pulling us toward a disturbed world beyond our quiet cove. . . . Maybe this was due to the subject, which was "Peace." (289)

Mrs. W. W. Martin . . . gave "Progress toward Peace," taking the place of "our dear Mrs. [R. B.] Oliver, unable to attend because of anxiety over her daughter, Marguerite, who has been at the scene of the war." . . .

[Mrs. Martin] was in her element, linking woman's sphere to public problems. Having recently attended a convention in Chicago . . . all about women being the ones to prevent war, because they alone who bore life with suffering and blood knew what it was to see it laid down in a murderous war. . . . At this point she veered off to stress woman's chief business in life, the bearing and rearing of children. . . . In conclusion she said, "The time will come when mothers who bear and rear men will not consent to anything except defensive war unless it be to fight for some great principle." (291–93)

OCTOBER 6, 1916

Anna records her usual observations about club members, decor in Mrs. Duckworth's newly redecorated home, and the program on prison conditions with readings from Crime and Punishment. *In a note, presumably added in 1963, Dierssen tells that Miss Marston never returned after a leave of absence to visit her parents in Springfield.*

This was because of not having a degree, a requirement not yet set up when she came to the Normal. Precipitated to the top in her chosen field at an early age because of her extraordinary brilliance, she was never afterwards free to go back to school until she felt it was too late.

To her students and friends the idea of her career being interrupted by some arbitrary rule seemed the height of absurdity, for she was not only saturated with her subject but had it all at tongue's end and in addition the matchless personality to carry it to her classes. Then her out-reaching influence beyond the call of duty. It was she who was the inspiration of the four literary societies, she who coached the oratorical contestants, she who was constantly back of the laggard as well as the eager, urging each one on to achievement. . . .

When she lay ill of a final malady in a distant state some years later, students from far and wide showered her with tributes; and at her passing the President of the Normal said he had never known a teacher who had been so closely associated with so many students and whose influence had been more deep and lasting. (307)

[Undated entry]

My active interest in the Wednesday Club, which ended because of circumstances rather than lack or regard, continued for some years after the final diary entry.

For quite awhile other matters had been claiming my attention and vying for the hours I could spare from home duties. We were starting a Sunday school in our church, which heretofore had left religious instruction to the pulpit and the catechism classes. . . . In addition, I became a sort of ex-officio leader and entertainment planner for a youth organization of the church. . . . Then there were things incidental to the War as soon as we were engaged. . . .

Anna felt that she made a significant contribution to the club during 1917–1918, calling it her "best year." As program chairman, she put forward the theme she had proposed in 1913, "Our Own People—Past and Present." The members agreed "that since the world was in turmoil and we were facing ordeals that would try our mettle, this was a time to assess our people against the background of their national blessings." The yearbook contained a quotation appropriate to both the Wednesday Club and Anna Dierssen's career in education:

> *With kindly mien and hearts that lead,*
> *They did this thing right well indeed. (308–10)*

Mary Margaret Ellis (b. 1911)

"$\mathcal{I}$ hope that whoever reads this story will become aware of what 'family' meant to the people of the Soulard area in south St. Louis during the early part of this century."[1] Family and neighborhood are the themes of Mary Margaret Ellis's unpublished memoirs, "That's the Way It Was." Her father, born Walter Baker in Festus, Missouri, was adopted by the Aubuchon family and grew up on their farm at Mineral Point. At the age of seventeen, now called Walter Lincoln Aubuchon, he came to St. Louis and found a factory job. His future bride was Julia Bohan, the daughter of Margaret Haggerty and John Bohan. Although Mary would later enjoy occasional visits to the Aubuchon farm, she identified with her mother's family. They saw each other frequently, at times of crisis, informal family gatherings, and holiday celebrations. From the Bohans Mary learned of Irish folklore and traditions.

Early in the nineteenth century a number of Irish immigrants settled in St. Louis, and the business and political leaders among them became known as the "Irish Crowd." By 1860 almost sixty percent of the city's inhabitants were foreign born. The majority came from Germany, while the second largest group was Irish, including many who left Ireland in the 1840s because of the potato famine and political rebellion. Martin G. Towey writes that the Irish in St. Louis, like those in San Francisco and in contrast to those in Boston, were accepted with tolerance and many of them prospered. It helped that Catholicism had been established in the city by the early French settlers. The Bohans were typical of the majority of the Irish who found jobs as unskilled laborers when they first arrived in St. Louis. As the years went by, the Irish in general made "steady progress."[2] In Mary's family progress was measured by the increasing size of each new home, and by such things as lace curtains, a set of living room furniture, a Victrola, and a player piano.

The 1910 census shows that Walter Aubuchon had by then married Julia. With their infant son Walter John, they were living with the Bohan family. Julia's sisters still at home were Margaret (19), Gotham (12), and Helen (9). Margaret had a job as a factory hand at a hemp mill. Both her

---

1. Ellis, "That's the Way It Was," preface. A typed copy of "That's the Way It Was, 1914–1930" was donated to the Western Historical Manuscript Collection, University of Missouri–St. Louis. Reprinted with the permission of the archive and the author. References to page numbers in the manuscript appear in the text. Information about Mary Margaret Ellis and her family has been obtained through phone interviews and correspondence, September–October, 1995.

2. Martin G. Towey, "Kerry Patch Revisited: Irish Americans in St. Louis in the Turn of the Century Era." For population statistics, see James Neal Primm, *Lion of the Valley, St. Louis, Missouri*, 171, 332, 357, and 441.

father, John Bohan, and her brother, John J. (15), were laborers working at a "plaining mill," which seems to have been the same factory where Walter Aubuchon was identified as a "box maker."[3] After proving his mechanical aptitude to the management of the Loy-Lange Box Factory, at Third Street and Russell Avenue, Walter had secure employment for a lifetime.

In some respects Mary's memoirs resemble those of Margaret Gilmore Kelso. The stories present a contrast of rural and urban life; yet they are alike in emphasizing family and the sense of belonging to a specific place. The Aubuchon family always lived in the Soulard area.[4] Mary attended the Lafayette School from the first through the eighth grades. After that she went out to work, finding jobs in a spaghetti factory and in shoe factories.

Beyond the passages selected for this anthology, Mary continued to write about her life up to the year 1930. She recalled her father's first automobile in 1920, Prohibition, silent movies, the Charleston, "Lucky Lindbergh's flight, the stock market crash, the Great Depression and then despair." Through it all, she wrote, "we stayed together as a family." She met Walter Emmel Ellis (1907–1991), who had grown up in Ellington, Missouri, when his family moved to her neighborhood in about 1929. Mary and Walter were married in 1930, and had two children, Dianne and Robert.[5]

Mary Ellis wrote her memoirs in the late 1970s, recapturing the innocence of childhood, a time when poverty, illness, and death occasionally intruded. The editors have selected episodes that give an impression of life in a working-class, immigrant neighborhood. Just as the children she recalls could not stay sad for long, the author also prefers to focus on colorful characters, on mischievous pranks, carnivals, and holidays. She presents herself as a member of a family that managed without "the

3. The census contains some errors regarding the family, such as the spelling "Bahan," but the ages given may be correct. Both John and Margaret Bohan were 48, Walter Aubuchon was 27, and Julia, 22. Julia lived until 1943; Walter died in 1959.

4. Mary's first home was at Eighth Street and Rutger Avenue. She and her family lived next at 2111 South Fourth Street. In the 1920s they moved three blocks away to 314 Lesperance. These houses were in the Soulard neighborhood, which developed between 1838 and 1869. The land, south of downtown St. Louis, originally belonged to Antoine and Julia Soulard. Following the original French settlers came working-class immigrants, including Germans, Irish, and Bohemians. Many houses are row buildings with a distinctive European appearance. By 1920–1940 the ethnic character of the neighborhood changed; however, there has been an effort to preserve the historic atmosphere of the neighborhood. The Soulard Farmer's Market, founded in 1843, still operates.

5. Walter Ellis was employed first by the Hager & Sons Hinge Manufacturing Company, then Century Electric, and finally the Charles Todd Uniform Company. Dianne (Donnie) Ellis Kraus is a customer service representative for Pitney Bowes. Robert G. Ellis administrates the Radiology Department of the Lutheran Hospital in St. Louis. Mary Margaret Ellis has seven grandchildren and four great-grandchildren.

material possessions that many enjoy today, but got great enjoyment out of the simple things in life."[6]

—————————————— THAT'S THE WAY IT WAS ——————————————

. . . We were a typical Irish family, one of many who lived in the Soulard area of St. Louis. We were loving, affectionate and close and we enjoyed life.

My maternal grandfather, John Bohan, was a native of County Cork, Ireland. He was tall and proud and always kept his hair and mustache neatly trimmed. Like most grandfathers in those days, he expected grandchildren to have good manners and to be very obedient. Walter, my brother, and I seldom called him anything but "Pal" because as long as he lived, he was always our close pal. We loved to listen to him tell stories about Ireland and the leprechauns he said he often saw in the woods. . . .

Each Saturday night after being paid, his custom was to stop at the corner saloon for a few drinks.[7] After he came home he brought out his fiddle, which he had brought from Ireland, and proceeded to play, much to the dismay of the neighborhood.

Grandma, whom we called Nanny, was a tall, gentle Irish woman who enjoyed living nearby because it gave her an excuse to help my mother. The former Maggie Haggerty was a devout Catholic who attended daily Mass.[8] Often when my father would see her passing through the yard on her way to church, he would say, "There goes Grandma. If she has a nickel left in her purse, she will put it in the collection basket." She did, too.

We seldom saw my paternal grandparents since they lived on a farm at Mineral Point, near Potosi, Missouri, miles and miles from St. Louis. My father was their adopted son.

Dad was of average size but one of the handsomest men I have ever seen. He had deep blue eyes and black curly hair. Each morning he wet his hair thoroughly with cold water and combed it flat but by the time he had finished breakfast, his hair would be dry and curly again. While he didn't have much formal education, he was very knowledgeable. He was an excellent machinist, mechanic, electrician and builder. Nothing

6. Ellis, "That's the Way It Was," preface.

7. After Prohibition went into effect, John Bohan had the misfortune of drinking some liquor containing wood alcohol. He lost his memory and became almost blind (Ellis, "That's the Way It Was," 71).

8. Margaret (Maggie) Haggerty was born in Springfield, Illinois, to Irish parents. In her first marriage she had a daughter, Mary Braun. After moving to St. Louis she worked in the rectory of the St. Vincent dePaul Church. With her second husband, John Bohan, Margaret had six children.

daunted him and he was ingenious in solving mechanical problems of any kind.

Mom was an Irish beauty with jet black hair and blue eyes that seemed to sparkle with a million tiny stars when she laughed. She was tiny, frail, and shy. She really didn't enjoy going out but loved to have friends to the house for singing and dancing. The men would play their mandolins while the women would harmonize on such songs as "My Wild Irish Rose," "Did Your Mother Come from Ireland," "Danny Boy," "The Curse of an Aching Heart" and many other Irish songs and ballads. There was always a half-barrel of beer for the men and a pot of chili for everybody. I remember one time when Johnny Nicholson, a family friend, wore a dress to have some fun but his joke nearly turned into a beer disaster for the men. He was carrying the half-barrel of beer up the stairs when the tip of his shoe caught in the dress's hem and down he went, the barrel bouncing along with him. But except for making a racket, he escaped uninjured. Of course, with all of us looking down at him and laughing uproariously, he was quite embarrassed.

Children in 1914 had as much fun as children today and without the money and commercial outlets available today. We also had our close calls. [One] day when Walter and I were scrounging for scrap iron proved to be one of our close calls.[9] One minute everything was fine; the next, a policeman was frantically waving his arms at us. Walter shouted, "Run for your life. We're going to be arrested." It was hot and we were barefoot but we didn't worry about nails, glass or rocks hurting our feet as we scooted like scared rabbits from the iron yard and down the alley. We lived in the rear flat because the rent was cheaper so, once in the alley, it was no problem racing up the steps and into the house. Without a word but with the same thought, we slipped under a dresser and tried to make ourselves as small as possible. Well, we didn't have long to wait. A minute later the policeman was at the door. We heard him tell Mom, "I'd like to see the little boy and girl who were in the iron yard." Walter and I had seen movies of people in jail and just knew that was where we were going to be taken. We cried and pleaded but to no avail. Mom had us come out and face the policeman. But instead of being arrested, the policeman patted us on our heads and smiled. "Kids," he said, "I've seen you in the iron yard several times and you worry me. There are large cranes there, moving huge pieces of iron and if a piece would fall on you, begorra, you'd be dead." Mom also got a warning. He said, "Mother, if you want to keep your children safe, make sure they stay away from that yard."

9. Walter John Aubuchon (1909–1979) was the oldest of six children. Mary was the second child, born in 1911. There were two younger brothers, Albert (1916–1970) and Gene (1918–1994). Mary's sisters are Catherine Aubuchon Krygiel, born in 1916, and Dorothy Aubuchon Ragan, born in 1927.

While we never wasted our pennies letting the trolley cars flatten them on the tracks, we did waste two of Mom's eggs that way one day. It wasn't as much fun as we had thought it would be. (5–9)

Dad came home from work one day and told Mom he had found a flat that was closer to his work and we were going to move. I don't remember moving the furniture but do recall Mom sitting in the kitchen of our new place nursing Catherine. Even though she was an infant, Catherine had on long black stockings and high-top button shoes. My shoes, when I wore them, were the same style as my baby sister's and I was forever losing the button hook. This was a long curved piece of steel with a hook on the end with which to catch the button and slide it through, closing the shoe. But a closed safety pin worked about as well. . . .

Our flat had three rooms, the front room, a middle room, and the kitchen. . . . Three other families lived in the building; we were on the first floor. Along with offering some room for playing, the back yard had four wood sheds, one for each family, an ash pit and two toilets. There was no inside plumbing in that neighborhood and, of course, no house had hot water. Everybody used coal for heating, so everybody had ash pits in their yards. Coal oil lamps supplied light. People either used coal or wood for cooking.

Our neighbors to the north were a family of seven, a blind man, his wife, three sons and two daughters. . . . The blind man watched his children while his wife worked in a factory. I used to feel so sorry for him because whenever we were playing and he would come just outside the door and call for some of his children, his daughter Jane would place her hand over her mouth, motioning to us we were not to say she was standing nearby. . . .

Joe, the oldest child, would often disappear for many weeks at a time and we would be told, "He's sick in the hospital again." Being kids, we didn't question the absences but years later we learned that Joe wasn't quite honest and when he was gone, he was actually spending some time in the reform school. Jane wasn't too honest either. That first summer she got a job in a candy store and soon had Bill, her brother, and me talked into putting Josie in the baby buggy and wheeling her up to the store just about each day. Jane would straddle the buggy and drop candy from her dress and then tell us to go straight home. It was such an easy way to get candy, none of us really considered it stealing but, of course, it was. One day Jane's employer caught her hiding candy in her dress and she was fired. (10–13)

The streets and outdoors were important to us when we were growing up. There was always something to do for kids. I remember the large coal yard next to Dad's factory. Since everybody had coal stoves for cooking and heating, the yard was always busy and there were always several men on the job. Trains would bring in cars filled with coal and the workers would shovel it into large wagons for delivery. We loved to watch them working. After the wagons were loaded, the men would hitch up their teams of horses and start up the cobblestone street. I remember how the horses strained to pull their loads and how the drivers would often have to use whips to keep them moving.

We kids had a bushel basket and would follow a wagon, picking up the lumps of coal that would bounce onto the street. Sometimes a driver would push a large chunk of coal onto the street and laugh, showing his white teeth against his black face, as we scrambled to pick it up. But this was one way we helped our parents save money on their coal bill.

One day we were all playing in the street when the ice man came with his delivery for our house. We had an old wooden icebox with three doors, two for storing food and the other for the block of ice. . . .

On this particular day the ice man was cutting his big block of ice into chunks that would sell for ten, fifteen and twenty-five cents. I decided I would make the ice man think we were rich. I called to my brother, "Hey, I lost my ball. Will you go inside and look on the piano for it? If it isn't there, check the sideboard and if it isn't there, look on the library table." The ice man stopped chipping the ice and turned around and looked me up and down, standing there dirty and without shoes. I can still see that funny look on his face. And wouldn't you know, my brother really cooked my goose when he said, "What's the matter with you? We don't have a piano or a sideboard." I guess he couldn't say "library table" because he didn't mention it. Right then I felt a little ashamed because I knew I was pretending to be something I wasn't. After the ice man left to deliver his ice, we all scrambled into the wagon for some ice chips to eat and I forgot all about being so deceitful.

Then there was an Easter Sunday when several of us, dirty and ragged, were playing in the street. Suddenly I saw some people coming along the street, the men dressed in their new Easter suits, and the women in their beautiful dresses and large hats, their white shoes and carrying their delicate-looking parasols. They were on their way to visit neighbors up the street and as they passed by, I was actually ashamed of myself because I was so dirty and ragged. That was one time when I was sure we were the poorest family in the world. I ran into the house, then through it and into the back yard, feeling ashamed. But when I looked up and saw Sidney [a neighbor boy] with some grasshoppers, I began wondering if one of the insects would actually make it to the top of the bannister and became so interested in watching the neighbor boy, I forgot all about being poor, dirty and ashamed. (17–20)

[One] time [Walter and I] were punished for something we did and Mom put us to bed without supper. Then she felt sorry for us and brought us some crackers to eat. After she left the room we pushed open the shutters and put on a show for the neighborhood kids. We danced and clowned around on the quilts on the floor and then began hitting each other with the pillows. They were old pillows and soon feathers began flying all over the room. Mom heard all the kids laughing and looked in to see what was going on. My memory doesn't recall what she did but I'm sure we got the razor strap that night. I do remember those cracker crumbs and the feathers kept me from sleeping half the night.

Summer passed and in September it was time for Walter and me to start school. Even though he was a year older, we were going to kindergarten together. I think the reason for that was because Mom couldn't buy us shoes and clothes when we needed them. I remember Mom telling Dad she would have to ask the Provident Association to furnish us with some clothes if we were to go to school that year.[10] Even though it meant swallowing some pride, it had to be done if we kids were to make it to classes that year. The association gave us a huge box of clothing. I still remember those shiny black shoes that buttoned up beyond the ankles and the long black stockings that went up over the knees. I also remember Mom tying a string around the tops of the stockings because she didn't have any garters for us. To this day when I smell the leather of new shoes, my mind flashes back to that day when I got my new shoes. We had so many cuts and bruises on our feet from going barefoot all summer that the shoes really didn't feel all that comfortable but we kept them on.

Mom took us to school, signed the register and then was told to take us to the kindergarten room. I remember my first glance around the room. There was a huge piano and three large circles of small chairs, about twenty chairs to a circle. Mom told us goodbye and as soon as she left, Walter and I began to cry and wrapped our arms around each other. We were really frightened. The teacher began to play the piano and told us we had to carry a chair and march around in a circle. We were screaming and crying and really disrupting the other children but we weren't the only kids acting up. Finally, the teacher stopped playing the piano and told Walter he had to go to the last circle and I had to go to the first circle. That was the first time in our lives we had ever been separated by someone we didn't know. Even though we were unhappy, our teacher taught us a lesson in independence. (22–24)

One day we were all coming home from school when the ice truck came along the street. Bill, the youngest [child] of the blind man, began running after it. However, just as he reached its side, he fell to the roadway when he tried to jump on the running board and the back wheels of the

---

10. The Provident Association was sponsored by St. Vincent dePaul Church. Bryan Mullanphy, who was mayor of St. Louis in 1847, "introduced the St. Vincent dePaul Society to respond to the charitable needs of the city" (Towey, "Kerry Patch," 141).

vehicle ran over his stomach. His stomach suddenly began swelling and got so large, the ice man had to cut his belt with a knife. When he asked if anyone knew the boy, I said I did and would run home to tell his mother. I ran as fast as I could and told his father because his mother was working. The father began crying and said, "I knew something like this would happen. He would never listen to me when I told him not to jump on trucks." Bill died that night and I remember thinking that if the truck had been an ice wagon being pulled by a horse, maybe it wouldn't have been so heavy and Bill might have lived.

My friend and I went around the neighborhood and asked all the neighbors if they would like to donate twenty-five cents for a flower for Bill. We collected fifteen dollars and were able to buy a beautiful wreath which we took to his mother. In those days funeral services were held from the home, partly because of custom and because having the services at home was less expensive. They had Bill lying in his casket in the front room. The shutters were closed and the shades were drawn. They even had the mirrors covered with cloth. Bill's mother and father were crying and it was so dark and spooky looking that I ran out in the yard and sat down and cried.

We missed Bill a great deal for several weeks but as the months passed and because we were kids, we eventually stopped thinking about him all the time.

One day we were all playing on the corner of Bismar[c]k and Russell Avenue, about a half-block from our house, when some men came with a tall ladder and took down the sign that said "Bismark." They replaced it with a sign that said "Fourth Street." We later asked Dad why they had changed the name of the street and he said, "We're at war with Germany . . . and 'Bismark' . . . [is a] German name, and people thought the signs weren't proper. We don't want any German street names because too many of our boys are being killed over there."

Albert and Catherine were getting big enough to go outdoors and play with us now. Mom always put me in charge of them so that they wouldn't get hurt. In the evenings after supper, the parents in the neighborhood would bring their chairs out to the sidewalk and talk and visit. All the kids would meet on the corner under the lights and play games like London Bridge is Falling Down, BomBay, Lay Low Sheep, . . . and, oh, so many more. When it got late, we were all called home by our parents. Dad had a special whistle for us and whenever we heard it, we scooted. Then we all took turns climbing up on the sink board to wash our feet in the sink. That was the rule of the roost: You never went to bed with dirty feet and you always slept in your own bed. (24a-26a)

One night at the supper table Mom gave us the news that soon we would have a new baby in the family. When Gene was born in 1918, that meant we now had five children in the family, three boys and two girls. Gene was born during the great flu epidemic and he not only got the flu, but Mom did too. As a matter of fact, they nearly died. Nanny stayed with us, helping to take care of them. Poor Dad, he walked the floor many a night with the baby and soon was so exhausted, I thought he would die. Mom gradually regained her health and was able to get out of bed, but Gene was dying. He became so weak and frail that he had to be carried on a pillow. The doctor had been coming each day, but one day he told Mom, "I'm not coming back again. There's nothing more I can do for your son."

Of course I wondered why he didn't put Gene in the hospital, but I guess we couldn't afford it. Mom was really crying when Lisa's mother came down from the upstairs flat. She told Mom to stop crying because she would get a doctor who would help the baby. She was gone a short time and when she returned, she had a German doctor with her. After he examined Gene, he said, "This baby is starving to death." He told Nanny to get a piece of bacon and rub it inside of Gene's mouth each day, to give him barley water in a bottle, and for Mom to stop breast feeding him. He told Mom, "You're so weak and run-down from the flu that your milk isn't strong enough for him." This wonderful doctor came each day and soon Gene began to get some flesh on his bones and he didn't have to be carried on a pillow. Eventually, he began to sit up and watch us play. Needless to say, he was the family's pride and joy and we all loved him. . . .

When Gene was about a year old, a man came around the neighborhood with a beautiful pony. The pony had a beautiful saddle and bridle and we kids thought he had to be a pony from the circus. The man learned we five kids were brothers and sisters and told me to ask my mother if he could take our picture on the pony. Knowing Mom's limited income, I told him we didn't have any money to have pictures made. But he laughed and said, "That's all right. Let me put you on the pony and the others around it, and take your picture. If your mother doesn't have any money, I won't charge her for it." When Mom saw the picture she soon found enough money around the house to pay for it. . . .

In those days, all the girls and women had long hair. Somehow we all began to get lice in our hair. . . .

Mom used to wash our hair in vinegar and coal oil once a week to get rid of the lice. Thank goodness she never shaved us down to the skull. . . .

Once a week we would have to go to the nurse's office in school and she would run a comb through our hair looking for lice and nits. If she found any, she would send us home with a note, telling our mother to do something about the problem before she would allow us to return to school. I was really embarrassed when I would get one of the notes. . . .

We heard about the *Lusitania* being sunk from newsboys shouting their "Extra," and from what Dad said to Mom, our beautiful country would soon be involved in World War I. (27–30)

This was another year when we were told not to expect much for Christmas because of doctor bills and other expenses. Mom said we might have a tree but nothing else. She told me to write to our friend, the old German doctor, and ask if he would submit our name to the Christmas fund. The Fund was an organization that donated baskets of food and toys to poor people. I wrote to the doctor and for days and days we waited for his reply. Christmas drew near and finally Mom said that maybe there were many other poor people, people poorer than we were. But since we did have enough money for a tree, Mom told us we had better get busy and begin making trimmings for it. Each night we would all sit at the kitchen table and cut strips of paper about a quarter of an inch wide and two inches long. Mom had bought us a box of crayons and we colored the strips all different shades. Then Mom made paste from flour and water and we pasted the strips together, one inside the other, to make a long chain that would wind around the tree. . . .

. . . [Dad] usually put a box of apples and oranges on the mantel at Christmas and only at Christmas because we couldn't afford fruit other times during the year. Every year, a day or two before Christmas, my grandparents from the farm would send us a basket of food. Mom said, "I hope they don't forget about us this year." Sure enough, the basket of food arrived, a chicken that was ready to eat, some canned fruit and vegetables, some nuts, a fruit cake, coffee, sugar, flour and other goodies. Mom said, "God bless Grandma and Grandpa." . . .

Christmas Eve came and we were all so excited, we had forgotten about the letter to the doctor. . . . Dad would light all the candles on the tree. . . . As soon as the candles burned low, Dad would have to take them off and replace them with new ones. Sometimes the tree would catch fire and we would run and open the front door so Dad could toss it in the street. Needless to say, on Christmas Eve the bells of the beautiful fire horses and the fire engines were clanging all evening.

Now it was time for Santa [Uncle Ange] to come. All the kids had to go into the kitchen to wait for him. Soon we would hear his "Ho, ho, ho," and then we would dash into the front room. Santa's suit and whiskers must have been at least ten years old but he looked beautiful to us. Dad stood guard beside the lighted tree. The bowl of apples and oranges was on the mantel. Santa gave us each the usual peppermint stick and under the tree were two boxes wrapped in Christmas paper. A note, one for me and the other for the family, was on each box. Mom said the German doctor had brought the boxes earlier in the evening. She let me open mine first since I had written the letter. When I had it all unwrapped, I saw the most beautiful doll in the world, the first one I had ever owned. The doll had brown hair and a little straw hat, sleeping blue eyes and a china face, a beautiful dress, white stockings and black patent leather shoes. After all the "Oh's" and "Ah's" had been said, someone shouted, "Open the other package." That honor was given to Walter. The box contained more chocolate candy than I had ever seen. On the card the doctor had written: "Dear Mary, I was so busy due to the flu epidemic and other diseases, I forgot to mail your letter to the Christmas Fund. However, I hope you like the two little gifts I was able to send to you and the family."

It was truly a memorable Christmas. (31–34)

During the winter we had to find ways to entertain ourselves. . . .

Since we didn't have a piano at the house, I improvised. I would get all the forks from the kitchen cupboard drawer and put them in a straight line on the table. Then I would pretend they were piano keys and while I would pretend to be playing, the other kids would sing. After each song, we would straighten the row of forks and begin again. (38)

We also played jumping on the beds. We would jump from one bed to another. One night we grew so wild, we knocked Albert against the iron bed post and knocked out all of his front teeth. You can imagine what happened to us after that incident. . . .

. . . One day we were in the back yard and I heard a woman screaming in the next yard. I climbed up on the fence and saw a woman running through the yard with blood streaming down her face. It was a very bad sight. The woman was a Polish woman who had moved into an upstairs flat about a week before. One of the neighbors said her husband had just hit her in the head with a hatchet. First the ambulance came and took the woman away, then the police came and took the husband away. I learned that the couple had four children, three boys and a girl. . . . The youngest boy, Lester, was about two. The girl, Brenda, became my best friend and we played together whenever we could. (42–43)

One day we put Lester in the wagon and went to Lyons Park. There were train tracks on one side of the park and often there was at least one empty box car waiting to be coupled to a train and hauled away. It was very hot and we decided to swim in the little pool but first we put Lester in the box car where it was cool and told him to watch us swimming. We didn't have bathing suits and jumped in the water wearing our clothes, knowing they would dry before we got home. We were having so much fun, we forgot about Lester and when we remembered, the box car was gone with Lester in it. You can imagine how frightened we were. Since we didn't know what to do, we went home. But Brenda's mother was already there and when she saw us coming, she began screaming in Polish at Brenda. When she asked about Lester, we told her about leaving him in the box car. That woman went crazy. The veins on her neck stood out and she grabbed Brenda by her long pigtail and swung her around on the sidewalk. I ran for home, frightened to death, and told Dad. He came right out and told the woman he would take her to the police station and she could report Lester. But when they got there, the police already had the boy. It seemed they had received a call from someone at a depot about three miles from the park. No one had noticed Lester when the car had been hitched up but when it reached the station, someone heard Lester crying. . . . Lester wasn't crying with the police. He was enjoying a big bag of candy a policeman had bought for him. (45–46)

I got a good slap from Mom one day and I don't think I deserved it. It was wash day and we had the two tubs sitting on the wringer bench on the back porch. The night before we had filled the wash boiler with water and put it on top of the cook stove. While Mom was cooking our breakfast, the water would get boiling hot and we would transfer it to the tub, add some cold water, put in the washboard and start scrubbing the dirty clothes. . . .

Lisa, the girl from upstairs, came down one wash morning to watch us. She said to me, "You didn't turn the socks inside out when you washed them." Without thinking, I said, "Oh, my Mom never turns the socks. We only wash them on one side." When I went into the kitchen to get more soap, Mom grabbed me and slapped me hard, saying, "Don't you ever tell the neighbors we don't turn our socks when we wash them." I said, "But Mom, we don't." She said, "Even if we don't, you don't have to tell the neighbors about it." (49–50)

. . . Sometimes when we didn't have gloves and wanted to go sleigh riding, Mom would let us wear Dad's old woolen socks for gloves. Mom was sick a great deal during the winter months and I always had to stay home from school on wash day to help take care of Gene and help scrub the clothes on the washboard. During the cold months we had to carry the wash up to the attic and hang them on the lines but by then they were nothing more than frozen pieces of cloth. (60)

Life changed for the Aubuchon family as more money became available for larger homes, household furnishings, and entertainment. The brothers and sisters were confirmed in the Catholic faith, finished school in the 1920s, found jobs, and enjoyed silent movies and dances in large ballrooms. When life became difficult during the depression, members of the family helped each other, a tradition that has continued to the present day.

As each of us married, instead of drifting apart we became more closely knitted and more protective of each other. Our problems and our joys are shared and when one needs help, the rest are standing by. (95)

FANNIE HURST (1889–1968)

"*T*he unexplored continent of the female creative mind is an exciting frontier that remains to be crashed."[1] This is how Fannie Hurst described *other* women. She dedicated her own life to exploring the continent of the creative mind through her calling as a writer. Passages selected from her autobiography *Anatomy of Me* spotlight the two most vivid features of Hurst's early life: an intense ambition to become a professional writer and her relationship to her family. Hurst resembles Marian Wright Powers in longing to use her artistic talent, but their situations were different. Powers felt that responsibilities to her husband and child held her in her hometown, while Hurst dared to break away from her protective parents.

Being Jewish was part of Hurst's self-image, although her mother declined to join the Jewish women's literary society, the Pioneers, and her parents did not attend a temple. There is a history of Jewish congregations in St. Louis, such as the Emanu-El, organized in 1847, and the B'nai B'rith, organized in 1849. The two congregations united in 1852, combining their names to become B'nai El. In 1855, members dedicated their temple, the first one built in the Mississippi valley.[2] By 1880 it is estimated that the St. Louis population included 6,200 Jews.[3]

Fannie's father Sam had some difficult years financially, but was a modestly successful Jewish businessman. Born in Vicksburg, Mississippi, and raised in Memphis, Tennessee, Sam was working in St. Louis as a salesman when he met his future wife, Rose Koppel. Rose's parents emigrated from Bavaria and established a farm near Hamilton, Ohio. After returning to Hamilton for the birth of her daughter Fannie in 1889, Rose brought the baby back to St. Louis at the age of two weeks. Since the Hursts did not observe holidays or participate in congregational activities, Fannie was slow to appreciate her heritage. "It was to take me almost half a lifetime of the Biblical three score and ten to evaluate properly the richness of that heritage" (235).[4]

While she lived for many years in New York and used that city as the setting for most of her fiction, Hurst said that often "the characters and locale really belonged to St. Louis."[5] She enjoyed outstanding financial

---

1. Fannie Hurst, *Anatomy of Me: A Wonderer in Search of Herself,* 355. Subsequent references will be noted in the text.

2. Nini Harris, *A Grand Heritage: A History of St. Louis Southside Neighborhoods and Citizens,* 44.

3. Anne Hessler, "German Jews in Small Towns in Missouri, 1850–1920," 4.

4. To read about the experiences of other Jewish women in Missouri, see Sara L. Hart, chapter 6 of *The Pleasure Is Mine: An Autobiography;* Frank J. Adler, *Roots in a Moving Stream . . . ;* and Jack Nusan Porter, "Rosa Sonneschein and *The American Jewess* Revisited."

5. Catharine Cranmer, "Little Visits with Literary Missourians: Fannie Hurst," 392.

success, with her books translated into many languages and adapted into film scripts. Hurst wrote with imagination and sympathy, but wanted her writing to be truthful, even photographic. She would observe and take notes on people in various neighborhoods of New York, sometimes working as a waitress, store clerk, or factory laborer to search for material.[6] Among the best known Hurst novels are *Back Street* (1931) and *Imitation of Life* (1933).

As a public figure Hurst became active in politics and social issues and met interesting people, including Eleanor Roosevelt, who became a close friend. In private life Fannie Hurst was married to Jacques S. Danielson, a pianist and composer. Danielson was Russian, which distressed her parents, who lamented that she had fallen in love with someone who was not "American-born" (233). Fannie and Jacques enjoyed a harmonious marriage with independent careers and separate social lives until his death in 1952. Following her own death in 1968, Hurst was buried in the New Mount Sinai Cemetery, St. Louis.

Anatomy of Me: A Wonderer in Search of Herself has scenes and dialogue that might have come from one of Fannie Hurst's novels. Despite its somewhat affected style and rambling sequence of events, the autobiography is convincing when the author reveals her worries, doubts, and regrets. Reviews were mixed. Iola Haverstick in the *New York Times* cast doubt on the book's literary quality, finding its analyses and revelations "self-conscious and tedious." Others praised *Anatomy of Me* for "an objectivity rarely achieved in personal narrative" *(Christian Science Monitor)*, described it as a "heart-warming, zestful autobiography" *(New York Herald Tribune)*, and recommended it as "fascinating" and "enriching" *(Chicago Sunday Tribune)*.

Hurst produced the novel *Family!* two years after publishing her autobiography. As with the story of her own life, she set *Family!* in St. Louis and drew upon her acquaintance with the city's places and people. When describing certain female characters she might have been pondering what her life would have been like if ambition and talent had not turned her thoughts to New York and a demanding career. Perhaps acknowledging her Jewish heritage in *Anatomy* inspired her to create *Family!*'s Yetta Goldonsky and the widower Topel, who observe steadfastly the orthodox practices of their faith and decide after more than eighteen years of being neighbors and friends to marry and travel to Israel. Visiting that country had been a powerful experience for Hurst: "In Israel when I saw the tribal men and women out of Yemen and the long-eyed Sephardic Jews, and Jews who for the first time in their history were not walking the desert

---

6. Some biographical information has been drawn from Anne André-Johnson, *Notable Women of St. Louis*, 105–9; and Cynthia Ann Brandimarte, "Fannie Hurst: A Missouri Girl Makes Good."

sands but the storied streets of the homeland to which they had returned, it came to me as if up from the biblical soil: These are my people, and Mama and Papa and I from Cates Avenue in St. Louis are their people" (351).

Because this anthology emphasizes events that took place in Missouri, the editors have selected passages from *Anatomy of Me* about Hurst's early life. The book was published by Doubleday in 1958. With the permission of the co-holders of the copyrights, Brandeis University and Washington University, the editors feature scenes from Hurst's home and experiences as a student at Central High School and Washington University, where she was graduated in 1909. After months of tempestuous scenes with her grieving parents, Fannie Hurst left for New York. "Looking back, I marvel at the ruthlessness which drove me" (143).

ANATOMY OF ME

A Wonderer in Search of Herself

From the hour I gave Mama my first stare from her bed of my birth, I must have braced my new spine against being overpowered by the rush of her personality.

When Mama walked into a room filled with ladies, she doused them like so many candles blown out on a birthday cake.

Yet, on the other hand, no sooner had I left the warm cove of her body than we committed the anachronism of becoming one again.

Despite the fact that we had neither temperamental nor intellectual compatibility, I loved her in a deep uncomplicated way that was never to waver throughout storm and stress.

And storm and stress it was. Mama's temper, fiery as lightning, terrible as thunder, was a matter of periodic blitz in our home, my own kitten of a temper, like Papa's, managing to keep its claws in.

In a way, however, Papa and I were a pair of terrible meeks, huddling and waiting for the storm to pass like a pair of wayfarers, our mute surrender to her fury serving only to increase the gale which could rage out of a trifling or fancied hurt, and a clear sky.

Mama, who emerged from these outbursts contrite, darling, and her usual warm self, was a "natural"; uninhibited, sparkling with a wit both unique and exhilarating, an "extrovert" in a community that had never heard the word.

Bashful, and what Papa termed "reserved," I grew up in the lavishness of her maternalism, recipient of the heavy spill of her easy emotions. (3–4)

For a decade after the century had turned, St. Louis was still vying with Chicago for the majestic place of "Gateway to the West." Destined ultimately to lose the race, she nevertheless maintained her identity as a highly respected and well-to-do member of the summit cities of the nation. Her interesting compound of German and French beginnings is probably the answer to the stability and conservatism which characterize her.

Papa fitted into that stability and conservatism like a round peg into a round hole. His compatibility with environment must have been part of his capacity for monotony. Intellectual curiosity was languid at our house.

Looking back, I realize that the insulation of our lives could scarcely be equalled today, even on a desert island. Local and national issues, the temper and temperature of the world found slow if any entry into our house or consciousness. . . .

However, at the mention of business conditions between Papa and his porch confreres, a listening look would come into Mama's face and she would stop rocking.

Every evening she met Papa with the same anxious question: How is business, Sam?

I never knew him to answer other than cheerfully. All right.

It is not. I can tell by your voice.

All right, if you prefer it that way, then it isn't.

I heard you talking to the men across the porch the other evening. From what you said to them, things aren't so good.

Mama's dread of poverty was little short of obsessive. Money matters plagued her out of all proportion.

The paradox of a woman generous to the extreme in so many ways, yet parsimonious to that same extreme, was to harass Papa and me all through the years.

The circumstance of dwelling in the same city with various relatives on her father's side, who lived in those fine private places enclosed in stone gates, was humiliating to her.

They only invite me out of charity. I'm a poor relation. I can't entertain the way they do, and I don't intend to be beholden.

But Rose, these people go out of their way to be nice to you. For Fannie's sake, we should cultivate more Jewish people.

My child is not going to be humiliated by having her cousins visit her here. . . .

Because of Mama's repetitive indoctrination, I too felt insecure among our eager-to-be-friendly "rich relatives." Their fine homes impressed but did not depress me as they did Mama. (13–14)

A cloud no larger than my pudgy hand began to form on the horizon.

A chain of us girls were walking arm in arm in the bricked schoolyard at recess.

Suddenly, one of them—I recall her name, Hazel Thompson—sang out: What religion is everybody? I'm Lutheran! Instantly the line took it up like a singing regiment. Left foot, right foot, each girl snapping out in turn: Lutheran, Catholic, Baptist, Lutheran, Presbyterian. The exception was the girl at the far end. Me. I opened my mouth to speak in turn, but no sound came. I opened my mouth again, in the silence that had fallen, unloosed my encircling arm from the girl next to me and stood apart. Suddenly I had become different.

That night at the dinner table I asked a difficult question.

Is being Jewish one's religion?

Certainly, said Mama with prompt sureness. Why do you ask such a question?

Can you be the Jewish race and be Lutheran or a Catholic the way you can be American and also be a Lutheran or a Catholic?

Of course not.

Why not?

Because you can't.

But why?

Ask your father.

Papa began to moralize. That's a mighty difficult question, Fannie, and I'm glad you are thinking about such matters. I hope you say your prayers nightly. Always be proud of your religion.

I wasn't. It was difficult to be what no one else was, even though it was never talked about.

Your mother and I aren't as observing as we might be. I think the time has come, Rose, when we should join the temple and Fannie attend Sunday school.

I don't intend to join the temple and be stuck in the back pew so I can see my rich relatives up front. Besides, aren't you the one who always says you can say your prayers as well at home as in temple?

A child should have religious training.

But I don't want to join the temple, Papa, I hastened to intervene. I can learn Bible history at school if I want to. I was just asking . . .

Since you are a great reader, Fannie, I am sure your teacher or the librarian can give you books on the subject. I don't feel competent to answer your question, except to impress upon you that the Jews are both a race and a religion, and you are both.

I'm an American.

Always be proud of being that, too.

I notice, Sam, interposed Mama, you always say of yourself that when men you meet in business speak of "that damn Jew" you keep silent. That does not sound as if you are proud.

This kind of repudiation, especially in my presence, must have been bitter to Papa. He gave no sign.

When there is nothing to be accomplished, Rose, except embarrass the other fellow into admitting that he has his "pet Jews," I keep quiet.

But when Papa was not present, Mama would speak admiringly to her Jewish friends: Mr. Hurst never makes it an issue when someone in business who doesn't know his religion refers to the damn Jews. He says the embarrassment caused only increases prejudice.

I realized that I was not proud but furtive, or I would have answered Hazel Thompson's question in the schoolyard.

In our middle-western world of assimilated German Jews, and comparatively few of them, this race consciousness had been slow to awaken and then only languidly. The small incident of the schoolyard was quickly laid back into the silence, although I was to come to know from talk at home that prejudice could lift its head.

Our neighbor, a Mrs. McCaffry, had once made a disparaging remark to which Mama had been the one to reply proudly: You may as well know, Mrs. McCaffry, that we are Jews.

Oh, Mrs. Hurst, I was only speaking generally. I knew a lovely girl in Keokuk before I was married. Babette Levy. You couldn't meet a lovelier person.

I always suspected, said Mama relating the incident to Papa, that she had *richus*.[7]

Such people are to [be] pitied for their ignorance.

I could tell a few things about the Irish Catholics, too. And I wish you could see the condition of her kitchen. Unwashed dishes piled to the ceiling.

That's no way to talk, Rose. It puts you in a class with her.

That's right, make me small.

You make yourself that way by using her methods.

We can't all be as noble as you are.

All right, Rose, you win. Get into an argument with such people and belittle us all, if that's what you prefer.

No, I want to be made small by my husband. Everybody in the world is in the right but me. If it wasn't for my child, I would wish myself out of it altogether . . .

This was typical of the kind of circumstance that would send Mama off into one of her volcanic eruptions that could last for an hour or a day, as the case might be. The quarrels in our house began that way.

---

7. "To have *richus,* I knew from Mama's and my Aunts' lips, was to have 'race prejudice,' a phrase which never failed to strike dread and humiliation into me" (43).

People tell me what a fine husband I have. They should know. Fine words outside his home, but abuse on the inside. The mistake of my life was not to have gone home to Hamilton with my child, while my parents were alive. Thank God they never knew. . . . My child—what comfort is she! I sacrifice my life for her and she takes sides with her father.

The psychology of Mama's quick temper fascinated me. The explosion would seem to come out of the blue from an innocent remark or unintended implication. Housemaids scurried before the gale of Mama like chickens before a storm, and we too hurried before the hurricane, closing windows and doors.

There must have been times when the spectacle of Papa and me, fearful for rather than of her, presented a sorry sight. . . .

. . . [E]xcept for Mama's eruptions I grew up in a quiet house of evenly drawn window shades, impeccable cleanliness, geometrically placed conventional furniture, middle-class respectability.

I adored Mama. I liked Papa. I hated the quiet house. (16–19)

This matter of overweight.

Had it ever occurred to Mama and Papa to analyze beyond: I don't know what ails the child; she mopes; they might have hit upon one or two contributory causes.

First, the special climate that surrounds the only child. Usually, they move in an adult world of overemphasis upon them. Their oneness invites introspection, and for want of the sharing family life of brothers and sisters, the give and take, rather special conflicts set in.

Second, and by no means less in my case, was the psychology of the fat child.

Intimations of my rotundity came to me slowly. Occasionally a small boy would call out as I passed: Hello, Fatty. Mr. Lazarus Scharff, a rotund friend of Papa's, used to pinch my cheek and say: Hello, little Fatso. In the beginning, this made no more impression upon me than the yanking of one of my heavy brown braids by one of the small boy pests, which I met with a glare or a stuck-out tongue.

Three healthy uninhibited appetites had their way at our house and enough was left over of Mama's rich cookery to send out to the neighbors as much again as we consumed. Little wonder that girth consciousness came to me slowly.

The first conscious prick I recall was on the occasion of Mama's decision to send me to Mr. Jacob Mahler's select dancing school.

I protested.

But I thought you wanted it.

I did last year, but not now.

Why?

I'm too—fat.

I think it must have been about the first time the humiliating phrase crossed my lips.

What do you want to be, a skinflint like Marian Flitcraft!

That evening Mama said to Papa in my presence: Your daughter doesn't want to go to Mahler's now that she has pestered me into it.

Papa, reading his newspapers, looked up over his eyeglasses.

Well, I don't know that I blame her. Fannie is serious-minded.

Oh, so you want her to be a wallflower. Your daughter's reason is that she thinks she is too fat.

Why, Fannie, said Papa gently, handsome is as handsome does. Besides, you should be grateful that you are healthy. You have flesh on your bones and that is nice. Surely you don't want to look sickly.

In the end I attended Mr. Mahler's dancing school, but immediately I began to scrutinize the other girls. They were slender, with small waists and no dimples in their hands, and their legs, above black patent-leather dancing pumps, were slim.

When we knew our steps sufficiently to have partners for the waltz and schottische, I began to notice with sinking heart that when Mr. Mahler clicked his cricket and snapped, Take partners! the boys broke row on the opposite side of the room and began to slide across the polished floor, each racing for the girl of his choice. I was not among the first they made for. Sometimes the last, or almost.

That was terrible. I not only wanted to be among the first, but the first. That or nothing, and any old little boy would have sufficed.

Dancing school began to be a dread. When I demurred, Mama said: I have paid Mr. Mahler one hundred dollars in advance and I don't intend to throw it away. Money doesn't grow on trees.

Once, when I had been left over, Mr. Mahler drew me out on the floor to dance with him.

Fannie is very light on her feet, he said, addressing the class. If she can handle herself gracefully, there is no excuse for the rest of you. Watch us.

I knew what he meant! If a fat girl could do it, the thin ones surely could.

Nevertheless, I continued to be chosen last, or among the last, and that major frustration of childhood, feeling out of the herd, began to take shape. . . .

It never occurred to me that you could do anything about it. You were fat as uncompromisingly as your eyes were brown.

It helped make me a tight little island. I was fat and all the other girls in the world were thin. To isolate me further, everybody else had sisters or brothers or both.

Not that I coveted them, but nevertheless it was another difference. There was still another. We were Jews. Almost everybody was not Jewish. (28–30)

After three unhappy months at Harperly Hall, a private school, Fannie became one of the 1,400 students at Central High School.

One day I realized I had indeed broken through the ice of anonymity, when one teacher remarked to another as I passed in a throng: There she goes! That is Fannie Hurst, the heavy-set girl in the checked dress.

At last! "Heavy-set" or not, once they knew of my existence and the way I was, we could share thoughts. It did not matter to me so much that the boys passed me by. I wanted the attention of these teachers who, I believed, lived in the world of the mind.

I wanted them to regard me as the most interesting girl in the school. I felt and thought so much that I could never discuss with the girls on my block or in my classes, or at home with Mama and Papa. No one except me really knew the kind of person I was. I wanted to share me, to exhibit me, the way I was . . . inside. . . .

I became outstanding quickly enough, but not in the manner I craved. Overdressed, overglib in class, my recitations laboriously "different," I too often excited the laughter of class or teacher or both. But it was laughter at me rather than with me. I realized it, and the fires of my tortured teens burned high.

Perversely I went my way, hating the reasons for my becoming a conspicuous pupil among the fourteen hundred. Nevertheless, even if ignominiously, outstanding I was.

Periodically, Mr. Bryan, principal of Central High School, sent word to Mama he would like to see her. In a strange way I exulted in these conferences, which took place in my presence, and I don't think Mama or Papa minded too much.

Fannie has a good mind except for the fact . . .

When a strong personality like Fannie sets a bad example to her classmates . . .

Fannie is quite exceptional in some respects but . . .

I felt secretly flattered.

Mama and Papa did too. I could tell by the indulgent way in which they voiced disapproval of me. (48–49)

Planning to major in journalism, Fannie enrolled at the University of Missouri in Columbia. Secretly relieved when her mother begged, "Don't leave us, Fannie," she decided to live at home and study at Washington University.

So far as [Mama] was concerned, I was crossing over, by way of college, into the barren wastelands of the Tillie Strausses, where femininity died on the vine, where no eligible man entered, where parents of erudite unmarried daughters buried their dead hopes.

Only a small percentage of young ladies, principally those with the ultimate purpose of teaching and self-support, were entering institutions of higher learning at that period.

But generally the bridge-of-sighs beyond a girl's graduation from finishing or secondary school was as brief a span as possible. Parents saw to it, to the limit of their financial abilities and often beyond, that daughters were placed promptly on the market.

During the period when my college plans still hung in the balance, Mama attempted to reach me with offers to move into a finer home, even build one, travel, follow the current fashion and take lessons in burnt wood, have a little Model T Ford car of my own, extend my piano education at the finest conservatory in town.

To add degrees to Mama's fever, Irene Wertheim, a featureless girl in my graduation class, became engaged to the son of the president of a mammoth burlap bag concern in East St. Louis. At Mama's urging, Aunt Jennie came to visit us. An obsessive matchmaker and advocate of early marriage, she dared be even more outspoken than Mama.

I am ashamed for the people in Hamilton. I brag about my brilliant niece and, meanwhile, the nieces of most of the women I know marry off, while you are still without even an admirer. Your mother tells me that Milton Jelenko, who is marrying that Wertheim girl, would have been glad to call on you if you had ever given him the opportunity. Your mother is right. Tillie Strauss is written all over you.

Now, *Gensbebla*, you and Rose leave Fannie to work it out her own way. There is no hurry about such things.[8]

Sam doesn't talk that way, Jennie, when we're alone. That child and her father just aren't themselves before one another.

That was the way it went, up to the hour I became a freshman at Washington University. (79–80)

Now, for the first time, it seems to me, I become intellectually awake, where before I had only dragged back my eyelids. I select courses close to my interest, based on my need to know, rather than for convenience.

Shades of the halls of learning began to close in my growing self. The university buildings were massive Gothic, the men of the faculty, in my fancy, Olympians who had temporarily descended to the lecture halls.

Interest in the outer world receded. After the day's lectures I lingered on the campus, in the library or on its great stone porch, filling composition books with vaporings. A course in the major Elizabethan poets drenched me in the reflected light of the era. My freshman year I submitted a masque in blank verse to *The Saturday Evening Post*. That

---

8. *Gensbebla* might be translated as "silly goose"—a person who prattles without thinking.

same year I offered twice the required number of assigned "themes" to my English professor.

This struggle to capture the winged words that seemed to fly through my mind in flocks was almost as old as I was. It did not matter that once on paper they lost much of their iridescence—there was always the next clean page of the composition book.

As I examine those days under the microscope, I recapture the adult anguishes that went with them. Tormented, violently ambitious, jealous of the achievements of others, I slashed about in all directions at once.

I recall, when I was no more than five, Papa remarking to a business associate who was visiting our house: By the way, my little daughter has written some verse. Would you like to read it? Extracting a bit of paper from his waistcoat pocket, he watched anxiously the guest's face for reaction. So did I. It came promptly, in an m-m-m. Thus Papa's guest handed me my first rejection slip.

At this period of my freshman year, the march of the long envelope containing the returned manuscript with a rejection slip was uninterrupted. For years our faithful Willie had been marching upstairs mornings with the mail: Miss Fannie, here's another story come back, and each time, as every writer must know, that plop down into the bottomless pit. (83–84)

Certain of the girls usually lingered after class in English composition to talk with Mr. Starbuck. . . . I would have given much to do the same. Instead, I would leave the lecture room, head up, heart down, casting proud cold glances upon a procedure I longed to share. Someday I would show them! Show them what?

In the spare time inflicted by aloneness, I dug my pencil into paper and wrote, using up what Mama called a round-trip fortune in stamps and long self-addressed envelopes. East they went and westward they returned—"not up to our standard."

Once Mama, so bored by the proceedings, so eager to gratify my slightest whim, suggested: Fannie, offer to pay to have your story printed. I'll bet you that's what many of the writers who are in the magazines do. I'll give you the money.

Papa said: Rose, you should be ashamed to even make such a suggestion.

Mama said: Anything that costs money makes you ashamed. Fannie, do you want fifty dollars?

Oh, Mama, you're just terrible.

I wish I was dead, said Mama. What do I get out of it but abuse.

These ridiculous moments live on in heartache and regrets. Mama meant so well. She would have schemed to get me the moon had I expressed a wish for it. Yet time and time again I turned on her: Oh, Mama, please keep out of it.

Mama is gone now, but as the years pass, her warmth, her humor, her tempestuousnes[s] linger on as if she had just passed through the room.

Fannie, take off your good clothes when you come home from school! Today, the adult me changes clothes immediately upon entering the house.

No woman who leaves a dish unwashed overnight is worth her salt. Still a cardinal sin in my eyes. Don't sit on the bed. I no more would!

With your kind of father, Mama used to say out of his hearing, you can afford to hold up your head with the best. I might have retorted, but did not: And with my kind of mother, all her this-and-that to the contrary notwithstanding.

People say: How much pleasure you must have given your parents. Wonderful that they lived to see it.

Yes, but how much more I might have given. In my middle-class world of that era it was no small thing for a daughter to break the pattern of fitting into the home for as short as possible an interlude between graduation and marriage.

Both Mama and Papa did live to enjoy some of the results of my nonconformity, but looking back, I marvel at my capacity for ruthlessness in leaving the home so concentrated on me. The fierceness of that concentration was doubtless part of the compulsion.

I left, hurting with the gentle resignation of my father and wetted with Mama's tears. (88–89)

Mary Ezit Bulkley (1856–1947)

"Grandmother, Mother, and Me" is the title of the final selection in this anthology. The story begins, "Me, if you please, is one Mary Ezit Bulkley, now in my ninetieth year and surely one of those who with delightful malice have been described as 'indestructible old ladies,' cluttering up the earth" (4).[1] Although she claimed there was "not one single thrill of adventure in this whole sheaf of remembrances" (5), Miss Bulkley wrote a memoir demonstrating both her individuality and her kinship with many of the other women represented in this anthology. At her home in Carmel, California, she looked back on her life and beyond it, examining political, economic, and religious changes she had witnessed and reflecting on what they had meant to her personally. Using the framework of the century and a half from the birth of her grandmother in Somerset, England, to the year following World War II, she told about the trio of women whose lives and beliefs were different because of the impact of historic events, changing social conditions, and private circumstances.

Mary Ezit Bulkley became an independent and energetic individual, living in a way unimaginable to her grandmother and mother. Bulkley admits she was never fond of her grandmother, Ezit Moody Carpenter (1798–1882), who was pious, sober, and uncompromising. Her husband died shortly after they arrived in the New World. She remarried and made a home for her daughter and two stepchildren on a farm near New Rochelle, New York. Ezit's daughter, Mary Moody Bulkley (1829–1916), was a subdued and dutiful woman, who "seldom laughed and never hummed a tune as she sat and sewed" (21). Mary Ezit was born in 1856 in New York City, where her father, Peter C. Bulkley, conducted a real estate business. There were frequent visits to the grandparents in New Rochelle, where the children enjoyed berry picking in summer and sleigh rides in the winter. In 1866 the Bulkley family moved to St. Louis.[2]

Mary Ezit Bulkley received a private education at home in her earlier years, and then completed elementary and high school in St. Louis. She also had lessons in piano and dance. A disappointing romance and the family's financial problems changed the course of Bulkley's life. After her father lost the money he had invested in an iron foundry, she had to give up plans to attend Vassar College. She studied interior decorating in New York at Cooper Union School, but found herself frustrated at being taught only to adapt historical designs from books rather than working with the

---

1. References to page numbers in the memoir appear in the text.
2. In the St. Louis census for 1870, we find Peter C. Bulkley, age 40, a real estate agent, his wife Mary, age 38, and their children: Minnie, age 13, Willie, age 11, and Louis, age 7. In addition to "Minnie," Mary was sometimes also called by the nickname "Mamie."

materials herself. On a trip to Italy as chaperone for two girls, she became interested in the art of bookbinding. On her return to the United States, she worked diligently on the craft, studying with several teachers. She went to Chicago to study her craft with one of the top bookbinders in the country, Ellen Gates Starr, who with Jane Addams founded Hull House.[3]

Returning to St. Louis, Bulkley pursued the craft of bookbinding for over fifteen years. She also became involved in social work of the type she had observed at Hull House. Being exposed there to the problems of the "very poor" awakened an interest in social activism that she pursued throughout her life. Bulkley served on the board of the St. Louis Children's Hospital and became involved with a settlement house organized by the Ethical Society to teach basic classes in hygiene, language, and other skills to the disadvantaged. Through this work Bulkley met Roger Baldwin, a recent Harvard University graduate who served as resident director at the settlement house. He taught sociology at Washington University and organized its Sociology Department. During World War I Baldwin spent a year in prison in New Jersey for refusing to serve in the military. He went on to found the American Civil Liberties Union. Bulkley and Baldwin worked together when he was Executive Secretary of the Civic League of St. Louis. Her association with Baldwin and with certain revolutionaries led authorities to search her home without a warrant and to keep her under surveillance on a trip to England. Roger Baldwin, who was like a son to Bulkley, always valued their friendship.[4]

Taking part in meetings of a woman's club and the Women's Trade Union League prepared Bulkley to work for women's rights as a prominent member of the St. Louis Equal Suffrage League, starting in 1910. She also helped to establish and served as a contributing editor for the magazine, *The Missouri Woman*.[5] Anticipating passage of the suffrage amendment, Bulkley in 1918 published a highly regarded handbook entitled *Aid to the Woman Voter in Missouri*. In order to help women "use their vote intelligently," she explained political parties, the process of voting, and the organization of city, county, state, and federal governments. Presenting clear explanations, organizational charts, and space for the reader to fill in

3. Located in a poor, multiethnic neighborhood on the southwest side of Chicago, Hull House was founded by Jane Addams and Ellen Gates Starr in 1889. It became a center for meeting the needs of the surrounding community by providing day care, special classes, and a residence for working women. It also supported social reform activities in areas such as child labor, sanitation, and housing.

4. Baldwin visited Bulkley in California for three months in 1925 or 1926. On Baldwin, see Peggy Lamson, *Roger Baldwin: Founder of the American Civil Liberties Union*, and Charles Lam Markmann, *The Noblest Cry: A History of the American Civil Liberties Union*.

5. Among the articles written by Bulkley for *The Missouri Woman* were: "Do Women Bear a Citizen's Responsibility?" (May 1916, 5); "Reflections on the Last Elections" (December 1916, 5–6); "Rule-of-Thumb Justice" (April 1917, 6–7); and "What Is Americanization?," (March 1918, 5, 25–26).

names of officials, *Aid to the Woman Voter* served as a "textbook in general voter preparation classes for many years."[6] In 1919 she wrote a play for the Suffrage League entitled *The Trial,* which portrayed the 1873 trial of Susan B. Anthony after her arrest for registering and voting under the Fourteenth Amendment.[7] Bulkley's dramatic account in her memoir of the ratification of the women's suffrage amendment by the Missouri Legislature reminds the reader that many people worked hard and gave of themselves to ensure basic voting rights to women—and that it was a battle not easily won.

In 1920 Mary Ezit Bulkley moved, because of her health, to California, where she did some writing and reflected on economic, political, and social issues. She also did weaving and worked with metal and other materials. On the theme of aging, she wrote a book of poetry entitled *Speaking at Seventy.*[8] She died on May 8, 1947, at the age of ninety-one. Annora Koetting has called Bulkley "an unheralded prophet."[9]

In 1946 Bulkley wrote her memoir, which she called "Grandmother, Mother, and Me."[10] The editors have selected passages from this memoir that present some of the highlights of Mary Ezit Bulkley's private life and a sampling of her varied interests and concerns. The emphasis, however, is on her account of the work for suffrage and her assessment of the impact of passage of the Nineteenth Amendment. In that way we mark the significance of 1920 as the time in women's history with which we close this survey of the lives of Missouri women.

"Grandmother, Mother, and Me" in its entirety is what Roger Baldwin called a "really remarkable piece of self-revelation." He found the account of events from his years in St. Louis to be quite accurate, but thought his friend was overly modest about her position "among a wide circle of artists, intellectuals and club women." The passages selected convey the qualities Baldwin appreciated:

> But what to me is so unusual about her story of her family and life is the perception and objectivity of an understanding—and the expression of it so

6. From the introduction; the word "woman" was cut from the title for the second edition.

7. Arrested after she registered and voted in Rochester, New York, in November 1872, Anthony was tried in Canandaigua in June 1873. Bulkley opens with a prologue in the garden of Judge Ward Hunt the day before the trial. In the courthouse scene Anthony's lawyer Henry Selden, who encouraged her to register and vote, argues in her behalf. After the Judge instructs the jury to find Anthony guilty, she protests eloquently.

8. San Francisco: Gelber, Lilienthal, Inc., 1931.

9. Annora K. Koetting, "Mary Ezit Bulkley," in *Show Me Missouri Women,* 2:226. Koetting also wrote about Bulkley in her thesis, "Four St. Louis Women."

10. Bulkley mimeographed several typed copies and gave them to friends. The editors have used the copy received by the Missouri Historical Society in 1952. In 1972 Roger Baldwin gave the society a second copy, which they in turn gave to Radcliffe College. There is also a copy at the St. Louis Public Library.

clearly—that I would not have suspected. She talked so rarely of herself and her family that this was a revelation to me, and as a piece of writing it must be to others, whether they ever heard of her.[11]

"GRANDMOTHER, MOTHER, AND ME"

. . . [A]lthough I have spent one-third of my ninety years as a citizen of a confessedly peace-loving nation, yet that nation had been at war for one third of my life. War, for that time, has been either going on, or immediately in prospect, or just past.

And yet—in spite of all this frightful wastage of time, of life, and of natural resources, see what we have managed to do in the 150 years since Grandmother was born in her little Somerset village! I refrain from the catalogue so easily made. But while steam, electric energy, and the power of the atom have changed the whole environment, I ask if I, after ninety years, am correspondingly as developed a human being as I should be. There has, I convince myself, been some betterment in my outlook. I am not quite so ready to accept Things As They Are as my grandmother was. I am not so much concerned with my soul's salvation as she and her mother were. I have other ideas than my mother as to what women should or should not do. But on the whole the change in my spirit is not marked, although it shows differently. If perhaps a group of friends and I could go back the hundred odd years and settle in my grandmother's village, if we went to church on Sunday and kept our mouths shut on week days, we need be considered by them as only slightly cracked. (8)

While I am day-dreaming in this fashion as to what the world might have developed had we not spent so much time destroying each other and wasting our resources, why not also consider what our development could have been had we not, in our inhuman haste to destroy our natural resources as speedily as possible, merely allowed the dwellers in this rich and fertile land to develop its resources from a natural increase of population and normal immigration and not called the world in to help us. This was really no benevolence on our part. True, we gave them a percentage of what they cut down and grubbed up, but we took the most of it for ourselves. If there had been a release of pressure from the eastern side of the Alleghenies, there perhaps would be no Dust Bowl and no exhausted farms. But War and Unlimited Immigration kept us in a very great hurry to Do It and Do It Now.

What has all this to do with me today? I suspect much more than, try as best I can, I am at all able to realize. The wastage and destruction have

---

11. "A Note on the Auto-Biography of Mary E. Bulkley," 1972, Bulkley Family Papers, Missouri Historical Society, St. Louis.

gone on in geometrical progression. For after World War II we see the possible end of timber, pasture, oil, coal, water power and sea fisheries. I claim that this haste, this greed and this threat of depletion have helped to circumscribe me, and if you do not stop it will dwarf your children. (9–10)

[Grandmother] was never the cuddly kind. I was seldom on her knee and then terribly conscious of her bony processes. She was tall as well as gaunt, with piercing dark eyes and a ruddy skin. She followed the English custom and always wore a cap. These purple ribbon strings concealed the ridges of her throat. Her voice seemed sharp and could penetrate across the garden to the tall grass of the meadow lot where I lay hidden with a book "wasting time." Now I may have misunderstood her, but I never could have misunderstood her bony structure nor her grasp of my arms as she took away my book and ordered me to go to some job flagrantly made up on the spur of the moment in order that her interference might have apparent justification. She was very religious; that is, a bigoted sectarian. She was Baptist and set her immortal status on the fact that she had been dipped and not just sprinkled. Whatever she did, she did thoroughly. (12)

. . . For many years I was so indoctrinated with the belief that the main reason for a daughter's existence was to assist her mother that I was almost grown before I realized what this outrageous notion had done to my mother. Never did I know her to complain; she took it simply as an unhappy matter of course. (13)

. . . All my most usual memories of my mother are with her needle. She worked incessantly when we were children to give us what she thought was best for us. She did all the household sewing and gave endlessly of time and strength. She seldom called us to her to read us stories or poems. She had no time for this. She never talked to us of her feelings or of anything except very external experiences.

My father liked the poems of Sir Walter Scott and used to read "Marmion" and "The Lady of the Lake" to us. Also he used to play with us and my mother never did. He was always held up to us as a Court of Last Resort, and his displeasure was crushing. Many times since I began to try to recall incidents of my earliest childhood, I have wondered why the figure of my father appears so seldom in the foreground of my remembered picture. Not that he was not always in the picture, for he was pervasive. Yet the stage was always set to hold Mother, Grandmother and various aunts. I was always very close to my father; yet he does not take a major place until my adolescence. Now, I can see that this was according to the pattern of the time and because of this pattern most fathers were deprived of the pleasures as well as the proper duties. Occasionally a father overstepped the bounds and indulged himself. This, if not carried too far, was considered an amiable weakness. In the public eye, the father was the indubitable ruler of his household. He was the economic support, The Provider. He usually did the marketing on his way down town and at home handed out the required cash. Household money usually had to be asked for. A very few progressive wives had established allowances; but the man was regarded as the source from which all household blessings flowed. If in this realm the husband was the King, the wife was the Prime Minister. . . . I know my Mother would have felt herself disgraced had her husband ever been required to dry a dish or manage a safety pin, although he might have been perfectly willing to give needed assistance. In my early time the free give-and-take of today, where the wife works in the office and the two, arriving at home, collaborate in cooking and clearing away the dinner, was entirely unknown. (27–29)

Bulkley recalls her school days in St. Louis.

Being filled with self-conceit and also really better informed at my age than my fellows I can now chuckle over my having become that detestable creature known as "Teacher's Pet." I had been trained to obedience and taught not to be mischievous. "Lessons" had always been serious matters and this attitude was transferred to the school. And since the children made me feel myself ostracized for "queerness," I compensated for this by outstripping them and remained for most of the time at the "head of the class." For in those mistaken days this "headship" was no idle phrase. We stood to recite in a long line at the side of the room below the skirting blackboard. Questions were propounded from the teacher's dais, and were given out usually in turn. If there was a silence or a wrong response the question was taken on by the next in line. An immediate change in position marked a correct reply. It seems astonishing that at that time people did not see that in this performance was an implicit acknowledgment that no one could improve his own status except at the expense of some one else. There was little cooperation and the very rankest competition. (43–44)

. . . There were absolutely no commercial amusements for the respectable adolescent, unless in the winter a few days of ice skating at the rink. It was after my time that there were roller skates; and in Saint Louis ice was not to be depended on. There were no places where one could go to dance except in each other's houses—and there it was always a question of getting music. . . . When dancing was planned the music was violin and piano. We played games a great deal: "Going to Jerusalem" and "Blind Man's Buff," and I am now amused to find "Twenty Questions" being carried to its last extreme difficulty on the radio today.

Why all this did not seem dull then, I do not know, unless it is because everything is comparative. But I can assure you we did have "a good time." (45–46)

Even in those days a few women known as "strong minded" began to make an increasing sound of protest. My mother knew of them but had no interest in them except as a social phenomenon. My grandmother was outspokenly scornful. That many of these women were "nice" was not to be disputed. A wealthy young cousin of my father's had married a niece of the Quaker, Lucretia Mott, and we knew all about her. Mrs. Mott was one of the most prominent of the early women and one of the most outspoken. Her younger friend, Elizabeth Cady Stanton, told of her amazement at Mrs. Mott's free discussion of things which she, Elizabeth, had "really reproached myself for daring to entertain in my mind." Mrs. Stanton was herself emphatically a "nice" woman and married to a husband who was sympathetic with her. . . . Susan [B.] Anthony was in evidence wherever her friend and co-worker, Mrs. Stanton, appeared. . . . [I]t does seem to me that Susan Anthony and Mrs. Stanton did more than any others to bring equal rights for women out of the domain of theory into practical politics . . . .

There was no doubt where to place the occupants of a handsome barouche with a liveried driver. These two women were pointed out to me as horrible examples of what was to be expected when women left their proper sphere. They were [the sisters] Victoria Woodhull and Tennessee Claflin. They had a business office somewhere in Wall Street and were reported to be very disreputably connected with prominent financiers. The dubious position they held could not really be blamed on their desire to vote, though was probably a contributory cause. These two not only practiced Free Love but openly upheld it as a theory. This was a proceeding quite at variance with the custom of that day. If these two women gave the scale of public opinion a slant on the downward side, this was measurably counterbalanced by the excellent reputation of Anna Dickinson, who although a spinster and a public character, was nevertheless a "nice" woman. . . .

Late in the Sixties the Woman's Club movement began. The members were less daring than the Suffragists. However, the first club, Sorosis, was an important landmark. The membership was carefully chosen and was referred to colloquially as "Sorosisters." They were the objects of envy or hatred, or both, from those who, although they considered themselves eligible, were not invited. The Club was supposed to have all culture for its field but not to go out of bounds in the dangerous precincts of either religion or politics, which inhibition still largely prevails in the General Federation [of Women's Clubs] of today. I doubt if membership in any club would have appealed to my mother. She was not only firm in her belief that woman's place was in the home, but also that it was a very busy place, indeed. She was never intolerant about such conduct but was absolutely superior to it, being certain not only that it was not for her, but just as sure it never could be for any of hers. (46–49)

. . . In 1873 I finished all I ever had of formal education, one year in the grade and four in the High School. . . . [A]t graduation I was given, through my fellow students' vote, "the last essay" on the program. This was supposed to be the highest honor which a girl could carry off, for of course only a boy could represent the class in the valedictory. I know the teaching staff made these selections, but they had also to have a certain acceptance by the class itself.

So, all togged out in a preposterous, befrilled, be-bustled long frock containing uncounted rows and rows of machine hemming and stitching, my silly head a mass of braids and curls, some belonging, some applied, I stood before my audience and read what I meant for a versified (I called it poetic) *résumé* of Progress. Progress was what we all believed in then as much as we believed in God.

Both my brother and I had aspired to go to college; he, to Cornell; I, to Vassar, the best known of the few colleges for girls. My father's financial failure made this impossible; the lean years were upon us. . . . My mother's health broke and I had to take charge. . . . We still kept one maid, for in so dirty a city my young shoulders were really too slight both to keep house and to nurse, unassisted. I did try to learn to do this in more scientific ways than my farm-bred mother had done. . . . To the mingled admiration and disgust of the family, I found out that we were spending too much money on expensive food, put us on a budget and introduced what my father contemptuously called "grocery store breakfasts."

In those days there was little that a middle class girl could do except teach. I secured one or two pupils, youngsters who needed coaching. What with teaching and learning, housekeeping and nursing, I was kept fully occupied. This was not to the exclusion of a certain amount of dancing and theater going. (52–54)

. . . I [felt] a growing irritation and annoyance that the world appeared to be turning into a different and not nearly so agreeable place as I had supposed it to be. My previous acceptance of an essential right to economic privilege was now perhaps also questionable. I had to agree that as a family we were really poor. Things were sure to right themselves and we must come into better times. Perhaps these difficulties were just part of the paradox which I was beginning to find everywhere and which I could not explain. "All men are created free and equal"—I knew they were not; and I knew that it had very recently taken many years and many lives to do away with actual slavery. We accepted the saying of Jesus, even though he commanded us to sell what we had and give to the poor; and did we not turn the tramp from the door, saying we had nothing for him when I knew the larder was full? All these things had indeed been puzzles,—so much so that one just stopped bothering and took them for granted just as one took the weather, something to be endured and not to be changed. (62)

The "frigid woman" was a phrase not heard then because frigidity was supposed to be a normal condition for all "nice women." The world was neatly divided into women who were "nice" and women who were not so nice. In order that the race might go on, man was a ravaging creature upon the altar of whose appetite nice women were sacrificed. Even "nice women" recognized that children were not only necessary but were highly desirable, although the Lord God had been very inconsiderate to one half of the race in His approved method of bringing them to birth. . . . Not one of [my] young friends ever confessed to any joy in the actual marriage relationship. Had they done so, they would have confessed to being "not nice," and that would never do. They loved their husbands and because of this submitted to indignities from them. Was it not a wonder, with this so often in the background, that being built on so paradoxic and inhuman a relationship there were any happy marriages at all?

Outside of marriage, even to be kissed was justified only when the strains of the Wedding March were almost audible in the thrilling atmosphere. . . .

While all these confused and contradictory notions were in my mind, I met a youth a little older than I and whose profile, as I afterward recognized, was very like that of my father. (This was before psychoanalysis.) He had a lovely deep voice and what immediately seemed a very inflammable heart. He was very assiduous; and I began to like him very much. He and his family, whom I met and found fairly agreeable, had lately come from New England to live in Saint Louis and he was about to graduate from Law School. He made a brilliant record and soon entered the office of a well-known lawyer. Everything seemed to me to be more or less . . . "going according to plan," my plan! My plan seemed to be his also. To be sure there was but little money in sight, but I could be a famous housekeeper and stretch his nickels farther than most; of course there would soon be dollars instead of small change. He convinced my father that this would be so and after this preliminary we were engaged. I think at this time he really wanted to marry. Of course if this was to be soon he could not wait to build a law practice but must take a business offer made him by a wealthy friend. . . . This meant long absences from town. . . . For two years we had to depend on letters, except for occasional short visits home. When we were together everything seemed satisfactory, but the longer intervals seemed very hard. And not just because we could not see each other, but altho letters were warm and frequent I knew there was something radically wrong, some need of his I did not seem to fill. This disturbed me very much, for I was sure he was a lucky man— and he had frequently mentioned this fact himself. The only question

I had ever put to myself was whether he could make me happy; and I was certain that after we were married I could be all he could want. After a while I could see that he was filled with growing discomfort at the rigors of the pedestal on which my lofty and persistent ideas had placed him. Like many youngsters we really were in love with love and not with each other. We were neither of us thinking of mutual gains through mutual sacrifice. I knew what I wanted from him; he definitely knew what he wanted from me. In this there was no unity. Within a brief time before the date set for marriage, the engagement was broken. . . .

He soon left town permanently and I never saw or heard from him again. When he later married, I am sure it was to a girl less demanding and much less romantic. (63–66)

Bulkley spent some time in New York serving as a governess for a cousin and staying with an aunt while studying interior design. Back in St. Louis, her brothers established a construction business, and she devoted herself to her family.

. . . [F]or the first time I became rather involved in the affairs of a large Club. I realized that such an institution was truthfully described as a "University for Gray-haired Women." Of course, since the club had recently been formed, they at once tackled the study of the Italian Renaissance. They all did. Since politics and religion had been, by their constitutions, barred from the programs, this was as good as anything. Girls coming back from college had been well drilled in parliamentary law and we felt that above everything we must be correct in our smallest procedure. Every section chairman slept with Robert's Rules under her pillow and the general chairman had a parliamentarian sitting beside her on the platform. Limited as they were, these clubs did for the comfortable woman at that time what the Trade Union Local was doing for her working sister. Although we did not know it and probably would have shuddered if we had, it was a needed and worthwhile preparation for "votes for women." At even our least important meetings everything was carried on with the utmost elaboration and decorum. We learned to "move the previous question" with no one batting an eyelash at such sophisticated temerity. About this time there was a general Convention of Women's Clubs at Washington, [D.C.], so delegates and alternates took their good clothes and went. During the rare intervals of leisure from our own work, several of the most earnest of us eschewed the planned parties and managed to attend sessions of Congress. On our return to our own place of business, we were almost too shocked to report on what we had seen with our own eyes; a loud-voiced man gesticulating as he made a speech to which no one even pretended to listen; page boys running around calling out names; other men standing in groups and talking in ordinary tones just as if nothing was happening! We did things much better,—at least more decently.

All our parliamentary punctilio did come in handy after we had the vote and had had more experience of the way things did or did not get themselves done, for in these clubs women were able for almost the first time to work with a basis of common aims to certain ends. We tried ourselves out in competition with one another and thus found who had real qualities of leadership. And, although "politics" in its particular sense was banned, yet, as far as running the club was concerned, it was very much in evidence. The General Federation [of Women's Clubs] is too often a splendid, well-oiled and smoothly-running machine turning a pin wheel, valuable mostly because it gathers a friendly group for study of various problems. (94–96)

During all [the] years when I was coquetting with benevolence and general "uplift," with settlements and trade union auxiliaries, with pacifism and charity hospitals, etc., I did not see that what I really wanted was to help to bring about some measure of social justice, in which everyone might have a fighting chance to develop himself.

. . . I do take credit to myself, let me say, that by this time I had lost any notion of finding a panacea and considered "Votes for Women" as something which might be of real use only if it were intelligently administered as a means of a larger end. But when I read of the selfless devotion of these well-bred English [suffragettes], their struggles with police and bitter terms in filthy jails, they made me feel self-conscious and uncomfortable. I had an annoying feeling that they were suffering because of the likes of me; also that their work was not only necessary but praiseworthy. I knew that I should be willing to do the little that I could to help. . . .

. . . [W]hen the first meeting was called at her own house by Mrs. Florence Wyman Richardson to establish a Saint Louis suffrage league,[12] I was there—and after this first plunge went about declaring "the water was fine" and urging others to come on in. For the first time, I began to understand the "wild women" in England and their tactics. I realized that those English Suffragettes were most of them women with better educations and better social advantages than I had; that they did not do these things from choice but from a reasoned necessity; that, although the work which women had done and were doing in the war was proving even to the most stubborn how the status of women had changed, unless

12. For accounts of the suffrage movement in Missouri and identification of the women who played leading roles, see Mary K. Dains, "The Fight for Woman Suffrage," in *Show Me Missouri Women*, 2:222–24, and Mary Semple Scott et al., "History of Woman Suffrage in Missouri."

this realization was driven home by something new and unforgettable women would be allowed to drop back into the patient Griseldas of long tradition.[13] It dawned upon me that in all their publicity stunts, jails, and fights, no one had ever been hurt except the women themselves. I saw the same capacity for zeal and self sacrifice when, later, I was sent as a missionary to meetings of the W.C.T.U.

The advocates of "Votes for Women" had to be very cagey with the W.C.T.U. If we could have annexed them, their numbers would have done a great deal to help get the vote. But on the other hand, had we had their active support, this would have alienated many who did not believe that legislation of such a sumptuary nature was worthwhile. We were sure espousal of it would alienate as many as were gained. Addressing a W.C.T.U. meeting was not an easy job. There would be forty or fifty women meeting in summer time in the side yards of small houses; in winter, in their stuffy little parlors. Nearly every one showed in her wrinkled worn face that her own struggles were the basis of her zeal to try by legislation to save son or husband from the Demon Rum. Poor dears, they had not the slightest notion that a few years after they got their bills signed and sealed, they would have to take to praying for their daughters too. When to the tune of Old Black Joe, they sang "The saloon has *got* to go," I had a very clear conviction that it would. There was little emotional appeal in our asking support for suffrage. We wanted justice— and they mostly wanted revenge, and they very much wanted the power to make everyone do as they thought that they should.

Suffrage by now had become so much in controversy that one could no longer be dubbed a "suffrage crank" and cut dead; suffrage workers had become too respectable. The average woman had a very odd attitude as she watched to see which way the cat was going to jump. . . .

There were many men among the prohibitionists who were very skillful in the use of political pressure. We learned a good deal from them, especially that our best chance was to cease trying to work directly with State Legislatures and to make suffrage a national issue. It is more than likely that, had we stuck to forty-eight separate groups of women working to get what we wanted from forty-eight groups of men, we might be at it yet. For all the State Assemblies had worked out an efficient technique which they, in our age of innocence, put over on us successfully. We were divided into groups, each functioning in her most suitable field. Some took on the difficult task of raising the needed funds. This was the most basic of all. Another group arranged lectures by well known out-of-town speakers. I shall never forget Mrs. [Emmeline] Pankhurst, who was

13. The story of Griselda, which first appeared in the last tale of the *Decameron* by Boccaccio, was retold by Petrarch, Chaucer, and other authors. Griselda became the symbol of endurance, patience, and wifely submission.

at her best when she was handling rather rude heckling from the floor. Her wit fairly crackled around the worried supporter of things as they were. Our own great Anna Howard Shaw was equally witty and ready. Some of our local women were rather surprised to find how well they could handle street meetings, although they never had anything harder than jeers to encounter. I had the very carrying voice for such a role but I did not have the needed intestinal fortitude and just couldn't participate.

But I did find a way, all my own, to do what proved to be needed just as much. In order that women might not have their ignorance of the processes of government thrown up at us, I compiled and gave to the League a little volume: *An Aid to the Woman Voter in Missouri.* This aroused considerable notice when its publication was announced because at that particular time there "just wasn't no such animal." . . .

When I began to make the charts for it, I found a good one of the City of Saint Louis which was made by the former Secretary of the Civic League. That for the County was not difficult. None had been ever made for the State Government, and, when these various bureaus and departments which had, like Topsy, "just growed" for a century, were laid out in graphs, the arrangement of the State showed itself for the patchwork it was. It was a troublesome job to correlate the functions of Missouri. . . .

. . . If the lines of the graph for Missouri State suggested a crazy quilt, the Federal was a mess of wrecked spider webs. Lines which showed connections and subordinations might have been made by independent spiders working at cross purposes,—the lines intersected one another so thickly and so strangely. Finally this graph was made. It has been copied and reprinted in several manuals on government. . . .

Suffrage work in Saint Louis was well coordinated. Of course it all was concentrated on the Missouri Legislature. Long before its regular biennial sessions, we would make arrangements with a friendly member of each house to introduce and back our bill. It would usually make its appearance early in the session and there was always a delegation of "the ladies" to grace the occasion. We did not send the worst looking ones either. If our bill was first brought up in the House, the committee to which it would be referred would tell us how glad they were to help so righteous a cause and our bill would go through that chamber as if on skids. Upon its passage, there would be jubilant headlines in the papers at the state capital. These would be hopefully copied in the suffrage journals everywhere. If easy passage were its history in the House, the Senate would receive it rather coldly. Then in its regular procedure our bill would be referred to a committee and it would just stick there. No ants from any hill ever worked harder over an obstruction than the women would to get that bill reported out. Since we could no longer be laughed at, since it was not good politics to report it unfavorably, the safe and easy thing was to let it find its finish by death from inanition. Our suffrage bill in the next session might go through the Senate as if greased and come to a silent death in the House. On investigation, we found that the political Steering Committee of the legislature would always hold a pre-session caucus and decide which branch should "jolly the ladies."

After the Federal Amendment [the "Presidential Suffrage Bill"] had been passed by both houses of the National Congress, it still had to be ratified by three-fourths of the legislatures of the states. There again it suffered every form of delay, misrepresentation and sharp practice. However, the innocent handful of wishful thinkers who had first gone to work trustfully had through the years learned several things. They now had a membership behind them of respectable size with influential women who had learned in a hard school to be seasoned campaigners.

The crucial moment for Missouri came when the legislature was to decide whether or not to give Presidential Suffrage. The convention of the State Suffrage League was being held in Saint Louis and the officers were of course obliged to be at their posts.[14] Our most astute politicians were a sort of roving commission to be sent where needed and of course they were at Jefferson City. Our bill had already passed the House and we knew the usual technique would be to have it knifed in the Senate. This body had of course been well canvassed by the women as well as by the opposition. If now it were to be defeated, we knew it would be by a very small margin. Every vote counted. The time when it would be called up was therefore of great importance and, since this was more or less in the hands of those who were unfavorable to us, incessant watchfulness was needed. Events proved that the few women there on the job were quite equal to the situation.

The National Democratic Party under Woodrow Wilson had been slowly awaking to the fact that the past years of Republican indifference to the possibilities of "Votes for Women" as a party asset could be utilized to its own advantage. They were as a party no more anxious to give us the vote than were the Republicans; but they were clever enough to try to put one woman as window dressing on each State National Committee. Our member was an enthusiastic young matron, Mrs. David O'Neil. At this time it happened that the National Democratic Committeeman for Missouri, Mr. Edward F. Goltra, was really a sympathizer, as well as astute enough to capitalize on what he believed might be an asset for his party. Mrs. George Bass, of Chicago, who was at this time our national chairman, suggested to Mr. Goltra that it was indicated that an immediate change from compliments and polite conversation was now overdue. Mr. Goltra saw the point and determined to do his best for us. It happened that just at this time two of our supporters in the Missouri Senate, not realizing the

14. During the last week of March 1919, the National American Woman Suffrage Association was holding its fiftieth annual convention in St. Louis. Scott et al., "History of Woman Suffrage," 341.

turn things were about to take nor how precarious was the situation, left the session at Jefferson City to attend to some pressing personal business. Judge Gray had been summoned to try a murder case and Mr. Stark to sell some hogs.[15] Our opponents were very influential. They represented the railroads, the breweries and other industries. Many of them were large employers of women. Their senators decided to bring the bill up just at this juncture; and it seemed as if we were caught. This was especially so since, when we returned to Mr. Goltra, we found he had just left town to go to Washington. Our telegram caught him on the train. To our joy he left the train, and went at once to Jefferson City, where he took counsel with Mrs. O'Neil, Mrs. [Helen Guthrie] Miller, our state President, and some up-state women who were on guard. Together they worked out a bit of drama. Our two senator friends were communicated with by telephone and saw at once that they must return, if they could possibly do so in time. I doubt if we women, so used to pinching pennies, would have been able to stretch our imaginations to pull off the coup that Mr. Goltra made possible. He had an engine and car sent for Judge Gray, who was outside regular train connections; and Mrs. Stark hustled her husband to catch the one train available to him, although he had to board it unshaven and, in his farm clothes, sit up all the remainder of that night to make the proper connection.

The foes on the floor who had counted noses and knew that we needed just two votes were urbane, even sympathetic. "It is going to be a close call, ladies; too bad your friends could not be here." The session was to begin as usual at ten in the morning and our bill was already set as the first order of business. The train bringing our farmer, if on schedule, would arrive in time but the "special" for which Mr. Goltra had arranged was less predictable. What if it should come even one minute too late? No suspicion that there was anything up must be evoked by anxious women fluttering in and out of telephone booths. It seemed as if our reinforcements would be on hand a very few minutes after the Senate was called to order; but every moment counted.

[On the morning of March 28, 1919,] Mrs. O'Neil and Mrs. Miller went to the office of the President of the Senate with some important questions on which they must have immediate advice. They played up to him so well that he forgot to be absolutely punctual; besides he knew what the outcome of the vote would be. Probably he also hated to administer so heavy a blow as he was about to give to two such agreeable ladies. At any rate, he did not hasten. After a little the two women got the "all clear" signal from their scout, took a friendly farewell and scurried for the

15. Howard Gray of Carthage, a Republican, was the senator from the 18th District. He served as judge of the circuit court and of the Springfield Court of Appeals. David W. Stark, a Democrat, represented the 17th District. He did farming and raised stock at West Line in Cass County.

gallery in time to get the picture when, just as the roll was being called, in came Judge Gray from Mr. Goltra's five hundred dollar special train, and Mr. Stark, still in his blue jeans and dishevelled from his train ride. From their seats the suffragists could see the surprise and dismay frozen on the faces of the enemy.[16] The women said later that the only thing which detracted from one of the most perfect moments which life had had to offer them was that the rest of us who were holding things down in Saint Louis could not have been there with them. After we gained complete suffrage, there were many celebrations. We had our own fun at these to see wives of many of the men who had fought us long and hard, sitting on the front row of platforms with their ample fronts covered with yellow and white ribbons. They themselves had never lifted a finger nor contributed a penny. I suspect our laughter was a little grim.

Of course the question now is in order: "Now you have it, what have you done with it?" I am free to confess that the millennial state which many of our speakers confidently prophesied has not come about. In my turn, I make bold to ask, "What of it?" There have been results even if small; how much or how little is beside the point. As a measure of justice, it is worth all it cost and, in bringing about such justice in the national framework, men have benefitted by it just as much as women. It was another case of a national survival "half slave, half free." It has helped to remove false sentimentality between men and women; removed foolish one-sided "chivalry" which put a privileged man's own kind of woman on a silly pedestal and could not see the office scrubwoman as also eligible to such a position. To their greater glory, women became just folks. We learned the worth of organization but we have not used our knowledge. It is especially to our discredit that the maternity death rate is ghastly in our land and also that there is little protection from fraud in the children's bread or medicines. Twenty years is a short time in which to revolutionize an ingrained attitude. It is too soon to judge results in concrete terms. (140–51)

During the twenty-seven years she lived in California, Bulkley occupied herself with crafts, writing, and the study of economic theory.

Almost all old people, when they are appealed to for their particular prescription for longevity, deliver themselves of categories of what to do

16. The Missouri House of Representatives passed the same bill a week after the Senate vote. The "Susan B. Anthony Amendment" to the U.S. Constitution, the 19th, was passed by the U.S. House of Representatives on May 21, 1919, and by the Senate on June 4. It reads, "The Right of Citizens of the United States to vote shall not be denied or abridged by the United States or by any state on account of sex." This amendment was ratified by the Fiftieth General Assembly of the State of Missouri at a special session on July 2, 1919. Scott et al., "History of Woman Suffrage," 350–54.

and not to do. Sometimes I am treated to such an inquiry, and all I can say is that they should eat what agrees with them, should neither under nor over do, should have a once-over from a good doctor rather often and follow his advice. Also I can, on my own, say that if you eat very simple food your appetite will stay hearty enough to enjoy it. This sounds like a beneficent circle—and it is.

And as a final dictum, I advise something which no one need tell you that I practice. Keep on good terms with yourself. If you are a bit smug, so is everyone else; if you are too much interested in your own doings, you are no exception; if you think you know yourself, be sure other people know you better; and be content to get on without remorse or worry. Especially remorse. Crying over spilled milk is the worst possible way to waste time. . . .

I have to confess that my more than fourscore years and ten have taught me to realize that, if given the same opportunities to re-live my life, I would make the same mistakes. (183–84)

As I see it now, the stern and continually placated God of my grandmother was in my youth masquerading as "Inevitable Progress," the Sweetness and Light of Matthew Arnold. Progress was a product of material betterment. It could be depended on to bring Universal Brotherhood. This was a matter for Human Reason untainted by Emotions and would be initiated by Scientific Advance. Thus my parents' generation suffered two terrible impacts: the increasing mastery of the physical world and a decreasing ability to feel any unity with the closed world of the church into which they had been born. What they did was what we all tend to do, as they refused to consider their losses and turned their attention to what seemed illimitable gains.

It was true that there were many at the turn of the century who had begun to suspect that our vaunted civilization was very lopsided and that there were very inadequate foundations for our Temple of Congress. We had done away with chattel slavery but was our wage slavery any better? Were children working a twelve-hour day in cotton mills any better off than those who in former days used to work from dawn to dusk in the fields? Was the woman who "needle in hand sang the song of the shirt"[17] really any worse off than her granddaughters who ran power machines in lofts for ten hours a day and never sang at all? . . .

I think we are today a little more realistic and less hopeful. We know very well we have neglected the things of the spirit and have been sunk in the love of luxury and soft, pleasurable living. We now know we must write into the American Constitution a Bill of Duties to take precedence over our Bill of Rights. (183–88)

17. From Thomas Hood, "The Song of the Shirt," first published in the Christmas issue of *Punch* in 1843.

BIBLIOGRAPHY

―――――――――――――――― SOURCES ――――――――――――――――

Bruns, Henriette Geisberg. *Hold Dear, As Always: Jette, a German Immigrant Life in Letters.* Trans. Adolf E. Schroeder; ed. Adolf E. Schroeder and Carla Schulz-Geisberg. Columbia: University of Missouri Press, 1988.

Bulkley, Mary Ezit. "Grandmother, Mother, and Me: 1856–1946." Bulkley Family Papers. Missouri Historical Society, St. Louis.

Chopin, Kate. "On Certain Brisk, Bright Days." *St. Louis Post-Dispatch,* November 26, 1899.

Clark, Genevieve Bennett. Diary and essays [including "I Married a Politician"]. Champ and Bennett Champ Clark Papers, 1853–1973. WHMC-C.

Couzins, Phoebe. Speech [newspaper clipping]. *J. E. D. Couzins Papers,* Box M77. Missouri Historical Society, St. Louis.

Creel, Virginia Fackler. Virginia Fackler Creel Diary, 1864. WHMC-C.

Dierssen, Anna. "Wednesday Club in Person: A Diary." Anna Dierssen Papers, 1907–1965. WHMC-C.

Duchesne, Philippine. *Philippine Duchesne: Frontier Missionary of the Sacred Heart, 1769–1852.* Ed. Louise Callan. Westminster, Md.: The Newman Press, 1957.

Ellis, Mary Margaret. "That's the Way It Was, 1914–1930." Western Historical Manuscript Collection, University of Missouri–St. Louis.

Hurst, Fannie. *Anatomy of Me: A Wonderer in Search of Herself.* Garden City, N.Y.: Doubleday, 1958.

Keckley, Elizabeth. *Behind the Scenes, or, Thirty Years a Slave and Four Years in the White House.* New York: G. W. Carleton, 1868.

Kelso, Margaret Gilmore. "Family History." History Museum for Springfield–Greene County. Springfield, Mo.

Nation, Carry. *The Use and Need of the Life of Carry A. Nation.* Topeka, Kans.: F. M. Steves & Sons, 1904, 1908, 1909.

Oliver, Marie Watkins. Letters. Oliver Family Papers, 1805–1977. WHMC-C.

Powers, Marian Wright. "Talks on Self." Powers Museum. Carthage, Mo.

Ray, Emma J. *Twice Sold, Twice Ransomed: Autobiography of Mr. and Mrs. L. P. Ray.* Chicago: Free Methodist Publishing House, 1926.

Scott, Elvira. Elvira Ascenith Weir Scott Diary, 1860–1887. WHMC-C.

Stephens, Margaret Nelson. Margaret Nelson Stephens Diary, 1897–1903. WHMC-C.

Vanarsdale, Susan B. Susan D. [B.] Vanarsdale Diary, 1847–1855. WHMC-C.

Wilder, Laura Ingalls. Diary (microfilm). Laura Ingalls Wilder Papers, 1894–1943. WHMC-C. [Originals in the possession of the Laura Ingalls Wilder Home Association, Mansfield, Mo.]

———. *On the Way Home: The Diary of a Trip from South Dakota to Mansfield, Missouri, in 1894,* with a setting by Rose Wilder Lane. New York: Harper & Row, 1962.

Willis, Frances D. Letters. Willis Family Papers, 1843–1908. WHMC-C.

Wood [Woods], Martha J. Diary. Arrow Rock Tavern Board Papers, 1826–1923. WHMC-C.

REFERENCES

Adler, Frank J. *Roots in a Moving Stream: The Centennial History of Congregation B'Nai Jehudah of Kansas City, 1870–1970.* Kansas City: The Temple, Congregation B'Nai Jehudah, 1972.

Alexander, Adele Logan. "White House Confidante of Mrs. Lincoln." *American Visions* 10 (February–March 1995): 18–19.

Andrews, William L. "Reunion in the Postbellum Slave Narrative: Frederick Douglass and Elizabeth Keckley." *Black American Literature Forum* 23 (Spring 1989): 5–16.

Asbury, Herbert. *Carry Nation.* New York: Alfred A. Knopf, 1929.

Bader, Robert Smith. *Prohibition in Kansas: A History.* Lawrence: University Press of Kansas, 1986.

Beals, Carleton. *Cyclone Carry: The Story of Carry Nation.* Philadelphia: Chilton, 1962.

Black Women in America. Ed. Darlene Clark Hine. 2 vols. Brooklyn: Carlson Publishing, 1993.

Blair, Karen. *The Clubwoman as Feminist: True Womanhood Redefined, 1868–1914.* New York: Holmes and Meier, 1980.

Bloom, Harold, ed. *Kate Chopin.* New York: Chelsea House, 1987.

Boren, Lynda S., and Sara de Saussure Davis, eds. *Kate Chopin Reconsidered: Beyond the Bayou.* Baton Rouge: Louisiana State University Press, 1992.

Brandimarte, Cynthia Ann. "Fannie Hurst: A Missouri Girl Makes Good." *Missouri Historical Review* 81 (April 1987): 275–95.

Brown, Earl Kent. *Women of Mr. Wesley's Methodism.* Studies in Women and Religion, no. 11. New York: Edwin Mellen Press, 1983.

Bulkley, Mary E. *An Aid to the Woman Voter in Missouri.* [St. Louis: Garrison-Wagner Printing Company,] 1918, 1920.

———. *The Trial: An Episode in American Suffrage History More or Less Dramatically Presented.* [St. Louis]: n.p., 1919.

Callan, Louise, ed. *Philippine Duchesne: Frontier Missionary of the Sacred Heart, 1769–1852.* Westminster, Md.: The Newman Press, 1957.

Chapman, Carl H., and Eleanor F. Chapman. *Indians and Archaeology of Missouri.* Rev. ed. Columbia: University of Missouri Press, 1983.

Chopin, Kate. *The Complete Works of Kate Chopin.* Ed. Per Seyerstad. 2 vols. Baton Rouge: Louisiana State University Press, 1969.

————. *A Kate Chopin Miscellany.* Ed. Per Seyerstad, asst. Emily Toth. Natchitoches, La.: Northwestern State University Press, 1979.

Clark, Champ. *My Quarter Century of American Politics.* 2 vols. New York: Harper & Brothers, 1920.

Clevenger, Martha R. "From Lay Practitioner to Doctor of Medicine: Woman Physicians in St. Louis, 1860–1920." *Gateway Heritage,* Winter 1987–1988, 13–21.

Coalier, Paula. "Beyond Sympathy: The St. Louis Ladies' Union Aid Society and the Civil War." *Gateway Heritage,* Summer 1990, 38–51.

Cogan, Frances B. *All-American Girl: The Ideal of Real Womanhood in Mid-Nineteenth-Century America.* Athens: University of Georgia Press, 1989.

Coleman, Nadine Mills. *Mistress of Ravenswood.* Columbia, Mo.: Tribune Publishing Company, 1992.

Conway, Jill. *The Female Experience in Eighteenth- and Nineteenth-Century America: A Guide to the History of American Women.* New York: Garland Publishing, 1982.

Coulter, Hope Norman. Introduction to *Civil War Women: The Civil War Seen through Women's Eyes . . . ,* ed. Frank McSherry, Jr., Charles G. Waugh, and Martin Greenberg. New York: Touchstone/Simon and Schuster, 1990.

Cranmer, Catharine. "Little Visits with Literary Missourians: Fannie Hurst." *Missouri Historical Review* 19 (April 1925): 389–96.

Creel, George. *Rebel at Large: Recollections of Fifty Crowded Years.* New York: G. P. Putnam's Sons, 1947.

Croly, Jane Cunningham. *The History of the Woman's Club Movement in America.* New York: H. G. Allen, 1898.

Davis, Elizabeth Lindsay. *Lifting as They Climb.* Washington, D.C.: National Association of Colored Women, 1933.

Dierssen, Anna. "Missouri University and I: 1907–1908." WHMC-C.

Duden, Gottfried. *Report on a Journey to the Western States of North America and a Stay of Several Years Along the Missouri. . . .* Ed. James W. Goodrich et al. Columbia: The State Historical Society of Missouri and University of Missouri Press, 1980.

Dunne, Gerald T. *The Missouri Supreme Court: From Dred Scott to Nancy Cruzan.* Columbia: University of Missouri Press, 1993.

Dyer, Robert L. *Boonville: An Illustrated History.* Boonville: Peleitanoui Publications, 1987.

Evans, Sara M. *Born for Liberty: A History of Women in America.* New York: The Free Press, 1989.

Ewens, Mary. *The Role of the Nun in Nineteenth-Century America.* New York: Arno, 1979.

Faragher, John Mack. *Women and Men on the Overland Trail.* New Haven, Conn.: Yale University Press, 1979.

Foley, William E. *A History of Missouri.* Vol. 1. Columbia: University of Missouri Press, 1971.

Frémont, Jessie Benton. *The Letters of Jessie Benton Frémont.* Ed. Pamela Herr and Mary Lee Spence. Urbana: University of Illinois Press, 1993.

————. *The Story of the Guard: A Chronicle of the War.* Boston: Ticknor & Fields, 1863.

Furnas, J. C. *The Life and Times of the Late Demon Rum.* New York: G. P. Putnam's Sons, 1965.

Gerlach, Russel L. *Immigrants in the Ozarks: A Study in Ethnic Geography.* University of Missouri Studies, no. 64. Columbia: University of Missouri Press, 1976.

The German-American Experience in Missouri. Ed. Howard Wight Marshall and James W. Goodrich. Publications of the Missouri Cultural Heritage Center, no. 2. Columbia: University of Missouri–Columbia, 1986.

Goodrich, Thomas. *Black Flag: Guerrilla Warfare on the Western Border, 1861–1865.* Bloomington: Indiana University Press, 1995.

Grant, Julia Dent. *The Personal Memoirs of Julia Dent Grant.* Ed. John Y. Simon. New York: G. P. Putnam's Sons, 1975.

Greene, Lorenzo J., Gary R. Kremer, and Antonio F. Holland. *Missouri's Black Heritage.* Rev. ed. Columbia: University of Missouri Press, 1993.

Grimké, Sarah. *Letters on the Equality of the Sexes, and Other Essays.* Ed. Elizabeth Ann Bartlett. New Haven, Conn.: Yale University Press, 1988.

Hagood, J. Hurley, and Roberta (Roland) Hagood. *The Story of Hannibal: A Bicentennial History, 1976.* Hannibal: n.p., 1976.

Harris, Nini. *A Grand Heritage: A History of the St. Louis Southside Neighborhoods and Citizens.* [St. Louis]: De Sales Community Housing Corporation, 1984.

Hart, Sara L. *The Pleasure Is Mine: An Autobiography.* Chicago: Valentine-Newman, 1947.

Heilbrun, Carolyn. *Writing a Woman's Life.* New York: Norton, 1988.

Hessler, Anne. "German Jews in Small Towns in Missouri, 1850–1920." M.A. thesis, University of Missouri–Columbia, 1991.

Hine, Darlene Clark. " 'In the Kingdom of Culture': Black Women and the Intersection of Race, Gender, and Class." In *Lure and Loathing: Essays on Race, Identity, and the Ambivalence of Assimilation,* ed. Gerald Early, 337–51. New York: Allen Lane/Penguin Press, 1993.

————. "Rape and the Inner Lives of Black Women in the Middle West: Preliminary Thoughts on the Culture of Dissemblance." *Signs* 14 (Summer 1989): 912–20.

History of Greene County, Missouri. Ed. R. L. Holcombe. St. Louis: Western Historical Company, 1883.

History of Saline County. [Marshall, Mo.: Saline County Historical Society], 1967.

History of Saline County, Missouri. . . . St. Louis: Missouri Historical Company, 1881.

History of Saline County Missouri. Marshall, Mo.: Saline County Historical Society, 1983.

History of Southeast Missouri. Chicago: Goodspeed Publishing, 1888.

Holtz, William. "Closing the Circle: The American Optimism of Laura Ingalls Wilder." *Great Plains Quarterly* 4 (Spring 1984): 79–90.

———. *The Ghost in the Little House: A Life of Rose Wilder Lane.* Columbia, Mo.: University of Missouri Press, 1993.

Hunt, Marion. "Woman's Place in Medicine: The Career of Dr. Mary Hancock McLean." *Missouri Historical Society Bulletin* 26 (July 1980): 255–63.

An Illustrated Historical Atlas Map of Greene County, Mo. N.p.: Brink, McDonough & Co., 1876.

Jackson, Donald Dale. *Gold Dust.* New York: Alfred A. Knopf, 1980.

Johnson, Anne André- [Mrs. Charles P. Johnson]. *Notable Women of St. Louis.* [St. Louis: Woodward, 1914.]

Kelley, Mary. *Woman's Being, Woman's Place.* Boston: G. K. Hall, 1979.

Kessler-Harris, Alice. *Out to Work: A History of Wage-Earning Women in the United States.* New York: Oxford University Press, 1982.

Koetting, A. K. "Four St. Louis Women: Precursors of Reform." M.A. thesis, St. Louis University, 1973.

Korner, Barbara O. "Philippine Duchesne: A Model of Action." *Missouri Historical Review* 86 (July 1992): 341–62.

Kremer, Gary R., and Cindy M. Mackey. " 'Yours for the Race': The Life and Work of Josephine Silone Yates." *Missouri Historical Review* 90 (January 1996): 199–215.

Lamson, Peggy. *Roger Baldwin: Founder of the American Civil Liberties Union.* Boston: Houghton Mifflin Company, 1976.

Leach, Blanche S. [Mrs. Frank Sayre]. *Missouri State History of the Daughters of the American Revolution.* Sedalia: n.p., 1929.

Levens, Henry C., and Nathaniel M. Drake. *A History of Cooper County, Missouri.* St. Louis: Perrin & Smith, 1876.

Levy, Joann. *They Saw the Elephant: Women in the California Gold Rush.* Hamden, Conn.: Archon Books, 1990.

Logan, Shirley Wilson, ed. *With Pen and Voice: a Critical Anthology of Nineteenth-Century African-American Women.* Carbondale: Southern Illinois University Press, 1995.

Luchetti, Cathy. *Women of the West.* St. George, Utah: Antelope Island Press, 1982.

Madison, Arnold. *Carry Nation*. Nashville: Thomas Nelson, 1977.

Markmann, Charles Lam. *The Noblest Cry: A History of the American Civil Liberties Union*. New York: St. Martin's Press, 1965.

Marston, Leslie R. *From Age to Age a Living Witness*. Winona Lake, Ind.: Light and Life Press, 1960.

Mattes, Merrill J. *The Great Platte River Road: The Covered Wagon Mainline via Fort Kearney to Fort Laramie*. 2d ed. Lincoln: University of Nebraska Press, 1987.

McClain, William B. *Black People in the Methodist Church: Whither Thou Goest?* Nashville: Abingdon Press, 1984.

McCluen, Marilyn Neathery. "Andrew Jackson Willis." Typescript.

McLaurin, Melton A. *Celia, a Slave*. Athens: University of Georgia Press, 1991.

McMillen, Sally G. *Motherhood in the Old South: Pregnancy, Childbirth, and Infant Rearing*. Baton Rouge: Louisiana State University Press, 1990.

Miller, Sally M. *From Prairie to Prison: The Life of Social Activist Kate Richards O'Hare*. Columbia: University of Missouri Press, 1993.

Mooney, Catherine M. *Philippine Duchesne: A Woman with the Poor*. New York: Paulist Press, 1990.

Moore, Rosa Ann. "Laura Ingalls Wilder and Rose Wilder Lane: The Chemistry of Collaboration." *Children's Literature in Education* 11 (Autumn 1980): 101–9.

———. "Laura Ingalls Wilder's Orange Notebooks and the Art of the Little House Books." In *Children's Literature*, 105–19. Annual of the Modern Language Association Seminar on Children's Literature and The Children's Literature Association, vol. 4. Philadelphia: Temple University Press, 1975.

———. "The Little House Books: Rose-Colored Classics." In *Children's Literature*, 8–16. Annual of the Modern Language Association Seminar on Children's Literature and The Children's Literature Association, vol. 7. Philadelphia: Temple University Press, 1978.

Morello, Karen Berger. *The Invisible Bar: The Woman Lawyer in America, 1638 to the Present*. New York: Random House, 1986.

Muncy, Robyn. *Creating a Female Dominion in American Reform: 1890–1935*. New York: Oxford University Press, 1991.

Myres, Sandra L. *Westering Women and the Frontier Experience, 1800–1915*. Albuquerque: University of New Mexico Press, 1982.

Napton, William Barclay. *Past and Present of Saline County Missouri*. Indianapolis: B. F. Bowen, 1910.

Owens, J. Adolphus, ed. *Anywhere I Wander I Find Facts and Legends Relating to the Creel Family*. 2 vols. N.p.: Diversified Endeavors, 1975.

Papke, Mary E. *Verging on the Abyss: The Social Fiction of Kate Chopin and Edith Wharton*. Contributions in Women's Studies 119. New York: Greenwood Press, 1990.

Park, Eleanora G., and Kate S. Morrow. *Women of the Mansion*. Jefferson City, Mo.: Midland Printing Company, 1936.

Parrish, William E. *A History of Missouri*. Vol. 3. Columbia: University of Missouri Press, 1973.

————. *Turbulent Partnership: Missouri and the Union, 1861–1865*. Columbia: University of Missouri Press, 1963.

Past & Repast: The History and Hospitality of the Missouri Governor's Mansion. Jefferson City: Missouri Mansion Preservation, 1983.

Peavy, Linda, and Ursula Smith. *Women in Waiting in the Westward Movement: Life on the Home Frontier*. Norman: University of Oklahoma Press, 1994.

Perspectives on Kate Chopin: Proceedings from the Kate Chopin International Conference, April 6, 7, 8, 1989. Natchitoches, La.: Northwestern State University Press, 1990.

Pickle, Linda S. "Stereotypes and Reality: Nineteenth-Century German Women in Missouri." *Missouri Historical Review* 79 (April 1985): 291–312.

Porter, Jack Nusan. "Rosa Sonneschein and *The American Jewess* Revisited: New Historical Information on an Early American Zionist and Jewish Feminist." *American Jewish Archives* 32 (November 1980): 124–31.

Portrait and Biographical Record of Lafayette and Saline Counties Missouri. Chicago: Chapman Brothers, 1893.

Primm, James Neal. *Lion of the Valley, St. Louis, Missouri*. Boulder, Colo.: Pruett, 1981.

Rainey, T. C. *Along the Old Trail: Pioneer Sketches of Arrow Rock and Vicinity*. Vol. 1. Marshall, Mo.: Marshall Chapter of the Daughters of the American Revolution, 1914.

Riley, Glenda. *The Feminine Frontier: A Comparative View of Women on the Prairie and the Plains*. Lawrence: University Press of Kansas, 1988.

Ruether, Rosemary, and Rosemary Keller, eds. *Women and Religion in America: The Nineteenth Century*. San Francisco: Harper and Row, 1981.

Sanford, Mollie Dorsey. *Mollie: The Journal of Mollie Dorsey Sanford in Nebraska and Colorado Territories, 1857–1866*. Ed. Donald F. Danker. Lincoln: University of Nebraska Press, 1959, 1976.

Santmyer, Helen Hooven. *" . . . And Ladies of the Club."* New York: Putnam's, 1982.

Schiavo, Giovanni. *The Italians in Missouri*. Chicago: Italian American Publishing Company, 1929.

Schlissel, Lillian. *Women's Diaries of the Westward Journey*. New York: Schocken Books, 1982.

Schroeder, Adolf E. "The Survival of German Traditions in Missouri." In *The German Contributions to the Building of the Americas: Studies in Honor of Karl J. R. Arndt*, ed. Gerhard K. Friesen and Walter Schatzberg, 289–313. [Worcester, Mass.]: Clark University Press, 1977.

Scott, Anne Firor. *Natural Allies: Women's Associations in American History.* Urbana: University of Illinois Press, 1991.

Scott, Mary Semple et al. "History of Woman Suffrage in Missouri." *Missouri Historical Review* 14 (April–July 1920): 281–384.

Seyersted, Per. *Kate Chopin.* Baton Rouge: Louisiana State University Press, 1980.

Show Me Missouri Women. Ed. Mary K. Dains and Sue Sadler. 2 vols. Missouri Women's History Project, American Association of University Women. Kirksville, Mo.: Thomas Jefferson University Press, 1989, 1993.

Stepenoff, Bonnie. "Kate Chopin in 'Out-At-The-Elbows' St. Louis." *Gateway Heritage,* Summer 1990, 62–67.

Stevens, Walter Barlow. *Centennial History of Missouri (the Center State): One Hundred Years in the Union, 1820–1921.* Vol. 3. St. Louis: S. J. Clarke, 1921.

Stratton, Joanna L. *Pioneer Women: Voices from the Kansas Frontier.* New York: Simon and Schuster, 1981.

Taylor, Robert Lewis. *Vessel of Wrath: The Life and Times of Carry Nation.* New York: New American Library, 1966.

Thompson, John. *The Life of John Thompson, a Fugitive Slave . . .* (1856). Reprint. New York: Negro Universities Press, 1968.

Tokarz, Karen L. "Opening the Way." *Law School Magazine* [Washington University], Winter 1990, 8–12.

———. "A Tribute to the Nation's First Women Law Students." *Washington University Law Quarterly* 68 (Spring 1990): 89–102.

Toth, Emily. *Kate Chopin.* New York: William Morrow, 1990.

Towey, Martin G. "Kerry Patch Revisited: Irish Americans in St. Louis in the Turn of the Century Era." In *From Paddy to Studs: Irish-American Communities in the Turn of the Century Era, 1880 to 1920,* ed. Timothy J. Meagher. Contributions in Ethnic Studies 13, 139–59. New York: Greenwood Press, 1986.

[Van Arsdall, Peter.] "Autobiography of Peter Van Arsdall." Harrodsburg [Ky.] Historical Society Library. Typescript.

Van Ravenswaay, Charles. "Arrow Rock, Missouri." *Missouri Historical Society Bulletin* 15 (April 1959): 203–23.

Watkins, Marie Oliver, and Helen (Hamacher) Watkins. *"Tearin' through the Wilderness": Missouri Pioneer Episodes, 1822–1885, and Genealogy of the Watkins Family.* Charleston, W.V.: n.p., 1957.

We Are Your Sisters: Black Women in the Nineteenth Century. Ed. Dorothy Sterling. New York: W. W. Norton, 1984.

Welsh, Donald H. "Martha J. Woods Visits Missouri in 1857." *Missouri Historical Review* 55 (January 1961): 109–23.

Welter, Barbara. "The Cult of True Womanhood: 1820–1860." *American Quarterly* 18 (Summer 1966): 151–74.

————. *Dimity Convictions: The American Woman in the Nineteenth Century.* Athens: Ohio University Press, 1976.

Wilder, Laura Ingalls. *The First Four Years.* New York: Harper & Row, 1971.

————. *Little House in the Ozarks: A Laura Ingalls Wilder Sampler, The Rediscovered Writings.* Ed. Stephen W. Hines. Nashville, Tenn.: Thomas Nelson, 1991.

————. *These Happy Golden Years.* New York: Harper & Brothers, 1943.

Woman's Being, Woman's Place: Female Identity and Vocation in American History. Ed. Mary Kelley. Boston: G. K. Hall, 1979.

The WPA Guide to 1930s Missouri. Foreword by Charles van Ravenswaay, introduction by Howard Wight Marshall and Walter A. Schroeder. 2d ed. Lawrence: University Press of Kansas, 1986.

ABOUT THE EDITORS

Carla Waal is Professor Emeritus of Theatre at the University of Missouri–Columbia and the author of *Harriet Bosse: Strindberg's Muse and Interpreter.*

Barbara Oliver Korner is Associate Professor of Theatre at Seattle Pacific University.